D0396486

Victory City

Also by John Strausbaugh

The Village:
400 Years of Beats and Bohemians, Radicals and Rogues,
a History of Greenwich Village

City of Sedition:
The History of New York City during the Civil War

Victory City

A History of New York and New Yorkers during World War II

JOHN STRAUSBAUGH

TWELVE

NEW YORK BOSTON

Twelve

Hachette Book Group

1290 Avenue of the Americas, New York, NY 10104

twelvebooks.com

twitter.com/twelvebooks

First Edition: December 2018

Twelve is an imprint of Grand Central Publishing. The Twelve name and logo are trademarks of Hachette Book Group, Inc.

Library of Congress Cataloging-in-Publication Data

Names: Strausbaugh, John, author.
Title: Victory City : a history of New York and New Yorkers during World War II / John Strausbaugh.
Description: New York : Twelve, 2018. | Includes bibliographical references and index.
Identifiers: LCCN 2018022866| ISBN 9781455567485 (hardcover) | ISBN 9781549194795 (audio download) | ISBN 9781455567461 (ebook)
Subjects: LCSH: New York (N.Y.)—History—1898–1951. | World War, 1939–1945—New York (State)—New York.
Classification: LCC F128.5 .S87 2018 | DDC 974.7/104—dc23
LC record available at https://lccn.loc.gov/2018022866

ISBNs: 978-1-4555-6748-5 (hardcover), 978-1-4555-6746-1 (ebook)

Printed in the United States of America

LSC-C

10 9 8 7 6 5 4 3 2 1

Contents

INTRODUCTION

Sunday, April 30, 1939, dawned bright and sunny in New York. But by lunchtime a lid of low, dark clouds had clamped over the city, and soon it was steadily and drearily pelting rain. Knowing what we know now, the historiographer James Mauro noted in *Twilight at the World of Tomorrow*, it's hard not to see this shift in the weather as ominously portentous.

April 30 was the day for the grand opening of the 1939 New York World's Fair. The fair's theme was "Building the World of Tomorrow." Starting in 1936, sixty nations, dozens of corporations, some of New York's finest architects and designers, and an army of workers had pitched in to transform an ash dump in Flushing Meadows, Queens, into a heroic, soaring vision of a utopian future, a world of peace and harmony, rocket ships and robots, orderly ribbons of highway and glittering forests of skyscrapers.

President Franklin D. Roosevelt, Mayor Fiorello La Guardia, Albert Einstein, and other dignitaries were on hand for the grand opening. The one million fairgoers organizers had predicted were not. The gloomy, wet weather reduced attendance to at best half that, and some estimates were as low as two hundred thousand.

On April 30, 1939, the future was cloudy indeed. Two of the world's fair's sixty original nations, Austria and Czechoslovakia, had recently ceased to exist as independent states, devoured by Hitler's Germany. Germany, another original participant, had pulled out of the fair in a fit of pique over increasing criticism from Americans, not least of them the outspoken La Guardia.

In September 1939, as the fair's first season was drawing to a close, Germany invaded another participating nation, Poland. Within weeks, Germany and the Soviet Union had divided the country. Two more nations at the fair, England and France, declared war.

New York's world's fair, like the world itself, was in shambles when it opened again in May 1940. From "The World of Tomorrow," which now seemed hopelessly naive, the official theme was changed to "For Peace and Freedom." Ten nations did not reopen their pavilions, most of them because they were now in Nazi hands. Finland, overrun by the Soviets, closed its pavilion. The Soviet Union had shut down its own pavilion, dismantled it, and shipped it away.

By July Hitler had established dominion over virtually all of western Europe, and his Luftwaffe was bombing England in preparation for an invasion. That July 4, a terrorist bomb at the fair killed two people and severely injured others. Japan, which had one of the more popular national pavilions at the fair, formally joined the Axis alliance with Germany and Italy that September. By the time the fair dispiritedly folded for good at the end of October 1940 its theme might as well have been "The World at War."

The conflict that began in September 1939 raged on around the world until August 1945. Fifty million to 85 million people died (estimates still vary). Millions more were injured, raped, enslaved, displaced, or otherwise brutalized. Many of the world's great cities were smashed to rubble. It all ended in the hellish flash of the most powerful weapon yet developed, the atom bomb.

Still, dreams of global peace and progress survived, and in 1946 they returned to Flushing Meadows. The only structure from the '39 world's fair still standing, the large New York City Building, was converted into a meeting hall for the first gathering of the General Assembly of the United Nations. While delegates conferred there, work on the UN's permanent home got under way in Turtle Bay, a former area of slaughterhouses and crumbling waterfront on the east side of midtown Manhattan. On October 24, 1949—just a week short of ten years since the first season of the New York World's Fair ended—President Truman, New York governor Thomas Dewey, various diplomats, and ten thousand onlookers gathered at the foot of the slim, elegant UN Secretariat tower, still under construction, to lay the granite cornerstone.

Becoming the home of the United Nations and the "capital of the world" was the crowning achievement for New York City when it was at the zenith of its power and influence. In the decades surrounding World War II, New York was a far larger presence in America and around the world than it is today.

To start with, there was its sheer size. In the 1920s it had eclipsed

London to become the largest city in the world. Its population of seven and a half million in 1940 was larger than the next three American cities—Chicago, Philadelphia, and Detroit—combined. It was bigger than the populations of the fourteen smallest states combined. Three of its five boroughs—Manhattan, Brooklyn, and the Bronx—would rank among the eight most populous cities in the country. Almost 6 percent of all Americans lived within its five boroughs, 10 percent in the greater metropolitan area. It was also an extraordinarily diverse and cosmopolitan population. More Jews lived in New York than in any other city in the world, more blacks than in any other city in America, more Irish than in Dublin, more Germans than anywhere outside Germany, almost as many Italians as in Rome.

While Washington was the nation's political capital, New York was the capital in just about every other way that mattered. Its port was the busiest in the world, shipping 40 percent of all imports and exports for the entire United States. It was the nation's wholesale and retail merchandising hub. It was its powerhouse of banking and international finance. There were more Fortune 500 headquarters in Manhattan than anywhere in the country. Although it had no giant steel mills or automobile plants, New York's tens of thousands of smaller factories employing a million workers made it the largest factory town in the world.

It was the nerve center of national media, headquarters of the national radio networks and the big national magazines. When the Japanese attacked Pearl Harbor, New Yorkers could read about it in a dozen English-language dailies: the *Daily News*, the *New York Times*, the *Herald Tribune*, the *Sun*, the *Wall Street Journal*, the *Mirror*, the *New York Post*, the *Journal-American*, the *World-Telegram*, the *Brooklyn Eagle*, the *Daily Worker*, and the new *PM*. The conservative *Daily News* was the largest-circulation paper in the country, selling two million copies a day during the week, four million on Sundays. The *New York Times* moved far fewer copies, but it was highly influential among the power elite in Washington as well as New York. There were also foreign-language dailies, including the *Forward* for Yiddish readers and *Il Progresso Italo-Americano*, and a number of weeklies, such as the archconservative *Examiner*, which, because it came out on Sundays, was the first New York paper to carry the Pearl Harbor news on Sunday, December 7, 1941.

Home to Tin Pan Alley and the Brill Building, Broadway and book publishing, the Harlem Renaissance and Greenwich Village bohemia,

New York City was the culture engine for the nation. It even styled and made the clothes Americans wore.

New York's political clout in Washington was at its height in this period. Having this massive population center in it gave New York State more electoral votes than any other—47 in 1940. Pennsylvania came second with 36. This made winning the state key in any presidential election—and the city, with half of the state's voters, was key to winning the state. In the first half of the twentieth century, getting elected governor of New York was a very good way to be taken seriously as a presidential candidate. From the mid-1880s to 1948 governors Grover Cleveland, Teddy Roosevelt, Charles Evans Hughes, Al Smith, Franklin Roosevelt, and Thomas Dewey won their parties' nominations, and three of them went to the White House.

It's no exaggeration to say that from the day President Roosevelt took office in 1933 to the day he died in 1945, New Yorkers ran the country. Washington, D.C., was virtually Gotham-on-the-Potomac. Franklin and Eleanor Roosevelt's family roots in New York reached back to the 1600s. Eleanor was born in the city, kept residences there throughout her life, and died there. Franklin was born and raised up the Hudson but lived in Manhattan on and off until moving into the White House. On arriving there he filled his administration with the best and brightest, the most powerful and influential people New York City had to offer: corporate leaders, judges, lawyers, bankers, academics, scientists, social workers, playwrights, composers, journalists, even advertising executives. Roosevelt's right-hand man, many of his closest advisers, and his speechwriters all came down from New York. He put New Yorkers in his cabinet and on the Supreme Court, and he had New Yorkers running many of his agencies. New York intellectuals formed the core of his "brains trust." New Yorkers played the principal roles in crafting the New Deal programs that gradually lifted the nation out of the Great Depression, and in guiding the nation's efforts in the war, and in holding together the Grand Alliance of Roosevelt-Churchill-Stalin to win the war. Some were salaried federal employees, others donated their time and skills as so-called dollar-a-year men, paid a symbolic salary of a dollar a year because U.S. law forbids the government from accepting the services of unpaid volunteers.

New York City's participation in the war can be gauged by other metrics. Some 850,000 New York City residents served in the armed forces during the war, more than from any other American city. Tens of thousands of U.S. Navy officers, male and female, were trained in New York City, more than anywhere else. New York State suffered some forty-three thousand war casualties, more than any other. The giant Manhattan Project that produced the Hiroshima and Nagasaki bombs was aptly named: it began in New York City and was led by an Upper West Side native, J. Robert Oppenheimer.

Tens of thousands of New Yorkers, from high school students to pensioners, volunteered as air raid wardens, as auxiliary police and firemen, as civilian sailors and pilots who patrolled the U-boat-infested Atlantic coast, and with the Red Cross, the USO (headquartered in New York), the Stage Door Canteen, and other support organizations. Thousands of black and female New Yorkers joined the war effort in defense plants and the Brooklyn Navy Yard, in hospitals and offices, driving buses and cabs. Everyone who could bought war bonds, contributed to scrap drives, and tended hundreds of thousands of Victory Gardens. Even New York's most notorious gangsters and mafiosi pitched in.

The giant, diverse city of New York rarely speaks with one mind on any topic, and World War II–era New Yorkers were no exception. Mussolini and Hitler had fans and supporters among all strata, from wealthy blue bloods to poor immigrants. Mayor La Guardia was one of the earliest and harshest American critics of Nazism, at the same time that the largest pro-Nazi group in America, the German American Bund, set up its headquarters in Manhattan. Several of the city's large corporations and banks, even as their dollar-a-year men were assisting President Roosevelt in preparing for and then conducting the war, hedged their bets and invested in the regimes of Hitler and Mussolini.

The Communist Party in America was headquartered in Manhattan. Native New Yorkers figured prominently among the traitors who fed Manhattan Project secrets to the Soviet Union. Black New Yorkers were reticent to help free the rest of the world from oppression when they were oppressed at home, and their resentment boiled over into a midwar riot in Harlem. New York's Jewish community was deeply divided over Roosevelt and the Allies' lack of response to the Holocaust as it unfolded.

New York City was also home to some of the most organized, influential antiwar and isolationist groups of the 1930s. Public expression of antiwar sentiments all but vanished after the Japanese attacked Pearl

Harbor, obscuring the fact that for most of the period between World War I and World War II Americans had been overwhelmingly, almost unanimously against ever again getting involved in foreign wars. Before Pearl Harbor propelled America into the conflict, Franklin Roosevelt and the New Yorkers he'd gathered around him expended considerable effort slowly and gingerly prodding the nation toward intervention.

Any history of World War II and New York City's role in it thus properly begins twenty years earlier.

PART ONE

Storm Clouds Gather

While the storm clouds gather far across the sea
Let us swear allegiance to a land that's free.
—"God Bless America," Irving Berlin (1938)

CHAPTER 1

Decades of Disaster

The period from 1914 through 1945 was a time of global death and destruction on a scale not seen in human history. The Great War was followed immediately by a worldwide influenza pandemic, then the Great Depression, horrific famine in the Soviet Union, and finally World War II and the Holocaust, ending with the apocalyptic specter of the A-bomb.

Some historians suggest that the Great War and World War II, which bookend the period, are best understood not as two wars at all but as a single long one, the twentieth century's Thirty Years' War, which flared from 1914 through 1918, smoldered through the next two decades, then roared back to full fury in 1939. The human race shocked itself with the scale and savagery of the first world war, a war that began by accident and then dragged on year after year with a terrible monotony, like a nightmare from which the world couldn't wake. It left at least 50 million people dead or maimed and large swaths of Europe in desolate ruin. It introduced new or improved technologies of slaughter—the tank, the airplane, chemical warfare, the U-boat, the giant dreadnought. It erased the traditional line separating combatant and noncombatant; in the Great War, everyone was fair game, everyone was cannon fodder. It toppled the old political regimes of Europe, only to clear the ground for the radical politics of Communism, Fascism, and Nazism.

The war was just sputtering to a close in the autumn of 1918 when influenza struck around the world, killing another 20 million to 40 million people by winter's end. Some 675,000 Americans died from it, more than all American deaths of World Wars I and II combined.

The chaotic Versailles peace conference that followed the Great War opened in January 1919, in the midst of the pandemic. A British delegate likened it to "a riot in a parrot house." The thousands of delegates and consultants disagreed about virtually everything. President Woodrow Wilson went with his hopelessly lofty ideas about a League of Nations and permanent world peace; the French wanted to reduce Germany to a weak and unthreatening neighbor; others wanted to maintain a relatively intact Germany as a buffer against bolshevism spreading out of Russia; and England continued its centuries-old policy of playing one continental power against another for its own security.

In the end, the "peace" conference only set the world on a course to further conflict. The victors redrew the map of Europe, carving away pieces of Germany, splitting up the Austro-Hungarian Empire, patching together new political entities, including Czechoslovakia and Yugoslavia, which seemed almost designed by intent to be future sites of contention. Germany was forced to give up more than 10 percent of its territory and population. Both its military and its armaments industry were to be dismantled. The war had cost the country hundreds of billions of marks; the victors demanded gigantic reparations on top of that. Under threat of invasion, Germany agreed. As a final slap, the country was blockaded while the negotiations dragged on, and thousands of Germans died of starvation before it was over.

It all had a cataclysmic impact on the German people. Intensely proud and nationalistic, they now felt just as intensely humiliated and betrayed. Kaiser Wilhelm abdicated and the monarchy collapsed, replaced by a weak parliamentary democracy nominally presided over by a coalition of squabbling political entities, the Weimar Republic. Inflation that started during the war accelerated into surreal hyperinflation that lasted into the early 1920s. At war's end 20 German marks equaled a British pound; by 1924 it had plummeted to 20 *billion* marks to the pound.

It was the average German citizen, the workers and the middle class, who suffered. The large industrialists and wealthy landowners actually benefited, because inflation wiped out their debts while sending the value of their properties soaring. Largely through a mighty influx of capital from America—principally Wall Street bankers and big corporations headquartered in Manhattan—the German economy stabilized by 1924, then went into a surge of fantastic growth, the halcyon time of Weimar art, culture, and decadent pleasures. The mood of the people relaxed. It helped that the rabble-rouser Adolf Hitler, who was jailed after his failed 1923 putsch, was forbidden to speak in public for several years.

But the world depression that followed the New York stock market crash of 1929 fell with particular force on Germany. Its industrial output was cut in half, banks failed, and millions of Germans were thrown into unemployment and wretched poverty. The republic was doomed. From the seething cauldron of extremist political movements vying to replace it, the industrialists chose to back Hitler and the National Socialists. Believing that they could maintain control over Hitler, they gave him the funding and the social prestige he needed to seize power in 1933, and then helped him build the military machine with which he intended to take back what Germany had lost in the Great War, and much more.

The outcome of World War I ultimately led Italy and Japan to join Germany in the Axis alliance. Benito Mussolini started out a fiery Socialist like his blacksmith father. When the Great War began, the Socialist Party condemned it as a squabble between the old monarchies and lobbied strenuously against Italy's joining in. Mussolini broke with them, arguing that participating in the war and sharing in the spoils would give Italians a sense of national pride and unity they'd never felt. (Italy had been a nation for only some fifty years.) When the other victors at Versailles largely denied Italy any spoils, Italians felt as cheated and dishonored as Germans did. Mussolini seized the chance to pull irate war veterans and others into his new Fascist movement, which brought him to power in 1922. He quickly established his dictatorship. His admirer Adolf Hitler would follow his example in the next decade.

Japan emerged from the Great War, and its earlier victories over Russia and China, as a bona fide world power. But as an island nation it was hemmed in by the Western powers' colonial interests in the Pacific and starved for the raw materials on which to build a modern economy and military. Hitler's Germany faced similar shortages, and each saw territorial conquest as the solution. Starting in 1931, Japan's program of military expansion into Manchuria, China, and French Indochina made a collision with the West inevitable. Hoping to curtail Japan's empire building without military confrontation, Roosevelt would wage economic war, embargoing exports of fuel, steel, and iron, then freezing all Japanese assets in the United States. At that stage Japan, which had allied with Germany and Italy, could either shrink back or attack. It would choose to attack.

⌣

For its part, although U.S. involvement in the Great War had been relatively brief and the nation was more or less physically unscathed, the appalling, pointless barbarity of it was deeply demoralizing to most Americans and it left the entire nation, in a sense, shell-shocked. After Pearl Harbor, "isolationism" would become a dirty and shameful word, a taint it has carried ever since. Americans quickly and conveniently forgot that from the end of the Great War through most of the 1930s virtually all of them—95 percent in some national opinion polls—were isolationists. Left wing and right, feckless college kids and gray-bearded veterans, Charles Lindbergh and John Kennedy and Gerald Ford—they all agreed that if the world ever went to war again, the United States must not get involved. Even President Roosevelt's wife was an isolationist. "How can we live through the things that we have lived through and complacently go on allowing the same causes over and over again to put us through these same horrible experiences?" Eleanor cried in a 1934 speech. "Anyone who thinks must think of the next war as they would of suicide." In an antiwar march down Fifth Avenue shortly thereafter, protesters carried placards that read MRS. F.D.R. SAYS: "WAR IS SUICIDE!"

Isolationism was one symptom of a much broader reaction to the world war, a rejection not just of foreign wars but of foreign influences, foreign ideas, and foreigners themselves. Fear of "alien" influences ranging from communism and anarchism to Roman Catholicism surged. Severe new restrictions on immigration were enacted in 1921 and 1924, slamming Emma Lazarus's "golden door" on the two largest groups of newcomers since the 1880s, southern Italians and eastern European Jews. (Lazarus herself was descended from Jewish immigrants.) Anti-Semitism, which had always percolated through American culture, rose to new levels in the 1920s and '30s. The postwar years saw a resurgence of the Ku Klux Klan and other hate groups that played on Americans' suspicions of anyone and anything nonwhite and non-Protestant.

Turning their backs on the world and its problems was very easy for Americans to do in the 1920s. While Europe lay in ruins and chaos, in America the 1920s was a decade of phenomenal economic growth. Industry surged as new technologies transformed everything from coal mining and the corporate office to automobile manufacturing (which shot up from just over half a million new cars a year in 1914 to more than five million in 1929). Productivity overall increased 70 percent. Millions of new homes were built in the 1920s, equipped with electricity and telephones.

In New York, Wall Street was borne aloft on winds of speculation and margin buying. The rich got richer and richer. But it was the spending of the masses that was revolutionary. Middle- and working-class consumers, egged on by vigorous advertising, spent like never before, using a new invention, the installment plan, to buy cars, furniture, clothing, Victrolas, washing machines, radios. The upward cycle of investment, production, and consumption seemed to have no ceiling. As newsman Eric Sevareid would later put it, America appeared to have found a "magic key to eternal prosperity."

Even Prohibition, virtually the decade's only gesture of austerity, incited giddy, mindless hedonism. In New York City, central casting could not have sent a better figurehead for the period than the hard-partying, hardly working, and breezily corrupt mayor Jimmy Walker, aka the Night Mayor. Son of one of Tammany's more upright citizens, Jimmy started out a songwriter, a friend of George M. Cohan and Ira Gershwin, and married a Broadway chorus girl. Then he obeyed his father and went into politics. In the state assembly he came under Al Smith's wing, and in January 1926 he entered the mayor's office. For the next four years he played affable host to the city's nonstop gaiety, more easily found in one of the better nightclubs or speakeasies than behind his desk.

The Roaring Twenties ended almost exactly on cue, in October 1929, with the total collapse of Wall Street. New York City was the epicenter from which shock waves of economic misery spread around the world in the following years. Before October 1929, national unemployment stood at around 3 percent. When Franklin Roosevelt took office in March 1933, it was around 25 percent. Of 130 million Americans, an astounding 34 million were without means of support.

In New York City, where it all began, the Great Depression came down like a sledgehammer. Half of the city's manufacturing facilities closed in the first two years. The usually overcrowded and bustling port fell quiet. Unemployment in the city reached 33 percent by 1932, and almost two million New Yorkers went on relief. Thousands, unable to pay their rents, were thrown out of their homes. Many built their own shanty jungles, known as Hoovervilles, all over the city; the Great Lawn of Central Park was covered in tar-paper shacks.

At the start of the Depression, the City of New York maintained a single homeless shelter, the Municipal Lodging House on East 25th Street, with some nine hundred beds. When it became clear that this was woefully inadequate, the city opened two annexes, one in the long shed on the nearby Pier 73, with three thousand beds, and the other in the South Ferry terminal at the foot of Manhattan, with almost two thousand beds. Breadlines ten men deep and blocks long formed outside the Lodging House every day for the free hot lunches. (Only men lined up. Women and children were let right in.) Men lucky enough to get cots in the Lodging House were woken up at 4:30 in the morning. They raced one another out to various street corners around the city where, again if they were lucky, they might climb into a truck and be carried away for a day's work, handing out circulars in the city or working on farms nearby.

In December 1930, some twenty-five thousand depositors gathered outside the Bronx branch of the Bank of the United States, withdrawing $2 million in one day. It was the fourth-largest bank in the country. When it failed, the first big bank in the city to do so, it started a run on other banks around the country. Three hundred banks failed within a month; more than ten thousand would be closed by 1933. A Brooklyn woman who had lost most of her savings when the Bank of the United States closed hung herself from a water pipe in her basement.

New York had suffered wrenching recessions and depressions before, but this one, slamming the city to the pavement after the high-flying 1920s, was particularly shocking and frightening. A political operative named Ernest Cuneo, who was an aide to Fiorello La Guardia at the time, later wrote that "it wasn't so much the hunger or the hardships of actual poverty itself that gave the haggard face of the thirties its haunted look; it was something less tangible and much worse: the universal loss of self-respect. Deprived of their function as breadwinner, men felt deeply ashamed and cruelly frustrated." And just as the ebullient speculation of the boom years could make paper tycoons of waiters and cabdrivers, the Depression, the journalist Lorena Hickok reported from New York in 1933, affected "a complete cross-section of the population...all thrown together in a vast pit of human misery." When construction ground to a halt, architects and engineers lost their jobs along with the bricklayers and hod carriers. Ad agencies cut their staffs by half or more. With two-thirds of the city's legitimate (nonburlesque) theaters going dark, three-fifths of professional musicians and 70 percent of professional actors lost their jobs. Many headed west, hoping to find work in Hollywood. Three out of ten doctors in Brooklyn had their office telephones taken out because they couldn't pay the bills anymore. Debutantes fought for jobs as chorus girls, Cuneo wrote, and the West 50s in Manhattan became notorious for its part-time prostitutes, "young women with cultivated accents, the residues of wardrobes of excellent tailoring, and bitter smiles of contemptuous resignation."

As the capital of capital as well as the epicenter of the crash, New York City responded with a few symbolic acts of defiant bravado. The Chrysler Building was completed in 1930, the Empire State Building in 1931, Rockefeller Center in 1933. Henry Luce launched his magazine *Fortune* in 1930, and he would locate its offices in the Chrysler Building. But these soaring expressions of hope hardly made an impact on most New Yorkers' lives; the Empire State Building, barely tenanted when it opened, was nicknamed the Empty State Building and bled red ink for the next twenty years. The artist George Ault called the new skyscrapers "tombstones of capitalism...with windows."

Like a biblical blight ravaging an already suffering people, the weather turned freakishly apocalyptic in the mid-1930s. During the miserably hot summer of 1934, immense dust storms raged across the continent. Known as "black blizzards" and "dry blizzards," they blew up in mountainous whirlwind clouds from the parched, eroded soil of the Southwest farmland dubbed the Dust Bowl, then marched east. On July 3 of that year, after several days of broiling heat that killed at least three New Yorkers, one of these blizzards of dust rolled across the city, reducing visibility to three feet. It was followed immediately by a thunderstorm that killed more people in flash flooding and paralyzed a seven-mile stretch of the Long Island Rail Road in Brooklyn and Queens with lightning that set the wooden ties on fire. An estimated 350,000 New Yorkers who had crowded the beach at Coney Island for some respite from the murderous heat were sent scrambling for cover. The heat had been so bad that the cops gave up arresting the thousands of men who wore "shirtless bathing suits," still a misdemeanor offense against public decency in 1934.

Where Jimmy Walker had seemed the perfect mayor for New York in the capricious 1920s, he proved perfectly incapable of dealing with the city's monumental problems in the 1930s. As the Depression ravaged the city in 1930 and 1931, he hid in what was in effect his own private speakeasy, Central Park's Casino, while a couple of thousand homeless people erected a shanty Hooverville nearby in the park. In his defense, aid to the city's needy had always been the province of private charities more than the municipal government. They pitched in now, but the scale of need soon overtaxed their resources, and the mayor did little to help.

Jimmy had to go. He would be forced to resign in 1932, to be followed by a mayor who seemed his complete opposite in most every way possible.

Something similar could be said for President Herbert Hoover. He'd first come to international fame during the Great War as a humanitarian, the organizer of crucial relief programs for ravaged Europe. He was a staunch but not hidebound Republican, a believer in free enterprise and individual achievement, and as secretary of commerce through most of the 1920s he'd tried to keep the government out of the way of the decade's fantastic economic boom. He was in the White House less than a year when it all came crashing down. Although he responded with some proto–New Deal public works programs like the Hoover Dam, he was inclined to hope that businessmen and bankers would figure out on their own how to correct the plunging economy. They did not. In the summer of 1932 he appeared to be hiding in the White House when the "Bonus Army," more than forty thousand Great War veterans and their families, camped out in Washington to demand benefits they felt were owed them. When the president let General Douglas MacArthur, along with officers including Dwight Eisenhower and George Patton, attack the camp with tanks and cavalry, killing two veterans, he condemned himself to lose the election that fall. Like Mayor Walker in New York, Hoover was succeeded by a man who couldn't have been or acted more unlike him.

CHAPTER 2

Gotham Goes to Washington

The Roosevelts were as Old New York as a family could get. They traced their line back to a van Rosenvelt who came to New Amsterdam in the 1640s. Over time the family tree split into two branches: one in Oyster Bay on Long Island, the other in Hyde Park up the Hudson. Teddy and his niece Eleanor were Oyster Bay and Franklin was Hyde Park. Oyster Bay Roosevelts had been Republican since Lincoln, while the Hyde Park clan were old-line Democrats. Teddy's progressive politics struck the aloof Hyde Park clan as déclassé—except for Franklin, who greatly admired and emulated his cousin. As Franklin rose to power, the Oyster Bay clan grew increasingly resentful.

Franklin's mother, Sara, was a Delano, another old family, sprung from Plymouth Rock Pilgrims. His father, James, was a quarter century older than she when they made their dynastic union in 1880. Franklin was born two years later. He grew up like an English lord, pampered and privileged, surrounded by tutors and Swedish and German servants. (No Irish or Negroes—James would not have them.) Franklin spent little time among people his age until he went off to Groton and then Harvard, where he was neither especially popular nor academically successful. He never did learn how to have really close friends, and he would always treat even his most respected colleagues and advisers with a patrician's unthinking condescension.

When James died in 1900 Sara focused all her fierce love and domineering will on her only son. Franklin was totally dependent on her financially, and would be until she died in 1941, when he was in his third term as president.

Eleanor was born in New York City, in 1884, to parents who, for all their wealth and rank, were doomed to a short, unhappy life together. Her father, Elliott, was Teddy's younger brother. Unlike Teddy, Elliott never found a purpose in life and struggled with alcoholism and melancholia. Eleanor's mother, Anna, was also Old New York, descended from Livingstons and Ludlows. She was a beauty who took it as a personal affront that her daughter was so homely and grave—"a very ugly little girl," Eleanor later said of herself. Anna called Eleanor Granny and mocked her for her lack of looks and grace. Anna died of diphtheria at the age of only twenty-nine, when Eleanor was eight. Elliott drank himself to death two years later.

Taken in by her mother's dour family, the orphaned Eleanor remained a painfully shy loner until she bloomed at finishing school near London. She returned to New York City in 1902 a cultivated seventeen-year-old of elegant manners, though still stiflingly insecure. Her uncle Teddy had recently become president following the assassination of William McKinley. Eleanor followed his reformist example, joining the Junior League, working at a settlement house for immigrant children on Rivington Street on the Lower East Side, getting involved in workplace issues.

Then her cousin Franklin started courting her. Though they'd known each other since they were toddlers, his advances caught her by surprise. She was guarded and skeptical. But he was looking ahead and felt he needed a smart, conscientious, and reliable partner. On meeting Franklin in 1933, Oliver Wendell Holmes Jr. would famously judge that FDR possessed a "first-class temperament" but a "second-class intellect." To his credit, Roosevelt was smart enough to understand this about himself, and to surround himself with people he thought were brighter or wiser than he was. Eleanor was one of the first. She came with an intellectual gravitas and awareness of social issues he lacked. For example, she took him to the Lower East Side, where he was shocked to see for the first time how the poor lived. He knew she was good for him. He could, and would, have prettier, more fun girls on the side.

Franklin's mother Sara was displeased and jealous. She fought hard against Eleanor's intrusion before giving in, and the cousins were married in 1905. Franklin was living in New York City by then, attending Columbia Law School. After passing the bar he worked a couple of desultory years as a clerk at a Wall Street law firm and tried his hand, erratically and disastrously, at investing. Children Anna and James, always called Jimmy, were born in the house where Eleanor and Franklin were then living on East 36th Street. In 1908 Sara gave them the town house at 49 East 65th Street as a Christmas present. She moved into 47, connected to 49 on every floor by sliding doors. She dominated the joint households, making Eleanor feel like a guest. Eleanor and Franklin would live there, on and off, until he went to the White House in the spring of 1933; they would sell both houses after Sara died in 1941.

In 1910 Franklin was elected to the state senate, and Eleanor was relieved to go, without Sara, to Albany. In 1913 Woodrow Wilson appointed Roosevelt an assistant secretary of the navy. In that capacity he was at the Brooklyn Navy Yard in 1914 when the keel was laid for the battleship USS *Arizona*, launched the following year.

In 1918 Eleanor discovered Franklin's romance with Lucy Mercer, her pretty former social secretary. She could not have been surprised—his flirtatious ways and a certain deviousness had worried her since their honeymoon—but she was devastated nonetheless. She threatened divorce, which would have killed his political career. Although she never left him, and they remained supportive political partners, it was the start of their living separate lives. Feeling betrayed and rejected by her husband, Eleanor developed close, loving relationships with several women. Among her closest friends were a Greenwich Village couple deeply involved in women's politics, Nancy Cook and Marion Dickerman. Eleanor, Nancy, and Marion were a trio for fifteen years, to the chagrin of her Oyster Bay relatives. But Franklin—who was spending much more private time with a new secretary, Missy LeHand, than with his semi-estranged wife—approved. He built the three women a stone cottage at Hyde Park, where they lived together for a few years. Eleanor would keep a foothold in Greenwich Village. From 1933 to 1942 she had a pied-à-terre at 20 East 11th Street. Then she bought another apartment in the Village, at 29 Washington Square West, which would be her city residence in the first few years after Franklin's death in 1945. Her last Manhattan home would be at 55 East 74th Street on the Upper East Side.

Roosevelt was chosen as the running mate of the Democratic presidential candidate James Cox in 1920. They were thrashed by Warren Harding and Calvin Coolidge. The following year, he was struck down by polio, paralyzed below the waist. In 1924 he visited Warm Springs, a spa in Georgia built around a mineral pool. He'd heard about its therapeutic powers from its owner, George Foster Peabody. Born in Georgia and raised in Brooklyn, Peabody had become wealthy on Wall Street, while involving himself in Democratic politics in New York State. He bought the rather dilapidated spa in 1923, then sold it to Roosevelt.

In 1924, the crippled Roosevelt struggled to the lectern at the Democratic National Convention in Madison Square Garden (which was then actually on Madison Square, soon to move uptown) to nominate for president New York's governor Al Smith. Smith, a cigar-chomping Irish Catholic and Tammany Hall leader who had worked his way up from the Lower East Side, could not have been more different from Roosevelt socially. Smith liked to tell a bitterly humorous story about the first time he called on Roosevelt at his mansion back in 1911, and the butler didn't want to let him in the door. But they shared some progressive political ideas. The delegates leapt to their feet and roared when Roosevelt called Smith "the happy warrior"—then they nominated someone else.

Four years later, Roosevelt put Smith forward again, this time successfully. At the same time, Smith suggested that Roosevelt run to follow him as governor. Roosevelt stumped around all sixty-two counties of the state seated in an open touring car. Traveling with him, filling him in on local politics and helping him write his speeches, was the state assemblyman Samuel Rosenman. Born to Russian Jewish immigrants in Texas, he'd grown up in New York City, graduated from Columbia Law, and been in the assembly as a non-Tammany Democrat since 1922. He would remain a friend and adviser until Roosevelt's death.

On election night they were all at campaign headquarters at the Biltmore Hotel (which, with the Commodore and the Roosevelt, towered over Grand Central, forming the complex they called Terminal City). They witnessed Smith's crushing defeat at the hands of Herbert Hoover. Roosevelt, however, was elected governor.

Covering Roosevelt's 1928 campaign, the accomplished Associated Press reporter Lorena Hickok met and fell in love with Eleanor, and Eleanor reciprocated. Hickok, whom Eleanor called Hick, quit her job because she couldn't write objectively about the Roosevelts anymore. She and Eleanor would be companions for thirty years, with Hick enjoying a small bedroom in the White House for much of the Roosevelts' time there. In 1934, *Time* snarkily described her as "a rotund lady with a husky voice, a peremptory manner, [and] baggy clothes" who "has gone around a lot with the First Lady."

⁓

While Mayor Walker hid from the Depression in New York City, in Albany Governor Roosevelt took an active approach. As he would do in the White House, he put some smart, dedicated people on the job and gave them what they needed to get things done in a hurry.

One of them was Frances Perkins. Born in Boston, she was twenty-nine when she moved to New York City in 1909 to get her master's in political science at Columbia. As director of the New York Consumers League, she lobbied in Albany for a fifty-four-hour workweek for women and youth, forming an alliance with Lower East Side assemblyman Al Smith and the state senator Robert Wagner. In 1911 she was at a party on Washington Square when the Triangle Shirtwaist fire broke out nearby and 146 workers, mostly women and girls, died horribly. Smith and Wagner chaired a state investigation that led to the Committee on Safety, and hired Perkins as its chief officer in 1912. Together they got dozens of new laws on worker safety passed in the next few years.

In 1926, Governor Al Smith appointed her to chair the state's Industrial Commission. Roosevelt kept her on when he became governor. When the Depression hit, Perkins suggested that he start statewide public works programs to provide New Yorkers with at least temporary jobs. In 1931 Governor Roosevelt doubled the state income tax to fund the $20 million Temporary Emergency Relief Administration (TERA), the first and largest state program of its type. A man named Harry Hopkins was tapped to run it. It was the start of a Roosevelt-Hopkins partnership that would last until Roosevelt's death.

Although thin and unhealthy from childhood, Harry Hopkins would always keep his wan candle blazing at both ends. He lived on coffee and Lucky Strikes, worked with an incandescent energy that astounded everyone who met him, then partied just as energetically, a man who loved days at the track and nights hobnobbing in swanky clubs with the wealthy and celebrated. By his early forties it was clear to all his friends and colleagues that he was working and playing himself into an early grave. He seemed to know it too, which made him a man in a great hurry.

He was born in 1890 and grew up in Grinnell, Iowa. He inherited equal parts of his father, Al, a harness salesman who liked to gamble and party, and his Methodist mother, Anna, who took seriously her Christian duty to help the less fortunate. At the Congregationalist Grinnell College, where he majored in political science and history, Hopkins, like his older sister Adah, took to heart the tenets of the Social Gospel, which sent waves of idealistic young Protestants to settlement houses in big-city slums to labor for the betterment of the poor. On graduating in 1912 he followed

Adah to Manhattan's Lower East Side to work at the Christodora ("Gift of Christ") House on Avenue B facing Tompkins Square Park. He was stunned to see the wretched poverty in the neighborhood's overstuffed tenements, the most crowded immigrant enclave in the country. In 1913 he married Ethel Gross, a Jewish girl from the neighborhood. They had three sons who would all serve in the military during the war. In the late 1920s Hopkins would start an affair with a coworker; Ethel divorced him in 1931 and he married his lover Barbara Duncan a month later.

From the Christodora, Hopkins moved on to the Association for Improving the Condition of the Poor, the oldest and most respected welfare charity in the city, and then to the American Red Cross. He was directing the New York Tuberculosis and Health Association when Perkins and Governor Roosevelt asked him to take on TERA. Within its first few months, Hopkins had spent all the money Roosevelt gave him, providing aid to 1.2 million New Yorkers—a tenth of the population—and creating public works jobs for eighty thousand.

⌣

Sam Rosenman is credited with coining the term "New Deal." It was in a line from Roosevelt's acceptance speech of the Democratic presidential nomination in 1932: "I pledge you, I pledge myself, to a new deal for the American people." Given the pervasive anti-Semitism of the era, had Americans known the slogan came from a New York Jew they might not have embraced it as warmly as they did.

It was also Rosenman who suggested that candidate Roosevelt recruit a circle of respected intellectuals from various fields to advise him. The original group was heavy with Columbia professors, including Raymond Moley and Adolf Berle (pronounced Burly), who both taught law, and agriculture professor Rexford Tugwell. A *Times* writer sarcastically called the group Roosevelt's "brains trust"—often rendered brain trust—as more and more intellectuals, many from New York, joined it.

Roosevelt rewarded Rosenman by appointing him, at the age of thirty-six, a justice of the Supreme Court of the State of New York. That job would keep Rosenman busy through FDR's first term in the White House, but as the 1936 election approached Roosevelt would bring Rosenman back into the fold to help him craft his speeches and campaign positions.

Roosevelt crushed Hoover in the 1932 election. At the same time, his lieutenant governor, Herbert Lehman, was elected to follow him in the governor's mansion. Lehman, the first Jewish governor of New York, would serve through 1942. His father was one of the Lehman Brothers of the Wall Street investment firm. Lehman's Republican opponent was a Word War I hero, William "Wild Bill" Donovan. Born in 1883 and raised in a middle-class Irish Catholic home in Buffalo, Donovan first encountered Franklin Roosevelt when they were classmates at Columbia Law School. In 1916, before the United States entered the Great War, he toured the front lines as a thirty-three-year-old lawyer representing the Rockefeller Foundation's War Relief Commission, which shipped food and clothing to citizens in countries ravaged by the conflict. When America did enter the war in 1917 Donovan joined New York City's famed 69th Regiment, the Fighting Irish. Lieutenant Colonel Donovan led his men with great courage through some of the bloodiest battles of 1918, earning a Medal of Honor and a chestful of others, plus his nickname, and celebrity status back home.

In the 1920s Donovan's celebrity propelled him up the ranks of the national Republican Party, but his Catholicism prevented him from getting higher than a stint in D.C. as an assistant attorney general in the criminal division. A young J. Edgar Hoover, a future rival, worked under him there. In 1932 Donovan, about to turn fifty, was running a prosperous law office at 2 Wall Street and living in a grand Beekman Place duplex staffed with live-in servants, when state Republicans invited him to challenge Lehman. Donovan fought hard, denouncing Roosevelt as "a new kind of red, white and blue dictator" and Lehman as his "Siamese twin," but he lost. He would cross paths with Roosevelt again, and in a very different way, a few years later.

⌒

In February 1933, the president-elect summoned Frances Perkins to his East 65th Street home and asked her to be his secretary of labor, making her the first female cabinet member in history. She had barely gotten settled in Washington when Hopkins took a train down to meet with her. He presented a plan to re-create New York's jobs program on a national scale. She presented it to the president, who had it put to the Democrat-controlled Congress as one of the fifteen major bills he pushed through in his legendary first one hundred days in office, kickstarting the New Deal. In May Congress passed the Federal Emergency Relief Act, and Roosevelt brought Hopkins to Washington to run it.

The typical Washington administrator might have spent weeks setting up an office, assembling a staff, and having meetings. Hopkins found an unmanned desk in an empty room, sat down, and in his first two hours on the job authorized more than $5 million in relief. In a capital city used to turgid bureaucracy, his head-spinning hurry made headlines. Once, when Hopkins was told one of his programs would likely get funded "in the long run," he snapped, "People don't eat in the long run, they eat every day." He would come to be known as Roosevelt's "minister of relief."

Hopkins believed that Americans didn't want handouts, they wanted jobs. In the fall of 1933 he got FDR's backing for a short-term jobs program, the Civil Works Administration. He invited another New Yorker down to Washington to help him design the program: the newly elected mayor Fiorello La Guardia.

CHAPTER 3

New Deal New York

Five-foot-two, shaped like a barrel, and fond of oversize cowboy hats, Fiorello La Guardia cut a comical public figure, the Lou Costello of politics. But the barrel was stuffed with dynamite that could explode at any instant into rage, into laughter, or just into manic rushing around. He was generally a friend to the poor and downtrodden, but to his staff he was an autocrat and slave driver who could be viciously insulting and abusive. People called him Butch and the Little Flower, but also Mussolini and Napoleon. Matching towering ambition, a limitless ego, and a motor always running at top speed, he was convinced there was no issue or problem, from the minuscule to the global, that he could not personally solve. In his early mayoral years he raced tirelessly around the city—smashing slot machines, padlocking burlesque houses, dashing into burning buildings, cutting ribbons, and tongue-lashing Tammany clock-watchers—until people joked there was not one mayor but several identical ones. Later, he would foil himself with his attempts to run the biggest city in the world while simultaneously participating and kibitzing in national and international affairs. By the end of World War II he would have exhausted himself nearly to the last atom.

He was born in Greenwich Village in 1882. His father was a musician from Foggia, in southern Italy, and a nonpracticing Catholic; his mother was from Trieste, then part of the Austro-Hungarian Empire, and from a highly respected Jewish family. They had three children: Gemma, Fiorello, and Richard.

When Fiorello was three his father became a U.S. Army bandleader and they left New York City for a succession of army bases, mostly in Arizona, which was still the Wild West. Fiorello would wear black Stetsons and string ties the rest of his life. At sixteen he followed his father to

Tampa, where the army was massing for the invasion of Cuba in the short-lived Spanish-American War. When his father took sick—Fiorello blamed the tinned army beef, nicknamed "embalmed beef" by the soldiers—the family left the United States for Trieste. His father never recovered and died in 1904. At eighteen Fiorello got a job as a clerk and translator in the American consulate in Fiume. He developed at least some fluency in half a dozen languages, including Yiddish, a skill that would serve him well in New York City.

He returned to New York in 1906, leaving his mother and older sister in Fiume, and got a job processing immigrants at Ellis Island. He studied law at night at NYU and took flying lessons on Long Island from the famed aircraft designer Giuseppe Bellanca. He ran for Congress as a progressive Republican in 1914, lost, but won two years later.

When the United States entered the Great War in 1917 Congressman La Guardia volunteered as a pilot and was sent to an Italian airfield near his father's hometown. He flew bombing missions over German and Austrian troops, survived a potentially deadly crash, had a medal pinned on his chest by King Victor Emmanuel III, and was hailed in the American press as the Flying Congressman. In 1918 the thirty-six-year-old assistant secretary of the navy Franklin Roosevelt went to Italy to ask for the Italian navy's assistance in fighting the German U-boats that were preying on Allied shipping. Stepping off a train he was met by Captain La Guardia. As very different as they were, the two men liked each other; later, when they were both much more powerful figures, they would fondly tell the story of this first meeting.

After the war La Guardia returned to Congress. In 1929 he tried to unseat Jimmy Walker, but his railing against Tammany corruption fell on deaf ears and Walker was reelected in the biggest landslide in the city's history. Then the Depression hit. While the catastrophe spread and the mayor hid, reform groups such as the City Affairs Committee pressured Governor Roosevelt until he appointed a blue ribbon commission to investigate what everyone already knew: that Walker's administration was putrid with fantastic levels of graft and corruption. Roosevelt convinced Jimmy to resign in September 1932. Tammany's John P. O'Brien won a special election to keep the mayor's chair warm until the next election in November 1933.

La Guardia chose to run again that year. He'd lost his congressional seat in the backlash against Hoover's Republicans that swept the country in 1932 and was available for a new job. To go up against a Tammany mayor in 1933 he joined the new City Fusion Party, a multiethnic, multiparty stew of Republicans and Socialists, wealthy WASPs and poor immigrants, Jews and Catholics and Protestants, Greenwich Village bohemians and renegade Democrats—all brought together by the common goal of ending Tammany's reign. La Guardia began the campaign with an enthusiastic rally at Cooper Union and ended it with a speech at Madison Square Garden—which by then had moved to Eighth Avenue between 49th and 50th Streets. He drew a crowd of at least fifty thousand. That was thirty thousand more than the venue could seat, so loudspeakers carried the event to a throng outside. An all-female band played "Who's Afraid of the Big Bad Wolf?" to which the crowd sang "Who's afraid of Tam-man-y?" On Eighth Avenue, the crowd scuffled with a passing parade of five hundred Tammany supporters. When La Guardia took the stage the crowd inside let out a roar that rattled the rafters. La Guardia beat O'Brien with almost 870,000 votes split fairly equally between Republican and Fusion voters.

⌣

In January 1934 La Guardia took over a city mired deep in Depression misery. But he had extremely powerful friends in Washington—Perkins, Hopkins, the president himself. FDR and La Guardia had similar ideas about government's responsibility to the people, and similarly expansive views of their power to make their government do what they wanted it to do. Only their managerial styles were different—La Guardia shouted and screamed, Roosevelt smiled and schemed.

Except in wartime, Washington had rarely gotten involved in municipal affairs. Now cities around the country were approaching bankruptcy and finding that their state governments, many of them more geared to rural than urban policy, were of no help. Mayors had formed the U.S. Conference of Mayors as an organized vehicle for appeals to the federal government. La Guardia vaulted to the head of the group, acting as its spokesman and direct link to the White House.

Harry Hopkins listened closely to La Guardia's ideas about the Civil Works Administration. La Guardia returned to New York with a couple hundred thousand short-term CWA jobs and put New Yorkers to work in the winter of 1934 repairing parks and waterfront and public buildings that had fallen into near ruin during the previous decades of Tammany neglect. They also razed slums to make space for the first public housing developments in the city's history.

Despite the alphabet soup of New Deal programs Roosevelt threw at it—the CWA, the CCC (Civilian Conservation Corps), FERA (Federal Emergency Relief Administration), PWA (the Public Works Administration), NRA (National Recovery Administration) et al.—the Depression ground on through the mid-1930s. Buoyed by the 1934 midterm elections in which the Democrats expanded their dominance in Congress, Hopkins told his staff, "Boys, this is our hour. We've got to get everything we want—a works program, social security, wages and hours, everything—now or never." Early in 1935, Roosevelt approved Hopkins's sweeping new jobs program, the Works Progress Administration, a larger and longer-term successor to the Civil Works Administration.

The WPA became one of the most visible of New Deal programs, and Hopkins the most championed and attacked New Deal administrator. In its first year it provided nearly three million jobs, and over its lifetime it employed eight million. Not everyone agreed this was a good thing. Republicans denounced it as creeping socialism and charged that many of the jobs were useless make-work. The recently-coined term "boondoggle" was soon applied.

In New York City, Mayor La Guardia and his parks commissioner Robert Moses pounced. They made the best team in the country for acquiring WPA funds and putting them to use, even though their egos clashed like continents. Monstrously arrogant and convinced of his superiority to nearly everyone he met, Moses was born in 1888 into a privileged household of prosperous uptown German Jews and educated at Yale, Oxford, and Columbia. Looking around the dirty, chaotic New York City of the 1910s, stuffed to bursting with wretchedly poor immigrants and being run into the ground by the tremendously corrupt Tammany Hall machine, the young Moses envisioned an entirely different city, a clean and well-ordered metropolis of gleaming residential and commercial towers, reaching out to sprawling suburbs and vast parks through an arterial network of parkways, expressways, and waterways. Then he set out to build it. He became a brilliant bureaucratic tactician, and by La Guardia's time he was creating his own nearly autonomous empire of multiple agencies, a power base easily rivaling the mayor's. He saw La Guardia as at best a helpmeet in realizing his grand plans for the city. They fought every time they met. "Someday I'm going to hit that son of a bitch and knock him through that door," La Guardia once said of Moses, whom he sarcastically called His Grace. Moses referred to the mayor as "that dago son of a bitch" and Rigoletto. Moses's utter lack of tact helped doom his one campaign for political office. In 1934, in the midst of working with La Guardia, he made a quixotic and failed run against Herbert Lehman for the governorship.

While Moses had a small army of architects and engineers crank out project applications, the city rented La Guardia an apartment in D.C. to facilitate frequent trips to the White House. "He comes to Washington and tells me a sad story," the president once said with a laugh. "The tears run down my cheeks and the tears run down his cheeks and the first thing I know, he has wangled another fifty million dollars." Soon New York City was filling so many jobs and receiving so much funding—almost a tenth of the WPA's national total—that Hopkins declared it the forty-ninth state and gave it its own WPA administration. To run it, Hopkins sent Lieutenant Colonel Brehon Somervell of the U.S. Army Corps of Engineers to the city. He was an Arkansas-born West Pointer who in his youth had served in the expedition against Pancho Villa and in France during the Great War. He would direct the city's WPA programs until 1940, then oversee a massive buildup of defense facilities around the country, including the Pentagon, as well as the start of the Manhattan Project.

Working with Somervell, La Guardia and Moses used WPA support to put thousands to work building or improving hospitals and post offices, schools and firehouses, beaches and parks, the Prospect Park and Staten Island zoos, the Bronx–Whitestone Bridge, and the New York Municipal Airport, later renamed for La Guardia. The airport was La Guardia's "baby," his wife said. It had rankled him that the greatest city in the world did not have a viable commercial airport. The nearest were in Newark and Floyd Bennett Field out near Coney Island, often fogged in and considered too far away to serve New York City well. The site La Guardia chose was North Beach, Queens, home of the small Glenn Curtiss Airport. It was just across the East River from Manhattan and, not coincidentally, a stone's throw from Flushing Meadows, where the 1939 world's fair would be. FDR, a promoter of commercial aviation, supported the mayor with $27 million in federal funds and thousands of WPA workers, who at peak construction periods labored around the clock in eight-hour shifts. La Guardia came by to watch their progress so often that smiling workers took to handing him their tools. They made the longest runway in the world at the time (6,000 feet) and beautiful art deco terminals. The airport opened in December 1939, too late for the first season of the world's fair. It was soon the busiest airport in the world, handling two hundred flights a day; coming and going, passengers would get spectacular aerial views of the fair's iconic Trylon and Perisphere.

⌒

The WPA also included a relatively small but highly visible and controversial component for arts funding, a program called Federal Project Number One—or "Federal One" for short. By the end of 1936 it employed some forty thousand artists, musicians, writers, and theater workers around the country. In New York, Colonel Somervell made it quite clear he had no patience for wrangling arts workers into some semblance of bureaucratic order. Many were used to lives of bohemian excess and license; some, especially among the writers, treated heavy drinking as a mark of their profession. Added to all that, the leftist ideals in much of the work they created for Federal One made it an easy target for conservatives at the newspapers and in Congress.

Directed by Holger Cahill, a curator at the new Museum of Modern Art (opened in 1929), the Federal Art Project created jobs for some five thousand visual artists. In New York it put bread on the table for a generation of young artists who would go on to make the city the art capital of the Western world after the war, including Jackson Pollock, Lee Krasner, Willem de Kooning, Mark Rothko, and Arshile Gorky. New York City had the highest concentration of writers in the country, so Hopkins gave them the Federal Writers' Project.

The Federal Theatre Project was the most controversial of the Federal One programs. As the Depression deepened, more and more Broadway theaters went dark or were taken over as burlesque houses, until La Guardia started closing those as well. From employing something like twenty-five thousand people before the crash, Broadway sank to around three thousand. Another thirteen thousand theater workers around the country were idled. Harry Hopkins asked the New York playwright Elmer Rice if he knew someone who could run a program to put some of those people back to work. Born Elmer Reizenstein on East 90th Street in 1892, Rice had written the gigantic 1929 hit *Street Scene*, a realistic drama about tenement life in New York, which earned him a Pulitzer and was adapted as a film and later an opera, with music by Kurt Weill and lyrics by Langston

Hughes. He referred Hopkins to Hallie Flanagan, who was teaching theater at Vassar up in Poughkeepsie. As it happened, Hopkins and Flanagan had been classmates and friends at Grinnell College. In August 1935 Flanagan was sworn in as the project's director, and she brought Rice on to help.

By January 1936 the FTP had hired nearly ten thousand theater workers around the country, some thirty-five hundred in New York City alone. But the program got off to a bumpy start. A pet project of Rice's, a ripped-from-the-headlines production condemning Mussolini's recent invasion of Ethiopia, was about to open in New York when the White House killed it, fearing the diplomatic fallout. It was a public relations fiasco for Flanagan, and Rice quit in a huff. Joseph Losey, a Communist sympathizer and later party member, directed a couple of productions marked by down-with-capitalism up-with-the-workers cant that drew the attention of Congress. The *New York Times* complained that the "Moscow stylization of writing and staging" reduced the shows to "adolescent gibberish," while William Randolph Hearst's conservative *Journal* attacked Hopkins for funding a "Communist-infested" program.

⌣

The WPA was also attacked from the left. In February 1936 a left-leaning New York City congressman managed to get himself roughed up and arrested by the NYPD for protesting the way the WPA was run under La Guardia's "Mussolini-like administration." To make matters worse, he had been a devoted protégé and aide to La Guardia.

Vito Marcantonio was born in a tenement in Italian East Harlem on East 112th Street. His father, a carpenter, was killed by a streetcar when Vito was a boy. After graduating from NYU Law School in 1925, Vito went to work for Congressman La Guardia, who was very fond of him. Marcantonio managed La Guardia's failed reelection campaign in 1932 and stumped hard for his election to mayor the following year. In 1934, with the mayor's backing, the thirty-one-year-old Marcantonio won La Guardia's old congressional seat as a Republican-Fusion candidate. He cut an odd figure in Washington, a small man—the press habitually described him as "diminutive," "slight," "spidery"—with a New Yawker's nasal voice and nervous hands, given to a cartoon gangster's fedoras and wide-striped suits. He was also a maverick, argumentative and combative, the bane of both parties, and so pro-labor, antimilitary, and soak-the-rich that most people just assumed he was, as one opponent put it, a "Communist stooge."

At a WPA protest rally in Madison Square Park, Marcantonio railed that La Guardia had shown his back to the little man he once championed. "A billion dollars for war and the munitions makers, but not one cent for the unemployed, starving workers!" he cried. It was inaccurate and nonsensical, but it fired up his thousands of listeners. He was trying to lead them in a march, without a police permit, across town to the WPA's offices when the cops moved in and, according to the *Herald Tribune*, Marcantonio was "cuffed, kicked, and thrown into a police wagon" with eleven others. The police commissioner Lewis Valentine released them all later that day. His blood still up, Marcantonio challenged Valentine to meet him "alone in a gymnasium." Valentine scoffed that he'd meet him "with a flit-gun," adding, "This is just another evidence of what happens when you elect a boy to do a man's job." La Guardia—who, after all, was no stranger to outbursts of populist theatrics himself—treated the incident as a fit of pique from a beloved wayward son. He merely asked him "to refrain from such conduct in the future." Marcantonio would lose his reelection bid that fall, but it was far from the end of his career.

As Roosevelt's own first reelection drew near, the WPA and especially Federal One made soft targets for his critics. The *Times* contrasted the solid achievements of the WPA's public works projects in the city—a hundred new playgrounds, more than one hundred miles of new roadways, eleven new public swimming pools, new traffic lights, new piers—to the arts programs, whose "usefulness has been widely doubted," and where the "boondoggling...tends to bring the engineering projects into discredit with it." To the *Times*, Federal One looked like preferential make-work for artists. "If unemployed tap dancers must be given Government jobs at tap dancing, why shouldn't the Government open new banks to give jobs to unemployed bank clerks?"

Bending to the criticism, Roosevelt ordered the WPA's overall budget cut by a quarter, and Federal One's by a third. In New York City, two thousand Federal One arts workers were laid off. They didn't take it quietly. More than two hundred artists barricaded themselves inside the Federal Art Project offices on East 39th Street. When a squadron of seventy-five policemen broke in the artists still refused to leave. The cops' batons came out, seven people were injured, and 219 artists were carted off to the Tombs. Two doors down, writers occupied the seventeenth-floor offices of the Writers' Project. Theater workers occupied the FTP offices as well. Colonel Somervell went to Washington, where he asked that funding for the public works programs be restored—but not Federal One. Artists marched in the streets carrying signs like "MERRY CHRISTMAS/ WISH YOU WELL/ HERE'S YOUR PINK SLIP/ SOMERVELL."

To quell the strife, La Guardia too went to Washington and worked his magic on Roosevelt. Somehow, in the end, the Federal One roster for the city actually went up from 10,560 employees to 10,566.

⌒

As early as the spring of 1934, Harry Hopkins had worked and played himself to exhaustion and an ulcer, the first signs of his physical decline. Roosevelt was genuinely concerned. Hopkins was proving to be not only his most trusted and loyal assistant but the nearest Roosevelt came to a close friend.

Hopkins had one quality Roosevelt found indispensable. Roosevelt's warm, charming affect was a dazzling facade behind which he hid his feelings and agendas. He was a master of misdirection. In meetings he was notoriously vague, discursive, and evasive. He had a way of nodding and smiling, as though he agreed with everything everyone in the meeting said, without actually committing himself to anything. New Yorker Henry Stimson, FDR's secretary of war through World War II, would complain in his diary that meeting with FDR was like "chasing a vagrant beam of sunshine around a vacant room." The journalist John Gunther observed, "I never met anyone who showed a greater capacity for avoiding a direct answer while giving the questioner a feeling he had been answered." His vice president Harry Truman would flat out call him a liar.

Hopkins, though, as Churchill later wrote, "always went to the root of the matter." With his restless need to get things done and make things happen, Hopkins cut through any red tape or obstructionism that got in his way. He was one of the few people in FDR's inner circle who could focus his wandering attention and clarify his vague intentions. Hopkins's impatience with dithering bureaucrats and posturing politicians earned him many enemies in Washington but made him indispensable to FDR for twelve years. People would take to calling him the deputy president or assistant president. He was also called the "Shadow," because he went everywhere Roosevelt did. *Time* would rate him “the second most powerful man in America,” and a senator once cracked, “If Roosevelt ever becomes Jesus Christ, he should have Harry Hopkins as his prophet.”

In the spring of 1934, Roosevelt sent Hopkins and his wife on a long European trip to get some rest. But—and this was typical of how Roosevelt treated even his closest friends—not *too* much rest. He asked Hopkins to visit U.S. embassies in Europe and report his assessments of their staffs. The Hopkinses were in Europe that summer when Adolf Hitler had his first meeting with Benito Mussolini, purged the Nazi Party of Ernst Röhm and his SA leaders in the “night of the long knives,” and further consolidated his power as Führer. Hopkins tried and failed to get an audience with the Führer, but he did meet Mussolini and reported his impressions of it all to FDR. He would make many more such trips for his wheelchair-bound boss in the coming years.

In 1937 both Barbara and Harry Hopkins would be diagnosed with cancer. She died that year, while surgeons at the Mayo Clinic removed two-thirds of Harry’s stomach. He would return to Mayo for more treatments in 1939, and he remained in ill health for what was left of his life, anemic, unable to properly absorb nutrients, often exhausted. Yet he remained an unstoppable worker for his boss, never hesitating to further damage his health to carry out any assignment or task Roosevelt handed him. As much as FDR worried for Harry, the president would come close more than once to working him to death.

CHAPTER 4

Franklin Rosenfeld of Jew York City

When Roosevelt entered the White House, there were more Jews in the United States—about 4.2 million—than in any other country in the world. About 1.75 million of them lived in New York City, far more than in any other city in the world. The next four largest Jewish communities combined—in Chicago, Warsaw, Budapest, and Vienna—didn't add up to New York's. It was not uncommon for Americans elsewhere to call it Jew York.

It followed that among the New Yorkers whom FDR attracted to Washington there were a number of Jews. During his twelve years in office he put Jews in his cabinet, his brains trust, on the Supreme Court, at other places of power around his administration. Jews had never been more influential or visible.

What's remarkable is that he did this at the same time that anti-Semitism was not only boiling into genocidal rage in Germany but peaking in America as well. The more power and influence Jews achieved in the 1930s, the more some Americans feared they were "taking control."

Anti-Semitism permeated American society in the 1930s. Its expressions ranged from mild prejudice to acts of violence. A 1938 Roper poll asked Americans, "What kinds of people do you object to?" Jews topped the list at 35 percent. Even the sort of powerful Jews in FDR's circle suffered frequent, insulting reminders that for all their success they were still, as the saying went, "not quite our sort." Top universities and colleges maintained strict quotas on Jewish admissions; country clubs and patriotic organizations including New York's Union Club barred them; Gentile employers limited how many Jews they hired, if any; intermarriage was severely discouraged. Even the progressive Eleanor Roosevelt once sniffed about an acquaintance acting too "Jewy." Depression-fueled resentments and the spread of Nazi and Nazi-inspired hate literature in the 1930s heated up attitudes that had been simmering since the world war.

For appearing to favor Jews in his government, Franklin Roosevelt was called Franklin Rosenfeld, his New Deal the Jew Deal. Privately, he would never entirely evolve past his wealthy WASP upbringing, with its offhanded and no-harm-meant condescension in matters of race, color, and creed. Eleanor was always far more progressive in such matters. But just as the young Franklin had married Eleanor because he recognized in her qualities he lacked, President Roosevelt intuited that he needed to surround himself with the best and brightest he could get, whether they were Jewish, Catholic, Republicans, female, or black (at a time when Washington, D.C., was still segregated in many respects).

⌒

New York's Jews in the 1930s lived in two distinct and mutually rather exclusive communities. One community was Reform Jews, mostly of German descent. They'd begun immigrating to the city in the 1840s. Generally they'd been literate, sophisticated urbanites in Europe, and they were able gradually to ease their way in and up the social ladder in the city. They tended to be nonreligious or follow the Reform practices established by Rabbi Isaac Wise in the nineteenth century. Wise insisted that Jews were not a people, a nation, or a race, they just happened to share a form of worship. You couldn't speak of a "Jewish race" any more than you could a "Presbyterian race." German Jews were Germans, American Jews Americans, and so on. It followed that Wise considered the Zionist dream of a homeland for the Jewish people folly built on a false premise. By the 1930s these German descendants were the "uptown" Jews, living prosperously on the Upper West and Upper East Sides. They did their best to fit in with the WASPs around them. Some would change their names to ones that sounded less Jewish.

One distinct subset of German Jews in the 1930s were newcomers fleeing from the Nazis. By the start of the war they'd number some twenty thousand. They formed their own community in the far northern tip of Manhattan, in Washington Heights, where they came to represent about a tenth of the neighborhood's total population. Because many of them were from the city of Frankfurt am Main and surrounding towns, Washington Heights came to be known as "Frankfurt on the Hudson." Most of them had been fully assimilated in Germany, nonpracticing or Reform in religion, thinking of themselves as Germans first and Jews second. They were educated, liberal, and middle class. The first arrivals headed to Washington Heights because there was a small but well-established Jewish presence there already, and because it was less densely urban than the rest of Manhattan, more like where they'd lived all their lives. They acted as a magnet for the later immigrants. Although they clung to their German language and customs at first, they assimilated into American life quickly and took citizenship as soon as they could. They started small businesses and shops throughout the neighborhood. There would be no greater fans of FDR, and the young men among them would race to enlist in the armed services when the time came.

The second large group of Jews in New York were originally Yiddish-speaking, eastern European, Orthodox Jews. Nearly three quarters of the two and a half million of them who came to the United States from the 1880s to the mid-1920s got no farther than the Lower East Side of Manhattan. There they were mercilessly crowded into tiny rooms in the dark, crumbling tenements that lined streets such as Orchard and Hester, Ludlow and Rivington, Norfolk and Suffolk. The streets themselves were often impassable, with milling crowds seeking a little light and air, and with hundreds of pushcart peddlers selling fruit and vegetables, needles and pins, pocket watches and ties. (In the mid-1930s, Mayor La Guardia, sensitive about the ethnic stereotypes attached to both Jewish pushcart peddlers and Italian organ-grinders, began to clear the streets of both. The peddlers were moved into new municipal markets, the organ-grinders banned altogether.)

Poor, speaking little or no English, many of them country peasants back home, Orthodox Jews on the Lower East Side and in pockets in the other boroughs formed their own insular communities. The original immigrants (less so their New York–born children) were not particularly interested in assimilating into secular American life and therefore were less concerned about ingratiating themselves with Gentiles or upsetting anti-Semites. For some, America was just a stopover on the way to a Zionist homeland in Palestine. New York's German Jews, both the older and the newer arrivals, tended to look down on them for their incomprehensible Yiddish, their deeply old-fashioned ways, and their reluctance to assimilate.

In the 1930s, despite the bubbling anti-Semitism, New York Jews achieved unprecedented levels of political prominence. The governor was Jewish. The mayor was Jewish on his mother's side. In Washington, FDR's circle included, along with Sam Rosenman, the Jewish New Yorkers Felix Frankfurter, Henry Morgenthau Jr., and, though at arm's length, Bernard Baruch.

Born in Austria, Frankfurter had come to the Lower East Side with his family as a boy. After graduating from Harvard Law, he worked as an assistant to the U.S. attorney for the Southern District of New York (FDR's future secretary of war Henry Stimson). He later joined the Harvard Law faculty, and he was one of the founders of the ACLU. He was a supporter of and adviser to President Roosevelt from the start, a brains truster who recommended many bright young people to the president, including Dean Acheson and Alger Hiss. In 1938 Roosevelt appointed him to the Supreme Court.

Born and raised in New York City, Henry Morgenthau Jr. was a disappointment to his father, a highly successful German Jewish real estate magnate. Henry Jr. was big and clumsy, crushingly shy and inarticulate, and a poor student, possibly dyslexic, who never finished college. With his father's help he bought a farm in Dutchess County, making him a neighbor and friend to Franklin Roosevelt at nearby Hyde Park. He much preferred touring his apple orchards on horseback to working in the family business in Manhattan.

Many of his contemporaries believed him rather dim-witted. The *Saturday Evening Post* judged him "slow-thinking and slow-speaking," *Time* called him "a real cold fish," and in FDR's administration he was nicknamed Henry the Morgue. When Roosevelt appointed him secretary of the treasury in 1934 it was joked that he had hired the one Jew in New York who knew nothing about money. But Morgenthau had two qualities that endeared him to Roosevelt: he was deeply devoted to his president and he got things done. He would capably manage billions in federal bond issues to fund the New Deal without raising taxes or interest rates.

Bernard Baruch was, as his biographer James Grant noted, a looming figure in the American mind in the 1930s, yet he was also a rather nebulous one. He was half New York Jew and half patrician Southern gentleman. He advised several presidents but often in no official capacity, preferring to float as an independent consultant. He possessed an Apollonian intellect and a satyr's eye.

Baruch's father, a Jewish doctor from Prussia, immigrated to South Carolina in 1855, served as a surgeon with the Confederate army in the war, and married a ruined plantation owner's daughter. Bernard was born there in 1870, and when he was ten the family moved to New York City.

After graduating in 1891 from the College of the City of New York, at Lexington Avenue and East 24th Street—now site of Bernard M. Baruch College—he took a $3-a-week job running errands on Wall Street. He had grown to a towering, athletic six-foot-four, with blazing blue eyes and a sportily curled mustache. He was a sturdy amateur boxer with brains to match the brawn. He was extremely vain about it, but he had good reason, so most people forgave him. Men as well as women found him attractive; he would enjoy his fair share of the latter.

He also enjoyed gambling at cards, at the track, and on Wall Street. By 1897 he had done well enough at the last to buy his own seat on the Exchange. He'd made his first million by 1900, when a million dollars bought roughly twenty-five times what it does today. He piled more millions on that one and reveled in them. He owned racehorses, speedboats, and fast cars. To his Manhattan brownstone he added a baronial plantation in South Carolina, called Hobcaw, where his guests sipped mint juleps and murdered waterfowl in relaxed isolation—no telephone, though mail and telegrams were delivered. His wealth and success bought access to high levels of WASP society despite his being half Jewish; several of his WASP friends, who called him Barney, would say he was the least Jewish Jew they knew. Still, not every gentleman's club or golf club would accept him no matter how many millions or Gentile friends he had.

During the Great War, Woodrow Wilson appointed him chair of the War Industries Board (WIB). The United States had entered the war in a state of drastic unpreparedness. The WIB brought together industrialists, military men, and labor leaders and tasked them with standardizing military hardware, speeding up production, and minimizing discord between industrial employers and workers.

When the war ended, Baruch sailed with the American delegation to the peace conference at Versailles, where he argued, unsuccessfully, against the vindictive reparations England and France wanted to impose on Germany, and, more successfully, he threw sumptuous parties that were still being talked about years later. When he sailed with Wilson's party back to America, a flotilla of battleships and destroyers met their steamer at the New York harbor, banging off salutes. This was followed by a parade and a celebration at Carnegie Hall.

Baruch surfed the madly speculative stock market of the 1920s and held on to many of his millions when it crashed in 1929. Although Franklin Roosevelt was not his first choice for a Democratic candidate in 1932, he contributed generously to his campaign.

It says something about the era's anti-Semitism that Baruch was always presumed to be more influential with FDR than he was in reality. When Roosevelt was elected it was widely assumed that Baruch was a shoo-in for a cabinet post, but he never got one. To Roosevelt and his inner circle, Baruch was "too luminous a figure," best kept at a friendly distance. He would be in the cloud of experts surrounding the president, his advice sometimes heeded, just as often not. The idea also persisted that he was a chief architect of the New Deal, when in fact he thought it often gave the government too much power over the economy. As FDR rushed to build up America's defenses from 1940 on, it again would be widely assumed that he would tap Baruch, with his WIB experience, to head one of his larger wartime agencies; again, he did not.

Yet the legend of Baruch's shadowy power continued. The anti-Semitic demagogue Father Charles Coughlin would call him "Acting President of the United States." A French newspaper described him as "President Roosevelt's great financial adviser and semi-official chief of Jewish policy in America," and Joseph Goebbels's propaganda, which routinely referred to him as "the Jew Baruch," would paint him as one of America's leading warmongers and profiteers. In a skit at the Washington press corps' Gridiron Dinner, newsmen sang, to the tune of "Oh! Susanna":

When any problem gets too large
It might end in a fluke,
We take it straight to F.D.R.—
Who takes it to Baruch!

⁓

The *New York Times*, the most influential newspaper in the country by the 1930s, had been Jewish-owned since Adolph Ochs bought it in 1896. It was not the most widely read paper in the country, or even in the city. Its daily circulation was 435,000, twice that on Sunday. By comparison, the mighty *Daily News* sold nearly two million copies a day, the *Daily Mirror* 750,000, the *Tribune* 400,000, the *Post* 250,000. But, as the saying went, it wasn't how many people read the *Times*, it was who read it: everyone in the power elites of New York and Washington. The most influential people in the country were influenced by what they read in the *Times* every day. Roosevelt read it religiously, was pleased when it said nice things about him, miffed when it did not.

Ochs's parents were from Bavaria. He had relatives in Germany whom he often visited, and he felt a strong sentimental bond with German culture. He married the daughter of Rabbi Isaac Wise and thoroughly agreed with his Reform principles. Ochs made his last trip to Germany in 1930. He visited with relatives and went to the little town his father was from. Hitler's rise to power in 1933, followed shortly by the start of his purge of Jews from Germany, shattered Ochs (who had a previous history of depressive incidents). He ceded the running of the *Times* to his son-in-law, Arthur Hays Sulzberger, and died in 1935.

Sulzberger's family was also from Germany. If anything, he was even more assimilationist than his in-laws. Judaism played little part in his personal life, and he went to great lengths to give anti-Semites no excuse to criticize the *Times* as a Jewish paper. He carefully monitored news about Jews and Jewish issues in the paper, even restricting the use of the words "Jew" and "Jewish." Staff writers with Jewish names were encouraged to use their initials. Zionism was effectively banned from its pages. Most important, Sulzberger's concerns about how the *Times* was perceived would lead inevitably to a conscious and methodical downplaying of news about the persecution and massacre of Jews in Europe.

⌣

No one represented the aspirations and concerns of the uptown Jews more than Rabbi Stephen Wise (no relation to Rabbi Isaac), the leading voice of mainstream Reform Judaism for decades. To his supporters he was one of the Jews whose access to the inner sanctums of power in the Roosevelt years benefited all Jews, and one of the first voices in the early 1930s to speak out against Hitler. To his detractors, however, he was a craven apple-polisher who abetted Roosevelt's slow (or non-) response to the massacre of eastern European Jews during World War II. There was justification for both views.

He was born in Hungary in 1874 to a long line of Orthodox rabbis and brought to New York as an infant. He grew up on East 5th Street in today's East Village, but in a family milieu much closer to the German Jews uptown than to the Yiddish Jews in the neighborhood. He went to

CCNY and Columbia, then completed his rabbinical studies in Vienna. As a young rabbi he embraced Zionism, a pursuit so outré it smacks of youthful rebellion on his part. His Reform community expressed nearly no interest in Palestine before Hitler's rise. America was their Zion.

Nevertheless, Wise grew in repute as a speaker and preacher. He was a master of the theatrical, imitation-British delivery that was considered the apex of oratory at the time. At thirty-two he was approached by Emanu-El, the flagship Reform synagogue. But after a contretemps with the synagogue's board—its members wanted to approve his sermon topics (especially on Palestine) beforehand, which he denounced as censorship—he started his own Free Synagogue. He would also found and/or direct the American Jewish Congress, the World Jewish Congress, the Zionist Organization of America, and other Jewish institutions, and he cofounded the NAACP, the ACLU, and the City Affairs Committee, which needled a reticent Governor Roosevelt into dealing with Mayor Jimmy Walker.

Because of that flinty relationship, when Roosevelt went to Washington and brought so many New Yorkers with him, Rabbi Wise was not among them. Governor Roosevelt had considered Wise a nuisance, and Wise had thought Roosevelt shifty. It was only in 1936 that they would patch up their differences, and even then it was a lopsided relationship. Wise never had the influence with FDR that a Rosenman or Morgenthau enjoyed. In his patronizing way, FDR called Wise, who was in his sixties, "Stevey," while Wise fawned and addressed Roosevelt as "Boss" or "Chief."

When Hitler came to power in 1933, Wise took a more aggressive stand than many other of New York's uptown Jews were willing to adopt in public. In March 1933, a month after Hitler became chancellor, Wise organized a public meeting of the city's Jewish leaders that packed the eighth-floor ballroom of the Hotel Astor in Times Square to overflowing. It was tumultuous. Wise wanted to hold a mass rally at Madison Square Garden to protest "the damnable outrages of Hitlerism." Others cautioned, amid boos and catcalls, against doing anything to further provoke the Nazis. "I ask you to think whether you want Jewish blood to be seen in the gutters of Germany," one of them urged. Wise, in full oratorical splendor, quashed them.

A week later, more than twenty thousand people jammed into the Garden, with an estimated thirty-five thousand more out on the streets. Wise, Al Smith, New York's senator Robert Wagner, and others gave speeches. The state's Jewish governor Herbert Lehman declined an invitation to speak, saying that he was worried about German retaliation against Jews over there. By implication, former governor Al Smith lambasted Lehman when he declared that there should be no "pussyfooting" about the Nazis. He compared them to the Ku Klux Klan, who had fiercely propagandized against his presidential candidacy in the 1920s because he was Irish and Catholic. "It don't make any difference to me whether it is a brown shirt or a night shirt," he quipped.

On April 1, the Nazis launched a boycott of all Jewish shops and services in Germany. Jews around the world responded with their own boycotts of German goods and services. Two New Yorkers, the wealthy German Jewish lawyer Samuel Untermyer and the Russian Yiddish newspaperman Abram Coralnik, organized the national boycott in the United States. Rabbi Wise joined. But other prominent organizations, including B'nai B'rith, still argued against any provocative public actions the Nazis could use as pretext for further punishing Jews in Germany. Wise took to calling these groups the "Sh-Sh Jews."

The American boycott targeted everything from the transatlantic German cruise ship line the Hamburg-American, which did brisk business in New York, to Macy's, run by a German Jewish family. In a radio address broadcast by WABC and syndicated nationally, Untermyer denounced the "black clouds of bigotry, race hatred and fanaticism that have descended upon what was once Germany, but is now medieval Hitlerland...a country that has reverted to barbarism." He warned that the Nazis were already taking the first steps in a "devilishly, deliberately, cold-bloodedly planned" elimination of German Jews and called the boycott a "holy war."

As Untermyer's predictions became nightmarish reality in the coming years, Rabbi Wise would continue to give speeches and hold rallies. Some of New York's Jews, particularly in the Orthodox community, would condemn merely speaking out as weak and craven. To them, Rabbi Wise would look and sound increasingly like a Sh-Sh Jew himself.

The Jewish New Yorker who was in some ways Roosevelt's most powerful and influential supporter wasn't a banker, a lawyer, a rabbi, or a politician. He was the nastiest, most powerful gossip columnist and radio personality in the country. From the time FDR was elected onward, no one adored him more than Walter Winchell did.

Born in 1897, Winchell (originally Weinschel), a grandson of Russian Jewish immigrants, grew up poor in Harlem tenements. In 1910 he and another adolescent, the future star George Jessel, who was already smoking what became his trademark stogies, started touring with a vaudeville troupe. Winchell came back to New York in 1920, stopped performing, and started writing insider Broadway gossip for trade publications and the bottom-feeding tabloid the *Evening Graphic*. As he grew bolder through the decade he increasingly mixed his innocuous backstage tidbits with venomous rumor and innuendo about the private lives of performers, producers, and their backers. Much of what he passed on he heard sitting all night in speakeasies and nightclubs, where he developed friendly relations with the gangsters who ran them. He eventually made table 50 at Sherman Billingsley's Stork Club on West 58th Street (later East 53rd Street) his universally known HQ—"New York's New Yorkiest place," he called it. Table 50 was in the Cub Room, a VIP inner sanctum only the rich, powerful, and famous could enter, from movie stars to mobsters to the Duke of Windsor.

By the end of the 1920s Winchell could make or break a show, a career, or a marriage, a power that rendered him the most courted and most feared man in New York show business. In 1929 he stepped up to Hearst's *Mirror*; his column, "Walter Winchell On Broadway," nationally syndicated by King Features, became the most widely read in the country. In 1932 CBS gave him a national fifteen-minute slot on Sunday nights, and it was a giant hit as well.

By then Winchell yearned to be more than the top gossipmonger in the land. With the simultaneous rise of Hitler and Roosevelt in 1933, he started working politics into his writing, in his own way. Deciding that "the best way to fight a person like Hitler is to ridicule him," he took his initial angle of attack from a remark by the New York journalist Quentin Reynolds: "Hitler is a fag." In column after column Winchell mocked the Führer as "an out and out fairy" and called him "Adele Hitler." To Winchell, Nazis were Ratzis and swastinkas. When the *Völkischer Beobachter* railed against him, he wrote, "It is so nice to know that my efforts haven't altogether been snubbed."

A week after Roosevelt's inauguration in March 1933, Winchell was excited to receive an invitation to a private meeting at the White House. He and the president spoke for only ten minutes, but it was enough; Winchell, his biographer Neal Gabler has written, "suddenly became a rabid Roosevelt enthusiast." For the rest of the 1930s he rhapsodized about FDR like a starstruck fan. It repeatedly got him into hot water with his boss, the conservative Hearst, but Winchell was far too popular to rein in.

Starting in 1938, readers and listeners would notice a new depth to Winchell's political items. He seemed to be getting the same sort of insider dope on Washington that he'd always gotten on Broadway. It was because he had a new ghostwriter for his political items.

Ernest Cuneo was a lawyer by trade, but his real skills lay in shadowy backroom politics. He was a resourceful fixer, legman, deal broker, and matchmaker, a guy the Democrats and the White House called on when they needed something done and didn't necessarily want to hear how.

Born in 1905 in New Jersey to an Italian immigrant metalworker, he was built stocky and thick. He played football from high school through a couple of years in the NFL with the Orange Tornadoes and the Brooklyn Dodgers, who shared Ebbets Field with the baseball Dodgers in the 1930s. With age he softened to nearly 300 pounds of jolly fat. He studied at Columbia Law School under Adolf Berle, and in 1931 he got a job as a law clerk in Congressman Fiorello La Guardia's office. Working for the hyperactively mercurial congressman was his political birth by fire.

When he met Winchell at "21" on West 52nd Street one night in 1938, Cuneo was legal counsel to the Democratic National Committee. The husky, affable party hack and the sharp, garrulous gossip hound forged a productive partnership. Cuneo fed Winchell a constant stream of inside-Washington scoops, and Winchell happily let himself be used as a platform and mouthpiece for whatever position Franklin Roosevelt wanted him to promote. Given his enormous and faithful following, Winchell was arguably the single most effective propaganda tool ever wielded by Roosevelt's White House.

CHAPTER 5

If It Can Happen There . . .

In August 1934, the *New York Evening Post*'s Dorothy Thompson was the first American journalist expelled from Nazi Germany, on Hitler's direct order. It made the front page of the *Times*, and she returned to New York a star. She was on her way to being one of the most widely read, discussed, and argued about journalists of the era.

Thompson had grown up in various small towns around Buffalo, daughter of a Methodist minister who went from one parsonage to another, and came to New York City as a young suffragette in the time of the Great War. For much of the 1920s she roamed Europe as a freelance journalist, writing for various papers back home. At a time when many Americans turned their backs on Europe, she experienced the political and social bedlam the world war had left in its wake.

By 1924 she was living in Berlin, where her circle would come to include Arnold Schönberg, Bertolt Brecht, Lotte Lenya, Kurt Weill, and the playwright Ernst Toller. All would flee to America after Hitler took power; Toller, unable to adjust to life in New York City and depressed by news that a brother and sister back home had been sent to a concentration camp, would hang himself in his room at the Mayflower Hotel on Central Park West in 1939.

In 1927, turning thirty-four and just divorced from her first husband, Thompson met Sinclair Lewis in Berlin. He was going through a divorce himself. Born and raised in rural Minnesota, he had gone to Yale in 1903 and from there to New York to pursue a writing career. In 1927, at forty-two, he was among the best-selling American novelists of his time, the author of *Main Street*, *Arrowsmith*, *Babbitt*, and the just published *Elmer Gantry*. He was also a notorious drunk, prone to brooding, and fabulously homely. Nevertheless, Thompson fell for him in a single night.

They came back to America and were married in 1928. He finished his novel *Dodsworth* that year, when they were living on West 10th Street in Greenwich Village.

In 1930 they returned to Europe, to Stockholm, where he was immensely proud to accept the Nobel Prize for literature, but also gloomily terrified that he couldn't live up to it. (His best years were in fact behind him.) The following year Thompson got an interview with Hitler in Munich. It appeared in *Cosmopolitan*, followed in 1932 by a book with the cheeky title *I Saw Hitler!* "When I finally walked into Adolph Hitler's salon in the Kaiserhof Hotel, I was convinced that I was meeting the future dictator of Germany. In something less than fifty seconds I was quite sure I was not. It took just about that time to measure the startling insignificance of this man who has set the world agog...He is the very prototype of the Little Man."

She was far from the only outsider who saw Hitler pre-1933 and wondered what all the fuss was about, but later she took a terrific drubbing from fellow journalists for what one called her "comico-terrible gaffe."

As if to make up for it, when Hitler came to power she turned obsessive in her warnings about him, in print (now for the *Saturday Evening Post*) and in lectures and at parties. That led to her expulsion from Germany in the summer of 1934. As soon as she returned to New York she set out on a thirty-six-city lecture tour, drawing two or three thousand people a night to listen to her dark views on Hitler and the future of Europe.

Two star writers under one roof was one too many for Thompson's husband. Lewis was envious that Dorothy's career was soaring while his seemed to have crested. He resented her now universally acknowledged expertise on international affairs, which he complained made him feel like an ignorant bumpkin. He came to so hate hearing her speak about Nazism and fascism that he could only refer to the topic as "It," as in, "Is she talking about It again?"

So there was clearly some measure of competitiveness behind his next novel, *It Can't Happen Here*, published in 1935, a dark fantasy about what might happen if "It" came to power in the United States. He set it one year in the future, in 1936, when Senator Berzelius "Buzz" Windrip is vying for the Democratic presidential nomination. Buzz combines the homespun demagoguery of a Huey Long with the racism, anticommunism, and anti-Semitism of the various American Nazi and fascist groups. Windrip fields goon squads whose uniforms and tactics of violent intimidation are directly borrowed from Hitler's SS. Like Hitler, he crafts distinct messages to appeal to different classes, promising one thing to unemployed Depression victims and another to industrialists and bankers, one of whom says it might not be so bad "to have a real Strong Man, like Hitler or Mussolini—like Napoleon or Bismarck in the good old days—and have 'em really *run* the country and make it efficient and prosperous again."

When he gets into the White House, Windrip reveals himself to be a full-on American Führer. He makes himself the supreme ruler of a totalitarian police state, disempowers Congress and the courts, establishes martial law, and fills concentration camps. Many Americans go along with it all; those who oppose Windrip flee to Canada or join an underground resistance movement.

MGM bought the film rights but then backed out, fearing that not only Germany and Italy but other foreign markets would ban all MGM films. The controversy propelled the book onto the *Times* bestseller list, despite cool responses from most reviewers, who found it overlong and implausible.

The controversy gave Hallie Flanagan an idea. In August 1936, a front-page *Times* article announced that the Federal Theatre Project would mount a multicity, multilingual stage adaptation of *It Can't Happen Here*. To condense the sprawling novel for the stage, Flanagan put Lewis and a cowriter, a relatively untried Hollywood screenwriter named Jack Moffitt, in the Essex House on Central Park West. They feuded, forcing Flanagan to ferry pages back and forth from Lewis's room on the twenty-second floor to Moffitt's on the thirty-eighth. Moffitt eventually fled, and Vincent Sherman, who would direct the New York production, helped Lewis finish the play at the eleventh hour.

On October 27, 1936, twenty-one simultaneous productions of *It Can't Happen Here* hit the boards around the country. There were separate English and Yiddish productions in New York, a Spanish production for Cuban audiences in Florida, a "Negro" production with white actors playing all the bad guys in Seattle. Critical response was again lukewarm, but audiences loved it; it was the signal triumph of the FTP, running into the war years and seen by more than a quarter million people.

In 1936 Dorothy Thompson also scored a great victory. She got a column in the *New York Herald Tribune*, the national platform for East Coast Republicanism. Helen Reid, wife of the publisher Ogden Mills Reid, made the offer. She and Thompson had been suffragettes together. The Reids started out a team, but through the 1930s Ogden spent more and more time at the bar of the Artist and Writers restaurant, next door to the *Tribune*'s offices on West 40th Street and a watering hole for *Trib* staffers for many years. It was colloquially known as Bleeck's ("pronounced to rhyme with shakes," *Life* helpfully pointed out) for its proprietor, the German-American Jack Bleeck. As Mr. Reid sank into uselessness, his wife took the reins. She hired the preeminent liberal columnist of the day, New York native Walter Lippmann, who would be syndicated worldwide and win two Pulitzers. In addition to Thompson, she hired other women writers including Irita Van Doren. She allowed both Thompson and Lippmann the freedom of their opinions, loosening up what had been a very starched-collar conservative paper.

Thompson's column, "On the Record," ran three times a week, alternating with Lippmann's "Today and Tomorrow." It would run in various venues for the next twenty-two years and was soon syndicated in some 150 papers nationwide, reaching up to ten million readers. *Tribune* publicity defined her politics as "liberal conservatism." As her biographer Peter Kurth pointed out, it might be more precise to say that she attacked fascism wherever she thought she spied it, whether at home or abroad. Domestically she was very suspicious of Roosevelt and the New Deal. On the international scene she devoted many columns to railing against the Nazis, warning of the grave danger they represented, and pillorying American isolationists. She denounced Hitler's "terrible barbarities," declared that "the civilized world has had its face slapped and turned the other cheek so often that it's become rotary," and proclaimed "the necessity of either taking a last stand against heavy odds, or going under for generations." She repeated the message in a weekly NBC radio show heard in an estimated five and a half million homes.

She was also one of the earliest, clearest voices in America speaking out for European Jewish refugees, at a time when the United States, like most nations, severely limited their entry, and even American Jewish leaders hesitated to say anything for fear of rousing the country's many anti-Semites. She proposed a clever though diplomatically doomed plan to use the frozen foreign assets of Germany and other offending nations to fund the resettlement of their exiles. Anti-Semitic hate mail poured in.

Time would put her on the cover in 1939 and call her and Eleanor Roosevelt "undoubtedly the most influential women in the U.S." *Fortune* ranked her the most read columnist in the country after Winchell. Other journalists criticized and lampooned Thompson for her obsessive stridency, the emotional intensity of her opinions, the way she always seemed to be writing at full volume. When Houghton Mifflin published a collection of her writings in 1939 titled *Let the Record Speak*, a reviewer called it *Let the Record Shout*. She was called a Valkyrie, a Fury, a Cassandra, and worse; Mencken called her an "ignorant bitch." But she had millions of faithful followers, especially but not exclusively among women.

It was too much for Lewis. Blaming the reflected glare of her career for his struggles to maintain his own, he moved out. Angry and hurt, she made him beg for a divorce for years. Spencer Tracy and Katharine Hepburn's troubled relationship in the 1942 movie *Woman of the Year* was a thinly veiled portrait of the Lewis-Thompson marriage.

⁓

In the summer of 1934, at about the time that Thompson was being kicked out of Germany, her friend from her early Berlin days Kurt Weill made a trip to Austria. He met up with the internationally acclaimed Austrian theater and film director Max Reinhardt, the Prague-born playwright and novelist Franz Werfel, and a New York emigrant theater impresario named Meyer Weisgal. The place was Schloss Leopoldskron, Reinhardt's palatial estate near Salzburg. (The film version of *The Sound of Music* would be shot on location there thirty years later.) Weisgal, a Zionist, had an idea for a lavish musical pageant based on the Old Testament stories of the Hebrews' journey out of Egypt to the Promised Land. The others had agreed to create it for him, and now they were meeting up as a group for the first time. The irony was not lost on them that they were four Jews planning a spectacle glorifying their Hebrew heritage not 30 kilometers from the town of Berchtesgaden, where Adolf Hitler had his Berghof retreat. Weisgal very much intended his pageant as a response to Hitler's rabid anti-Semitism.

Weill's name had given Weisgal a bit of pause when Reinhardt first proposed him. All Weisgal or most Americans knew of Weill in 1934 was *The Threepenny Opera*, which seemed the very antithesis of the grand, stately pageant he envisioned.

A cantor's son from the city of Dessau, Weill was composing by adolescence. He and his new wife, Lotte Lenya, met Bertolt Brecht in Berlin in 1927. Thompson met them all soon after. Over the next few years the quiet, bespectacled composer and the riffraffish writer collaborated on *Mahagonny* and *Threepenny Opera* before falling out with each other. As Jews, Weill and Lenya fled Berlin for Paris within three months of Hitler's becoming chancellor in 1933. Brecht, a Communist, also left.

Werfel set the Old Testament stories in a modern synagogue in an unnamed country from which the congregation is about to be expelled, starting their own trek to the Promised Land. He titled it *Der Weg der Verheissung*, which was translated as *The Eternal Road*. Weill set it to serious operatic music, very different from the raucous songs he'd written for Brecht's satires.

In New York City, Weisgal and Reinhardt engaged the industrial designer Norman Bel Geddes to do the sets. Manhattan had only a few venues big enough for the giant spectacle they wanted. One was the old Hippodrome, a mammoth barn of a space taking up the whole block of Sixth Avenue between 43rd and 44th Streets, but there was already a spectacle being staged there, the circus-themed *Jumbo*. Weisgal settled for the Manhattan Opera House, built by Oscar Hammerstein in 1906, on West 34th Street near Eighth Avenue. Bel Geddes had to gut and redesign the interior for *The Eternal Road* to fit inside it.

Weill and Lenya arrived in September 1935. Weisgal put them up at the grand St. Moritz hotel on Central Park South, and Weill was warmly greeted by the city's music elite, including George and Ira Gershwin. The first Broadway production of *The Threepenny Opera*, in 1933, had closed after only two weeks, but aficionados had admired Weill's music. The Gershwins paid him the great compliment of inviting him to a rehearsal of *Porgy and Bess*, which would open on Broadway in 1935.

After numerous production hurdles, *The Eternal Road* would finally open in January 1937, with a cast of more than two hundred fifty. It earned favorable reviews and ran for more than a hundred and fifty performances, but it was so expensive that Weisgal was essentially bankrupted by it. By that point Weill and Lenya had settled in the city, deciding that given what was going on in Europe it was foolish to return there. For a while they'd live in a de facto artists' commune in a ramshackle house on Middagh Street in Brooklyn Heights, where other tenants would include the expatriate English poet W. H. Auden, young novelist Carson McCullers, and the stripper/author Gypsy Rose Lee. Weill began composing for

Broadway, where he'd collaborate with Ira Gershwin, Robert Sherwood, Elmer Rice, and others.

Max Reinhardt and Franz Werfel would flee Austria for good after Hitler annexed it in 1938. They'd both go to Hollywood.

⌒

On the evening of July 15, 1935, almost a year after Thompson was ejected from Germany, twenty-seven-year-old Varian Fry stepped out of his hotel in Berlin. He had come from New York to Nazi Germany to see conditions for himself before taking over the editorship of the prestigious journal of international affairs *The Living Age*.

The education he got this night was shocking. On the front page of the next day's *New York Times*, he described seeing "a band of some 200 Nazis, clad in civilian clothing but many of them wearing Storm Troop boots and trousers," surge along the fashionable Kurfürstendamm, attacking anyone they thought was Jewish. They yanked people out of cars and cafés to beat and kick them senseless. They smashed the windows of Jewish shops and restaurants, as they sang the "Horst Wessel Song" and chanted anti-Semitic slogans. Fry saw one young man "whose eyes became filled with blood so that he could not see where he was running," and the Jewish proprietor of an ice cream shop badly beaten as his shop was wrecked.

Fry returned to his hotel room, telephoned his report to a wire service, and the next day it was in the *Times* and other newspapers. When he sailed back into New York a few weeks later on the German liner *Bremen*, the press was waiting for him as the ship docked at its midtown Hudson pier.

On the surface he seemed an unlikely antifascist crusader, a prissy and mannered literary aesthete who peered arrogantly at the world from behind owlish spectacles. But he was also, as his biographer Andy Marino put it, a man who "was not truly happy unless he was in some way outraged," and that outrage, beginning with what he saw in Berlin that night, would propel him to political action.

He had been a pampered only child, born into a middle-class home in Harlem in 1907, son of a former schoolteacher and a man who worked on Wall Street. The family later moved to suburban Ridgewood, New Jersey. A loner, Fry was hazed mercilessly by other boys at the elite Hotchkiss prep school, but he thrived when he transferred to the Riverdale Country School in the Bronx. He could read and write in six languages when he scored in the top 10 percent on the Harvard entrance exams in 1926. At twenty-three he graduated and married Eileen Hughes, who was thirty and already established as an editor at the *Atlantic Monthly*. They spent a few years being knocked from job to job by the Depression. Then came the offer to edit *The Living Age* in 1935 and the trip to Germany.

The *Völkischer Beobachter*, unsurprisingly, blamed Jews for inciting the riot Fry witnessed, supposedly because they outraged good Germans by hissing at an anti-Semitic Swedish film in a Kurfürstendamm theater. To Fry, the riot "gave every evidence of careful planning" and was clearly led by Nazi storm troopers. The morning after, he went to Goebbels's Ministry of Propaganda for some answers and was ushered into the office of the National Socialists' foreign press representative Ernst Franz Sedgwick Hanfstaengl.

Hanfstaengl might have been an imposing, even frightening, presence: a six-foot-four giant with broad shoulders, a barrel chest, huge hands, and a boulder of a head with a lantern jaw and lidded eyes designed for the threatening glower. Instead, he was more often a clown. He was a big man who wanted only to be liked, aggressively ingratiating as a golden retriever, universally known by his childhood nickname, Putzi. He approached his job of explaining the odious activities of the Nazis to the world as an ongoing exercise in full-bore obsequiousness and overbearing charm. When Fry entered his office, Putzi went straight into hail-fellow boola-boola schmooze—because Putzi Hanfstaengl, like Varian Fry, was a Harvard man, as well as an erstwhile New Yorker.

Putzi was born into a prosperous and cultured home in Munich in 1887. His German father was a well-known dealer in fine art reproductions, with galleries in London and on Fifth Avenue in Manhattan. His mother was an American of fine New England pedigree, with a Civil War general in her family tree. They sent him to Harvard in 1905. In 1911, at twenty-four, he moved to Manhattan to run Galerie Hanfstaengl at the corner of Fifth Avenue and 45th Street. His first love was really music. He was an accomplished pianist if a sometimes overenthusiastic one who, it was said, occasionally banged the keys so hard with his sledgehammer hands that he broke strings. Many mornings before opening the gallery he could be found at the Harvard Club around the corner, playing the piano there. That was where he met another grad, state senator Franklin Roosevelt, who breakfasted at the club.

The coming of the Great War made life very difficult for Putzi in New York, as it did for other German-Americans. The Justice Department investigated him; his Harvard Club fellows turned cold; the gallery's windows were smashed more than once; and then, toward the end of the war, the government seized the gallery as "enemy property" and auctioned it off for a pittance.

In 1921 he returned to Munich with his wife and infant son. The following year, a Harvard classmate at the American embassy asked Putzi to go hear a political speech and give his impression. The speaker was Adolf Hitler, and Putzi was definitely impressed. He immediately ingratiated himself with Hitler, becoming his constant companion, his court minstrel and court jester. He saw his role as introducing some culture and cosmopolitanism to the rough, snarlingly parochial movement that was Nazism in its early years. He played Wagner and Liszt to soothe Hitler's nerves, and he tried to get him to grow out his mustache, which Putzi called his "snot catcher." He provided Hitler an entrée to upper-crust Germans and their money and personally footed the bill for expanding the *Beobachter* from a thin weekly to a thriving daily.

On November 8, 1923, he was inside Munich's Bürgerbräukeller when Hitler launched his failed putsch. Escaping the chaos of the next day, Hitler fled to Putzi's country home some forty miles south of the city. Dorothy Thompson, who knew Putzi, pursued Hitler there, hoping for an interview, but the police had gotten there first and taken Hitler away. "Hitler Seized Near Munich," the front page of the November 13 *Times* reported. "Found in Home of E. F. Hanfstaengl, Ex–New York Art Dealer."

Putzi maintained loose ties with the Nazis during their low ebb in the 1920s; then, when Hitler's fortunes seemed to be reviving in 1931, Putzi rehitched his wagon, joining the party—a commitment he'd resisted until then—and convincing Hitler to let him be his foreign press spokesman. He certainly had the international press contacts, from Thompson to William Randolph Hearst, though Thompson would dismiss him as "an immense, high-strung, incoherent clown," and another journalist sneered, "You had to know Putzi to really dislike him."

By the time Fry entered his office in the summer of 1935 Putzi was apparently finding his job rather daunting and frustrating. He was remarkably, even recklessly candid with Fry. He confessed that it was most likely storm troopers who had hissed at the Swedish film as a pretext for the rioting. More amazing still, he told Fry that two factions in the Nazi Party leadership were arguing over how to deal with Germany's Jews. The moderates, in which he counted himself, maintained that the answer was to segregate them or send them all away, perhaps to Madagascar. The radicals, who he said included Hitler and Goebbels, preferred exterminating them. Fry reported this conversation to the *Times* as well, nearly seven years before the Nazi hierarchy formally adopted the Final Solution.

Fry's encounters with the storm troopers and Putzi in 1935 left him deeply concerned about the spread of fascism. During the Spanish Civil War he would help raise funds for the loyalists. When Japan seized Peking in 1937, he would write a well-received pamphlet about it for the Foreign Policy Association, and when Hitler seized the Sudetenland the following year he'd write another, *The Peace That Failed*, about how the coming war in Europe was the inevitable result of the vindictive Versailles Treaty.

When France fell to the Nazis in the summer of 1940, Fry would go from observing and writing to direct, heroic action. Some of Europe's greatest artists and writers would owe their lives to him.

CHAPTER 6

Life and Death

In 1927, twenty-three-year-old Margaret Bourke-White wrote in her diary: "I want to become famous and I want to become wealthy." She pursued these goals with great talent and undeflectable ambition, displaying a genius for using men to help her get what she needed.

She had started out plain Margaret White. Her Irish mother, Minnie Bourke, was from Manhattan, her Jewish father Joseph White from the Bronx, where Margaret was born in 1904. He was an industrial engineer, an inventor and tinkerer, and an avid amateur photographer. When Margaret was little he took her to work with him, where he engineered improvements to the giant Hoe rotary printing presses used by newspapers and magazines. It was the start of her long fascination with industry and machinery. He was also a member of the New York Society for Ethical Culture, the secular, progressive movement that developed out of the assimilationist yearnings of Reform Jews on the Upper West Side. Born Weiss to Orthodox parents, he renamed himself White, practiced no religion, and hid his Jewish background from coworkers. Margaret adored her father and kept his secret; the name Weiss does not appear in her charming but cagey 1963 memoir *Portrait of Myself*. In many ways her life and career were her tribute to him.

In 1927, she hyphenated her parents' surnames to give herself the classy-sounding professional handle Bourke-White, and she achieved quick success shooting skyscrapers, steel mills, and industrial sites. She made machines and buildings look romantic and heroic—the perfect imagery for the magazine *Fortune*, launched by Henry "Harry" Luce at the start of 1930.

No man was more helpful to Bourke-White's career than Harry Luce. He was born in China in 1898 to a Protestant missionary couple and grew up there through the Boxer Rebellion and Sun Yat-sen's revolution. When he was fifteen the family sent him to America to attend Hotchkiss, the Yale prep school. He and a Hotchkiss friend, Briton Hadden of Brooklyn Heights, went on to Yale together. In 1923 they started a magazine, *Time.* Unlike the straightforward news digest it later became, *Time* in the 1920s was marked by an elitist college-boy sarcasm and a Mencken-inspired skepticism not much unlike that of the *New Yorker,* founded two years later. For a while their offices were in the same building at 25 West 45th Street. Their similarities and proximity made for an unfriendly rivalry that was carried on for years.

When Hadden died suddenly in 1929 at the age of thirty-one, Luce assumed sole control of the business and soon launched *Fortune*, intended to survey the landscape of American industrial capitalism in the Machine Age. Although the stock market crashed just before the first issue appeared in February 1930, Luce steamed on. His most innovative idea was to hire brilliant writers with no business backgrounds—James Agee; poet and playwright Archibald MacLeish; even a former Trotskyist, the lifelong New Yorker Dwight Macdonald. As the Depression rolled on, their increasingly anticapitalist, pro-labor attitudes often brought them into conflict with their boss. Macdonald would nickname Luce "Il Luce."

Luce made another bold and smart step when he hired the young Bourke-White to be *Fortune*'s star photographer. In 1930 she was the first American photographer allowed into the Soviet Union. She was invited back in '31 and again in '32. She was very impressed by the apparent results of Stalin's first Five Year Plan to industrialize the nation, but she saw and heard only what he wanted her to—nothing about the millions of farmworkers he had allowed to starve to death while he was building all his new factories.

In the middle of 1930 Luce brought on an eccentric named Ralph Ingersoll to edit *Fortune.* Son of an engineer who helped build the Queensboro Bridge, Ingersoll started out in engineering himself, then switched to journalism. He was the managing editor of the *New Yorker* when Luce hired him away. He was very bright and creative, which he used as license to be very arrogant and egotistical. Bursting with bluster and blarney, he made many enemies during his decade at Time Inc., then went on to make more elsewhere. He was given to unspooling lofty ideas, some good and others half-baked, carpet bombing his staff with heart-sinkingly long memoranda that made them duck and cringe. When burying his opposition under mountains of verbiage didn't work he resorted to lies. An officer who would serve with him during the war later recalled, "I've never met anyone who was such a bright guy who was such a goddamned liar. He'd say anything to get what he wanted." In 1935 Luce would make Ingersoll general manager of Time Inc., and, one insider said, "a great groan" went up around the Chrysler Building offices.

—

In 1934 another notable woman came into the Time Inc. circle. Clare Boothe was born in an apartment on West 124th Street in 1903, the second illegitimate child of a woman who had started out an actress and singer and, like so many women of the theater in the Gilded Age, ended up a courtesan. Clare's mother depended on a long string of men, most of them married, to provide for her and her children. Clare grew up a cool alabaster beauty, very smart and determined to overcome her tawdry background; as her biographer Sylvia Jukes Morris put it, she would aim for the best of everything, and usually get it.

When she was twenty she met and married the millionaire George Brokaw, "a forty-three-year-old dandy rumored to be New York's most eligible bachelor." She soon discovered he was "one of the most spectacular drunks in New York" as well. He was her conduit to New York society. She took it from there, appearing at all the right balls and openings, aggressively courting the famous and wealthy, while perfecting a chill, regal poise that made it seem they had gathered for her. Her skill for co-opting the center of all attention dazzled many, mostly male, and aggravated many, mostly female.

She divorced Brokaw in 1929, winning a handsome alimony that would help her sail relatively unscathed through the Depression. That year she met the magazine publisher Condé Nast, who gave her a job writing photo captions for *Vogue*. By 1932 she had ascended to managing editor of *Vanity Fair*. That year she also started a not very discreet affair with one of the most famous men in America, Bernard Baruch, who was sixty-one years old and unhappily married. For Clare, her eye always on the main chance, it was a smart alliance.

Though Baruch would remain a kindly mentor, Clare found another older and influential man to align herself with in 1934. One night that December a few hundred of New York's top names assembled at the

Starlight Rooftop Garden of the Waldorf-Astoria to celebrate the Broadway opening of Cole Porter's *Anything Goes.* Clare was there; so were Luce and his wife of eleven years. He and Clare sat and talked for a long time, at the end of which he shocked her by declaring that he had just fallen hopelessly in love with her. They carried on an affair while he arranged a relatively painless if expensive divorce.

She had left Condé Nast Publishing by then to pursue a new career as a playwright. Her first play on Broadway, *Abide with Me*, a seething potboiler about the murder of an alcoholic husband, opened in November 1935. When she took her bow at the end of it the audience booed her. The reviews were vicious. She and Luce were married two days later.

In 1936, Ingersoll and Clare convinced Luce to launch a new weekly photojournalism magazine for the masses—or "gum-chewers," as Ingersoll called them. *Life* debuted in November of that year. It went on to be the most popular news magazine in America. Staff photographers included Bourke-White, who had the first cover image, and Alfred Eisenstaedt. Eisenstaedt had been taking pictures since he was a kid in Berlin in the 1910s. As a Jew, he fled Germany in 1935 and arrived in New York City just in time to join *Life*'s staff. He'd be there for some thirty-five years and shoot nearly a hundred covers, plus one image from Times Square in 1945 that's one of the most iconic photographs of the twentieth century.

Five weeks after *Life* debuted, Clare returned to Broadway with a new play. Bernard Baruch had gotten his friend Max Gordon (born Mechel Salpeter, son of Yiddish-speaking Polish immigrants, on the Lower East Side) to produce it. Gordon brought in George S. Kaufman and Moss Hart to help Clare polish her play. *The Women* premiered on December 26, 1936. The first Broadway play ever with an all-female cast, it was a colossal success, running into mid-1938, touring the nation, adapted for a hit movie, and going on to be a staple of the American stage.

The Luces were now one of New York's most-watched power couples. They, Bourke-White, and Ingersoll would all play influential roles as America went to war.

⌒

Two other plays that hit Broadway in 1936 are notable for their strong antiwar sentiments: Irwin Shaw's *Bury the Dead* and Robert Sherwood's *Idiot's Delight.* Shaw, whose actual surname was Shamforoff, was born in the Bronx in 1913 and raised in Brooklyn, where he graduated from Brooklyn College. He was twenty-three when he wrote *Bury the Dead*, a bitterly absurdist fantasy that ran from April to July 1936 at the Ethel Barrymore Theatre. It was set in "the second year of the war that is to begin tomorrow night." The corpses of six young soldiers who died in battle stand up in their shrouds and refuse to be buried. This causes all sorts of problems for their wives, the army brass, the warmongering businessmen, and the clergy, while the news media spin it as a sign of "the indomitable spirit of the American doughboy." When no one can convince them to lie back down, a frustrated general grabs a gun and tries to kill them all over again, but they simply walk off.

Bury the Dead was a critical sensation. In the *Times*, Brooks Atkinson raved about "the genius of Mr. Shaw's lacerating drama. It is a rebellious dance of scabrous death on the battlefield. Take it also as a warning from the young." Eleanor Roosevelt had just begun writing a nationally syndicated daily newspaper column, "My Day," which, incredibly, she would keep up until a few months before her death in 1962. After seeing *Bury the Dead* in May 1936, she wrote that "the thoughts hit you like hammer blows," adding that it would "long be remembered by anyone who sees it and its strength lies, I think, in the fact that it is the expression of the thought and feeling of thousands upon thousands of people today."

Towering at six and a half gangling feet, with a long face that drooped like a pensive sunflower over everyone he met, Robert Sherwood loomed large in New York culture, in more than one sense, from the 1930s through the war and beyond. He grew up in Manhattan at the beginning of the century, son of a prosperous Wall Streeter and an artist. In 1917 Robert volunteered for the American Expeditionary Forces, but he was rejected as too tall for combat—the standard depth for frontline trenches during the Great War was only six feet. So he crossed the border and joined the kilted Canadian Black Watch. On an infantry charge in France he was gassed and got hung up in barbed wire. Like many other young Americans, he went "over there" convinced of the righteousness of the war and came back shocked by its obscene futility.

His first big Broadway success was a meditation on violence and mortality titled *The Petrified Forest*. It opened at the Broadhurst Theatre in 1935 with Humphrey Bogart and Leslie Howard in the roles they would reprise in the Warner Bros. movie the following year. His next play, *Idiot's*

Delight, opened on Broadway at the Shubert Theatre in April 1936, when *Bury the Dead* was running nearby, and went on for three hundred performances. In a setup similar to the one in *Forest*, an international gaggle of characters gets stuck at a ski lodge in the Italian Alps. Principal among them are a down-at-heels American showman named Harry Van, a wealthy arms merchant named Weber, and the mysterious Russian countess Irene, who is really a showgirl and con artist Harry spent a night with years ago. Just as they congregate, war breaks out again among the European powers, giving Sherwood the opportunity to have the characters voice different points of view, from Harry's naive American optimism to Weber's worldly cynicism.

Irene says to Weber, "I'm so happy for you. All this great, wonderful death and destruction, everywhere. And you promoted it!"

"Ask yourself: why shouldn't they die?" Weber replies. "And who are the greater criminals—those who sell the instruments of death, or those who buy them, and use them?" He argues that she shouldn't blame men like him for war, but the millions of "little people" who allow themselves to be goaded into fighting with cheap appeals to patriotism and duty.

Sherwood was citing an idea that was central to isolationism and the antiwar movement in the mid-1930s: the notion that international munitions dealers like Weber, the "merchants of death," had used propaganda and political influence to manipulate nations into a worldwide war. The remarkable Marine Corps general and two-time Medal of Honor recipient Smedley Butler put this notion succinctly in a speech and later book, *War Is a Racket*, published in 1935. He argued that modern war was choreographed by the arms dealers, steel companies, bankers, and other capitalists for their own immense profit and everyone else's terrible loss. In 1934 this idea led to a Senate Special Committee on Investigation of the Munitions Industry, better known as the Nye Committee for its chairman, the isolationist North Dakota senator Gerald Nye. The later-infamous Alger Hiss served as its chief counsel. The committee not only put an official stamp on the antiwar movement; it helped prod Congress into passing a series of Neutrality Acts beginning in 1935 that prohibited the export of arms to warring nations; banned loans to warring nations; and forbade U.S. merchant ships from carrying arms to belligerents, even if manufactured elsewhere.

Idiot's Delight won Sherwood his first Pulitzer. He wrote the screenplay for the MGM film adaptation that appeared in 1939, with Clark Gable as Harry Van and Norma Shearer as Irene.

The situation in Europe had changed a great deal between 1936 and 1939, however, and the film was dated the day it opened. Hitler had made his intentions unmistakably clear by then, forcing Sherwood to reassess his antiwar stance of just three years earlier.

CHAPTER 7

Springtime for Mussolini

With its very large Italian and German immigrant communities, New York City was fertile ground for pro-Fascist and pro-Nazi agitation. Yet support for Mussolini and Hitler could be found all over the city, not just in those neighborhoods but also in some surprising places: on Wall Street and Madison Avenue and in corporate headquarters; at some of the city's largest newspapers and magazines; among some of the wealthiest and WASPiest blue bloods on Park Avenue; in Irish Catholic parishes.

Mussolini came first. Today's common image of Il Duce as the clownish thug and posturing autocrat who dragged the Italian people to near-total disaster began to develop with his brutal invasion of Ethiopia in 1935. But he'd been in power for more than a decade by then, and had enjoyed a very different reputation in America and elsewhere—an almost entirely positive and often adulatory fame.

Washington, from the Republican 1920s of Harding, Coolidge, and Hoover well into the Roosevelt years, viewed Mussolini as a forceful leader who brought order to Italy's postwar chaos, stabilized the economy, and was a partner in the fight against international bolshevism. Early on, Roosevelt referred to Mussolini as "that admirable Italian gentleman," and even as Italy drew closer with Nazi Germany he clung to the hope that Il Duce would exert a softening influence on Der Führer. He didn't finally give up on Mussolini until Italy declared war on France in June 1940.

Despite some skepticism and derision in a few places—the always cheeky *New Yorker*, for example—the New York press treatment of Mussolini through the 1920s ranged from cautiously positive to positively infatuated. The *New York Times*' foreign columnist Anne O'Hare McCormick, who would be the first female journalist to win a Pulitzer, wrote rapturously about Mussolini and his economic and social transformations of Italy well into the 1930s. The *Saturday Evening Post* serialized Mussolini's autobiography in 1928. William Randolph Hearst's newspaper chain courted Mussolini through the 1920s. Mussolini had barely come to power in 1922 when Hearst sent one of his star writers, Louise Bryant (the former Greenwich Village leftist), to interview him. Hearst's wife, Millicent, a native New Yorker whom he'd first seen performing in vaudeville at the Herald Square Theatre, met and was wowed by Mussolini in 1923. She wrote a number of flattering, flirtatious portraits for Hearst's publications. In 1930 Hearst retained Il Duce himself to write articles. (Through most of the 1930s, Hearst's newspapers would also be not only anti–New Deal and anticommunist—Hearst more or less equated the two—but openly admiring of Hitler as well, praising the "amazing economic recovery" he had achieved in Germany. For a while his papers would run a column signed by Hermann Göring.)

New York academia felt the lure as well. Columbia University's Casa Italiana, housing Italian studies programs, opened in 1927 with funding from the city's Italian-American business leaders and with a largely pro-Fascist faculty. It enjoyed warm relations with Il Duce, who, according to a 1926 *Times* article, offered to "equip the entire house with Italian furniture of various periods, paintings and art objects obtained from the old royal palaces of Italy." (Decades later Casa Italiana would serve as a stand-in for the Soviet Rezidentura in the TV series *The Americans*.)

No one applauded more heartily than Wall Street as Mussolini dissolved trade unions, announced plans to increase productivity both in factories and on farms, and set about stabilizing the lira. He'd been in power only a short time when a delegation of two hundred American business and banking leaders hailed him at a lavish international conference in Rome, then came home convinced he would save Italy from, as one put it, "the blighting hand of radical socialism." The business press, including *Barron's* and the *Wall Street Journal*, spread the word. Thomas W. Lamont of J. P. Morgan (who for a while rented the Roosevelts' former home on East 65th Street) put together a $100 million loan for Italy. Wall Street wasn't necessarily pro-Fascist; it saw potential for growth in Italy (and in Germany and the Soviet Union too) and invested in it.

Mussolini's high standing was a source of considerable pride in Italian neighborhoods throughout New York City, especially among the older immigrants. Their largest communities were in Little Italy, which stretched across lower Manhattan from Greenwich Village to today's East Village; in Italian East Harlem; and in Brooklyn, with pockets in the Bronx and Queens as well.

The Order Sons of Italy in America (*Ordine Figli d'Italia in America*), founded in Little Italy in 1905, was the oldest and largest Italian fraternal organization in America, with some three hundred thousand members in the 1920s. In 1922, when Mussolini designated it his official representative in America, its members crowed with pride. There were only a few notable dissenters, including Congressman Fiorello La Guardia. A 1923 survey showed that of 136 Italian-American newspapers, only eight criticized Il Duce. New York's *Il Progresso Italo-Americano*, by far the largest with a circulation of a hundred thousand, staunchly supported him. Only a handful of tiny leftist publications, such as *Il Martello* (The Hammer), were anti-Fascist. Radio brought pro-Mussolini propaganda, including broadcasts of his speeches, into many Italian-American homes. So did the Italian Library of Information, the Mussolini government's prolific propaganda office in Manhattan.

⌣

In this context of general goodwill, it did not take long for grassroots pro-Fascist groups to organize and take to the city's streets in black uniforms imitating those worn by Mussolini's troops. The largest, the Fascist League of North America (FLNA), claimed more than twelve thousand members at its peak. Many were immigrants who had fought in the Italian army in the Great War. Some worked in industries with large numbers of immigrant laborers, such as the needle trades and the Brooklyn waterfront. These "blackshirts" marched on Columbus Day, Garibaldi's birthday (which happened to be July 4), and Memorial Day. Two hundred formed an honor guard in City Hall Park at a celebration for the Italian long-distance flier Francesco de Pinedo, while a crowd of thousands cheered and gave the stiff-arm "Roman salute" (which the Nazis copied).

The first organized resistance, the Anti-Fascist Alliance of North America (AFANA), came in 1923 from the left wing of Italian-American politics in New York. A fractious coalition of socialists, communists, and anarchists, also with Italian garment workers at its core, it published the first anti-Fascist newspaper in America, *Il Nuovo Mondo*. Public confrontations were inevitable and quickly turned violent, as both sides wielded clubs, whips, knives, and pistols. In 1925, anti-Fascists rumbled with FLNA blackshirts in Newark, putting six in the hospital with stab wounds. When another celebrated Italian flier, the polar explorer and airship designer Umberto Nobile, tried to give a talk at a high school on Manhattan's east side in 1926, five hundred anti-Fascists burst into the hall and scuffled with the audience and police. There was another row at a fete for Nobile in Lewisohn Stadium on CCNY's Harlem campus, which the *Times* said drew an audience of twelve thousand, "mostly Mussolini sympathizers," some of whom gave the Fascist salute at the mention of Il Duce's name.

No one in New York was more vituperatively anti-Fascist than Carlo Tresca, the publisher of *Il Martello*. Tresca was a star of the radical left for decades before World War II. He was an easy focus for media attention, tall and handsome, with old world flair, sporting a pointy Vandyke beard, pince-nez glasses, and the heavy accent of a cartoon Italian waiter.

Tresca was born in Abruzzo in 1879 into a prosperous family that lost everything as he was growing up. By 1900 he had joined the growing socialist and unionist movements. Hounded by the authorities in Italy, he fled to Switzerland; there he met another young socialist, Benito Mussolini. Tresca thought him a blowhard.

Tresca sailed steerage for New York City in 1904. He joined forces with the Industrial Workers of the World—the IWW, or Wobblies—the most radical union movement of the era, embracing its code of "direct action," which included matching the businessmen's strikebreaking police and Pinkertons fist for fist and club for club. When New York hotel workers went on strike in 1913, Tresca stood up at a meeting and railed, "Fellow workers, a strike, that is not a course of lectures, but a fight! . . . I say we stop talking. I say we act." He then led them on rock- and bottle-throwing attacks on the finer hotels around Times Square. When Tresca was arrested, strikers attacked the police station to try and free him.

While much of America was praising Mussolini and his Fascists in the 1920s, Tresca viciously denounced them in *Il Martello*, calling them "an army of degenerate, perverted criminals" and "the most savage bloodthirsty gangsters" who "fight the poor at the order of the rich." He was as harshly critical of New York's wealthy pro-Fascist Italians, the *prominenti*. At the top of Tresca's list was the owner of the pro-Mussolini *Il Progresso*, Generoso Pope. Pope was in many ways a classic immigrant success story. Raised in a small village near Naples, he arrived in New York in 1906 as a teenager, speaking no English, carrying $10. By 1930 he was said to be the wealthiest Italian in the city, owner of the largest building supply company in America, as well as the largest-circulation chain of Italian-language newspapers. Very effective in getting out the Italian vote, he was a welcome guest in Mayor La Guardia's office and at Roosevelt's White House. Meanwhile his newspaper chain functioned, according to the historian Nunzio Pernicone, as "the most pervasive and influential purveyor of Fascist propaganda" in America, and Pope himself as "Mussolini's unofficial emissary to the American government." In return, Mussolini showered him with "medals, honors, and special privileges," feeding not only Pope's ego but his standing as a *grand'uomo* in the Italian community.

All of this made him a fat, juicy target for Tresca, who skewered him as an "illiterate quadruped," a "golden ass," and "king of the *cafoni*" (oafs or boors). In return, Tresca was a target of violent retaliation. Armed thugs smashed the *Il Martello* printing presses. One night in 1926, when Tresca was to address a rally in Italian Harlem, a bomb went off in a car that had been seen circling the block outside the hall. The three men in the car were all killed. Evidently the bomb was meant for Tresca but detonated prematurely. He publicly accused the FLNA.

On Memorial Day in 1927, two FLNA members in full blackshirt regalia, waiting at the 183rd Street platform for a Third Avenue El to head downtown to the parade, were murdered, one shot and the other stabbed twenty-one times. Ten thousand mourners stood bareheaded in the rain outside the Bronx headquarters of the FLNA when the two lay in state. A large floral display spelled "Mussolini" in white flowers on red roses.

Police raided the *Il Martello* office and arrested everyone present but found no cause to hold them. Later two Italian garment workers from Brooklyn who were known anti-Fascists were arrested. Tresca and a committee of the city's prominent leftists and civil libertarians raised $20,000 and hired Clarence Darrow to defend the men, who were acquitted. In the aftermath, the NYPD banned blackshirts (and the KKK) from marching in city parades, and Mussolini sent orders that the FLNA should disband.

American public opinion began to turn against Mussolini with his brutal war on Ethiopia in 1935. His promulgation of new anti-Semitic laws in 1938 sent a flood of refugees to New York City, including scholars, scientists, writers, and artists. In 1939 they formed the Mazzini Society.

Headquartered at Broadway and West 57th Street, with offices in fifty other cities nationwide, it became one of the most powerful anti-Fascist organizations in America.

Carlo Tresca, characteristically, considered the Mazzini Society too bourgeois and centrist and continued his own parallel anti-Fascist campaigning. A wartime intelligence file would sum him up well in a single line: "A great individualist, he held tenaciously to his hatreds." It would be the death of him.

CHAPTER 8

Hitler's New York Friends

There were Nazi sympathizers and imitators in America almost from the moment there were Nazis in Germany. In New York City, where roughly a tenth of the residents were either German immigrants or German-American, pro-Hitler groups openly gathered and paraded in the neighborhoods of Yorkville, on Manhattan's Upper East Side from 79th to 96th Street between Third Avenue and the East River; Ridgewood and Glendale in Queens; and Bushwick in Brooklyn. Yorkville was home to one of the largest German communities in the world outside the Fatherland. German immigrants had originally settled in today's East Village, called *Kleindeutschland* in the 1800s, then migrated uptown early in the twentieth century. It was said that one heard German spoken in Yorkville, or Germantown, as often as English. Both sides of East 86th Street were lined with so many German establishments—Café Geiger, Kleine Konditorei, Maxl's Brauhaus, the Lorelei dance hall, the Yorkville Casino—that it was nicknamed Sauerkraut Boulevard. Strong support for the Nazi cause was a minority position in Germantown, but a very visible one, and if not tacitly approved of at least tolerated in the neighborhood. Swastikas and portraits of Der Führer adorned some shops. It was no coincidence that the largest pro-Nazi organization in the country would locate its headquarters there.

One of the first small pro-Nazi groups in New York was run by a Colonel Edwin Emerson Jr. He was born to American parents in Dresden in 1869. After graduating from Harvard he took up journalism in New York City, then rode with Teddy Roosevelt at San Juan Hill (he later wrote a biography of Teddy published by E. P. Dutton). During the Great War he went back to Germany to edit a pro-German propaganda sheet, the *English Continental News*. After the war he remained in the pay of the

German government and was kicked out of several countries as a spy. When Hitler became chancellor in 1933, Emerson and his organization, the Friends of Germany, kept an office in the Whitehall Building at 17 Battery Place, also home to the German consulate.

In the spring of 1933, shortly after Hitler took power, his aide Rudolf Hess sent a man named Heinz Spanknöbel to New York to coordinate the U.S. pro-Nazi movement. Hess recognized that one in four Americans was of German ancestry, representing a large pool of potential support, or at least sympathy, when the Nazis started on their crusade of European conquest. Settling in Yorkville, Spanknöbel absorbed Emerson's group, renamed it the Friends of the New Germany, and declared himself its *Bundesleiter*, or leader.

The Friends attracted some Americans of German descent, but more of its members were disgruntled German nationals, many of them veterans of the disastrous Great War, who'd come to the United States not so much to seek the American way of life as to find jobs and escape the abysmal postwar conditions in their homeland. Spanknöbel openly modeled the group on the Nazi Party. Members wore similar uniforms and gave the stiff-armed *Sieg Heil* salute. They had their own version of storm troopers, the *Ordnungsdienst* or OD, their own anti-Semitic propaganda wing, and their own kind of Hitler Youth programs.

On April 20, 1934, some two thousand Friends of the New Germany met at Schwaben Hall in Bushwick to celebrate Hitler's forty-fifth birthday. Outside, several hundred Jewish veterans of the Great War, calling themselves the National Blue Shirt Minutemen, marched behind a burning effigy of Der Führer. A police cordon kept them at a distance from the Friends. Bushwick had a long history as a German neighborhood, including a period when there was one brewery per block for fourteen blocks. The Friends had offices just down the street from the hall. Prospect Hall (now Grand Prospect Hall) in Park Slope was another regular meeting place.

Spanknöbel proved to be high-handed and abrasive, and he made more enemies than friends. He was once tossed out of the *New Yorker Staats-Zeitung* offices for demanding favorable coverage of Hitler. In 1934 he came to the attention of a federal grand jury investigating foreign agents in the United States and slipped out of the country on the SS *Europa*.

The "New Germany" had a smoother, more erudite friend in George Sylvester Viereck. He's forgotten now, but at the start of the twentieth century he was one of the brightest young stars in New York's literary firmament. He was born in Munich in 1884. His father, Louis, was the illegitimate son of a beautiful actress in Berlin and a royal lover, rumored to be Kaiser Wilhelm himself. Sylvester (he spurned the pedestrian-sounding "George") was nicknamed Putty, for Lilliput, because he was so petite.

Louis dragged his family around the map, landing them in New York City in 1896, where he taught German and wrote for the *Berliner Tageblatt*. After graduating from City College, Sylvester was twenty-two when his first volume of verses, entitled *Nineveh* (his trope for Manhattan), was published in 1907. Decadent and romantic, with a titillating bisexual eroticism, *Nineveh* made him, according to the *Saturday Evening Post*, "the most discussed young literary man in the U.S. today," and "unanimously accused of being a genius." His fans ranged from Theodore Roosevelt to Nikola Tesla.

That moment quickly passed. Literature was moving into the new century, while Viereck's style—"Beyond the sea a land of heroes lies,/ Of fairy heaths and rivers, mountains steep"—seemed stuck in the previous. He turned to fiction and journalism. When the world war broke out he started a magazine, *The Fatherland*, to counter the hate-filled coverage Germany was getting in the American press. Even though he changed the name to *Viereck's American Monthly*, it got him ejected from a few literary societies and gentlemen's clubs, along with some threats of vigilante violence. He also engaged in disseminating outright pro-German propaganda. During the war the Justice Department investigated claims that Viereck was paid by the German government for this work, but no formal charges came of it.

In 1922 he made his first postwar trip to Europe, conducting numerous interviews with political and intellectual leaders for William Randolph Hearst's *Daily American*. They included Kaiser Wilhelm, Sigmund Freud, Havelock Ellis, George Bernard Shaw, Oswald Spengler—and Adolf Hitler. Hitler explained his vision of a Germany cleansed of all Bolsheviks, Jews, and other "aliens." To Viereck, he seemed "more like a poet than a politician" and an "idealist, however mistaken." The interview was rejected by the newspaper, possibly less because of what Hitler said than because until the failed putsch a year later Hitler was still such a nonentity in America.

Viereck grew increasingly sympathetic to the Nazis through the 1920s. In 1932 he entered a paid arrangement with the New York public relations firm Carl Byoir and Associates to serve business clients in Germany. (It's worth noting that Byoir was the son of Jewish immigrants, and his other clients included Franklin Roosevelt.) For the German consulate in New York, Viereck edited a book of essays titled *Germany Speaks*, with a foreword signed by Adolf Hitler that Viereck may have ghostwritten.

As Samuel Untermyer's boycott continued into 1934, German businesses in New York and elsewhere sorely felt the effects. In May 1934, the Friends of the New Germany held a rally at the Garden to protest the boycott and packed it with twenty thousand pro-Germans. Swastikas were everywhere—a large one behind the stage, smaller ones on the armbands of the several hundred grim-faced OD men in their imitation storm trooper uniforms who patrolled the aisles. A long line of speakers took the stage and denounced the boycott. One of them was Walter Kappe, a devout Nazi from the movement's earliest years. He came to the United States when the Nazis were at a low ebb in 1925 and was now the editor of the Friends' newspaper, the *Deutsche Zeitung*. He railed at Untermyer and other Jewish leaders to loud boos and shouts of "Hang them!" Demanding an immediate end to the boycott, which had "poisoned American public opinion against Germany," he threatened that "if you continue the battle, you shall find us fully armed and then you will have to bear the consequences."

George Sylvester Viereck gave the most measured address of the evening. He claimed to speak for all 35 million German-Americans when he said that one could embrace National Socialism without being anti-Semitic or anti-American. "Whatever our attitude toward Hitler may be, there is no doubt that there was no alternative for Germany except Hitler—or chaos. Hitler saved not only Germany but all Europe from being inundated by the red sea of bolshevism." He called the boycott of German businesses a "reign of terror foisted upon the United States and especially the city of New York by certain professional Jews and their bolshevist confederates," and even said he "resented" it mostly because it hampered President Roosevelt's efforts to lift the nation out of the Depression.

"The meeting ended," the *Times* noted, "with the singing of the Horst Wessel Song, the official song of the National Socialists in Germany, shouts of 'Heil, Hitler,' and the Nazi salute for President Roosevelt and for President von Hindenburg of Germany."

The event turned out to be the last hurrah for the Friends of the New Germany. At the time of the rally, the recently formed House Special Committee on Un-American Activities Authorized to Investigate Nazi Propaganda and Certain Other Propaganda Activities was holding hearings not far from the Garden, in an auditorium on the second floor of the New York City Bar Association's building on West 44th Street. The chair of the committee was a Massachusetts Democrat, John McCormack, but its driving force was Congressman Samuel Dickstein from Manhattan. Born in Lithuania in 1885, Dickstein came to the Lower East Side with his family at the age of six. His father was a cantor on Norfolk Street. Samuel graduated from NYU Law and worked his way up in politics, first elected to represent the Lower East Side in Congress in 1922. He'd stay in office through most of the war. As a Jew representing a heavily Jewish constituency, Dickstein was an early and very loud voice against the Nazis. The committee roamed the country in 1934, holding twenty-four hearings in closed sessions and seven in public. Dickstein always took the lead, badgering and arguing with witnesses. The proceedings were so identified with him that people called it the Dickstein Committee.

A month after the Friends rally, the Dickstein Committee called Viereck to the Bar Association hearings to explain his and Byoir's publicity work for Germany. The committee also heard from another prominent New York publicist doing similar work, Ivy Lee. Lee was a pioneer of modern public relations—and propaganda. He devoted decades to reversing the Rockefeller family's public image from the evil robber baron's despised spawn to beloved, beneficent philanthropists. When the liberal Greenwich Village pastor Harry Emerson Fosdick left his downtown parish, Lee convinced John D. Jr. to donate $26 million to build Fosdick a new church of his own, the soaring neo-Gothic Riverside Church near Grant's Tomb in Morningside Heights. It featured (and still does) the largest set of carillon bells in the world. Reputedly it was Lee who convinced the family to name Rockefeller Center, begun in 1930, after themselves, rather than the originally intended name, Radio City.

Dickstein's committee learned that Lee's firm was advising Nazi Germany on how to present itself and its interests, especially its interest in rearmament, to Americans. (Lee's well-known theories about what he called the "psychology of the multitude" had a large impact on Joseph Goebbels. Lee argued that the masses "can only be organized and stimulated through symbols and phrases" that catch "the imagination or emotion of the public." He also stated that "the crowd craves leadership." Goebbels put these ideas to deadly effective use.) Grilled by Dickstein about the purpose of his travels to Germany, Lee said he had met Hitler "to size him up," and that his son was now stationed in Berlin to maintain constant contact. He insisted that he counseled the Germans that "anything savoring of Nazi propaganda in this country was a mistake," and that "they could never in the world get the American people reconciled to their treatment of the Jews." The news of Lee's involvement with the Nazis was not well received. In some circles, he was nicknamed Poison Ivy. He died soon after the hearings, of a brain hemorrhage, at the age of fifty-seven.

At the committee's last Bar Association meeting, the Friends packed the gallery with four hundred members who continually disrupted the proceedings with "outbursts of laughter, jeers and shouts, whenever evidence damaging to the Nazi cause was introduced," the *Times* reported. They gave the Nazi salute and chanted "Heil Hitler!" and "Down with Dickstein!" until a squad of policemen could muscle them out.

The committee released a report on its findings in 1935. One result would be the Foreign Agents Registration Act (FARA) of 1938, requiring anyone serving the interests of foreign governments to report it. This law would be used against Viereck and others.

The more immediate impact of the report was the embarrassment it caused Hitler. In 1935 he was busily building up his military forces and planning the conquest of Europe. He very much wanted America to remain neutral and uninvolved when that happened. The massive Friends of the New Germany rally and Dickstein's hearings were stirring up far too much press and public enmity. Der Führer had the contracts with Byoir and Lee canceled and ordered German nationals in America to quit the Friends.

⌣

At that unruly last Bar Association hearing, a pro-Hitler woman had rushed Dickstein, shouting, "Why don't you examine Communists?" It was, in fact, a good question, and one that wouldn't be answered for sixty years.

Although Dickstein had ostensibly formed his committee to investigate the un-American activities of both Nazis and Communists, the bulk of its attention was on the Nazis. The reason presumed at the time was that the congressman's Jewish constituents were far more concerned about Nazis, and anyway many of them were Communists or sympathizers themselves. Only in the 1990s, after the collapse of the Soviet Union and the declassification of secret documents, did another possible motive surface. Apparently, from 1937 until 1940, Dickstein was on the payroll of Soviet intelligence, receiving monthly payments of $1,250, more than $20,000 in today's currency. One of his tasks was to provide insider information on any congressional investigations into Communist activities in the United States. The Soviets considered him so greedy that his code name was Crook.

CHAPTER 9

The Rise and Fall of Fritz Kuhn

Fritz Kuhn arrived in the Yorkville neighborhood with grand plans. He saw the collapse of the Friends of the New Germany as an opportunity for personal advancement; he came to New York to replace the Friends with a new organization and declare himself the Führer of American Nazism.

Kuhn was born in Munich in 1896. He enlisted in the German army at the start of World War I, fought throughout the conflict, and was awarded the Iron Cross First Class. He joined the new Nazi party in 1921, was married two years later, then moved with his wife to Mexico seeking work. In 1928 he took his family to Detroit. He got a job as an X-ray technician at Henry Ford Hospital, which had a policy against Jewish doctors, and worked on and off for Ford Motor Corporation through 1936.

In 1934, Kuhn took American citizenship. That same year he joined the Friends of the New Germany. Detroit was a natural center for the Friends in the Midwest. It was home to a large German community; to the institutionally anti-Semitic Ford; and, in the poor suburb of Royal Oaks (a Klan stronghold), to Father Charles Coughlin, the immensely popular Irish Catholic priest who used radio and print to preach a far-right gospel that was anticommunist, anti-Roosevelt, anti-Semitic, and fascist. Kuhn rose to be the Detroit leader of the Friends in 1935—just as Hitler was withdrawing his support.

As an American citizen now, Kuhn considered himself exempt from the Führer's edict against Germans participating. In 1936 he rebranded the Friends as *Der Amerikadeutscher Volksbund*, the German American Bund (league). He declared it open "to all Americans and prospective citizens of Aryan blood of German extraction and good reputation." The "prospective citizens" was another way of getting around Hitler's ban. He moved to New York, installing his family in an apartment in Jackson

Heights, Queens, and established the Bund's headquarters in the nondescript building at 178 East 85th Street in Yorkville.

As he consolidated his position, Kuhn easily muscled out one rival, Walter Kappe. Kappe and Kuhn were natural competitors, both big-bellied blowhards with grandiose self-images. The Bund was big enough for only one of them, and Kuhn shoved Kappe out. Kappe went home to Germany in 1937. He'd never return to New York, but in a few years he'd send minions, with spectacular results.

Under Kuhn, the Bund quickly rose to be the largest, most visible, and best-organized of the country's many pseudo-Nazi organizations, with a peak membership estimated at between ten thousand and twenty-five thousand nationwide. (Kuhn claimed two hundred thousand.) Bund members were often seen marching up and down the avenues of Yorkville; if you squinted they looked almost like real Nazis as they passed before large crowds of admirers or just gawkers from the neighborhood. Their uniforms were black breeches and boots, gray shirts with black ties, black Sam Browne belts with shoulder straps. Swastikas adorned everything.

Rather like his idol back home, Kuhn was physically unimpressive. To his detractors he was a clown, a jowly middle-aged man with a comical Otto Preminger accent prancing around in a fake officer's uniform, his Sam Browne belt straining to encircle his potbelly. But to his followers and fans he was as close as they came to a Führer of their very own, and because power, or even the appearance of it, is the ultimate aphrodisiac he had many female admirers. With his wife and kids stuck out in Queens, he was often seen squiring the ladies around Manhattan. The best known was named Florence Kamp; someone in the press nicknamed her Mein Kamp. Coming to New York put Kuhn in Winchell's backyard, and Winchell lit into him with relish, calling him a long list of names like Phffftz Kuhn and the Shamerican. He cackled when Kuhn grumbled about "dot Chew Vinchell."

Bund members and their families even had a summer camp of their own, Camp Siegfried. It was sixty miles out on Long Island, in Suffolk County, near the village of Yaphank. The U.S. Army's Camp Upton, where many recruits from New York City had gotten their first training for the Great War, was just four miles away. The Brooklyn-based German-American Settlement League started the camp on farmland bought in 1935 by Ernst Mueller, who became a high-ranking Bundist. Like Kuhn and many other men of some authority in Nazidom and pseudo-Nazidom, Mueller was no archetype of the Aryan physique. He was short and round, with the sweetly chubby face of a well-fed child.

Camp Siegfried grew up around a small lake, with adult cabins on one shore and cabins for youth on the other. As it developed from 1936 on, the camp transformed an area of Yaphank into an exclusive little German village, called German Gardens, with cottages, sold to people of good German heritage only, that had swastikas inlaid in stone over some of the front doors. Street signs bore the names of Hitler, Göring, and Goebbels. A large, wood-framed inn that served solid German meals was bedecked with more swastikas, American flags, and portraits of Der Führer. At the camp entrance a flower garden featured yet another swastika, fifteen feet wide, of salvia and trimmed box hedge. A statue of Hindenburg graced an open plaza inside the camp; he was revered by Bundists for having the wisdom to turn the Fatherland over to Der Führer.

Siegfrieders came from Yorkville, of course, but also from German neighborhoods in Brooklyn and Queens, Suffolk and Nassau Counties. Some of what went on at Camp Siegfried looked like harmless summer fun—wiener roasts, archery, swimming, hiking. Oktoberfest was celebrated with much beer and sausages and the singing of old songs. But there was also open Nazi propagandizing by speakers including Fritz Kuhn, vendors hawking Nazi and anti-Semitic books and pamphlets, and Bund recruiting and fund-raising. Most troubling to outside observers, boys and girls were uniformed and trained like Hitler Youth.

Nonetheless, the Long Island Rail Road was soon offering a weekly Camp Siegfried Special, which left Penn Station at 8 a.m. on Sunday carrying as many as fifteen hundred jolly Bundists and others from Yorkville. At Yaphank's little whistle-stop station—the same one where American soldiers disembarked for Upton—fellow Bundists lined up and greeted them with the stiff-armed salute and an oompah band, then they marched along Yaphank's Main Street to the camp, swastikas and American flags snapping. Women dressed like the St. Pauli girl greeted them again at the camp entrance.

Life and various newspapers around the country sent photographers. Pathé shot a newsreel. One interloper, a Brooklyn high school student named Murray Cohen, used an assumed name and sneaked a camera in; his pictures appeared in the *Daily Worker* in 1938 as "Inside a Nazi Summer Camp."

On any given summer weekend there could be several thousand people at the camp. But on special occasions the gatherings were very much larger. A celebration of Hindenburg's birthday in the summer of 1937 drew twenty-five thousand, who cheered and sieg heiled as Kuhn and the Bundists marched along with members of the anti-Soviet National Russian-American League and fifty black-shirted members of a pro-Mussolini club from Italian Harlem, Circolo Mario Morgantini, named for the first officer who fell in Ethiopia.

On German Day in August 1938 the crowd swelled to an estimated forty thousand, plus two thousand OD storm trooping guards. There were speeches from Mueller and Kuhn, who declared the camp an "Aryan paradise and part of Germany in America." By that point locals were feeling overrun. Yaphank was a quiet village in the midst of potato and cauliflower farms. It wasn't just all the swastikas and sieg heiling but the hordes and the traffic and the trampled strawberry patches that got to them. For the first couple of years, local businesses—restaurants, service stations, groceries, laundries, farmers with fields for parking—had welcomed the Siegfrieders and their money, and many advertised in the Bund's newspaper *Deutsche Weckruf und Beobachter* (Wake-Up Call and Observer). Some were happy to put "ABC" signs (Always Buy Christian) in their windows. After all, the overwhelmingly white Anglo-Saxon Protestant Suffolk County was also home to a contingent of the Ku Klux Klan; a KKK group sometimes met in Yaphank's Presbyterian church.

Now resistance to the Siegfrieders gained momentum. In 1937, Congressman Dickstein had claimed that the Bund was using Camp Siegfried and others like it around the country to train and arm homegrown Nazis for a planned insurrection. The FBI conducted an investigation and reported that it had found no evidence of such activity.

A more serious challenge came in May 1938, when the state of New York charged Ernst Mueller and other camp founders with forcing Siegfrieders to swear an oath of allegiance to Adolf Hitler, which was illegal for American citizens to do. Despite thin evidence, a Suffolk County jury found them guilty in July. Mueller was sentenced to a year in prison, the others drew suspended sentences, and the Settlement League was fined $10,000, the equivalent of more than $170,000 today. An appellate court overturned the convictions that fall, on the grounds that Siegfrieders merely pledged support for Hitler, not outright allegiance. But it was too late to save the camp. The Suffolk County Sherriff's Office seized the property when the Settlement League couldn't pay the fine.

⌒

Opposition to the Bund was building in Manhattan as well in 1938. The Yorkville Casino on the south side of East 86th Street near Third Avenue was not a gambling establishment but a six-story social center for the neighborhood's German and Irish, with ballrooms, meeting halls, German catering, and the only movie theater in Manhattan showing German-language films. On April 20 a crowd of more than three thousand jammed into one of the meeting halls, where the Bund was celebrating Hitler's birthday again, as well as cheering his forced annexation of Austria the previous month. A group of one hundred or more hostile American Legion members infiltrated the audience and proceeded to shout at speakers. OD men descended on the hecklers swinging blackjacks and the heavy buckles of their Sam Browne belts and a wild melee broke out. Seven Legionnaires were led out bleeding, which incensed the crowd outside, who attacked Bundists as they left the hall later. Police struggled to keep the two groups apart and made a handful of arrests. One of those collared was Otto Geisler, a seventeen-year-old Bundist from the neighborhood, who was charged with wielding a knife. Two days later his court-appointed lawyer, a Jewish attorney from the Legal Aid Society, got the charges dismissed.

Two nights after the Yorkville scuffle, Charles Weiss, the thirty-one-year-old editor of *Uncle Sam*, a magazine published in Brooklyn by a group called the Anti-Communist Anti-Fascist and Anti-Nazi League, was working alone in his office on Flatbush Avenue when four burly young men he said were "of German appearance" broke in. Apparently retaliating for the Casino event, they beat Weiss, tried to make him kiss a swastika flag, then ripped his shirt off and etched swastikas in black ink on his back. They left after trashing the office and ripping an American flag off the wall.

In October of that year, Kuhn and about nine hundred Bundists marched in a short parade across 86th Street and down Lexington Avenue in Yorkville. According to the *Herald Tribune*, about half were gray-shirted men, the rest boys in brown uniforms and girls in white blouses and black skirts, like Hitler Youth. They marched behind American and swastika flags. "Spectators were lined four and five deep... Cheers, clapping, hisses and boos were about equal in volume. *Thousands of spectators lifted their arms in the Nazi salute* [emphasis added]; a few raised clenched fists in Communist salute, and others saluted by raising the right hand with fingers outspread and placing the thumb to the nose." Mayor La Guardia had arranged for fifteen hundred policemen to line the route and keep the peace, and only a few scuffles broke out. In one, when a young observer from Queens gave the marchers the Nazi salute, the man next to him punched him in the nose. At the cavernous Hippodrome that evening, a crowd of about three thousand heard Kuhn and other Nazis attack Dickstein and Untermyer and describe the Jew as "an alien microbe in our midst."

⌢

By then the Bund was becoming a problem for the Führer, just as the Friends of the New Germany had. Hitler was making his first moves of conquest—after the annexation of Austria that spring, his troops occupied Czechoslovakia's Sudetenland in October—and he still very much wanted the United States to stay neutral. He sent orders through the embassy in D.C. once again directing German nationals to quit groups like the Bund, leaving them entirely in the hands of American citizens.

But Fritz Kuhn's biggest triumph was still to come. On February 20, 1939, the German American Bund drew twenty-two thousand people to a massive "Pro-America" rally at Madison Square Garden, with another hundred thousand gawkers and protesters out on the street. The hall was draped with American flags, swastikas, and a giant portrait of George Washington. Bundists in their jackbooted OD uniforms lined the aisles as speakers denounced Franklin Rosenfeld and the Jewish Communist conspiracy to turn America into "a bolshevik paradise." Many in the audience gave the sieg heil salute.

Out on the street afterward, angry protesters kept cops busy as they scuffled with people leaving the hall. But during the rally there had been only two disruptions of note. As Kuhn spoke, a twenty-six-year-old plumber's helper from Brooklyn, Isadore Greenbaum, rushed the stage, shouting "Down with Hitler!" With newspaper and newsreel cameras whirring, Bundists tackled and beat him before the police hauled him away.

The other disruption came from the press gallery. Sitting in the first row, Dorothy Thompson interrupted speakers by "laughing in a superior and exasperating manner," as the *New Yorker* put it. Bundists surrounded her, but cops hustled her out of the building. *Newsweek* complained that she had violated journalistic decorum; the *New Yorker*, on the other hand, crowed that her "performance...was more damaging to the composure of Herr Kuhn and his mob than all the angry clamor on the streets," adding that "we would like to hear more such public merriment around the town...We live in merry times, Dorothy. Take care of your larynx."

It was Fritz Kuhn's finest hour—and his swan song. La Guardia had had enough. He directed the police and the Manhattan district attorney Thomas E. Dewey to bear down on the Bund. The FBI stepped up investigations as well.

⌒

In the month after Fritz's big rally, an actual Hitler came to the city. On March 30, 1939, Bridget Elizabeth Dowling, aged forty-seven, a roomy matron with a slight Irish brogue, stepped off the French liner *Normandie* at the midtown Pier 88 on the Hudson. She was accompanied by her twenty-eight-year-old son, William Patrick Hitler—Adolf Hitler's nephew. Called Willy or Willie, he was the first blood relative of the chancellor to visit America. He and his mother had traveled under an assumed name so as not to draw any unwanted attention on the voyage. But now attention is what they craved. They had come to New York City, center of media, to cash in on the family connection to the Führer.

Bridget Dowling had met Alois Matzelsberger Hitler, Adolf's older half brother, at a Dublin horse show in 1910. The dashing Austrian, who told her he was a rich hotelier, bowled over the pretty nineteen-year-old. Her family was against the marriage, especially when her father learned that Alois was actually a hotel waiter, so they eloped to London. They lived together three stormy years in Liverpool and had William Patrick before Alois returned to Germany. Because Bridget was Catholic there was no divorce, which didn't stop Alois from marrying again in Germany. In 1937, allegedly with help from his now all-powerful half brother, Alois was able to open his own bar restaurant in Berlin, which he called Alois. He would never join the Nazi Party.

Willy, who had grown up to be an accountant, went to Germany in 1931 to see if his uncle Adolf would give him a job. Hitler had a brief and cool meeting with him and offered to arrange a low-level government position. Willy turned down the job and worked at a bank and then for the Opel auto company, a division of GM. Around 1937, the Nazi Party began pressuring Willy to renounce his British citizenship and join his uncle's cause. Instead, Willy tried to blackmail the Führer, threatening to publicly "confirm the long-held rumor that Hitler's paternal grandfather was, in fact, a Jewish merchant, Leopold Frankenberger, who had had an affair with his grandmother, Maria." Hitler started to speak of him as "my loathsome nephew." Willy got the hint and fled back to England.

From the minute he stepped down the *Normandie* gangplank, Willy was badmouthing his uncle. He told the *Times*, "I believe he has created a Frankenstein which even he perhaps cannot stop. I think he has it in his power to destroy European civilization and perhaps that of the entire world." In July, the *New Yorker* visited with him and his mother in the small furnished house they'd rented in Hollis, Queens. The magazine described Willy as "a pleasant, relaxed young man, with jaunty clothes and nice manners. He looks like Hitler, but you can't blame him for that." That same month, *Look* published a six-page spread, "Why I Hate My Uncle." That fall, he went on a lecture tour.

When the United States instituted conscription in 1940, Willy's Long Island City draft board would classify him 1-A. The military, understandably cool to the idea of having a Hitler in the ranks, would keep rejecting him until 1944, when the navy finally took him. After the war, Willy would disappear. He moved to Patchogue out on Long Island under the assumed name William Stuart-Houston, married a German woman, quietly raised a family, and died in 1987.

⌒

Because Fritz Kuhn was an American citizen exercising his free speech rights, Thomas Dewey used an oblique attack he'd successfully deployed against the mobster Lucky Luciano: he had his investigators seize and pore over the Bund's financial records. On May 25, 1939, a grand jury indicted Kuhn on charges of grand larceny and forgery for embezzling some $15,000 from Bund bank accounts. That day, Dewey's agents followed Kuhn as he piled into a car with a few of his followers and hightailed it out of the state. They grabbed him when he stopped for gas in Pennsylvania and hauled him back to New York City. The next day he was fingerprinted, booked, and released on bail.

Making life worse for him, *Confessions of a Nazi Spy* had just hit New York screens. It not only was the first Hollywood film that specifically named Nazi Germany as a threat to American security but depicted the Bund as a front organization for Nazi espionage and propaganda, suggesting, as Congressman Dickstein had charged, that Kuhn and his Bundists were training a secret army to rise up against the government. This was publicity Kuhn did not need. He filed a $5 million libel suit against Warner Bros. studio. It went nowhere.

Kuhn's trial began in November of '39. Winchell attended every day and had a ball satirizing it. The jury found Kuhn guilty on five counts of larceny and forgery. On December 6 he drew a sentence of two and a half to five years in prison. He'd spend the next forty-three months behind bars, during which time his American citizenship would be revoked. That meant that on his release in 1943 he could be immediately rearrested as an enemy agent. Hitler would be dead and the war over before Fritz Kuhn breathed free air again.

The German American Bund would limp on without him, shedding members. A week after the United States declared war on Germany in December 1941, what little was left of the group quietly atomized. The FBI began rounding up former Bundists, as well as Siegfrieders, as enemy aliens, and the U.S. government seized Camp Siegfried as alien property.

The Bund was dead but Camp Siegfried would go on to a long and curious second life. In 1957, the German-American Settlement League, its Nazi years ostensibly long behind it, was able to buy the land back. Hitler Street and Göring Boulevard had been renamed back in 1941, and Camp Siegfried was now Siegfried Park. But one legacy remained: the Settlement League continued to sell German Garden homes only to people of good German heritage. It would do so until a federal discrimination lawsuit forced it to abandon the policy—in 2016.

CHAPTER 10

Paradise for Spies

Bundists and their kind were not the only Nazis in New York City in the prewar years. New York was also infested with Nazi spies.

The Versailles Treaty had no sooner been signed than Germany's military leaders began scheming how to get around the severe restrictions placed on them. The treaty allowed Germany no air force, no tanks, a tiny navy, and an army limited to one hundred thousand citizen volunteers. The generals' first ruse was to fill those slots with trained, battle-hardened veterans, a core around which a future army could be built. Forbidden a modern air force, they formed the Fliegenzentrale ("flight center") and trained future Luftwaffe pilots in harmless-seeming gliders.

Planning ahead in another way, they sent scouts to other countries to see what modern aviation designs and devices could be bought—or, better yet, stolen—for future use. In this regard the United States was a fat and easy target. The American aviation industry of the 1920s was booming and innovating, and the country had in effect no counterespionage capabilities to guard against thieving spies. Its military intelligence units were minuscule, and the FBI had its hands full chasing gangsters. It was, as the writer William Breuer has put it, "a spy's paradise."

Germany's military intelligence agency, the Abwehr, sent its first spies to New York City as early as 1927. A skilled mechanic, the spy Wilhelm Lonkowski got a job at an aircraft plant on Long Island and was able to build up a network of other German émigrés with jobs in the industry who stole designs and blueprints for him. Another spy, Dr. Ignatz Griebl, was on the surface a respected surgeon in Yorkville. Born in Bavaria, he'd served in the kaiser's army in the Great War. He and his wife came to New York in the mid-1920s and quickly took U.S. citizenship. He also joined the U.S. Army's medical reserve. Yet he remained patriotic to Germany and wrote to Goebbels offering to collect intelligence for the Reich.

He built his own spy ring, specializing in pilfering warship designs. His most glamorous agent, Kate Moog, was also his mistress. Born into wealth in Germany and raised in America, the tall and elegant Moog draped herself in diamonds and furs and lived in a huge fourteen-room apartment on the Upper West Side's Riverside Drive.

Griebl and Lonkowski merged their efforts into an intelligence-gathering machine that operated all along the East Coast. To get their information to Germany they used Abwehr couriers who had cover jobs as stewards and waiters on the German ocean liners that made regular trips between Manhattan's Hudson River piers and European ports.

In September 1935 Lonkowski went to Pier 86 at the foot of West 46th Street (where the Intrepid Sea, Air & Space Museum is now) to meet one of those couriers, Karl Schlueter, a steward on the German luxury liner *Europa*. Lonkowski was carrying a violin case. A customs man who had an interest in music innocently asked if he could see the violin. As Schlueter scuttled away, Lonkowski opened the case. When the officer lifted the violin from the case, he saw papers and blueprints underneath. In their office on the pier, customs men also found film negatives and letters in German in Lonkowski's pockets. There was information on Boeing's new B-17 bomber, experimental fighters, and an automatic gunsight. Lonkowski claimed he was a reporter for a German aviation magazine, sending the info to his editors. The customs men scratched their heads and called G-2, U.S. Army intelligence, at the army's base on Governors Island in the harbor. The G-2 man, Major Joseph Dalton, spent all night questioning Lonkowski. Then, incredibly, he told him he was free to go home but asked him to report back the next day. Dalton didn't even get his address.

Astounded at his luck and the Americans' naiveté, Lonkowski ran to Griebl, who got him across the border to Canada, whence he sailed home to Germany. He had managed to spy on the Americans for seven years unmolested, and even when he was caught red-handed they had no clue.

By 1935 Hitler was confident enough to renounce the Versailles Treaty. He instituted national conscription and an amazingly rapid campaign of rebuilding Germany's army, navy, and air force. German industry turned out planes, tanks, warships. The Abwehr redoubled its efforts to pilfer useful military secrets in America.

In the fall of 1937 a German named Nikolaus Ritter stepped off the ocean liner *Bremen* onto Pier 86. The customs inspector was intrigued by Ritter's unusual umbrella, which slipped into a wooden tube to double as a cane. The inspector noted that it would be a handy place for a spy or smuggler to hide something, and both men chuckled. Ritter vanished into the city, and in a few days his cover identity, a textile merchant named Alfred Landing, emerged.

Ritter knew the city well. Born and raised in the Prussian city of Essen, a veteran of the Great War, he had first come to New York in 1924. He stayed for twelve years, married an American, learned to speak nearly perfect American English, and professed to like the United States very much. Still, when the Fatherland called him home in 1936 he dutifully went. In Hamburg he was recruited and trained by the Abwehr, which sent him back to New York to set up a new spy ring.

Within a few days he had already scored a stunning coup. Starting in 1936, Hermann Göring used the Spanish Civil War as a testing ground for his brand-new Luftwaffe. His fighters performed brilliantly, but German bombers proved wildly inaccurate in dropping their payloads. The destruction of the town of Guernica in April 1937, widely interpreted as a despicable Nazi experiment in carpet bombing civilians to oblivion (a tactic the Allies would adopt themselves), was more likely the product of poor targeting: the bombers were aiming for a strategic bridge outside the city and missed. Although Göring and other German military men were happily impressed by the destruction of the town, the central lesson taken from the event was that the Luftwaffe needed a much more accurate bombsight.

The answer was in New York City, and that's why Ritter had come. Since the 1920s, a naturalized Dutch engineer named Carl Lukas Norden had been perfecting an automated, precision apparatus for bomb targeting that eliminated human error as much as possible. His Carl L. Norden, Inc., occupied the large building at 80 Lafayette Street between White and Franklin Streets. (It's now an NYU residence hall.) Norden's bombsight was one of the most valued military secrets of the period. It was a complex and intricate combination of gyroscopes, motor-driven optics, and an analog computer, many of its more than two thousand parts handcrafted to minute specifications by Norden employees. To maintain secrecy, each bombsight was assembled bit by bit in separate locations, with the employees knowing only the bits they worked on. Just a very small circle of trusted craftsmen and supervisors were involved in the final assembly, on the sixteenth floor of the Lafayette Street building. The process was so painstaking that Norden produced only one hundred bombsights a year, which were eagerly snapped up by the U.S. Navy and Army.

Norden had a preference for hiring skilled northern European machinists and engineers, which meant that a number of his employees were Germans who had come to America fleeing the tumult back home in the Weimar 1920s. One of them was thirty-six-year-old Herman Lang, a final assembly inspector on the sixteenth floor. He'd come to New York in 1927 and worked at Norden since 1929. He lived in the German enclave of Ridgewood in Queens and had applied for U.S. citizenship.

He was also a Nazi, proud to have been one of the four thousand or so who'd participated in the failed 1923 putsch. Just a few days after arriving in October 1937, Ritter met Lang. For a few weeks by then Lang had been sneaking plans for the bombsight home. At night, while his wife was asleep, he spread the plans out on the kitchen table and drew precise copies. He now handed Ritter the final drawings. Ritter, excited to receive such a windfall just days after entering the country, offered Lang $1,500, a tidy sum in 1937. Lang proudly rebuffed the offer, insisting that he was motivated by patriotism, not profit.

In November, Ritter went to the drugstore soda fountain in the Times Square Hotel Astor and met up with a steward/courier from the *Bremen.* The steward was carrying an umbrella. He exchanged it for Ritter's umbrella cane—the one that had intrigued the customs official. It had the final bombsight plans rolled up in it. They were soon in Germany. It would be three years before the Americans discovered the theft.

Ritter continued to expand his operation. He recruited his brother Hans, who had followed him to New York in the 1920s and now worked at the Chase National Bank. Then Ritter looked up Fritz Duquesne, a man so celebrated and notorious by the late 1930s that one might consider his usefulness as a spy highly dubious. Still, he did have traits handy for a spy. Not since Baron Munchausen had a man told so many outrageous lies, generated so much lore about himself, or created so many false identities. To this day biographers struggle to tease the facts from the myth.

⌒

Frederick "Fritz" Duquesne was born to a Dutch farm family in South Africa in 1877. Fighting in the Second Boer War (1899–1902) as an officer, guerrilla, terrorist, and spy, he developed a lifelong hatred for the British and an early legend as the self-styled "Black Panther of the Veld." Captured and sent to a POW camp in Bermuda, he escaped in 1902 and stowed away aboard an American yacht that brought him into the port of Baltimore. From there he made his way to New York, where he found an apartment in Brooklyn and a job as a reporter for the *New York Sun*. In later life he would tell amazing tales of his adventures as a young journalist spanning the globe to cover the biggest and most exciting stories of the early 1900s. According to his biographer Art Ronnie in *Counterfeit Hero* (1995) it was all lies. But in January 1909 a series of articles Duquesne wrote on big game hunting did get him invited to the White House, where the outgoing president Teddy Roosevelt was planning an African safari. Duquesne used his association with Teddy to promote his adventure stories and lectures for the next several years.

After TR went on his nearly fatal trip to the Amazon in 1913, Duquesne also traveled to South America, purportedly to film a documentary following in Roosevelt's footsteps. He was in Brazil when the Great War broke out in 1914 and was soon hired as a saboteur by a German naval intelligence officer in Manaus. For the next two years he was evidently all over South and Central America, using various aliases and disguises. He would later claim to have sunk twenty-two British ships and done other damage during that time. Ronnie says he's known to have blown up at least one British cargo steamer.

In 1916 he was in Buenos Aires, on the run from British intelligence, when a two-column article ran in the April 27 *Times*: "Captain Duquesne Is Slain in Bolivia. Hostile Indians Descend on His Expedition and Kill Soldier of Fortune." He had cabled the story himself to throw his pursuers off the scent. Then a few weeks later, now in Montevideo, he wired the *Times* a new story: Captain Duquesne had been found! Not dead but "in a badly wounded state," yet "expected to recover."

Soon after that Duquesne was back in New York City, sneaking around under various aliases. That June a ship carrying Lord Kitchener—whom Duquesne hated above all Englishmen for his scorched-earth tactics in the Boer War—blew up off the coast of Scotland. Kitchener and most of the crew died. For the rest of his life Duquesne would claim that he'd been aboard the ship, signaled the U-boat that laid the mine that sank it, then jumped overboard. A sensationalist 1932 biography was titled *The Man Who Killed Kitchener*. Ronnie judged the story pure fabrication.

Duquesne's next exploit was to tour the United States impersonating an Australian war veteran selling liberty bonds. He was arrested for fraud and remanded to the Tombs, the dismal city jail in lower Manhattan. Fearing extradition to England, where he might well be executed for his activities as a saboteur, he put on a new act and feigned insanity. This got him moved to Bellevue Hospital, from which he promptly escaped.

Using new aliases, he lived relatively freely and prosperously through the 1920s, with a nice apartment near Central Park and a job writing publicity for Joseph Kennedy and David Sarnoff's new RKO. Ritter first met him at this stage, drinking with him in private clubs and speakeasies and reveling in his wild storytelling, as most listeners did. Duquesne was unmasked again in 1932 and arrested, but lawyers for Great Britain lost their case for extradition. The Black Panther roamed free once more. He dropped the aliases and took to wearing a monocle and a uniform encrusted with bogus medals. He also promoted himself from captain to colonel.

When Ritter reconnected with him, "Colonel" Duquesne, now sixty, was still a charmer, staying in nice rooms four doors down from Carnegie Hall on West 57th Street with a pretty thirty-four-year-old artist from the Southwest named Evelyn Lewis. He was living above his means and happy to take Ritter's Abwehr money to be a spy.

After hiring a few more recruits, Ritter spent a last night in New York taking in a vaudeville show in Times Square and visiting a Nedick's hot dog stand. Then in December 1937 he returned to Germany to run his operation from there.

⁓

On December 31 of that year, a handful of Abwehr spies blended in with the innocent New Year's Eve revelers at Maxl's, a popular German restaurant in the basement of a town house on East 86th Street. Among them was Karl Schlueter, the Abwehr courier from the *Europa*, and his assistant Jenni Hofman, a flirty young hairdresser on the ship. Kate Moog was there. So was Guenther Rumrich. Rumrich was born in Chicago, raised in Germany, and returned to the United States at the age of eighteen in 1929. He enlisted in the army, went AWOL, was court-martialed, and was jailed for six months. When he got out he reenlisted, served for a while at the Panama Canal, then went AWOL again. He landed in New York City, where he got an apartment in the Bronx and a job translating for a company downtown on Varick Street. "A curious mixture of shiftlessness, arrogance, and brains," as William Breuer described him in *Nazi Spies in America*, Rumrich had a perpetual need of cash. In 1936 he decided to supplement his income by spying for the Abwehr, which gave him the code name Crown. Schlueter was his handler. Rumrich proved to be a busy and productive agent, though most of the information he sent to Germany was of no great value.

At Maxl's, Schlueter took Rumrich aside and showed him an Abwehr shopping list: blueprints to the new aircraft carriers *Yorktown* and *Lexington*; information on coastal defenses and on an experimental aircraft detection device (which would soon come to be known as radar); and fifty blank American passports. The Abwehr would pay him handsomely for results. Rumrich got right to work—and in doing so he brought down the whole spy ring.

Earlier in 1937 a postman in Dundee, Scotland, had noticed that he was delivering strangely high volumes of mail from around the world to Mrs. Jennie Jordan, a fifty-one-year-old hairdresser. She was also sending a lot of mail to Germany. The mailman alerted his superiors, who called in the British intelligence service MI-5, which under British law was allowed to intercept and open suspicious mail. MI-5 was astounded to learn that Jordan was acting as a mail relay station for an international circuit of Nazi spies. Particularly alarming was the high volume of letters she was getting from someone in New York City who signed himself "Crown," detailing various espionage plots for his Abwehr handlers in Germany.

An MI-5 man flew to New York and showed the evidence to Major Joseph Dalton, the G-2 man who had earlier let Lonkowski slip through his fingers. Dalton rushed to Foley Square to enlist the aid of the FBI. The FBI men were as shocked as MI-5 had been. One plot Crown described in his letters to Germany was to kidnap the commander of the army's antiaircraft station at Fort Totten in Queens and grill him for information about coastal defenses. In other mail Crown asked his Abwehr handlers to send fifty sheets of counterfeit White House letterhead to a postal box in the Bronx.

It was the blank passports that tipped Rumrich's hand. In February 1938, from a phone booth at Grand Central, he called the State Department's passport office down near Wall Street, claiming to be the undersecretary of state. He said he needed fifty passport blanks messengered instantly to the lobby of the Taft Hotel near Times Square. The passport official was puzzled. Blank passports would have been a strange enough request, but "passport blanks" were forms anyone could pick up at the counter of any passport office. He called the NYPD, who assigned detectives. They put together a dummy package, and when Rumrich picked it up he was arrested.

At Foley Square, Rumrich crumpled under interrogation by Special Agent Leon Turrou. Born in Belarus in 1895 and soon orphaned, Turrou had made his way to New York City at eighteen and was a translator at the *New York Times* before joining the FBI. After Rumrich gave him the names of Schlueter (who was not in the country) and Jenni Hofman (who was), Turrou could follow trails of clues that led to Kate Moog and Dr. Griebl. Griebl totally caved under interrogation and talked for six straight days, telling the stunned G-man everything he knew about the length and breadth of Nazi espionage activities in the United States. Then Turrou let him go, hoping he'd lead him to other agents; instead, he fled the country by stowing away on a German liner.

In June 1938 a federal grand jury indicted eighteen people for conspiring to steal U.S. military secrets. Only Rumrich, Hofman, and two others were in hand; of the fourteen others, thirteen were safely back in Germany (including Lonkowski, long gone), and Mrs. Jordan was already serving time in Scotland. The *Times* called it "the stuff of dime novels and spy thrillers."

Turrou added another layer of titillating controversy by resigning from the FBI right after the indictments and selling his story to the *New York Post*. When the paper ran a two-page ad ballyhooing "the most astounding revelation ever published by any newspaper," J. Edgar Hoover went ballistic. If any G-man was going to earn riches and fame from his service to the Bureau, it was J. Edgar himself. He refused to accept Turrou's resignation so that he could have the pleasure of firing him. At the same time the U.S. attorney in the case got a judge to block publication of Turrou's story until after the trial, with the White House's backing.

The trial of the four suspects in hand began in October in the United States Court House on Foley Square and stretched on for seven weeks. The *Times* described the proceedings as "petty, sordid and often faintly humorous." The large crowds who lined up every day for the first-come first-served seating in the gallery were said to be salted with Nazi spies as well as FBI men keeping tabs on the Nazi spies. Defense counsel sought to discredit not just Turrou's ethics—charges he'd left himself open to—but his sanity and even his species, once telling reporters he was "a low illegal offspring of canine ancestry." At the end of November the jury returned convictions and the judge pronounced sentences on the four defendants of two to six years, light considering that the maximum was twenty years.

By then, the press and public had wearied of the trial. "The fact is that the peacetime spy has scant 'pickings,'" the *Times* editorialized. "There are few real secrets, military or otherwise, here or elsewhere. With such complicated instruments as anti-aircraft fire control directors being sold to other nations, with destroyers being built from American specifications in Brazilian yards, with American aircraft sold all over the world, the spy's role is limited. Much of his time, as the Rumrich testimony has shown, is spent in a desperate search for the obvious."

With the verdicts in, the *Post* could run Turrou's articles. Random House simultaneously published them as a three-hundred-page book, *The Nazi Spy Conspiracy in America*, which Warner Bros. quickly adapted as *Confessions of a Nazi Spy*, the movie for which Fritz Kuhn would bootlessly sue.

The spy network Ritter had set up, using Fritz Duquesne and others, would manage to operate another two years undiscovered, then collapse in its own spectacle.

⁀

The Nazis weren't the only ones running spies in New York in the late 1930s. With war clouds gathering around the world, Franklin Roosevelt was severely disappointed with the state of the U.S. intelligence community. The navy, the army, the State Department, and the War Department all ran their own "primitive and parochial intelligence units," in espionage author Douglas Waller's description, that were "underfunded and undermanned dumping grounds for poor performers." They were "feuding fiefdoms," each jealously guarding its turf from the others. J. Edgar Hoover's FBI was an autonomous principality that held itself aloof from all of them. The welter of competing and contradicting tidbits these agencies fed FDR was so confusing it sometimes made him physically ill with frustration. He called it the "twilight zone."

Roosevelt harbored a lifelong fascination with espionage. His favorite chore as assistant secretary of the navy during the Great War had been involving himself in the affairs of the Office of Naval Intelligence (ONI). Now he used the mess of existing agencies as an opportunity to start his own spy outfit, answerable directly to him. Characteristically, he would end up engaging not one but several, adding to the confusion and bureaucratic infighting.

He turned first to an old friend. William Vincent Astor, called Vincent and known as "the richest boy in the world," was raised in a Fifth Avenue mansion and on a baronial estate in the Hudson Valley, Ferncliff, where he knew another lonely little prince just downriver, Franklin Roosevelt. In 1912, when his father, John Jacob Astor IV, went down with the *Titanic*, Vincent, twenty years old and a mediocre student at Harvard, inherited an estimated $87 million, much of it tied up in the family's immense real estate holdings in Manhattan. Franklin Roosevelt's older half brother James was the estate's executor. Like Franklin, Vincent was a wealthy young patrician who developed a social conscience. He would involve himself in philanthropy and divest himself of the family's slum properties in Manhattan.

During the Great War, after consulting with Roosevelt, Astor loaned the navy his steam yacht the *Noma* and served aboard it as a junior officer. Fitted out with guns and depth charges, it patrolled the Atlantic and got into several fights with U-boats. In the early 1920s, when Roosevelt was stricken with polio, Astor offered him the use of his heated pool at Ferncliff as part of a failed physical therapy regimen. Astor backed Franklin for governor and then in 1932 for president. In February 1933, after a would-be assassin emptied a pistol at the president-elect during a speech in Miami, Roosevelt went to Astor's luxurious yacht the *Nourmahal*, tied up nearby, to calm his nerves. They enjoyed many happy cruises on the *Nourmahal* over the years.

Besides blue blood, sailing, and an interest in social welfare, Astor shared Roosevelt's fascination with espionage. In 1927 he started a secret society of amateur spies, all wealthy men and friends of Roosevelt as well, called the Room. They met once a month in an apartment in a stately 1880s brownstone at 34 East 62nd Street and swapped scraps of intelligence they'd picked up in their world travels. (Other tenants in the town house included an actor, a stenographer, and the industrialist Siegfried Bechhold, who would help develop the Sherman tank.)

One of the few members with actual espionage experience was Allen Dulles. Born far upstate in Watertown in 1893, he had served in the diplomatic corps during the Great War, stationed all over Europe, where he dealt with spies of every description and nation. In the 1920s he joined his older brother, John Foster Dulles, at the Wall Street law firm Sullivan & Cromwell, a large presence in the world of international finance, including an office in Berlin. He was also a member of the Council on Foreign Relations. In 1933 he was part of a diplomatic team who met with Hitler at FDR's request, trying to determine the new chancellor's intentions regarding the rearming of his nation. Dulles returned convinced that Hitler was on a path to war, shocked by his treatment of Jews. When he argued that Sullivan & Cromwell should close its Berlin office, his brother scoffed that he was being an alarmist.

By 1938 Roosevelt was very concerned to know the state of Japan's military buildup in the Pacific, but the intelligence he was getting from the various services was bedevilingly murky. He secretly enlisted Astor and Room member Kermit Roosevelt, Teddy's son, to sail the *Nourmahal* to the Pacific and nose around, reporting back for Roosevelt's eyes only any signs they saw of Japanese military, naval, or air activities. The trip was largely a bust, but with the outbreak of war in Europe in 1939 Roosevelt would feel an urgent need for reliable intelligence from there, and he called on Astor again. "Composed of world travellers, important bankers and the directors of some of New York's most important cable companies and international business houses, all intensely loyal and personally obligated to FDR, The Room seemed the ideal semi-official and highly confidential agency to carry out clandestine operations," according to the historian Jeffery M. Dorwart.

The Room took on a new code name, the Club. The international dealings of Club members' businesses proved fruitful avenues for snooping. For example, Winthrop Aldrich was director of Chase National Bank, where both the Japanese and Soviet governments did business. Astor himself, as the director of Western Union, engaged in some highly illegal prying into international cable traffic. The Club struck up a working relationship with the British intelligence office in New York. It also crossed paths with the local offices of the FBI, the ONI, the army's Military Information Division (MID), and the State Department.

When they all complained about Astor, Roosevelt pulled his presidential trump card. In 1941, he would flabbergast them all by designating Astor his "Area Controller" for New York, with authority "to assign intelligence priorities, resolve conflicts, act as a clearinghouse, and be informed before the other four agencies could make any new espionage conflicts." Astor got an office in the lordly Hudson Terminal building at

50 Church Street (later demolished to make way for the World Trade Center), and a commission as a commander of the U.S. Navy. It only intensified the internecine squabbling.

For all his connections, Astor was a dilettante spymaster, and his actions would betray the same naiveté and amateurism that characterized prewar U.S. counterintelligence operations in general. For instance, Roosevelt once received a letter from a woman who claimed to know that copies of the Norden bombsight plans had been taken to Germany. He asked Astor to look into it. Astor assured him it was bunk.

CHAPTER 11

Red, Pink, Pacifist

May Day, a traditional spring holiday as well as International Workers' Day, was freighted with extra political significance in 1933. In Berlin, a crowd of one million massed to hear their new chancellor Hitler speak, and the whole rest of Germany listened on their radios. In Moscow, a million soldiers and workers filled Red Square for Stalin.

New York City was home to both the Communist Party USA (CPUSA) and the American Socialist Party, and they held separate marches that day. The Socialists marched on Fifth Avenue behind a rolling scaffold from which Hitler hanged in effigy. Their leader Norman Thomas was the son and grandson of Presbyterian ministers in Ohio, a conservative Republican when he graduated from Princeton in 1905. Coming to New York City and doing social work in some of the city's poorest neighborhoods converted him to the left.

Thomas first ran for office in 1924 as the Socialist candidate for governor, against the incumbent Al Smith. When he ran for mayor against Jimmy Walker the following year, Congressman Fiorello La Guardia endorsed him. As mayor himself in the 1930s, La Guardia would start programs for subsidized public housing first proposed by Thomas. When Thomas ran for president in 1928 it was a symbolic gesture. The party had peaked before the Great War and then faded through the boom years of the 1920s to only about eight thousand members. Thomas used the campaign as an opportunity to spread his ideas. He polled less than 1 percent of the vote but emerged a national figure, the man most identified with socialism in America.

The Communists had their own march on Seventh Avenue, under banners denouncing Hitler and Mussolini. The CPUSA was run by Earl Browder, a shy, gangly ectomorph who spoke softly with a midwestern twang and seemed the antithesis of the fiery Red. Decimated by the Red Scare that accompanied the Great War, then marginalized by the giddy prosperity of the 1920s, the CPUSA entered the 1930s nearly moribund, with fewer than ten thousand dues-paying members nationwide. With the crash of '29 and the universal suffering that followed it, the party's message, virtually unheard in the gay din of the 1920s, became much more persuasive. Party membership had increased tenfold by the mid-1930s.

Though still infinitesimal for a political party, in New York City Communists wielded influence far beyond their size. Large numbers of the city's intellectuals, writers, artists, and college students were, if they didn't actually join the party, sympathetic to its politics. These fellow travelers did a great service to the movement by disseminating its anticapitalist, antifascist ideas and romantic images of the Soviet Union in books, articles, plays, songs, and films. The New Yorkers who stole Manhattan Project secrets for Soviet intelligence all had Communist Party membership or sympathies.

Expecting trouble, police commissioner James Bolan had put his entire force of nineteen thousand on duty to monitor the May Day marches, but there was only a single arrest all day: a woman stood in the middle of the street trying to block the Communists' parade and got feisty when a cop told her to move along.

The two marches converged in a crowd of about fifty thousand at Union Square, where they listened peacefully to Thomas and other speakers, then went home. The general mood was hopeful about the new president. Since his inauguration just two months earlier, Roosevelt had already reopened three-fourths of the banks that had shuttered and moved to loosen up currency by taking it off the gold standard. He had started the Civilian Conservation Corps, while Harry Hopkins was cranking up the Federal Emergency Relief Administration. Roosevelt also seemed to be reversing decades of antiunion policy in Washington. The left was cautiously cheered.

⌣

Though some New Deal programs bore more than a passing resemblance to policies first advocated by Norman Thomas, no figure on the left would gain more influence in Roosevelt's administration than Sidney Hillman, a pro-Communist, pro-Soviet organizer from New York's garment district. His rise to national political prominence began with a punch in the mouth.

It happened at the American Federation of Labor's 1935 annual convention in Atlantic City. America's oldest and largest labor umbrella organization, the AFL was an alliance for skilled trades unions—electricians, carpenters, machinists unions, and the like—and was slow to include the masses of unskilled industrial workers in mines, in factories, and in the garment district. Tensions between the tradesmen's unions and the others boiled over in 1935 at Atlantic City, where the redoubtable John L. Lewis of the United Mine Workers clambered over some chairs and punched a carpenters' union delegate in the face. The next morning Lewis and a small group started the Committee for Industrial Organization (CIO), which would split from the AFL three years later and become the Congress of Industrial Organizations. His group included three union organizers from New York's garment industry: Hillman, David Dubinsky, and Max Zaritsky.

In one form or another, the garment industry had been a foundation of New York City's economy from its start in the 1600s as a fur-trading outpost. From 1800 to the Civil War, the city's economic growth was powered largely by extensive involvement in the international cotton trade. The manufacturing of ready-made clothing in America began in Manhattan in that era, and the city continued to dominate ready-to-wear clothing well into the twentieth century. The city's garment lofts and sweatshops employed mostly new immigrants, largely Italian and Jewish, many of them women and girls—as were, for example, almost all of the 146 who died in the Triangle Shirtwaist Factory fire in 1911. In the 1920s the industry concentrated in midtown, roughly from Herald Square to 42nd Street between Fifth and Ninth Avenues, tossing up new showrooms, lofts, and truck terminals to create the "garment district," a bustling hive of intense activity.

Like many of the workers they represented, Hillman, Dubinsky, and Zaritsky had come to New York as Yiddish-speaking Jewish immigrants—Hillman from Lithuania, Dubinsky from Poland, and Zaritsky from Russia. All three had fled a failed revolution against the czar in 1905. Hillman came to New York in 1914 and assumed leadership of the new and militant Amalgamated Clothing Workers of America (ACWA). Dubinsky, born Dobnievski, was nineteen when he sailed into New York harbor in 1911 and settled on the Lower East Side. He proceeded to fight and claw his way up the ranks of the largest union in New York City, the International Ladies' Garment Workers' Union (ILGWU), becoming its president in 1932. Zaritsky headed the newly formed United Hatters, Cap and Millinery Workers International (UHCMW).

Hillman's and Dubinsky's unions were both racked by factional wars between their pro-Soviet Communists and anti-Bolshevik Socialists. Dubinsky was an anti-Soviet Socialist. Hillman toured the Soviet Union more than once, met Lenin, and started an international joint project in which the ACWA helped to equip and organize new Soviet textile factories.

When the Depression hit, sales of all manner of new clothing, from off-the-rack suits to fur coats, quickly dropped. By 1932 the industry's output had fallen an astonishing 70 percent, thousands of companies had failed, half of the workers were unemployed, and those lucky enough to find any work were making half of what they had been. Union membership plummeted proportionally, their coffers emptied, and their negotiating position with remaining employers was severely weakened.

So when Roosevelt entered the White House in 1933 and kick-started his New Deal, labor leaders responded hopefully. At Hillman's suggestion, Frances Perkins convened a labor conference that spring at which Hillman, Dubinsky, Lewis, and others offered suggestions that helped shape the administration's National Industrial Recovery Act. The NIRA exempted businesses from antitrust laws, but it also protected workers' rights to collective contract bargaining and a minimum wage. When Roosevelt appointed a board of advisers for the National Recovery Administration (NRA), which supervised NIRA programs, Perkins made sure that Hillman and Lewis were on it.

The NIRA encouraged a flood of garment district workers into the unions. Dubinsky's ILGWU rocketed from around forty thousand to more than a hundred fifty thousand members in 1933, and it kept growing. Hillman's ACWA grew back as well. But employers resisted and got around NIRA regulations from the start. Its welter of codes left it open to constitutional challenges, on grounds that it was an executive branch usurpation of Congress's power to regulate interstate commerce. A challenge from a kosher poultry wholesaler in Brooklyn reached the Supreme Court, which in May 1935 ruled for the complainant, effectively declaring the NIRA unconstitutional. It was followed immediately by the National Labor Relations Act, also known as the Wagner Act for its sponsor, the New York senator Robert Wagner. A stronger rewrite of the NIRA, it guaranteed the right of industrial workers to join unions for collective bargaining, banned a list of employers' "unfair labor practices," and created a new agency, the National Labor Relations Board, to oversee and mediate.

It was in this period, flush with new members and with the federal government behind them, that Lewis, Hillman, et al., felt strong enough to break the CIO away from the AFL.

With so many new members, Hillman realized that running large workers' organizations could mean political clout. The 1936 elections gave him an opportunity to test it. There was concern that Roosevelt's support was softening in key sectors. On the one hand, Democrats could point to many solid returns from the three years of massive deficit spending on New Deal programs. Unemployment had eased below 20 percent, the manufacturing sector was slowly recovering, and the outlook for farmers was brightening. Yet business leaders who had clung gratefully to the life raft of the New Deal in 1933 and 1934 were now in open revolt against federal regulations they claimed were choking continued growth. The Supreme Court had ruled not just the NIRA but other New Deal programs unconstitutional, and the high court was reviewing more.

There were rumbles of rebellion even in FDR's home state. Given its 47 electoral votes, more than any other state's, winning in New York was crucial. Outside of New York City much of the state might easily go Republican. In the city, where half of the state's voters resided, Tammany's standard-bearer Al Smith, once FDR's strange bedfellow, had turned hostile. As a spokesman for the American Liberty League, a coalition of disaffected Democrats and anti–New Deal businessmen, Smith accused the president of leading the country toward socialism.

Roosevelt had key supporters in the city, including La Guardia and Hillman. By 1936, garment district workers practically worshipped Roosevelt. But Hillman worried that Smith and Tammany would make workers loath to vote Democrat; they might even throw their votes away on the spoiler Norman Thomas, handing the state to the Republicans' Alf Landon.

In a meeting at the venerable Hotel Brevoort on lower Fifth Avenue just up from Washington Square Park, Hillman proposed starting a third party, the American Labor Party. Through it, workers and other left-leaning New Yorkers could support FDR (and Governor Lehman, also up for reelection) without voting Democrat. Dubinsky, Zaritsky, and other industrial unionists joined. La Guardia and, of course, Roosevelt approved. The ALP went all out for Roosevelt and Lehman, and it worked. Much of the rest of the state did go for Landon, but with his combined Democratic and some quarter of a million ALP votes FDR won by a 3-to-1 margin in the city, giving him the state. The rest of the nation went much the same way, with the urban centers for FDR and rural areas for Landon. The result was that FDR won one of the most lopsided victories ever, 523 electoral votes to 8. The only two states that went for Landon were Maine and Vermont. Democratic National Committee chairman James Farley, a longtime party stalwart from Rockland County, New York, and adviser to FDR since his years as governor, joked, "As Maine goes, so goes Vermont."

With the great triumph of 1936, Hillman became one of Franklin Roosevelt's favorite labor leaders in the country. Over the next few years the president would often invite Hillman to the White House for chats, consult him on labor issues, and promote him to positions of national authority. In return, no unions would be more faithful to the president than the garment district's.

⌒

A thirty-five-year-old woman and three young male helpers worked their way through the Union Square crowd on May Day 1933, hawking the first issue of her eight-page tabloid, the *Catholic Worker*, for a penny. Dorothy Day would be one of the most consistent voices for pacifism in New York City through World War II and far beyond, as well as such a dedicated servant of the poor that she would be proposed for canonization.

No one who knew her in her youth would have predicted that. She was born in Brooklyn in 1897, raised there and in San Francisco, in a solidly middle-class, Republican, Episcopal family. On the family's return to New York, she threw herself headfirst into the bohemian milieu of Greenwich Village in the years around the Great War. She wrote for the leftist *Masses*, professed anarchist, pacifist, and suffragist politics, and drank and caroused with the best and worst of them.

Exhausted and disillusioned with the high life by the middle of the roaring twenties, she underwent a spiritual awakening and converted to Roman Catholicism. In 1932 she met Peter Maurin, a writer and former monk who had renounced all worldly goods and devoted himself to serving the poor and destitute, of which there were very many in New York at the time. They printed twenty-five hundred copies of the *Catholic Worker* in May 1933. Its messages of helping the poor, of "love in action," of pacifism, antifascism, and antiracism caught on quickly in the depths of the Depression. Circulation was up to twenty-five thousand a year later, and it would peak at nearly two hundred thousand in 1938. Meanwhile they opened the first of their dozens of "houses of hospitality" in a Lower East Side storefront; these had started as simple soup kitchens for the homeless and developed into something more like settlement houses. Day, Maurin, and their growing community of disciples lived in poverty themselves, following a Franciscan model.

During the Spanish Civil War, Day would declare that "Catholics should and must refuse to take part in any modern war." She would be harshly criticized by both leftists and the Church, who had taken opposing sides on the war. She would be even more roundly condemned when the United States went to war a few years later.

Operating out of a small office nearby, the War Resisters League was disseminating its own message of nonviolence. It was begun in 1923 by a handful of pacifists and Socialists, most notably the Brooklyn-born educator Jessie Wallace Hughan, who had earned her Ph.D. in economics at Columbia in 1910. From a tiny start the league grew in size and influence riding the widespread revulsion for war in the 1920s and '30s. Albert Einstein, a longtime pacifist, joined the league on his second visit to America in 1930. The league issued a pamphlet, "Einstein on War Resistance," that was widely read and discussed. Einstein resigned from the War Resisters League, however, when Hitler rose to power in 1933. In 1935, the league's No More War rally drew fifteen thousand people to Union Square, and the group's advocacy of noninvolvement in Europe's squabbles played a hand in Congress's passing the first Neutrality Act, followed by three more, all designed to hobble Roosevelt's attempts to send material support to the Allies before the United States entered the war. When America did get into it, the War Resisters League would be an important resource for conscientious objectors.

CHAPTER 12

Cinderella Men

On the night of Wednesday, June 22, 1938, the whole world was focused on Yankee Stadium. Joe Louis, the Brown Bomber, was fighting a rematch with Max Schmeling, Hitler's Superman. As David Margolick describes in *Beyond Glory*, this was much more than a prizefight, more than a title bout. Around the world, this was seen as a symbolic duel between democracy and fascism, freedom and slavery, white and black.

Sporting events were not usually freighted with such global political significance. In the Depression years they were a welcome distraction from one's miseries. Baseball, boxing, and horse racing were the most popular of the era. All three offered plucky underdogs and Cinderella stories to distract people from their own troubles. While the New York Yankees were winning the World Series with monotonous regularity, the scrappy, often hapless Brooklyn Dodgers had more, and more devoted, fans. When the smaller Seabiscuit outran the mighty War Admiral; when Jimmy Braddock made his amazing comeback; and when Joe Louis pounded Schmeling, it gave you a sense that you might come out all right yourself.

James Braddock's story was ready-made for the Depression. He was born in a Hell's Kitchen tenement in 1905; the following year, his poor Anglo-Irish immigrant parents moved their large family across the Hudson to New Jersey. He started boxing late, at eighteen, a fighter of tremendous heart and moxie but bad hands. In 1928, five years into a very promising professional career, he broke his right in two successive fights, and he would break it again later. His career slid, until by 1933 "he had gone from headline to breadline," as his biographer Michael C. DeLisa put it. He was taking what work he could get as a longshoreman on the Weehawken docks and accepting $6.40 a week from a New Jersey relief agency to feed his kids.

In June 1935 he made an astonishing comeback. In one of the biggest upsets in boxing history, he went up against the heavily favored world champion Max Baer at the Madison Square Garden Bowl, an outdoor arena in Queens, and won. Overnight he went from a has-been on the dole to world champion. It was the sort of story Depression America loved, and needed, to hear. Damon Runyon pegged him the Cinderella Man.

A month before Braddock's victory, on May 15, a young fighter named Joe Louis, on his first visit to New York City, stepped off a train in Grand Central to be engulfed by press, fans, and a police escort. Flashbulbs crackled. A group of Pullman porters lifted him in the air and doffed their caps for a photo as the fans cheered. The next day's *New York Post* ran a cartoon of a giant Louis bestriding Manhattan like a colossus, knocking the tops off the Empire State and Chrysler Buildings.

You might have thought Joe Louis was the reigning world champion, not Braddock, but in fact he'd been boxing professionally for less than a year. The hoopla had been orchestrated by his promoter, Michael Strauss Jacobs. And New Yorkers, not only but especially black New Yorkers, had proven to be a very receptive audience for it.

Jacobs, who preferred to be called Uncle Mike, was famously homely, with, according to *Life*, "beady eyes, a dead-pan face, a gruff voice, a set of badly fitting false teeth." He was born in 1880 into a large Jewish immigrant household on Manhattan's Lower West Side. As a kid he hawked popcorn and lemon drops on Coney Island excursion boats. By the 1920s he was scalping tickets and promoting events around the city, from Broadway revues to boxing matches. Failing to get the contract to book fights in Madison Square Garden, he forged an ingenious alliance with William Randolph Hearst's newspaper chain. He offered to promote fights at other venues as fund-raisers for Millicent Hearst's favorite charity, the Free Milk Fund for Babies. In return, writers for Hearst's papers, including Runyon, would beat the drums.

That deal in place, Jacobs headed west to investigate this new fighter he'd heard about. Joseph Louis Barrow was born a dirt-poor sharecropper's son in Alabama in 1914. He was twelve when the family moved to Detroit, part of the great diaspora of Southern blacks to the industrial

North in the 1920s. He started boxing in the Depression to bring in a dollar or two. Billed simply as Joe Louis, he was knocking down opponents at the rate of two a month in Detroit and Chicago when Jacobs signed him.

For Louis's first fight in New York, Jacobs got the former champion Primo Carnera. The Italian giant had a glass jaw and was rumored to have won most of his fights because his backers, who included the gangster and Cotton Club owner Owney Madden, paid the other fighters to tank. That didn't stop local and national press, with Hearst papers leading the way, from building up the match into one of the most highly anticipated sporting events in living memory.

⌣

No New Yorkers were more excited about Joe Louis than the three hundred thousand residents of Harlem. In 1935 they sorely needed something or someone to cheer about. Of all the city's neighborhoods, the Depression had fallen hardest on Harlem. Unemployment had already been higher there than in the rest of the city. The great majority of black New Yorkers who had jobs in the 1920s worked as unskilled or semiskilled laborers or in the service industries. Seventy percent of the working women were domestics. Those who worked in industry, such as the needle trades, consistently earned less than white women working at the same jobs. The city government made some token efforts to hire qualified blacks, but the Irish-dominated police, for instance, systematically prevented black cops from advancing, and no black doctors or nurses were allowed to work in any public hospital in the city except Harlem Hospital. Blacks who tried to run their own businesses always struggled against white competitors. Only one Harlem business in ten was black-owned. The stores that lined busy 125th Street were almost entirely white-owned and white-staffed.

Because black New Yorkers were ghettoized in Harlem and a few other areas, landlords could cruelly gouge them for outrageous rents. Harlem tenants consistently paid more for dilapidated housing where hot water, baths, and even heat were often missing. In the 1920s, rents citywide rose 10 percent but shot up 100 percent in some parts of Harlem. The poverty, crowding, terrible housing, and lack of services all combined to produce illness and mortality rates, especially from tuberculosis and pneumonia, that were shockingly higher than elsewhere in the city.

When the Depression hit, unemployment in Harlem rose to 25 percent in 1930, and steadily climbed to 50 percent. Anywhere blacks and whites worked together, blacks were fired first. Those who held on to their jobs saw their wages and hours cut. Domestics earned a maximum $15 a week, factory workers as little as $7. Average household incomes in the neighborhood dropped by almost half in the first two Depression years. All the problems the neighborhood had experienced even in boom times were now exacerbated: homelessness, malnutrition, petty crime, juvenile delinquency.

By the start of 1935 Harlem seethed with resentment and anger. That March it erupted. A Puerto Rican teen was caught shoplifting a cheap penknife in a five-and-dime on 125th Street. A minor scuffle ensued, but a rumor flashed around the neighborhood that the youth—now termed black—had been viciously beaten and/or killed. Protesters from the Communist Youth League and a group called the Young Liberators gathered outside the store, attracting a sullen crowd. Someone smashed a window and a full-scale riot broke out. It went on all night, as thousands of fed-up Harlemites raced up and down 125th Street, attacking and looting the white-owned shops. Mayor La Guardia rushed five hundred cops to the neighborhood. They made a thousand arrests, and by 4 a.m. it was over. La Guardia blamed the Communist protesters for causing it; leaders in the neighborhood said the causes were extreme poverty and hopelessness.

No one was surprised, then, when two months later Harlem greeted Joe Louis not just as a hero but, as *Time* later put it, "black Moses leading the children of Ham out of bondage." On the night of June 25, sixty-four thousand people crammed into Yankee Stadium to watch Louis knock the much larger Carnera down three times in the sixth round for a TKO. There was pandemonium in the stadium. Nearby, all Harlem erupted again—this time to dance and sing in the streets until dawn. Louis himself went to bed. He would always be the preternaturally still, calm center in the cyclone of adulation that whirled around him, a man so quiet and impassive in public that one reporter compared him to a wooden Indian.

When Louis returned to Yankee Stadium to face Max Baer in September, the crowd of ninety-five thousand included Babe Ruth, Cary Grant, Edward G. Robinson, Irving Berlin, Al Jolson, and Ernest Hemingway. Some thirty-five thousand blacks filled the bleachers and upper tiers. Baer was still rattled from his loss to Braddock, and Louis dispatched him in four rounds. "Town Goes Mad," the *Amsterdam News* reported, comparing the celebrations in Harlem to those at the end of the Great War. The revelers filled Seventh Avenue, banging washboards and tin cans, blowing horns and whistles. People danced on the roofs of parked cars and traffic-stalled taxis.

In June 1936, Louis faced the German former champion Max Schmeling. Schmeling had been the darling of Bertolt Brecht and Berlin café society in the Weimar 1920s, then easily adapted to Hitler's rise and was now a hero to the Nazis. Mike Jacobs and his newspaper pals ballyhooed it as a duel between America's sepia superman and Hitler's übermensch. But with most sportswriters predicting an easy Louis win, and Jews threatening to boycott, the crowd of forty-five thousand failed to fill up Yankee Stadium this time, though millions heard it on the radio. Schmeling's wife listened by shortwave in the home of Joseph Goebbels.

Schmeling had studied Louis carefully and trained hard, while Louis strolled into the ring unprepared and overconfident. To the increasing dismay of black Americans everywhere, the German pounded Louis mercilessly for eleven long rounds and then knocked him down for good in the twelfth. A few elderly black listeners, including one in Harlem, reportedly fell dead of heart attacks beside their radios. Langston Hughes would remember walking down Seventh Avenue and seeing "grown men weeping like children." Meanwhile, it was Yorkville's turn to party in the streets. The large German community there marched arm in arm along 86th Street, singing and cheering, and clinked steins in the Café Hindenburg and the brauhauses.

Schmeling flew back to Germany from Lakehurst Naval Air Station in New Jersey on the new zeppelin *Hindenburg*. The *Hindenburg* was the pride of Nazi Germany, the largest commercial airship ever built, almost three football fields long. New Yorkers gaped from the streets and windows of Manhattan as the immense silver lozenge—with swastikas emblazoned on its tail—floated overhead to and from Lakehurst. For all its awe-inspiring size, the *Hindenburg* carried fewer than one hundred passengers, who each paid more than $6,000 in today's currency to cross the Atlantic in two days, half the time it took an ocean liner.

Though they were at the peak of their romantic popularity in the 1930s, the gargantuan zeppelins were never practical. They needed huge, open airfields for takeoff and landing; the "mooring mast" at the top of the Empire State Building was a publicity stunt capitalizing on airships' allure, as no zeppelin could possibly have tethered there. For takeoff at Lakehurst, a large crew of midshipmen would actually toss a zeppelin into the air on the order "Up ship!" For landings, they hauled the hovering behemoth to the ground by dangling cables.

Also, zeppelins like the *Hindenburg* that were filled with hydrogen, as opposed to helium, were disastrously prone to explosive fires. When Schmeling returned to the United States in May 1937, he'd originally planned to fly again on the *Hindenburg*, but scheduling required that he take an ocean liner instead. So he was not on board when the *Hindenburg* exploded on arrival at Lakehurst that May 6.

⌣

Mike Jacobs had Louis back in the ring by August, knocking down a series of lesser fighters. In June 1937 he met the Cinderella Man in Chicago's Comiskey Park for the world heavyweight title. Braddock had not fought since beating Max Baer two years earlier. He was ten years older than Louis and still had the bad hands but great heart. He stood up to Louis's murderous assault into the seventh round, then went down on his face like a dead man. The headline of the June 26 *Amsterdam News* was "*KING LOUIS I*."

When Louis's rematch with Schmeling came to Yankee Stadium on the night of Wednesday, June 22, 1938, seventy thousand people packed the place. Mayor La Guardia was there, and J. Edgar Hoover with Clyde Tolson, and Tom Dewey, and Cab Calloway, Vincent Astor, Tallulah Bankhead, Louis Armstrong, Duke Ellington, Hemingway again, Jack Johnson. Some two thousand Germans had come over on the liners *Bremen* and *Europa*, swastikas snapping from their masts. Sixty million Americans, half the entire population, gathered around radios. All over New York City, deserted streets echoed to the sounds of radios tuned to NBC, announcer Clem McCarthy's gravelly voice rasping out of windows thrown open on a hot night. Twenty million Germans listened to their own broadcast, and another twenty million elsewhere around the globe, making it the largest audience for any event ever in the history of the world.

The stadium crowd exploded in cheers as Louis loped across the infield to the ring a few minutes before 10 p.m. Then Schmeling trudged out with a towel over his head for a little protection against the shower of cigarette butts and paper cups hurled at him. When the bell rang, Louis barreled out of his corner; Schmeling, who seemed to know what was coming, stood leadenly and braced for the assault. He looked like he wished he was anywhere else in the world. Louis charged into him, pummeling him with a whirlwind of punches. A minute into it, Schmeling was hanging on to the ropes. Louis's crashing right fist to the jaw knocked him down once, then again, then a third time in quick succession. Schmeling was on his hands and knees when the referee ended the fight, two minutes and four seconds after it began. It was over so quickly that some latecomers still filing into Yankee Stadium missed it.

An unearthly roar shot up from the crowd and was echoed around the world. At the Berlin Olympics two years earlier, another Alabama sharecropper's son, Jesse Owens, had embarrassed Hitler by beating his Aryan athletes for four gold medals. Now Joe Louis had pummeled the myth of Aryan supremacy to the canvas three times in two minutes and the world laughed and cheered.

All Harlem, plus a couple hundred thousand visitors, packed Seventh Avenue from 116th Street all the way up to 145th. Amid the singing and dancing and banging of pie tins, many raised their arms in mocking Nazi salutes. The gloom in Yorkville was funereal.

CHAPTER 13

God Bless America

In September 1938, Irving Berlin boarded the *Normandie* at Manhattan's Pier 88 on the Hudson and sailed to England to be at the London premiere of the new film *Alexander's Ragtime Band*, built around several of his songs. He was at the top of his game, his life a blueprint of the Lower East Side rags to riches legend. He was born Israel Baline in Belarus in 1888. Fleeing the pogroms, his father, a cantor, brought the family of eight in steerage to New York City when Israel was five. They settled in a cold-water flat on Cherry Street, lined with storefronts and houses crowded with poor Jewish, Italian, Irish, and other immigrants. After his father worked himself to death in a kosher meat market, Israel left home at fourteen—went "on the bum," as kids said then—and spent a year sleeping in a Bowery flophouse while working as a singing waiter in the Pelham Cafe and other Chinatown dives. He wrote his first published song with the piano player in the Pelham in 1907, now calling himself Irving Berlin, and earned 27 cents in royalties. He wrote a bunch more, knocking on every door on Tin Pan Alley, until he had his first bona fide hit in 1911 with "Alexander's Ragtime Band." He never learned to read or write music and used only the black keys on the piano, but after 1911 a year rarely went by without at least one big Irving Berlin hit. He started his own publishing company, had George Gershwin working for him for a while, and went on to conquer Broadway and Hollywood as well. In May 1934 *Time* put the "dark-skinned crickety little man" on its cover, simultaneous with a five-program NBC tribute that ran on Sunday nights at 9 p.m.—prime time—and played a hundred of his songs.

Berlin was in London, staying at Claridge's, when prime minister Neville Chamberlain returned on September 30 from Munich, where he had pledged that England would not intervene if Hitler annexed the Sudetenland, the "German" western half of Czechoslovakia. Chamberlain called the nonaggression pact "symbolic of the desire of our two peoples never to go to war with one another again." Irving Berlin was not so sure. He came home concerned about the "storm clouds" he believed were gathering over Europe and wanting to write a new song about how thankful he was to be an American. He had made a couple of false starts—one called "Thanks, America," and another called "Let's Talk About Liberty"—when he heard from Kate Smith's manager asking for a patriotic song she could sing on her November 10 radio show, *The Kate Smith Hour,* to celebrate the first officially observed Armistice Day the next day.

With a string of hit records and two popular radio programs, one daytime and one at night, Smith was at the top of her game as well. By the fall of 1938 she was as representative of old-fashioned American values as baseball and apple pie. If anyone could put over a new patriotic song it was Kate Smith.

Berlin still didn't have a new one, but he remembered a song he'd written twenty years earlier and set aside—what they called on Tin Pan Alley a "trunk song." In 1918, after the United States entered the Great War, he had unexpectedly found himself drafted into the army at the age of thirty. He was posted with some other New York entertainers to Camp Upton. Hating army life, he wrote a humorous complaint song, "Oh! How I Hate to Get Up in the Morning." It caught on with his fellow soldiers, which gave him an idea: a full-scale stage revue on army life called *Yip! Yip! Yaphank!*, with an all-soldier cast. His superior officers agreed, the show was built, and after opening at Camp Upton it went to Broadway.

Now he remembered a song he'd written for *Yaphank*'s finale but then replaced: "God Bless America." He dug it out, updated the lyrics, and gave it to Kate Smith. What happened with the song after that is interesting enough that an entire book has been written about it, Sheryl Kaskowitz's *God Bless America*, published in 2013. The version Smith first sang live on the radio differed in a small but very telling way from the one we know today. It included an introductory verse in which Berlin specifically made reference to the troubling signs he had just seen in Europe and said that Americans should be grateful that they were "far from there."

That line is key. In this version, "God Bless America" wasn't only a patriotic song, it was an isolationist one. Kate Smith, like so many Americans, shared the sentiment. She'd spoken out before about not sending American boys "to fight other nations' battles."

But timing is everything. On November 9, one night before Smith's broadcast, Nazis and their supporters throughout Germany and Austria began the rampage known as Kristallnacht, smashing and burning Jewish shops and synagogues, and arresting some thirty thousand Jews for deportation to concentration camps. The *New York Times* reported it on the front page the next day. On her daytime show, *Kate Smith Speaks*, Smith called it "a night of terror for German Jews."

Smith sang the introductory verse that night, but both she and Berlin were already reconsidering it. When the sheet music was published in February 1939 he had changed the wording to "grateful for a land so fair," and when Smith's recording came out shortly thereafter, the introduction had been cut altogether, the way it's usually been sung ever since.

Now an all-purpose, nonspecific anthem, "God Bless America" soared in popularity. Americans loved that it was so easy to remember and sing, unlike the official national anthem, and they started doing so everywhere—in classrooms and churches and synagogues, at meetings of clubs and civic groups, at company picnics and the 1939 world's fair in New York, and anywhere else they gathered. For a short time even Bundists, hoping to Americanize their image, sang it instead of "The Horst Wessel Song." Starting in 1939 it was played at every Dodgers ball game at Ebbets Field; the whole crowd stood and the males removed their hats, just as they did for "The Star-Spangled Banner." The following year both Republicans and Democrats sang it during their presidential campaigns. As people kept singing it straight through the war it completed a transit from an antiwar song to a victory song.

Not everyone liked it. It was criticized from the left for its complacent jingoism. Woody Guthrie despised it and wrote "This Land Is Your Land"—originally titled "God Blessed America"—as a retort. When it dawned on anti-Semites, including the Bund, that "God Bless America" had been written by a Jew York immigrant, they turned on it and booed when it was sung. But nothing could dent it.

As for Berlin and Smith, no civilians would do more to support the troops during the war. Smith would spearhead the most successful war bond drive of all, pulling in nearly $40 million in pledges, while Berlin would write, produce, and perform in a new version of *Yaphank*, called

This Is the Army, that toured around the world entertaining frontline troops for the duration and raised millions for the Army Emergency Relief Fund.

⌒

For German Jews who were able to flee after Kristallnacht, the supreme question was where to go. Nations around the world, including the United States, enforced strict immigration quotas. From the late 1930s through the war, Washington's policy toward European Jews rested on two fundamental ideas, shared in the White House, the Pentagon, and the State Department. One was that to make too much effort to save the victims of the Nazis would play into the hands of domestic anti-Semites, making it appear to be a "war for the Jews." The perception, undoubtedly correct, was that Americans could not be inspired to make the great sacrifices necessary to win the war if that were the rationale. They had to believe that it was a war to save the whole world from tyranny. The other understanding, often repeated, was that the best thing the Allies could do for the Jews was simply to defeat Hitler as quickly as possible. Any attention or resources diverted from the battlefield could actually be detrimental to the Jews.

Moreover, many U.S. policy makers saw the Nazi and Fascist dictatorships as regrettably necessary buffers against the spread of Soviet Communism. Even after the United States was dragged into the war against Hitler, many in Washington privately considered Communism the greater long-term threat. Because of the perceived need to deal with the Nazis now and the Soviets later, saving the Jews took a low priority.

New York's uptown German Jews and downtown Orthodox would argue bitterly over questions of how to aid Jewish refugees and influence FDR's policy toward them. Rabbi Wise naturally was the uptown spokesman.

Palestine, the traditional Jewish homeland and Zion, shone like a beacon of hope to Jews fleeing Europe in the 1930s. Yet the British, who administrated Palestine under a League of Nations charter following the Great War, turned back Jewish immigrants, wanting to keep peace with the majority Arab population. Nevertheless, between 1933 and 1936 European refugees doubled the Jewish population there. The Arabs revolted. The British, weighing the numbers and the balance of power in the Middle East, tacitly backed them.

Young Jews in Palestine formed the Irgun, a paramilitary organization that fought with both the Arabs and the British police during this period of unrest. One of them was Hillel Kook. He was born in Lithuania and left with his family in 1925. In 1937 the Irgun sent Kook to Poland, where he got involved in illegally smuggling refugees into Palestine in defiance of the strict quotas.

In New York, the refugee-smuggling effort, known as *aliyah bet* (the second immigration), galvanized Jews who might not have gotten involved before. William Ziff, of the Ziff-Davis publishing empire, had never shown any public interest in Jewish causes before. In 1935 he agreed to act as president of a Zionist organization, then wrote the 1938 book *The Rape of Palestine*, accusing the British of inciting the Arab violence against Jews. The British Foreign Office denounced it as a "violent and offensive" book by an "unscrupulous gangster."

Rabbi Wise and mainstream Jewish leaders condemned *aliyah bet* as provocative and reckless and urged going through official British immigration channels, as extremely restrictive as those were. Wise had grown more cautious since the days of the 1933 boycott rally. He was getting old and his health was fading. He now considered himself a friend of Roosevelt's, and like other Jewish supporters of FDR he was chary of making trouble for the chief with the anti-Semites.

That caution extended even to members of their own families. Sam Rosenman had a cousin who had escaped the Nazis but had to leave his wife and children behind. He was desperate to find out their status. Rosenman decided not to mention it to Roosevelt and went to Adolf Berle instead. In 1938, the Gestapo arrested an uncle of Felix Frankfurter's in Vienna. Frankfurter thought first about asking Roosevelt to intervene, but he went to the State Department instead and, not surprisingly, got nowhere. He reached out to the American-born Lady Nancy Astor, who spoke to the German ambassador in London, who arranged for the uncle's release. Roosevelt never lifted a finger and may never have heard a word about it.

Bernard Baruch acted privately to help a few relatives get out of Germany, but in terms of public policy he was both anti-Zionist and against lifting U.S. quotas on refugees. His proposed solution, oddly similar to the Nazis' Madagascar plan, was to carve a large area out of British-controlled Kenya, Rhodesia, and Tanganyika to create the "United States of Africa," a haven for European refugees of all faiths.

The trip of the ocean liner *St. Louis* in May–June 1939, known as "the voyage of the damned," was a watershed. A Hamburg-American liner, the *St. Louis* left Germany with more than nine hundred Jews fleeing the Nazis. Refused admission by Cuba and then the United States, they were forced to return to Britain and Europe. In New York the *St. Louis* affair further exposed the rift between the uptown Jews and the more confrontational Zionists downtown. The Orthodox community took note when Wise and Morgenthau exerted no pressure on the president to save the *St. Louis* refugees.

Almost a year later, in March 1940, a leading militant Zionist, Ze'ev Jabotinsky, would come to New York and address five thousand people at the Manhattan Center, describing his plan to raise an army of Palestinian Jews to fight Hitler alongside the British. The implication was that once the war was over they'd fight the British for a Jewish Palestine. Not surprisingly, Rabbi Wise denounced the idea.

Hillel Kook, now going by the nom de guerre Peter Bergson, came to New York with Jabotinsky and would stay there through the war. Appalled by the timidity of the Reform rabbis and the indifference of the U.S. government to the plight of European Jews, he would start the Emergency Committee to Save the Jewish People of Europe. It would come to be known simply as the Bergson Group, the angriest and most persistent advocates Hitler's victims had in New York or America.

PART TWO

The Storm Breaks

What we face is cold, hard fact. The first and fundamental fact is that what started as a European war has developed, as the Nazis always intended it should develop, into a world war for world domination.

—*Franklin D. Roosevelt (May 27, 1941)*

CHAPTER 14

Mr. New York's World's Fair

Of the dignitaries who gave speeches at the opening of the New York World's Fair on April 30, 1939—President Roosevelt, Mayor La Guardia, Albert Einstein, others—none spoke longer or more grandiloquently than Grover Whalen. His name is all but forgotten now, but at the time he was as familiar to New Yorkers as all those others. He'd been the city's master of ceremonies since the end of the Great War, its indefatigable booster and cheerleader. He could justifiably take the opening of the world's fair as a personal triumph, since no one had done more or worked harder to make it happen.

Whalen liked to call himself "Mr. New York," and for more than thirty years no individual seemed a better figure to represent the city—both its light side and its dark. Gregarious and affable, an inveterate glad-hander, a tall man with a movie star's pencil mustache and a mellifluous baritone that carried a pleasing hint of an Irish lilt, he looked as if he were born wearing a top hat and tails. But he had actually started out on the Lower East Side and could be tough and even brutal when he thought the occasion called for it.

He was born on June 2, 1886, the day of President Grover Cleveland's White House wedding. Hence the name given him by his father, whom he would call in his memoirs "a real New York Irish Democrat"—that is, a Tammany Hall man. Grover grew up at Montgomery and Henry Streets, studied at New York Law School but did not graduate, and went to work for Rodman Wanamaker's department stores. He joined a Democratic business committee that in 1917 helped oust Republican mayor John Mitchel (for whom Mitchel Field was named) and put Tammany's John Hylan in the job. Whalen left Wanamaker's to work for Hylan, nominally as his secretary, but mainly as the mayor's stand-in at official functions, which Hylan, who had little flair for public oratory or showmanship, disliked attending.

When the world war ended, Whalen was the master of ceremonies in the yearlong orgy of gigantic ticker-tape parades and other lavish festivities the city threw for General Pershing and returning troops. It was said that if Whalen did not actually invent the use of ticker tape, he perfected it. Among the local units feted were the 369th Infantry Regiment, the city's black regiment known as the Harlem Hellfighters. During the war they were seconded to the French army, because white American units didn't want to fight alongside them. (The 369th's commanding officer, who was white, did stick with them through the war. He was Hamilton Fish, who grew up near Franklin Roosevelt. As a conservative Republican congressman representing Roosevelt's home district in the 1930s, he'd be a staunch isolationist and one of FDR's bitterest foes.) The French were glad to have the Hellfighters. They distinguished themselves throughout that war, earning scores of medals, including a Croix de Guerre for Fish. Demobilized at Yaphank, they marched seven miles from Washington Square to Harlem as crowds cheered. Also marching were the city's beloved Fighting Irish of the 69th Infantry Regiment, led by Colonel Wild Bill Donovan and their famous chaplain Father Francis Duffy, who would get a statue and a piece of Times Square dedicated to him by Mayor La Guardia in 1937.

When Jimmy Walker followed Hylan as Tammany's man in the mayor's office in 1926, he kept Whalen around. It was Whalen who organized the mammoth parade for Charles Lindbergh in 1927, the biggest the city had ever seen. Whalen had actually planned it for Admiral Byrd, whose bid to be the first man to fly the Atlantic was sponsored by Whalen's former employer Rodman Wanamaker, but the dark horse Lindbergh beat Byrd across the ocean by five weeks.

Whalen showed his tougher side when Walker made him police commissioner in 1928. The former commish had failed to make much headway against a rising tide of gangland murders around the city, including one in crowded Herald Square in broad daylight that outraged and terrified the populace. Whalen entered the office promising to "teach these tough guys, these ruthless gangsters who respect no law, that there is still a lot of law at the end of a nightstick," and warned that his officers would use "plenty of lead." He threw the NYPD into raiding the gangs' speakeasies, hitting up to a hundred a night and using axes to smash up the premises, for which they earned the nickname Whalen's Whackers. It was good publicity for Mayor Walker, who had always been accused, rightly, of extreme laxity in prosecuting Prohibition, but it was little more than an annoyance to the gangsters.

Commissioner Whalen was harder on the city's Communists. As a businessman, a Tammany man, and an Irish Catholic, Whalen was anti-Red to his toenails. He formed a special "Red Squad," saying, "These enemies of society are to be driven out of New York regardless of their constitutional rights." On March 6, 1930, the CPUSA staged an International Unemployment Day rally in Union Square. Five thousand were expected and thirty-five thousand showed up, according to the next day's *Times*. After failing to talk CPUSA leaders out of their plans, Whalen showed up to personally supervise the more than one thousand cops with whom he ringed the square on foot and horse. When the rally organizers called for a march down to City Hall, for which they had no permit, Whalen took it as his cue to unleash hell. Cops charged the crowd with nightsticks flying in a brief but wild and bloody melee. The ensuing cries of police brutality forced Whalen to resign.

He went back to business life. By 1936 he was chairman of the liquor company Schenley, with offices in the Empire State Building. That year he became president of the nonprofit corporation formed by some of the city's top businessmen and bankers to plan a world's fair for New York. Based on the reported $800 million the 1933–34 Century of Progress pumped into Depression-ravaged Chicago's economy, they projected that a larger fair could generate a billion dollars or more for New York. The fact that world's fairs rarely turned a profit—ten of fourteen to then had lost money—did not deter them.

Whalen threw himself body and soul into making the fair happen. He was, as *Time* would put it, both its "figurehead and real head." He did all the wheeling and dealing, the hand shaking and arm twisting, the promoting and ballyhoo, and brought in the bulk of the funding. When the fair opened in 1939, *Time* called it "a $157,000,000 extroversion of Mr. Whalen's fantastic extrovert personality," which "gives him fair claim to the title of greatest salesman alive today." Terms like "Mr. Whalen's Fair" were common.

Whalen traveled to Europe and to embassies in Washington to recruit England, France, and the Soviet Union. Then he went to Rome to see Mussolini. Il Duce wasn't receiving Americans just then, miffed about the hostile coverage in the American press following his invasion of Ethiopia the year before. But as police commissioner, Whalen had done some favors for the Italian consul in New York, a close friend of Mussolini's, and had even been made a knight of the Order of the Crown of Italy. In white tie and tails, with his knight's gong glittering on his chest, Whalen was admitted to Mussolini's vast office in the Palazzo Venezia. After a rambling hour-long conversation—in English, which Il Duce spoke fairly well—Italy was in.

Whalen didn't get an audience with Hitler, but Germany did sign up in 1937. There was much outcry from anti-Nazi groups and individuals in America, none more vocal than Mayor La Guardia. He had been railing against Hitler since 1933, calling him a "perverted maniac" and predicting that he would try to annihilate "all the Jews in Germany." In March 1937 he spoke at a luncheon of the Women's Division of the American Jewish Congress at the Astor Hotel. The speaker before him, the editor of the Catholic magazine *Commonweal*, proposed erecting a "temple of tolerance" at the world's fair. La Guardia agreed, then added, off the cuff, that there should also be "a chamber of horrors" that included "a figure of that brown-shirted fanatic who is now menacing the peace of the world."

The Nazi press in Germany howled, calling La Guardia "a dirty Talmud Jew," a "Jewish lout," a "procurer," and "master of gangsters." The German ambassador in Washington issued a formal complaint. Secretary of State Cordell Hull apologized and asked Roosevelt to rein in the mayor. But the week after his first comment, La Guardia was at it again. Called onto the stage at an antifascist rally in Madison Square Garden, he showed off his facility for languages when he said that he paid no attention to the insults the Nazi press hurled at him, because Adolf Hitler was not *satisfaktionsfähig*. The German speakers in the crowd gasped. La Guardia was saying that Hitler was so beneath contempt that a gentleman would not bother to seek "satisfaction" for his remarks—a terribly cutting insult in Germany. The ambassador complained again, and Hull appealed to FDR once more.

The next time La Guardia visited the White House, FDR grinned, shot his arm out in the Nazi salute, and said, "Heil, Fiorello!"

"Heil, Franklin," La Guardia responded.

Commenting on the rather comical brouhaha, *Time* speculated that La Guardia, who was facing a reelection campaign that fall, was playing up to the large cache of Jewish voters in the city at the expense of the smaller

German vote. It's notable that La Guardia refused to speak out against Italy's participation in the fair, brushing off charges of hypocrisy from antifascists including Norman Thomas, Carlo Tresca, and the editors of the *New York Post.* The biographer H. Paul Jeffers explains: "In the arena of New York ethnic and nationalistic politics, where Italians greatly outnumbered Germans, and the Jewish vote often was decisive, it was easy and safe to excoriate Nazis, but not smart to alienate Italians by putting Mussolini in the same light as Hitler." Or as *Time* put it back then, "In New York City, as any political nose-counter knows, the hooked far outnumber the Aryan noses." There was similarly no great outcry against Japan's participating, despite its invasion of China in 1931 and its signing of an anti-Soviet pact with Germany in 1936. (When the fair opened, both the Italian pavilion, designed in Mussolini's favorite neoclassical fascist style, and the Japanese one, which evoked the restful serenity of a tea garden, were best known for their food and drink offerings. Mussolini liked the idea of the world's fair so much he planned one for Rome in 1942, but the war would intervene.)

In 1938 Germany withdrew. According to the *Times*, at least part of the reason was ill will generated not only by La Guardia's rants but by the U.S. government's refusal that year to permit the export of helium for German dirigibles "until Germany gives assurances that it will not be used for military purposes."

Whalen stalked industrial and business exhibitors as skillfully as he did nations. When Ford, General Motors, and Chrysler expressed little interest, he played them off against one another until all three built some of the most lavish and expensive exhibitions at the fair. GM spent $5 million on its Futurama; Ford put a figure-eight racetrack on the roof of its pavilion; and Chrysler's theater screened a 3-D movie of a car being assembled. Oil and gas companies, U.S. Steel and Corning Glass, B. F. Goodrich and Firestone, RCA and ATT, Consolidated Edison and Westinghouse and General Electric all signed on. Carrier's igloo-shaped, air-conditioned pavilion would pack in the summer crowds. The railroads agreed to show off the latest in streamlined engines, designed by the same men who created the futuristic look of the fair. The aviation industry bought in. Life Savers built the popular—if sometimes malfunctioning—Parachute Jump; later moved to Coney Island, it is one of the very few fair structures still standing, as well as the only remaining relic of Coney Island's Steeplechase Park.

Whalen had to lay down the law with a few exhibitors. When Heinz demanded a pickle-shaped building, which Whalen's design committee rejected as just too chintzy, "he signed up so many other food exhibitors that Heinz was finally glad to accept half of another, more prosaic building," *Time* noted.

In 1938, when Whalen heard that Howard Hughes was going to try to set a new record for an around-the-world flight, he got him to be a global rep for the fair. Hughes named his silver twin-motor Lockheed the *New York World's Fair.* Taking off and landing at Floyd Bennett, he circled the globe in three days and nineteen hours—an astonishing four days quicker than the previous record set just five years earlier. Twenty thousand people and all the media greeted him when he landed, and the world cheered. It was excellent free publicity.

⌒

Whalen turned the first spadeful of earth for the groundbreaking in July 1936. There are vying accounts about how Flushing Meadows in Queens was picked to be the site of the fair. Robert Moses would give his version in "The Saga of Flushing Meadows," a pamphlet he wrote in 1966, after the second world's fair was staged there.

Flushing Meadows was originally a handsome salt marsh on Flushing Bay and the Flushing River, where locals fished and crabbed. At the turn of the century, when most buildings throughout the city were heated by coal furnaces, New York engaged private contractors, usually with Tammany connections, to haul the resulting ashes to dumps and landfills. One of those was the Brooklyn Ash Removal Company, run by John A. "Fishhooks" McCarthy, who earned his nickname because when it came time to pitch in for drinks or a meal he couldn't seem to get his hands out of his pockets. Brooklyn Ash's first dump was on Barren Island in Jamaica Bay, where the ash went into landfill for what became Floyd Bennett Field. In 1909 the company expanded to Flushing Meadows, creating the smoking eyesore known as the Corona Ash Dump, which F. Scott Fitzgerald immortalized in his 1925 novel *The Great Gatsby* as "a valley of ashes." It was actually more like "a horrendous mountain," Moses wrote, of "accumulated clinkers, dust, offscourings, waste, and junk."

In the 1930s, Moses wrote in his pamphlet, he was trying unsuccessfully to get the city to buy the area so he could build his Grand Central Parkway through it. "Then the miracle happened—the idea of a World's Fair." The idea had first come to a man named Joseph Shadgen, who had immigrated to New York from Belgium during the Great War, done well as a civil engineer, but was now barely getting by in Depression-ridden Jackson Heights, Queens. Shadgen got a couple of Franklin and Eleanor Roosevelt's New York cousins interested, they talked it up among their circle of business and civic leaders, and it gained momentum.

Integral to Moses's plan was that when the fair was over the area would remain a large urban park. The city bought the 1,216-acre site from Fishhooks for $2.8 million, and Moses got to work terraforming it. Bulldozers and cranes leveled the mountains of ash and junk. The marsh was excavated to form what are now called Meadow Lake and Willow Lake. The Flushing River was diverted through tunnels. Landscaping involved planting some ten thousand trees, a couple of million shrubs and bushes, and a million and a half flowers. New plumbing, a sewage system, and electrical lines were laid.

To get people to and from the site, Moses—a great believer in highways, as were most planners in the 1930s—got to build some sixty miles of roadway. The Bronx–Whitestone Bridge (begun in 1937 and completed on April 29, 1939, the day before the fair opened), the Queens–Midtown Tunnel (begun in 1936 and opened in November 1940), and New York Municipal Airport (December 1939) were all, Moses wrote with some justification, "in a very real sense by-products of the Fair."

The fair wound up with two rather incongruous themes. Shadgen had suggested that it celebrate the fact that April 30, 1939, would be the 150th anniversary of George Washington's inauguration on Wall Street. But the dominant theme looked ahead to the "World of Tomorrow." Whalen wrote in a brochure that the fair "will predict, may even dictate, the shape of things to come."

So a traditional, 65-foot-tall statue of Washington by James Earle Fraser, who also designed the Indian head nickel, shared the fairgrounds with all the futuristic pavilions, the 610-foot-tall spike of the Trylon and the eighteen-story Perisphere next to it, both of which could easily be seen from as far away as Manhattan and the Bronx.

Some of the top industrial designers in New York City, the capital of industrial design in America, were hired to create pavilions and displays. Inside the Perisphere, in a space twice the size of Radio City Music Hall, visitors stood on two rotating balconies above a 100-foot model of the city of the future, Democracity. It was conceived by the Brooklyn-born industrial designer Henry Dreyfuss, one of the geniuses of the streamline age. In Democracity, central towers for government and business formed the hub of a wheel that radiated out to neat suburbs and farms. It was all orderly, rational, and well planned—the opposite of the unplanned chaos of the Brooklyn where Dreyfuss had grown up. The voice of H. V. Kaltenborn, the "dean of radio commentators," known (and often parodied) for his clipped, hifalutin delivery, rattled from speakers, explaining the wonder of it all.

The other and much more elaborate model of "the greater and better world of tomorrow" was Futurama in the General Motors pavilion, one of the most popular attractions of the fair. Created by Norman Bel Geddes, who gave futuristic flair to everything from appliances to ocean liners, it was promoted as "the wonder world of 1960" and, pointedly, as "a vivid tribute to the American scheme of living, whereby individual effort, the freedom to think, and the will to do have given birth to a generation of men who always want new fields for greater accomplishment." Ribbons of highway led from farmland into another planned city, where "residential, commercial, and industrial areas all have been separated for greater efficiency and greater convenience"—again, an implied rebuke to the cheek by jowl mixed-use chaos of New York City. Quarter-mile-high skyscrapers featured landing decks for helicopters—still brand-new and experimental in 1939—and autogyros.

For Chrysler's pavilion, the flamboyant, French-born Raymond Loewy, another giant of streamline design, created the Rocketport of the Future, a display in which a rocket carrying passengers from New York to London was shot out of a cannon, Jules Verne–style, to roaring sound effects and clouds of steam. Less visionary but still impressive, the industry pioneer Walter Teague's National Cash Register pavilion was an immense cash register that actually worked, adding up the number of visitors who passed through the turnstiles all summer.

Having envisioned a world of peace and prosperity, several of these men would soon be asked to design for a world at war.

⁓

In the weeks preceding the fair's opening, hundreds of black New Yorkers appeared with picket signs outside Whalen's office in the Empire State Building. They charged that the fair had hired few blacks, and those only to push mops and brooms, and that the so-called World of Tomorrow the fair promised to depict was a world almost completely devoid of blacks or their achievements.

The lead organizer and spokesman for the protest was the charismatic thirty-year-old pastor of the mighty Abyssinian Baptist Church in Harlem, Adam Clayton Powell Jr. He'd been born to the cloth, in his father's comfortable parsonage in New Haven. The family moved to Harlem six months later when his father took the pastorship of Abyssinian, then located on West 40th Street. When the Powells came to Harlem in 1908 it was still mostly white, but by 1920 a great influx of blacks had transformed it into the largest urban black community in the country. Powell Sr. moved his congregation there, building a magnificent new church on 138th Street between Seventh and Lenox Avenues (now Adam Clayton Powell Jr. and Malcolm X Boulevards).

In 1930, when Powell Jr. was twenty-one, he began assisting his ailing father at the church. He took over the pastorship fully in 1938. Light-skinned and of mixed-race heritage on both sides of the family, he had passed for white when it suited him in his teen years. As a young preacher he looked less like a clergyman than a matinee idol. He had the glistening hair, thin mustache, and faintly Mephistophelean good looks of a Warren William or William Powell, and some of the habits to match. He was as well known in the neighborhood's nightclubs as in the pulpit, loved parties and crowds, and would marry an older, divorced Cotton Club showgirl, then a jazz pianist. To his congregation he was refreshingly down to earth in the pulpit. He liked to say that a public address should be like a woman's skirt, "long enough to be respectable, but short enough to be interesting."

Powell took an activist approach to serving his flock in Depression-ravaged Harlem. Besides the usual soup kitchen and clothing drives, he organized a successful protest march on City Hall when the white management of Harlem Hospital fired five black doctors to make room for white ones whom the Depression had thrown out of work. He convinced Wall Street moguls to fund a church-run jobs bank. After the riot in 1935, Powell organized a boycott of the white-owned stores that lined 125th Street, with the slogan, "Don't shop where you can't work." He wrote a series of articles for the *New York Post*, stating that it wasn't a "race riot" incited by radicals, as La Guardia insisted, but a spontaneous protest against "empty stomachs, overcrowded tenements, filthy sanitation, rotten foodstuffs, chiseling landlords and merchants, discrimination in relief, disenfranchisement," and La Guardia's "disinterested" city government.

Powell tried talking to Whalen privately about the world's fair before going public. In his autobiography *Adam by Adam* he remembered telling Whalen, "You cannot have a world of tomorrow from which you have excluded black people," to which he said Mr. New York gave the steely reply, "I do not see why the world of today or tomorrow of necessity has to have colored people playing an important role." The picketing that ensued drew hundreds to the sidewalk below Whalen's office, including chorus girls from the Cotton Club. When cops arrested four picketers, the *Amsterdam News* made it a banner headline. The four were brought before Judge Myles Paige, who happened to be the first black criminal court judge in the city, appointed by La Guardia in 1936. Paige not only dismissed the charges, he joined the picket line. Powell sought a court order to prevent the fair's opening until its "Jim Crow" hiring policy was addressed, and he began planning mass demonstrations at the fair itself.

Some six hundred more blacks had jobs at the fair by the time it opened. But Powell was not through. Shortly after the fair opened, he would call for all blacks to boycott Chase & Sanborn coffee and other products of the Standard Brands corporation, because its pavilion had separate white and "colored" restrooms.

⁓

Sunday, April 30, started out sunny, but by the afternoon opening ceremonies it was steadily and drearily raining. Whalen had predicted attendance of one million; the *Times* estimated it at six hundred thousand, while other sources put it closer to two hundred thousand.

Two of the sixty nations Whalen signed up had come under Nazi rule by the time the fair opened. Hitler had annexed Austria in March 1938. In September the Munich Pact allowed Hitler to annex western Czechoslovakia, which he did the following month. The Czech president Edvard Beneš resigned and fled to London, where he would form a government in exile. The future of the republic turned increasingly bleak as construction on its pavilion continued. Mid-March 1939, six weeks before the fair was to open, German troops rolled into the rest of the country. Hitler himself was in Prague the next day. La Guardia thought the unfinished Czech pavilion should remain that way "as a silent monument to the tragedy."

But construction continued. The pavilion officially opened a month late, on May 31, with Beneš and La Guardia officiating. The facade had been emblazoned in large letters with a quote from one of Czechoslovakia's national heroes, the seventeenth-century educator and religious exile Jan Amos Comenius: AFTER THE TEMPEST OF WRATH HAS PASSED THE RULE OF THY COUNTRY WILL RETURN TO THEE O CZECH PEOPLE. The pavilion sold souvenirs and requested donations to fund Beneš's government. The pavilion would not reopen for the 1940 season.

At the opening ceremony, with Boy Scouts ranked behind him, President Roosevelt told the crowd that "the eyes of the United States are fixed on the future. Our wagon is hitched to a star. It is a star of good will, a star of progress for mankind, a star of greater happiness and less hardship... and, above all, a star of peace." Miles of newsreel film had been shot of FDR, but this was the first time a president was televised. The infant NBC television network had a single camera there and transmitted the event to an estimated two hundred receivers in a fifty-mile radius, including one at Radio City. The total audience was estimated at about a thousand.

Whalen, in signature top hat, tails, and striped pants, gave the longest speech of the day. He called the fair "an adventure along the frontiers of progress and world understanding." Recalling the hopes with which he and his group began planning the fair, he said: "The events of the past three years... have neither tampered with the ideals of the fair nor dampened the ardor of its creators. Rather have they contrived to set the international exposition in perspective by setting it in contrast."

La Guardia's speech was brief and pointed. After noting the New York City Building, he said that really "our exhibit to the whole world is that in a city of seven and one-half million people, coming from every land and every country... [we] live here together in peace and harmony... All we do is to let every man and woman have a say in their own government, and we have eliminated the artificial stimulus of hatred. That is New York City's contribution to the World's Fair."

In 1938, Albert Einstein had agreed to be the honorary chair of the fair's Science Advisory Committee. As the fair took shape, it became increasingly obvious that there would be little of his kind of pure, theoretical science on display. To the fair's corporate exhibitors—Westinghouse, DuPont, AT&T, and the rest—science meant wondrous industrial and consumer products like Plexiglas, nylon stockings, air-conditioning, and a robot named Elektro. By opening day Einstein had soured on the whole thing as mere hucksterism for gizmos and gadgets. Still, he had agreed to appear at the opening day's final ceremony, the dramatic switching on of the fair's newfangled fluorescent lights. The idea was that Einstein would deliver a brief talk on cosmic rays. As he did, ten beams of light representing the rays would gradually light the Trylon from bottom to top. Then he'd throw the switch and all the fair's fluorescents would bang on together.

Only straggling pockets of fairgoers had stuck it out through the wet afternoon to see and hear the world's most famous scientist. The damp loudspeakers crackled in the gloom and garbled his already thickly accented speech. Then when he pulled the switch, the fair's generators overloaded and threw the entire fairgrounds into a total blackout.

The World of Tomorrow was off to a bumpy start.

In the summer of 1939 England was reeling from the effects of the global depression. Production was down, unemployment high, military spending a trickle. Meanwhile Germany, with the help of American financial and industrial giants, had fully recovered and built up a powerful modern war machine. The British government had nowhere near enough money to build a force to match Hitler's if he decided to attack, which was looking increasingly likely. England's only hope was to get the Americans involved.

In June England made the unprecedented move of sending King George VI and Queen Elizabeth to America to meet—and plead with—President Roosevelt. They arrived in Washington on June 8, the first reigning British monarchs ever to set foot in the former colonies. On Saturday, June 10, they stepped off a U.S. destroyer onto the Battery in the New York harbor, with guns blasting a salute from Governors Island and fireboats jetting fountains of water into the air. Governor Lehman, Mayor La Guardia, and Grover Whalen greeted them in a short ceremony, then a motorcade got rolling through Manhattan and out to the world's fair. The king and queen had wanted to see Fifth Avenue and Broadway, the city's traditional parade route, but Scotland Yard forbade it for security reasons. Instead, they drove up the elevated West Side Highway, with rather dreary views of warehouses and pier sheds along the river and, because it was a foggy day, only dim views of the Empire State Building and midtown. La Guardia reported to the *Times* that they seemed disappointed. An estimated three million New Yorkers, who had sorely taxed the city's subways and bus lines that morning, lined the whole route uptown and across to the new Triborough Bridge. Police shut down traffic on the Grand Central Parkway, as well as closing overpasses to gawkers.

At the fair, another hundred thousand people tried to get a glimpse of the royals, while television cameras, the *Times* noted, broadcast the event to "about two hundred sight-sound receivers throughout the metropolitan area" and as far away as Schenectady. After a brief visit to the British pavilion, the king and queen were whisked away from the fair, back to Manhattan, to stop at Columbia University, founded as King's College during the reign of George II in the 1750s. Then they headed up to Hyde Park to spend the rest of the weekend with the Roosevelts. The newspapers made a great to-do over reports of a picnic (from which the press was barred) where the king of England ate hot dogs and drank bottled beer, just like a regular joe. "King Tries Hot Dog and Asks for More," the *Times* announced.

As a public relations spectacle, the trip was intended to bolster American voters' sympathies for doughty England and overcome their strong isolationist sentiments. Privately, the king won FDR's assurances that the U.S. Navy would help keep the Atlantic free, and that if the Germans attacked America "would come in."

∽

Despite the high-minded language Whalen and others used to describe their world's fair, the large amusement area was decidedly lowbrow, at times bordering on the sleazy. It combined the ambience of a carnival midway, a beer garden, and an open-air burlesque show. Besides the Parachute Jump, its attractions included the Little Miracle Town, featuring 125 midgets and dwarfs; Frank Buck's Jungleland, a menagerie of exotic animals; a freak show called Strange as It Seems; the Sun Worshipers Colony, where visitors could ogle topless women sitting around pretending to be at a nudist colony; and more topless ladies at Jack Sheridan's Living Magazine Covers. More eye-popping still was Salvador Dalí's Dream of Venus pavilion, with nude beauties swimming and cavorting in a surrealist undersea setting that someone dubbed "20,000 Legs Under the Sea."

The most spectacular attraction on the amusement midway was Billy Rose's Aquacade. In 1937, when La Guardia proposed his Nazi chamber of horrors, Billy had offered to run it. Somewhat like La Guardia in his way, Rose was a little guy—he stood five foot three in his handmade lifts—who made big things happen. He was born William Samuel Rosenberg in 1899 in a tenement on the Lower East Side, where his immigrant father peddled buttons from a pushcart. He left high school without graduating in 1917 to take a job in Washington as a stenographer at Bernard Baruch's War Industries Board. Baruch was everything Billy was not but would have liked to be: a tall, suave, rich assimilated Jew. He remained a role model to Rose for life.

On Tin Pan Alley in the 1920s, Billy cowrote novelty songs including "Barney Google" and the bona fide classic "Me and My Shadow." In 1934 he converted a Broadway theater that had gone dark in the Depression into Billy Rose's Music Hall. High up above it he placed an electric sign that could be seen glowing for blocks all around, with just two words in lighted fourteen-foot letters: BILLY ROSE. *Jumbo*, the circus-themed spectacle at the Hippodrome, was also his production.

He created the Aquacade for the 1937 Great Lakes Exposition in Cleveland, with a vast stage floating on Lake Erie and lots of girls in bathing suits swimming and diving. The star swimmer, Eleanor Holm, was a tall, pretty fireman's daughter from Brooklyn who'd won a gold medal for the backstroke at the 1932 Olympics. She was also a vivacious party girl who once told the press her training regimen was cigarettes and champagne. In 1936, sailing to Germany for her second Olympics, she was kicked off the U.S. team for carousing too much. It was a huge scandal, which only increased her celebrity. Billy married her, created the Aquacade as a mammoth showcase for her, and hired Johnny Weissmuller as her swimming partner.

When Billy offered to bring the Aquacade to the New York fair, he butted heads with Robert Moses, who looked down on him as a bottom-feeder. Billy went over Moses's head and schmoozed Whalen, who gave Billy Rose's Aquacade a prime spot in the amusement midway. Moses never forgave either of them for it. Rose built a beautiful ten-thousand-seat amphitheater, with a giant pool, a block-long stage, and a waterfall 40 feet high and more than 250 feet wide. Weissmuller (later replaced by Buster Crabbe), Eleanor (later replaced by Esther Williams), and seventy-two pretty girls in bathing suits did the swimming, with more than a hundred other performers singing and dancing. It was the top-grossing attraction at the fair in 1939. In the second year, the Aquacade's numbers would fall off a bit. A girlie revue nearby would prove stiff competition. The star was Gypsy Rose Lee.

⌣

Germany invaded Poland on September 1. Poland closed its pavilion and draped it in black cloth.

The English poet W. H. Auden, who had moved to New York the previous January, marked the event with a bleak poem. Simply titled "September 1, 1939," it begins:

I sit in one of the dives
On Fifty-second Street
Uncertain and afraid
As the clever hopes expire
Of a low dishonest decade

On September 3, two other fair participants, England and France, declared war on Germany and World War II began. Two weeks later Soviet troops also entered Poland.

The Soviet Union had been the first country Whalen signed up and had erected one of the most impressive, popular, and eventually controversial pavilions at the fair. The main building was a mammoth horseshoe shape. Spiking up from the middle of it was a 188-foot tower, and posed on top of that was a 79-foot sculpture of a heroic worker, holding aloft a huge, illuminated red star. The press called him Joe the Worker. Despite some protests that it was Communist propaganda on a grand scale, the pavilion was one of the most visited in 1939. Now that the Soviets were in league with Hitler and had joined in carving up Poland, the USSR's reputation among Americans plummeted. The Soviets would quietly dismantle their giant pavilion over the coming winter and haul it away.

When the fair shut down that October, the peaceful, orderly future it had so boldly and beautifully envisioned now looked less like a forecast than a forlorn hope. It had amazed, amused, thrilled, and exhausted almost 26 million visitors that summer, but the budget had planned for 40 million. The world's fair corporation fell a stunning $23 million short of projected income, and many concessionaires in the food and amusement areas lost money as well.

Given its poor financial performance, not to mention the dismal state of world affairs, organizers and exhibitors were uncertain about reopening the fair for a second season in the summer of 1940. They finally decided to do it, if nothing else in the hopes of recouping some of the first season losses. By the time the gates opened again in May 1940, the world would be in even more of a sorry state, and Mr. Whalen's fair would be a faint shadow of its former self.

CHAPTER 15

Einstein's Cottage

On Sunday, July 16, 1939, two men drove from Manhattan out to the forked tip of Long Island. They rolled onto Nassau Point, a pretty, quiet peninsula of summer cottages, beaches, and sailboats that poked out into Little Peconic Bay. They stopped and asked a few people for directions to an address on West Cove Road. No one recognized it. Then they asked a boy if he knew where "Professor Einstein's" cottage was. Oh sure, the kid replied, and pointed them the right way.

The two men were the physicists Leo Szilard and Eugene Wigner, both Hungarian-born refugees from Nazi Europe. Their visit with Albert Einstein this sunny Sunday afternoon was the first step in America's atomic bomb program.

As the Nazis and Fascists clamped down on Europe and imposed not only anti-Semitic but anti-intellectual regimes, many of the best scientific minds fled to America. Albert Einstein, the most famous of them all, sailed from Germany to California, where he was a guest lecturer at Caltech, in December 1932. By March 1933, when he and his wife Elsa were supposed to sail home, Hitler was in power. Einstein never set foot in Germany again. In October 1933 he and Elsa settled in Princeton. After Elsa died in 1936 he became reclusive, dividing his time between Princeton and rented summer cottages out on Long Island.

Einstein was in his early fifties when he relocated, and his important work was behind him. Most of the other physicists who came from Europe in the 1930s were in their peak twenties and thirties. Leo Szilard was born in Budapest in 1898. In 1921 he went to the University of Berlin, where Einstein was on the faculty. Through the 1920s they often partnered on patenting inventions, ranging from a refrigerator to the cyclotron. (Ernest Lawrence independently built the world's first at UC Berkeley in 1932.) Szilard fled Germany for England in 1933. In January 1938 he arrived in New York City, where he was hired by Columbia University.

In New York Szilard found an important financial backer for his continuing research in the prosperous Wall Street banker and philanthropist Leo Strauss (pronounced *straws*). Strauss was a partner at the Wall Street investment firm Kuhn, Loeb & Co. Two of his philanthropic causes were the plight of Jewish refugees (he was of German Jewish ancestry) and nuclear physics, which led him to Szilard.

In Berlin, Szilard had become a friend of another brilliant Jew from Budapest, Eugene Wigner. Wigner first came to America in 1930 to lecture at Princeton and stayed when Hitler rose to power. Hans Bethe, son of a university professor, was raised Protestant but was Jewish on his mother's side. He stayed on in Germany until 1935, then accepted a position at Cornell. The night he arrived in America he walked all around Manhattan, soaking it in. Edward Teller, another Hungarian Jew, got his Ph.D. at Leipzig under Werner Heisenberg in 1930. He left Germany in 1933 and came to America in 1935.

Enrico Fermi was a native of Rome, where he did groundbreaking work in nuclear physics that pointed the way to fission. He and his wife, Laura, first visited New York in the summer of 1930, when the Depression was just getting under way. "One of my earliest recollections of America," she later wrote, "is of standing with Fermi in Times Square and watching unemployment statistics among the glowing headlines that appeared in rapid succession high on top of the *New York Times* Building." In 1936 Fermi returned and spent the summer teaching a course at Columbia. Two years later, Italy adopted the first of its *leggi razziali*, its "race laws," aimed mostly at Jews. Laura was Jewish. That year, the Fermis traveled to Stockholm so that he could receive the Nobel; they did not go back to Rome. In January 1939 they stepped down off the liner *Franconia* in New York City, where he had a position waiting for him at Columbia.

Along with Europeans like Szilard and Fermi, the Columbia faculty boasted some great American scientists. Isidor Isaac Rabi had grown up speaking Yiddish on the Lower East Side, so steeped in old world Judaism that he found out the earth circled the sun only when he read it in a library book. He joined the physics faculty at Columbia in 1929. Harold Urey, raised in the Midwest and West, began teaching chemistry at Columbia that year. He was the world's leading scientist in the field of isotopes; in 1934 he won the Nobel for discovering the hydrogen isotope deuterium. John Dunning also came from the West and joined the Columbia faculty in 1929. When the neutron was discovered in 1932 its properties became his particular field of research.

One New York native would be associated in the public mind with atomic research above all others. Born in 1904, J. Robert Oppenheimer grew up in an apartment that took up the entire eleventh floor of 155 Riverside Drive at West 88th Street, with a panoramic view of the Hudson. His father, a German Jew, had come to America with no money and no English and was a prosperous textiles merchant by the age of thirty. His mother was a delicate and refined artist from Baltimore. They were representative of the Upper West Side's assimilated, secular German Jews who joined the progressive New York Society for Ethical Culture. Their son Julius, who attended the Ethical Culture school, styled himself J. Robert to sound less Jewish.

As a child he was brilliant, sickly, and ethereal. Surrounded by servants, petted and doted on by his loving parents, he rarely played with other kids. Instead, he did things like collect minerals. He'd remain aloof, studied, and a bit arrogant for the rest of his life.

He raced through Harvard in three years, devouring knowledge in huge gulps—not just science but philosophy, poetry, world religions. From there he went to Cambridge, and from there to the University of Göttingen in Germany. At Göttingen some of the best scientific minds of the century were cracking open the still new realm of quantum physics, discovering the laws and mechanics of the subatomic universe. Oppenheimer churned out one groundbreaking paper after another, making him a world star by the age of twenty-five. Harvard, Caltech, and UC Berkeley all offered him lecturing positions; he accepted the latter two, splitting his year between San Francisco and Los Angeles.

In 1922, hoping to improve Robert's health, his father had sent him for a summer to a dude ranch near Santa Fe, New Mexico, and he got his first sight of the area called Los Alamos. Five years later, his father bought him and his younger brother, Frank, a cabin and some land in the New Mexico wilderness they'd come to love. They named it Perro Caliente—Hot Dog.

⌒

Two weeks after the Fermis arrived in New York in January 1939, the physicist Niels Bohr came from Denmark with the news that the German scientists Otto Hahn and Fritz Strassmann, following up on Fermi's work, had split the nucleus of the uranium atom by bombarding it with neutrons—nuclear fission. The news hit physicists in America, and around the world, like a thunderclap. In the basement of Pupin Hall at Columbia, John Dunning had built a cyclotron a few years earlier. He used it to reproduce Hahn's results on January 25—the first nuclear fission in the United States.

Leo Szilard was in bed with a high fever when he heard the Hahn news. He sent a letter to Strauss, sprinkled with cautious words like "perhaps" and "potential" and "possibilities," suggesting that fission might lead to "atomic bombs." A handful of others drew the same conclusions. Oppenheimer was making the first crude drawings of a uranium bomb within a week of hearing the news. Gazing thoughtfully out a window at Columbia's campus, Fermi quietly cupped his hands as though holding a baseball and told a colleague, "A little bomb like that, and it would all disappear." By April the Associated Press was reporting that the debate among physicists was not over whether a uranium bomb was feasible but how big a bang it would make—enough for "blowing up a sizable portion of the earth" or just enough to "wreck as large an area as New York City."

Writing some thirty years later in her book *Illustrious Immigrants*, Laura Fermi claimed that a quartet of the refugee scientists from Europe—Szilard, Fermi, Wigner, and Teller—were the first to be deeply alarmed by the thought of Nazi Germany developing such a weapon. "In a sense this was natural," she wrote. "Hungarians and Italians knew dictators well," and were "well acquainted... with both Hitler's ruthlessness and the capabilities of German scientists." They were convinced the Allies must begin research and development instantly.

But the United States in the spring of 1939 was not one of the Allies. It was still neutral by law and almost unanimously isolationist in opinion. Szilard felt it would take more than a gaggle of scientists, many of them Jews from Europe, to budge the country. It would take the most famous scientist in the world.

When Szilard and Wigner met with Einstein that summer Sunday afternoon, he'd made two appearances at the world's fair, but otherwise he was spending his summer happily sitting on the beach (he could not swim), playing his violin, and fiddling with his small sailboat, which he'd named *Tinef.* (In Western European Yiddish, *tinef* means "junk"; in German slang, from which Einstein probably got it, it's spelled *tinnef.*)

Szilard was startled to discover that Einstein had not yet heard about the explosive potential of uranium. *"Daran habe ich gar nicht gedacht!"* Einstein exclaimed: "I never thought of that!" He agreed to help alert the government.

That same week in Manhattan Szilard met with Alexander Sachs, a distinguished biologist and economist who was also a vice president at the giant investment firm Lehman Corporation. Born in Lithuania in 1893, Sachs had come to New York City at the age of eleven. He studied at Columbia and Harvard, worked for a few years as an assistant to Louis Brandeis at the Zionist Organization of America, and served FDR in the NRA. Sachs told Szilard he could put a letter from Einstein in the president's hand.

Einstein's letter went through a few drafts, Einstein writing in German, with Szilard, Teller, and Sachs all contributing. It was translated and ready by mid-August, but with Hitler's invasion of Poland on September 1 FDR's appointment calendar was filled to overflowing. Sachs finally got into the Oval Office on October 11. Characteristically, Roosevelt didn't read Einstein's letter but instead chatted with Sachs over brandies. He got the gist—that what Sachs and the scientists wanted, he said, was "to see that the Nazis don't blow us up."

With the president's go-ahead, a Committee on Uranium met ten days later. It included Sachs, Szilard, Teller, Wigner, and an army and a navy officer. The military men were skeptical, but they grudgingly granted a few thousand dollars so that the Columbia physicists could do small-scale experimenting.

With so little government support, progress would be slow through 1940. In December of that year, scientists at Berkeley would create a new element, plutonium. The isotope plutonium 238 could also be used in weapons of enormous power, and it could be produced more quickly than fissionable uranium 235. At Columbia, Fermi and Szilard, with the help of husky football players, built a large uranium-graphite lattice in Schermerhorn Hall to continue investigating the potential of uranium.

Otherwise, nothing much would happen with atomic research in America until the Japanese woke the sleeping giant by bombing Pearl Harbor.

CHAPTER 16

Treason

American Communists called the autumn of 1939 their "nightmare season." The Hitler-Stalin pact in August and dual invasion of Poland in September ruined what goodwill the CPUSA had built up in the previous few years. Membership, already dropping because of the Great Purge, plummeted. Besieged in his East 12th Street office by downright mocking reporters, Earl Browder was close to tongue-tied.

New Yorker Whittaker Chambers was not just disillusioned by the Hitler-Stalin pact. He was panicked by it. He had served in the 1930s as a Soviet spy. Now he was horrified that U.S. government secrets he'd passed along might wind up in the hands of the hated Nazis.

Arthur Schlesinger Jr. later described Chambers as "a squat, lugubrious, unprepossessing, taciturn man." He was born Jay Vivian Chambers in Philadelphia on April Fools' Day, 1901, then in infancy moved to Brooklyn. When he was two the family moved twenty miles out on Long Island to the village of Lynbrook. His mother called him Vivian, which he hated; in high school he was nicknamed Girlie and Stinky. By the time he went to Columbia he was calling himself Whittaker, his mother's maiden name. Attending Columbia at the same time were such future lights as poet Langston Hughes, the literary critic Lionel Trilling, and editor Clifton Fadiman. They all agreed Chambers was the best and brightest among them, destined for a great literary career if he would only settle down and buckle up. He did not. He dropped out of Columbia twice and never earned a degree.

He joined the Communist Party in the 1920s. A devoted party apparatchik, he wrote and edited for the *Daily Worker*. In 1932 Moscow directed him to "go underground" and work for its espionage division, and he obeyed. For the next two years he was a courier, meeting agents all around the city and ferrying the envelopes they handed him to the operation's nerve center in an apartment at 17 Gay Street in Greenwich Village.

After he proved himself in that work, the Soviets sent him to Washington to run a ring of spies in the federal government. Most notable among them was Alger Hiss. Born in Baltimore, Hiss had come under the wing of Professor Felix Frankfurter at Harvard, who got him an appointment as an assistant to the venerable Supreme Court justice Oliver Wendell Holmes Jr. In 1933, after a year with a New York law firm, Hiss moved to Washington to take a job in the legal department of Roosevelt's new Agricultural Adjustment Administration.

Frustration with the pace and scope of the New Deal provoked Hiss, already a soft leftist, to join the CPUSA. From there, although he would deny it until his death in 1996, it was a short step to spying. By the mid-1930s he was at the State Department, an aide to one of the assistant secretaries. He was one of the fifty or sixty people in the federal government, mostly young left-wing idealists, doing various kinds of spy work for the CPUSA and the Soviets in the war years. They were all over Roosevelt's administration—at the Departments of State and the Treasury and Agriculture, the Pentagon, and other spots—broken up into cells.

In 1937 Hiss regularly stuffed his briefcase with classified or confidential State Department documents and brought them to Whittaker Chambers. Chambers had them photocopied overnight, then Hiss carried them back to his office the next morning.

Chambers began to fear for his life that year. Stalin's paranoid Great Purge had spilled outside of the Soviet Union by then. People involved in international Communism were disappearing or being assassinated for the slightest infractions, or for no reason at all discernible outside of Stalin's deranged mind. Being called to Moscow for meetings was seen as a death sentence. When Chambers got that call in the spring of 1938 he went into hiding, moving his family around from one safe house to another. For insurance he gave an envelope full of documents to an in-law, a lawyer in Brooklyn, and also stashed away some rolls of filmed documents.

By the spring of 1939 he felt safe enough to resurface. He went to work for *Time*, where at first he wrote book reviews. On September 2, the day after Hitler invaded Poland, Chambers went to Washington and met for two hours with Adolf Berle, FDR's intelligence adviser, naming Hiss and other government officials as spies. Berle sent a memo to Roosevelt, who shrugged it off. He was still hoping that Russia would be a partner in the fight against the Axis, and chasing Soviet sympathizers inside the federal government was not a priority.

⌣

Elizabeth Bentley, like many others, came to Communism in the Depression years with no proletarian background but a lot of romantic idealism and more than a trace of youthful rebellion. She was born into a strait-laced Connecticut family—Republican, Episcopalian, teetotaling—and earned a scholarship to Vassar, where from one of her teachers, Hallie Flanagan, she heard some progressive and socialist ideas.

She joined the CPUSA in the mid-1930s. In 1938, on her own initiative, she took a job at the Italian Library of Information in Manhattan, with the intention of spying on the Fascists. This interest in espionage led the CPUSA to arrange a meeting for her, on a street corner in Greenwich Village, with a nondescript-looking middle-aged man who called himself Timmy. Meeting him changed her life, and the lives of many others.

His real name was Jacob Raisin. A Jew born in Russia in 1889, he had been among the original Bolshevik revolutionaries, spent two years in a Siberian prison camp before escaping to Japan, then made his way to New York City in 1912, taking the name Golos, Russian for "voice." As a cofounder of the CPUSA he was watched by federal investigators as early as 1922. By the time Bentley met him he was forging passports and running a network of spies and informers, using a Russian travel agency, World Tourists, as a front. He and Bentley became lovers while he taught her espionage tradecraft and drew her into his operations. They spent their nights together either in her apartment at 53 Barrow Street in Greenwich Village or in his rooms at the massive Commodore Hotel, on East 42nd Street between Grand Central and the Chrysler Building (now site of a Grand Hyatt developed by Donald Trump early in his career).

In October 1939, agents of the Justice Department raided World Tourists and rifled Golos's files. Golos set up a new front, the U.S. Service and Shipping Corporation. He made Bentley vice president and expanded her role handling informants. Her first was a dyspeptic New York engineer named Abraham Brothman, whom Golos was cultivating for future industrial espionage. Bentley didn't work well with "the Penguin," as she called Brothman, and he was soon passed along to a different handler, a man named Harry Gold.

Golos had Bentley take over much of his work in the field. She was now a spymaster herself, and good at it—her Russian code name translates as Clever Girl. During the war she would run many spies inside the federal government, taking a train to Washington every couple of weeks and returning to New York with an innocent-looking knitting bag stuffed with microfilmed documents.

Bentley would later testify that one of her sources in the federal government was William Remington. He was born in New York City in 1917, an only child, and raised across the Hudson in Ridgewood, New Jersey. His Brooklyn-raised father was a midlevel executive for forty years at the Metropolitan Life Insurance Company on Madison Square. William grew up tall, sandy-haired, handsome, bright—the very model of all-American youth, according to a contemporary.

In 1934 he went to Dartmouth and fell in with a crowd calling themselves Socialists or Communists, which included the future *On the Waterfront* screenwriter Budd Schulberg. Together they brought a chapter of the Young Communist League to the campus. By 1936 Remington had apparently joined the CPUSA, though he'd later deny it. In 1940 he moved to Washington, where he appeared to settle down for the duration of the war into the life of a government economist, working in a series of departments, including the War Production Board, Naval Intelligence, the American embassy in London, and finally reaching his peak as an acting assistant secretary of commerce. Along the way, Bentley later testified, he was feeding her secrets on sensitive topics ranging from airplane design to synthetic rubber.

On Thanksgiving Day 1943, Jacob Golos would die of a heart attack on the couch in Bentley's apartment. It sent her into a tailspin that would eventually prove catastrophic for Hiss, Remington, and several others.

CHAPTER 17

Eagles and Doves

On September 4, 1939, the day after England declared war on Germany, New Yorker Clayton Knight got a call from a man in Canada named Homer Smith. In the Great War Smith had flown with the Royal Naval Air Service, while Knight had been one of the first American pilots who went to England to fly Sopwith Camels with the RAF. He was shot down in 1918 and spent the remainder of the war a POW. In 1939 Knight was a popular magazine and newspaper illustrator who specialized in heroic images of airplanes old and new. His work appeared in *Life*, the *Saturday Evening Post*, and boys' adventure magazines, and he was the illustrator for Eddie Rickenbacker's color comic strip *Ace Drummond* that was serialized in Sunday newspapers nationwide from 1935 into 1939. (His son Hilary would gain fame in the 1950s as the illustrator of Kay Thompson's Eloise books.)

The RAF wanted to recruit American pilots again. Because of American neutrality laws, it was illegal for pilots to go straight into the RAF, so the plan was to funnel them through the Royal Canadian Air Force. Knight thought this was a grand idea and set up an organization, the Clayton Knight Committee, operating out of the Waldorf-Astoria, to do the recruiting. President Roosevelt was informed and agreed to turn a blind eye. By the spring of 1940 more than three hundred Americans had signed up. As the war in Europe heated up that year and the next, the number of American pilots and ground crew in the RCAF would grow to more than six thousand.

In England, a cousin of Homer Smith's named Charles Sweeny was pursuing a parallel course. Sweeny was a wealthy New York investment banker, socialite, and playboy who had relocated to London. He played golf and partied with the highest echelons of British society, including

King George. Taking a cue from an uncle who had flown with the Lafayette Escadrille in the Great War, Sweeny began organizing American volunteers as the Eagle Squadrons of the RAF, using his connections to smooth the way. Three squadrons would be formed in 1941 and 1942; after the United States entered the war, they were transferred to the U.S. Army Air Forces. Many pilots came to the Eagle Squadrons through Knight's committee and the RCAF.

⌒

The alarming events in Europe in the autumn of 1939 raised the volume and heat in the debate between the numerically dominant American isolationists and the small but growing vanguard of interventionists such as Knight and Sweeny. Women, including several prominent New Yorkers, played leading roles in the isolationist movement, arguing that they did not want their husbands and sons to go fight and die in someone else's war the way they had in World War I.

Within a month of Hitler's invading Poland, three California mothers of draft-age sons saw where Europe was headed and formed the National League of Mothers of America, dedicated to keeping American boys out of foreigners' squabbles. In January 1940, the extremely popular New York novelist Kathleen Thompson Norris agreed to be the group's president. Seeing her involvement, women around the country raced by the tens of thousands to sign up. By February the group claimed one hundred thousand members in New York City, another seventy-five thousand in Los Angeles, and a million throughout the Midwest.

Kathleen Thompson was born and grew up in San Francisco, where she married Charles Norris, brother of the novelist Frank. They moved to New York in 1909 and both worked as magazine editors. She also began churning out romantic novels at a terrific clip; her last one, published in 1959, would be her eighty-fifth. They sold millions of copies, and many were adapted by Hollywood, making her the highest-paid woman writer in the country. She also wrote articles for magazines and newspapers, and covered the Lindbergh baby trial for the *New York Times* in 1935. Along the way she got involved in a number of causes, including Prohibition, the abolition of the death penalty, and pacifism.

The Hearst newspaper empire supported the League of Mothers with favorable coverage and funding. The organization published its own paper, the *American Mothers National Weekly*, believed to have reached several million readers. The mothers would oppose every measure by which FDR edged the country closer to war in 1940 and 1941.

As a moderate Republican, as well as a popular public figure with a career and reputation to protect, Norris hoped to keep the NLMA free of entanglements with right-wing extremists. In this she was quickly disappointed. Father Coughlin, George Viereck, and other questionable figures endorsed the group. Bundists and fascists soon dominated some local chapters.

Some members of the New York chapter migrated straight to the fringe. They believed that while America should stay out of others' conflicts, all Americans should be ready to defend the homeland if attacked. Calling themselves the Molly Pitcher Rifle Legion, they bought some uniforms, weapons, and ammo and got a couple of sharpshooters to give them target practice. In case of invasion, they intended to shoot enemy paratroopers out of the sky. They also printed up anti-Semitic literature, calling FDR, Thomas Dewey, and other politicians stooges of the Jews. Norris would leave the organization in exasperation in the spring of 1941.

Cathrine Curtis was one of the most capable businesswomen in America at a time when that was something rare. Mixing fascism and feminism, she taught other women how to achieve financial independence while espousing fiercely anticommunist, anti-Semitic, anti–New Deal, and Anglophobic ideas. She was an aloof and physically imposing presence, standing six straight feet tall and weighing nearly two hundred pounds.

Curtis was born into the Albany, New York, home of a wealthy stock and bond speculator who taught her the business. After studying at NYU she headed west, first to run a ranch in Arizona, then to Hollywood, where she was one of the very few women producers of the silent era. Along the way she built herself a handsome fortune through speculating on the frothy stock market of the 1920s, and she would go through three childless marriages without ever taking the men's names. Back in New York City by 1934, she started hosting a twice-weekly program on WMCA radio, *Women and Money*, but was so extremely anti–New Deal that WMCA canceled her contract. Angered but undaunted, she founded the Women Investors Research Institute, a nonprofit with swank offices in a Fifth Avenue building she owned. By 1939 she had three hundred thousand members. The organization ran seminars and published books and the weekly newspaper *Woman Courageous*, all combining financial advice and conservative politics. Her political associations stretched from congressional Republicans and the DAR to the fascist fringe. From the latter she heard conspiracy theories blaming the deteriorating world situation on the Jews, the Freemasons, the Communists, the British Empire, and FDR, the stooge of them all.

In 1939 Curtis created the Women's National Committee to Keep the U.S. Out of War. She was then approached by one of the most eccentric women of the far right, the star aviator Laura Ingalls. Ingalls grew up in a wealthy Brooklyn household that was German on her father's side and an old Knickerbocker dynasty, the Houghtaling tea merchants, on her mother's. She was educated in the finest private schools in Europe and learned seven languages. Petite, with an impishly boyish face, she was for brief spells a concert pianist, a ballerina, and a vaudeville dancer before she started taking flying lessons at Roosevelt Field on Long Island in the 1920s. She was only the fifteenth woman in the United States to earn a pilot's license, and then embarked on a glittering career as a stunt and race flier, the prime challenger to Amelia Earhart's celebrity. Often flying to and from either Glenn Curtiss Airport or Floyd Bennett Field not far from Coney Island—and living in hotel rooms nearby, so as not to be bothered with homemaking chores—she set a number of solo speed and distance records in the 1930s.

It was her politics—rabidly pro-Nazi, anti-Semitic, and isolationist—that brought her to Curtis. In September 1939, Ingalls flew over the White House, violating restrictions on airspace, and dropped isolationist leaflets written and printed by Curtis. When she landed she was arrested and her pilot's license was suspended for a week. Grounded but undeterred, she joined Curtis in trying to bull their way into a closed session of the Senate Foreign Relations Committee discussing an arms embargo.

Curtis would continue to lobby against U.S. involvement in Europe's war right up to Pearl Harbor, after which she disbanded her organization, though she still criticized Roosevelt. Ingalls would follow her pro-Nazi opinions all the way to treason.

⌒

After England and France declared war on Germany in September, not much fighting happened for eight months. There was some action on the North Atlantic, where the British hoped to keep the German navy from completely isolating and blockading them. The Soviets, with Hitler's backing, invaded Finland, bombing Helsinki on November 30, only to find themselves bogged down all winter by the much smaller but extraordinarily resourceful Finnish forces. Otherwise, no armies moved. The Allies hunkered behind the Maginot Line all winter into the spring, while Hitler's generals dickered with him about the best plan of attack. People took to calling it the Phony War, the Bore War, and the Sitzkrieg.

Most Americans were content to let the situation drag on that way and stay well clear of it. But not all. Robert Sherwood was "sickened" when the Soviets invaded Finland. Although he still considered himself a pacifist, he had now come to equate isolationism with escapism, reluctantly concluding, like his fellow playwright Irwin Shaw, that sooner or later the United States would be forced to defend itself and "save the human race from complete calamity." He had "consistently tried to plead the cause of pacifism," he wrote in a letter that December. "But the terrible truth is that when war comes to you, you have to fight it." As the outgunned Finns mounted a splendidly courageous defense that humiliated the Red Army through the winter, Sherwood churned out a play about a Finnish family and assorted others who join the resistance. His friends Alfred Lunt, who was of Finnish descent, and Lynn Fontanne agreed to star, and Lunt asked to direct. Montgomery Clift and Sydney Greenstreet were also cast. They were still in rehearsals when Finland finally capitulated in March 1940, but all felt the play should go on.

There Shall Be No Night opened on Broadway at the Alvin (now the Neil Simon) Theatre that April. In the *Times*, Brooks Atkinson was critical of the play's dramatic weaknesses but not its message, declaring that "the best parts of it speak for the truth with enkindling faith and passionate conviction." *Life* praised the "simple, poignant story" and said it had "chances of being an important hit."

Isolationists from the left, right, and middle attacked the play. The *Washington Post* assailed it as "a rank inflammatory job, pleading for intervention." The *Daily Worker* denounced Sherwood as a "stooge of the imperialist warmongers," while conservatives called him a stooge of international Communism (because the play theorized that the Soviets were merely Hitler's tools).

There Shall Be No Night ran for 181 performances on Broadway, went on a highly successful national tour, and would earn Sherwood his third Pulitzer. Isolationists picketed in Philadelphia, and Robert McCormick's conservative *Chicago Tribune* refused to run an ad or print a single word about it. It sold out in Chicago for three weeks anyway. In March 1941,

German-American members of New York City's bakers and butchers unions would announce plans to start an anti-Nazi Theatre of German Freemen and hoped to do the play as their first offering.

There Shall Be No Night was still doing good box office on the road when the Japanese attacked Pearl Harbor in December 1941. A week later, evidently responding to a personal request from FDR, Sherwood would abruptly cancel the tour. The United States and the Soviet Union were now allies against the Nazis—and against Finland, which had sided with the Axis in its struggle with the Soviets.

⌒

Clare Luce's latest play enjoyed its own success on Broadway in the 1939–40 season. After touring Europe in 1938 and 1939, she decided, perhaps taking a page from Winchell, that the best thing she could do to counter the Nazis in her own city would be to poke fun at them. She dashed off *Margin for Error*, a shotgun wedding of political satire and an Agatha Christie–style murder mystery.

In *Margin for Error*, a New York cop, Officer Finkelstein, is assigned guard duty at the German consulate in Manhattan. The German consul (played by Otto Preminger) and a Fritz Kuhn character named Horst (as in the Wessel song) are ridiculous caricatures. While listening to a Hitler speech on the radio, the consul is shot, stabbed, *and* poisoned. It's up to Finkelstein to unravel the absurd mystery.

Margin for Error seems strangely frivolous today, but it was a hit with both audiences and critics. It opened in November 1939, two months after the carving up of Poland, and ran into June 1940. A brief puff piece that ran in *Life* when the play opened suggested that its lightheartedness was its strength. It noted that eight anti-Nazi plays had opened on Broadway "in the past two years. All of them flopped, because the dramatists were too overwrought by their subject to write a good show." *Margin* was adapted for the screen in 1943, with Preminger reprising his role—and directing—and Milton Berle as the cop.

⌒

New York socialite Natalie Wales Latham was also not content to sit on the sidelines in the winter of 1940. She thought about the poor English sailors serving in the frigid North Atlantic and decided to pitch in.

Mrs. Latham was a born Anglophile. The first Wales in America had come over from Bristol in 1635. On a trip to England when she was seventeen she met and decided to marry a young English lord, but her mother broke it up and hustled her back to New York, where she went to Columbia. A pretty debutante, photographed by *Vogue*, she married a *Mayflower* descendant in 1929, when she was twenty, had two children with him, then got divorced. She married Edward Latham, a former diplomat, in 1937, and divorced him in 1939.

In January 1940 she was thirty years old, a well-known and extremely well-connected socialite, and "noticed that no one seemed to know how to help" the British defend themselves against the Nazis, she told *Life*. She "said to herself, 'This is the damnedest thing,' " and started her own little British aid society. She got the owner of a vacant storefront on Park Avenue to let her use it for free, gathered a few of her society friends, handed them wool and needles, and they started knitting sweaters, gloves, and socks for those shivering British sailors.

Other women strolling by the shopwindow stopped in and it snowballed. By mid-January Latham had given her group a name, Bundles for Britain. By the end of 1940 it was a national organization, with a million and a half volunteers knitting away in 270 cities and towns, and with offices in the fancy Squibb Building on Fifth Avenue at 58th Street. Along with tens of thousands of knit goods, they would ship X-ray machines, ambulances, surgical equipment, and hospital cots to England, each item bearing the label "From Your American Friends." Latham's connections in London, who included Clementine Churchill, helped on that end; Queen Elizabeth donated a bejeweled cigarette case for a fund-raising raffle. Bundles for Britain became so popular that Hollywood would base a Cary Grant movie on it, the 1943 *Mr. Lucky*, with Laraine Day as a fictionalized Natalie Latham.

Latham herself would go on to marry another *Mayflower* descendant, Edward Bragg Paine, with whom she would found Common Cause, an anticommunist group, in 1947. After he died suddenly in 1951 she would marry Lord Malcolm Douglas-Hamilton, making her Lady Douglas-Hamilton. He was Scottish, a former Spitfire pilot, and anticommunist. They lived on the Upper East Side and were best known for hosting the gala annual Scottish Ball at the Plaza Hotel. He was her last husband; after his death in a plane crash in 1964 she went on to be one of the grandest dames of New York Society, dying in 2013 at the age of 103.

CHAPTER 18

Downward, Christian Soldiers

On January 14, 1940, the FBI arrested eighteen men in New York City accused of plotting the overthrow of the U.S. government. Fourteen were snatched up in their homes in Brooklyn, the others in the Bronx and Queens. Searches yielded more than a dozen Springfield rifles, a shotgun, some handguns, thousands of rounds of ammunition, and the materials for homemade bombs. J. Edgar Hoover said they were plotting a terrorist campaign targeting transportation, power, and communications facilities; their goal was to rouse the military into staging a coup, placing a strong dictator like Hitler or Mussolini in power, and cleansing the country of Jews.

The men were mostly of German or Irish descent, and ranged in age from eighteen to thirty-eight. If employed (a few weren't), they held low-end jobs, including an elevator mechanic, a telephone lineman, a chauffeur, a couple of salesmen, a couple of office clerks. The eighteen-year-old was a student. Most troubling was the fact that six of them were National Guardsmen.

They were all followers of a Father Coughlin–inspired movement called the Christian Front. In his mid-1930s heyday, Coughlin was arguably the most powerful pro-fascist voice in America. An Irish Catholic originally from Canada, he had first turned to radio in the 1920s simply as a way to expand his ministry beyond his tiny congregation in Royal Oak. He had a strong radio voice, and when CBS started syndicating his weekly sermons in 1929 it was an instant success. The crash and the start of the Depression politicized him. His condemnations of Wall Street and President Herbert Hoover brought him tens of thousands of fan letters a week, and his high praises for Hoover's opponent FDR surely had an impact on the

1932 elections. Then, when the invitation he craved to sit among President Roosevelt's circle of advisers didn't come, he turned bitter as a jilted lover. He began denouncing Roosevelt, his New Deal, his Jew York advisers, and his friends in the labor movement as facets of an international Jewish-Communist conspiracy to destroy Christianity and democracy. He also praised Franco, Mussolini, and Hitler for defending their people against this spreading evil.

Coughlin's call for a "Christian Front," intended to combat the Communists' mid-1930s Popular Front coalition with other groups on the left, resonated with the Depression-driven anger and paranoia of many Americans, especially in the cities Boston and New York with their large communities of lower- and lower-middle-class Irish Catholics, who tended to be shut out of other right-wing movements precisely because they were Irish and Catholic. At his peak, Coughlin had tens of millions of listeners to his Sunday radio sermons, a million readers of his weekly magazine *Social Justice*, and he received millions of dollars in small donations.

By 1938 rabid anti-Semitism had become the centerpiece of Coughlin's message. That year, at a Christian Front rally in the Bronx, he allegedly gave the Nazi salute and declared, "When we get through with the Jews in America, they'll think the treatment they received in Germany was nothing." In *Social Justice* he reprinted the anti-Semitic hoax *The Protocols of the Elders of Zion*, which also topped Henry Ford's list of favorite reading. In the autumn of 1938, when Coughlin said the Jews had brought Kristallnacht on themselves, radio stations, including WMCA in New York, dropped him. Several thousand Fronters "picketed the station, its advertisers, and Jewish-owned stores throughout the city," the historian Robert A. Rosenbaum writes. "The pickets returned every Sunday afternoon for many months. In the meantime, gangs of Christian Fronters roamed the streets and subways, peddling copies of *Social Justice,* distributing anti-Semitic leaflets, and orating on street corners, while harassing and assaulting people they took to be Jewish." The city's police force, which was nearly two-thirds Irish, turned a blind eye; some number of them were Christian Fronters themselves.

The Christian Front thrived in parishes in all of New York City's boroughs. Some of the first Front meetings took place in a church hall near Columbus Circle, and some of the most frequent and well attended were in the Bronx. In Brooklyn, Father Francis Joseph Healy, the pastor of the St. Joseph's parish in Prospect Heights, was also the editor of the

Brooklyn diocese's weekly paper, the *Tablet*, which he made a platform for extremely anticommunist, pro-fascist, and pro-Coughlin thought. After Father Healy's death in 1940, his managing editor Patrick Scanlan continued the paper's reactionary slant. Scanlan ran Coughlin's rants on the front page. Healy's successor at St. Joseph's, Father Edward Curran, was also a major supporter of Father Coughlin and other fascist and isolationist groups. During the war in Spain Father Curran wrote dozens of pro-Franco columns for archconservative publications around the country.

By 1939 small cells of Fronters in Manhattan and Brooklyn were calling themselves "sports clubs," though the only sport they practiced was target shooting at rifle ranges. The National Guardsmen in the group evidently pilfered the rifles and ammo from their posts and trained other Fronters in how to use them.

Along with the cops and Guardsmen, the Christian Front cells were also peppered with spies. The FBI had informants keeping tabs on them. Two independent investigators would write very successful books in which they claimed to have infiltrated the Front as well as dozens of other underground hate groups. Richard Rollins's *I Find Treason* would be published by William Morrow in 1941; John Roy Carlson's similar *Under Cover* would be a runaway bestseller for E. P. Dutton two years later, galloping through sixteen printings in its first six months. Both writers used pseudonyms. Carlson was actually Arthur Derounian, an Armenian immigrant. Rollins was apparently Isidore Rothberg, an investigator for Congressman Dickstein. Partly because the writers used pseudonyms while naming scores of individuals they claimed were pro-Hitler and pro-Mussolini, both books were widely denounced on the right as fabrications and smear campaigns.

Derounian wrote that he was riding the subway one day in 1938 when he picked up a leaflet of "bitterly anti-Semitic quotations" published by something called the Nationalist Press Association on East 116th Street in Italian East Harlem. He decided to research and found himself exploring a vast underground world of wannabe Hitlers and Mussolinis, society matron superpatriots, racists, Anglophobes, White Russians, and assorted conspiracy theorists and kooks.

Born in 1909, Derounian had grown up in another world of hate. After struggling to stay alive as Armenians in Greece at a time of chaos and slaughter in the Balkans, his family fled to New York in 1921. Arthur learned English and earned a degree in journalism at NYU in 1926. In 1933 he learned that the turmoil in the Balkans had followed him across the ocean when the archbishop of New York's Armenian Orthodox Catholics, while serving Christmas Mass in his Washington Heights church, was stabbed to death by radical Armenian nationalists opposed to his politics.

So when Derounian read that hate sheet on the subway in 1938, he was primed to follow up. The 116th Street address was an old tenement with a barbershop on the ground floor. The Nationalist Press "office" was a dingy back room stacked to the stained ceiling with right-wing books, newspapers, and pamphlets. Poking around in the gloom were a few Italian men and Peter Stahrenberg, a tall blond Aryan type "with blunt features and a coarse-lipped, brutal mouth," who wore a khaki shirt and a black tie with a pearl-studded swastika tie tack. Stahrenberg was the publisher of the *National American*, a pro-Hitler newspaper whose striking logo was an American Indian giving the Nazi salute before a large swastika. He was also the head of the American National-Socialist Party. Derounian, calling himself George Pagnanelli and expressing interest in the "patriotic movement," wormed his way into Stahrenberg's confidence.

As he explored Stahrenberg's twilight world, Derounian claimed, he found pro-Nazis and pro-Fascists all over New York City, holding meetings and rallies in every borough. It was a topsy-turvy world where street thugs from the city's poorest neighborhoods mingled with wealthy Park Avenue crackpots, and Irish Catholic Fronters convinced that Communism was an international Jewish plot sat in the same meetings with Protestant zealots convinced that the Vatican was a Jewish front. He met rabidly anticommunist DAR socialites and retired military officers who were certain that FDR and the Jew Dealers were leading the nation to ruin. He met Cathrine Curtis, introducing himself as George Pagnanelli; she kept calling him Mr. Pagliacci. He even found black pro-Nazis in Harlem. Some were attracted by Hitler's anti-Semitism; others simply cheered the idea of a white man making trouble for other whites.

Most of the groups described in *I Find Treason* and *Under Cover* were as small and ridiculous-sounding as Stahrenberg's, just a self-declared Führer and a handful of disgruntled flunkies, meeting in back rooms and churning out mimeographed hate sheets to distribute to other hate groups. But then again, both writers noted, the Nazi Party itself had started small too. And when those smaller groups met up with large ones like the Bund and the Front the results could be ominously impressive.

When the Christian Front clique was arraigned in Brooklyn's federal courthouse in February, they all pleaded not guilty to charges of conspiracy and theft of government property. The lawyer for twelve of them was Leo Healy—Father Healy's brother. A crowd jeered and booed as they were perp-walked into the courthouse. Winchell and La Guardia both derided them as "bums," the mayor adding that, if they were the best the enemies of democracy could muster, no one need lose any sleep. But the defendants had their sympathizers. Father Curran was the keynote speaker at a large rally in Prospect Hall to express support for them.

Fourteen defendants were left when the trial began in April; one of the original eighteen had committed suicide and charges against three others were dropped. As the trial sputtered along through May, it began to appear that the FBI and prosecutors hadn't built a very strong case. When the proceedings stumbled to a close on Monday, June 24, the jury acquitted nine of the defendants and pronounced themselves hung on the other five.

It was a major embarrassment for Hoover. The Christian Front and its supporters cheered it as a great victory and would continue to spread hate and violence well into the war years. Through 1942 and 1943 there would be numerous reports in the press of roving gangs of young men, mostly identified as Irish and affiliated with the Front, beating and sometimes even knifing Jews in neighborhoods such as Flatbush, Washington Heights, and the South Bronx, where Irish and Jewish communities abutted. Many shops, synagogues, and cemeteries were vandalized. Jewish leaders pleaded with Mayor La Guardia and NYPD commissioner Valentine, but they took little action.

Coughlin would rant on into 1942, when the federal government shut down *Social Justice* as a seditious publication and the archbishop of Detroit finally ordered him to stop all political activity. Father Curran, however, continued undeterred, making anti-Semitic, antiwar speeches to Fronters and others through the entire war.

Around 8:45 on a hot night in August 1940, some six weeks after the Front trial had ended in Brooklyn, a pioneer-style Conestoga wagon, drawn by two white horses, pulled up to the corner of 88th Street and First Avenue in Yorkville. A crowd slowly gathered—mostly kids at first, attracted by the spectacle of it, then men in shirtsleeves and women in "cheap print dresses and straw hats," according to the *New Yorker*'s Robert Lewis Taylor. To him, four out of five looked like German immigrants, the rest Irish, which would be about right for Yorkville. A dozen or so cops arrived and stationed themselves at the four corners of the intersection, their nightsticks conspicuous, as was the paddy wagon parked close by. The crowd grew and milled around. At one point a short, stocky man shoved his way through them, shouting, "Let me through! Make way for a German! Get the damned Jews out of here!" As a pair of cops led him away, "several men and women in the vicinity began to chant, as if by prearrangement, 'Jew stooges, Jew stooges, Jew stooges.'" Other people wormed through the crowd hawking anti-Semitic, pro-Coughlin, and Christian Front pamphlets, including one written by the former army chaplain Father Edward Brophy, pastor of the working-class parish of Most Precious Blood in Long Island City.

When the crowd had reached an appropriate state of edgy anticipation, a man with a lantern appeared on the small platform at the rear of the wagon. "For the benefit of the hard of hearing," he boomed, "for the *Eskimos*, and for the Democrat *stooges*, this is a political meeting." The crowd laughed at "Eskimos"; it was a new code for "Jews" that they were all familiar with. He and two more speakers railed about how FDR and La Guardia and the Eskimos were selling America out to the Reds, working the crowd up for the main speaker, a thirty-six-year-old star of the far right, Joe McWilliams.

When he stepped out onto the little platform, he provoked "wild and prolonged cheering." Tall and square-shouldered, with the good looks and dazzling smile of a screen idol, he was called "the handsomest and meanest-talking man ever to run for a public office in the United States." He was also called "a glamor-boy fuehrer." Walter Winchell simply called him Joe McNazi. Four years earlier he'd been just another down-and-out victim of the Depression. Then he took a WPA course in public speaking and emerged as a self-made Buzz Windrip. After flirting with left-wing politics he veered far to the right. Rejecting the Christian Front as "too wishy-washy," he started his own, more extremist Christian Mobilizers. Operating mostly in the Bronx, where he then lived, he was soon near the equal of Fritz Kuhn in his popularity with the city's pro-Nazis. They made joint public appearances around the city and at Camp Siegfried, and there was talk of merging the Mobilizers and Bund. After Kuhn was jailed in 1939, McWilliams seized the opportunity to relocate to Yorkville.

By the summer of 1940 he had started his own American Destiny Party, with a small office over a German restaurant in the neighborhood, and announced his candidacy in the upcoming election for the 18th Congressional District. At first there was no talk of Eskimos in his stump speeches; he railed against the Jews and would invite hecklers to come up to the stage so he could "see how big your schnozzle is." After one such harangue in July he was arrested for disorderly conduct on a complaint from a Jewish man in the crowd.

By August he was back on the stump, but now he was using "Eskimos" in an attempt to keep from getting arrested again. Like his idol Hitler, he was running for office only as a first step to taking complete control of the country someday, purifying it of all Reds, Eskimos, and "effeminacy" and running it "like a factory."

It was not to be. In the September primary he would poll only 674 votes. When he was convicted on the disorderly conduct charge, the judge, instead of sending him to jail, had him taken to Bellevue for a week of psychiatric testing.

CHAPTER 19

Blitzkrieg

In April 1940, just as Robert Sherwood's *There Shall Be No Night* hit Broadway, the Phony War suddenly turned deadly real. The spring and summer of 1940 were catastrophic for Europe. In April Hitler's Blitzkrieg devoured Denmark and Norway. On May 10 German armies poured into Belgium, Luxembourg, and Holland. A few days later German armor was punching through French lines, and the French premier Reynaud told Churchill, "We are beaten." Millions of terrified civilian refugees glutted the roads, flooding south, strafed by German fighters. German troops reached the English Channel by May 20. At the end of the month more than three hundred thousand Allied soldiers had to be rescued at Dunkirk. Paris fell on June 14; Hitler forced the French to sign a humiliating armistice on June 22 and entered Paris, now his, on June 23.

Clare and Henry Luce were in Brussels on the morning of May 10 when the first German bombers flew overhead. She had convinced him to let her go alone to Europe as a war correspondent, but as the war grew more imminent he worried for her safety and joined her. They got out as German troops swept across Belgium. In Paris, on her own again, Clare was staying at the Ritz—of course—when the concierge told her she'd better flee because the Germans were almost to the city. When she asked how he knew that, he said, "Because they have reservations." She made it back to New York just before Paris fell and wrote up her observations as the book *Europe in the Spring*. When Knopf published it that September it was a bestseller and earned the most favorable responses she ever got from critics and intellectuals. Only the ever acerbic Dorothy Parker was skeptical and detected Luce's habitual scene stealing in it. Her review ran with the withering tagline "All Clare on the Western Front."

Henry meanwhile had joined with other prominent and influential men—Robert Sherwood, Rabbi Wise, leading Republicans Henry Stimson and Frank Knox, Luce's former employee Archibald MacLeish—in a prointervention group they gave the unwieldy name the Committee to Defend America by Aiding the Allies (CDAAA). For most of the 1930s, Luce and his magazines had watched the growth of fascism and militarism around the world with dispassion bordering on disinterest. *Time*'s reporting on Hitler and Mussolini, as in much American media, had sometimes approached fawning. *Fortune* barely mentioned world politics at all. Nearly being bombed by the Luftwaffe turned Luce into a dedicated interventionist. On his return from Belgium he and Sherwood placed a full-page ad in the *New York Times* and other newspapers nationwide, "Stop Hitler Now." Written by Sherwood, it asserted that only "an imbecile or a traitor" could fail to see that if Britain and France fell, America would find itself "alone in a barbaric world—a world ruled by Nazis."

In May *Collier's* sent the New York journalist Quentin Reynolds to France to cover the Germans' approach. "I arrived in Paris on May 10, 1940, which wasn't bad timing," he would write. "Hitler marched into Belgium just as I marched into the Ritz Bar. The first thing I did was to order a drink. I don't know what Hitler did first."

The breezy, conversational style of that passage is characteristic of Reynolds's writing. It distinguished him from other Americans who were covering the war, including Ed Murrow. They were reporting the grand sweep of history; he was recording how he and others lived and died against that grim background. A big, garrulous, hard-drinking Irish Catholic, he'd grown up in the Brooklyn neighborhoods of Bushwick and Flatbush. He was still in high school when he started writing for the *Brooklyn Eagle* at a dollar an article. When he was seventeen he crossed the Atlantic for the first time, working in the engine room of a freighter during his summer vacation before starting college.

Reynolds was one of the last foreigners to slip out of one end of Paris just as the German Panzers rolled in at the other.

⌒

On the evening of May 10 Roosevelt had dinner with Harry Hopkins, then the two of them sat talking into the night. "As always when the two were together," Hopkins's biographer David L. Roll writes, "the conversation ranged back and forth from the latest gossip to ribald stories to a relaxed but serious discussion of the newest developments in Europe."

Hopkins had recently been in and out of the Mayo Clinic again and looked awful. Roosevelt convinced him not to go home to Georgetown but to sleep in the White House. He lent him pajamas. The widowed Hopkins and his daughter Diana, born in 1932, would effectively live in the White House for the next three and a half years. His suite on the second floor "consisted of one large bedroom, with a huge four-poster double bed, a small bedroom (used at first as office for Hopkins' secretary) and a bath," Sherwood would write. It was Lincoln's study, "and there was a plaque over the fireplace stating that the Emancipation Proclamation was signed here. It was considered the best guest room and had been assigned to King George VI during his visit in 1939." Because Hopkins was so frequently ill and exhausted, many meetings took place in this room, with him, thin and emaciated, on the huge bed, surrounded by paperwork, and others gathered around. When Churchill visited during the war years he took the bedroom across the hall, so that he and Hopkins could sit up late into the night talking and smoking while everyone else slept.

Eleanor's bedroom and sitting room were at the other end of the hall, with Lorena Hickok's small bedroom next door. Rosenman and Sherwood frequently took smaller bedrooms in the middle of the same floor. On a wall in Sherwood's room was a cartoon ripped from a magazine that showed a little boy chalking something on a sidewalk. A girl pointed and cried, "Look, Mother—Wilfred wrote a bad word." The word was "ROOSEVELT." Diana Hopkins and Missy LeHand had rooms on the third floor. Other guests and family were frequently scattered around the place. Roosevelt, stuck in his wheelchair and largely housebound, was happiest when the house was crowded.

One of the developments that Roosevelt and Hopkins discussed on the evening of May 10 was the resignation of the British prime minister Neville Chamberlain, whose policy of appeasing Hitler was now seen as having led to this disastrous pass. The much more hawkish first lord of the admiralty Winston Churchill replaced him that day. Churchill had been warning for years against giving in to Hitler, but he'd been politically sidelined and treated as an alarmist crank. Now his day had come.

One of Churchill's first acts as prime minister was to send the remarkable William Stephenson to New York City that month. He was to take over British intelligence operations in North and South America to counter Nazi espionage and propaganda activities there. Churchill saw cultivating an Anglo-American intelligence partnership as one way of pulling the Americans into the war effort. He tasked Stephenson with making that happen.

To that end, Stephenson had barely stepped off the boat when he was meeting with two New Yorkers who had interests in intelligence gathering and direct access to the president: Vincent Astor and William Donovan. While Stephenson was setting up an office in Room 3603 of the International Building at Rockefeller Center (which just happened to be on the same floor as the Japanese consulate), using the bland cover name British Security Coordination, Astor put him up in the luxurious St. Regis Hotel at the corner of Fifth Avenue and East 55th Street. (It had come with Astor's inheritance when his father died.) Through Astor, Stephenson was soon visiting Hyde Park to meet Roosevelt.

Stephenson and William Donovan were old friends. People called them Big Bill (Donovan) and Little Bill. At the front in World War I, Donovan had met a slight, skinny kid from Manitoba, who though only twenty was an officer with the Royal Canadian Engineers. His lungs had been damaged in a gas attack. Donovan, thirty-four at the time, was impressed by the young man's courage and intelligence. It was Stephenson. Judged medically unfit to return to the trenches, he took five hours of flying lessons and transformed himself into an ace fighter pilot. He would earn medals, be shot down by friendly French fire and captured by the Germans, and escape. He was also a world champion amateur boxer.

In the 1920s and '30s Stephenson settled in England and demonstrated considerable skills as a businessman, inventor, and investor in technologies. He was a millionaire before thirty, at the center of an international web of companies pioneering developments in communications, aviation, steel, and other technologies. His steel business in Germany gave him a close view of the Nazis' rise and enabled him to track the buildup of German arms. It was partly through Stephenson that Churchill developed his keen interest in the Nazis. Intelligence officer Commander Ian Fleming was another of the like-minded individuals Churchill gathered around him.

In the summer of 1940, during long walks near Donovan's Wall Street legal offices and long lunches at "21," Stephenson spoke to Donovan about America's woefully inadequate intelligence operations. Someone, Stephenson argued, needed to go to Washington and be placed over the competing agencies, sifting and analyzing their reports into intelligence the president could actually use. It should be someone whom the more experienced

British intelligence services knew and with whom they could effectively collaborate. To Stephenson, that was not Vincent Astor but Bill Donovan.

Donovan resisted at first. He was convinced that the United States would be drawn into the war soon enough, and when it was he hoped to be reactivated and given command of combat troops. Commander Fleming and others came over from England to assist with the lobbying. They played on Donovan's ego and his nostalgia for his heroic younger days, and they promised him all the mentoring and support he would need. It would take them until the summer of 1941 to win him over.

Roosevelt addressed Congress on May 16. "These are ominous days," he said, "days whose swift and shocking developments force every neutral nation to look to its defenses in the light of new factors." He asked for huge appropriations "to turn out quickly infinitely greater supplies" of army, naval, and aviation equipment. After two decades of isolationism, America was barely equipped to defend itself. There was effectively no munitions industry. Germany was producing six times more armaments than the United States. The U.S. Army was the sixteenth largest in the world, down near Bulgaria's. The U.S. military could put only about two hundred fighters and bombers in the air in May 1940; Göring's Luftwaffe had around three thousand. Of all the services, the navy was the strongest, but it was concentrated in the Pacific to deter Japanese expansion. That left the Atlantic extremely vulnerable should the French and English navies come under Nazi control, which seemed inevitable. Roosevelt wanted a "two-ocean navy."

By the end of May the U.S. Senate had unanimously approved $1.8 billion for the army and $1.5 billion for the navy. By the end of summer, as events in Europe plunged from alarming to apocalyptic, defense appropriations for the year would rocket up to $13 billion.

The navy had been preparing for this moment since 1938, when it began an ambitious program to expand the Brooklyn Navy Yard and its other shipbuilding centers on both coasts. It was the start of boom times for the shipyard that would continue through the war.

The Navy Yard had grown as a presence in Brooklyn since the start of the nineteenth century, when the federal government bought Wallabout Bay, a half-moon-shaped indentation on the East River between today's Manhattan and Williamsburg bridges. The navy shipbuilding center that developed there went by several different official names but was and is most commonly known as the Brooklyn Navy Yard. In the Civil War it was the Union's chief shipyard. From the Spanish-American War through the Great War, the age of giant battleships, it grew into a major industrial center and built the *Maine*, the *Arizona*, and other famed behemoths. After that, activity at the yard dropped off during the antiwar, isolationist 1920s and early 1930s.

The neighborhood around the Navy Yard was known as Irishtown in the nineteenth century. It was a dense mix of working-class housing (bank robber Willie Sutton grew up there), waterfront dives catering to sailors and longshoremen, gasworks, and maritime industries. Food-related businesses also clustered there, from bakeries and candy factories to the big, handsome Wallabout Market, one of the largest wholesale food markets in the world, next door to the yard. More than seven hundred stalls sold fish, meat, produce, and dairy to grocers and restaurateurs. It was most active from midnight to dawn, with trucks and pushcarts beetling in and out of its large central piazza. Like much of the Brooklyn waterfront, it was a magnet for mobsters who extorted kickbacks and payoffs from stall owners and truckers alike.

The first sign of new life at the Navy Yard was the start of work on the battleship *North Carolina* in 1937. Over the next few years workers also started on the *Iowa* and the famed *Missouri*. But the juggernauts of the next war would be aircraft carriers more than battleships, and so in 1938 the navy began constructing two huge new dry docks, each large enough for the Chrysler Building to lie down in, and new structures such as the sixteen-story concrete monolith called Building 77. The expansion also meant razing the Wallabout Market, relocated out to Canarsie. By 1945 the Brooklyn Navy Yard would be the largest shipyard in the world.

In May 1940, a week after Roosevelt's address to Congress, the Navy Yard announced it was hiring, and thousands of men lined up to apply. Over the course of the war the yard would go from fewer than ten thousand workers to a peak of around seventy-five thousand. In 1942 alone, some thirty-two thousand new workers would be hired. They would be kept busy around-the-clock, building seventeen new warships, including five aircraft carriers (the last launched a month after the war ended), converting and modernizing two hundred fifty others, and repairing battle damage to five thousand more.

At the same time, the navy began negotiating the purchase of Brooklyn's

Floyd Bennett Field from the city so it could be converted into a naval air station. The handover would be completed in 1941. The navy built a huge hangar and ramp for large seaplanes, such as the PBY Catalina, which would patrol the near Atlantic for U-boats and provide air support for shipping in and out of New York harbor during the war. The station was also excellently situated to test and commission aircraft manufactured on Long Island, where Republic, Grumman, General Motors, and Vought would produce tens of thousands of fighters, bombers, and other craft. After they were fitted out at Bennett Field the naval planes would be flown to both the European and Pacific war zones. Late in the war the station would also train pilots for helicopters. It would all add up to make Floyd Bennett the U.S. Navy's busiest air station of the war years.

The army got busy as well. New York's harbor and the Long Island Sound were studded with defensive fortifications. Some dated as far back as the early 1800s, when they were built to keep British warships out, others from a period of intense defensive buildup around the start of the twentieth century. Among them, the lower entrance to the harbor was guarded by Fort Tilden out near Rockaway Beach, Fort Hamilton in Brooklyn, Fort Wadsworth on Staten Island, and Fort Hancock at New Jersey's Sandy Hook. Fort Totten in Queens and Fort Schuyler across the water from it in the Bronx guarded the upper entrance. Most had sat idle since the Great War. The army now began to reman and reequip them with giant guns that could hurl shells as far as twenty-eight miles out to sea (miles farther than any warship's guns could reach), antiaircraft batteries, and, starting in 1942, radar installations. Out at Montauk on the eastern tip of Long Island, the army built the new Camp Hero, with artillery batteries that were camouflaged to resemble a fishing village to fool any German bombers that might fly over. Although U-boats would seriously harass New York shipping in the early months of the war, the threat of surface warships or bombers never materialized, and as the war progressed the army would use its harbor installations mostly as recruitment and training centers.

Also, the New York harbor had been since the Great War the U.S. Army's largest port of embarkation. POE facilities were spread around the harbor, from Hoboken and Staten Island to the nerve center, the Brooklyn Army Terminal (also called the Army Base) on the waterfront in Sunset Park. After the United States entered the war in December 1941, 3 million troops and 63 million tons of supplies would pass through it—half of the men and a third of the matériel shipped to the European theater. A forty-eight-acre industrial mini-city, the Brooklyn base included the largest warehouse in the world, where as many as ten thousand troops a day would get off trains and march straight onto troopships that steamed out to the Atlantic. Tanks, artillery, and every type of military equipment also flowed through it. Its mammoth military postal facility was said to process some nine million letters and packages every day of the war.

⌒

The world's fair that reopened that May, as Hitler's forces were ravaging Europe, was a much reduced affair in most every sense. Grover Whalen remained its ceremonial figurehead, but the actual management passed to another businessman whose mandate was to produce a profit, or at least stanch the losses. He opened the fairground to any exhibitor or vendor who could pay the rent on a space and reduced ticket prices to increase volume. From "Building the World of Tomorrow," the official theme was changed to "For Peace and Freedom." Ten nations—half of the original European contingent—did not reopen their pavilions, most because they were now in Nazi hands. Finland, now overrun, closed its pavilion during the summer. Where Joe the Worker had hoisted his shining red star was now an open plaza, the red-white-and-blue American Common. Some buildings from the first year stood sadly empty, and others were oddly repurposed. For instance, the Bendix Lama Temple, a re-creation of a Buddhist temple, now housed another nudie show, with a Shangri-la theme.

On the Fourth of July, a quarter of a million visitors flooded onto the fairgrounds, attracted by the cheaper prices and the promise of grand celebrations. It turned out to be a day of violent death.

The first hint of trouble had come in Manhattan, on the afternoon of Thursday, June 20, when two small bombs on timers detonated. The first went off at 4:10 in the hallway outside the offices of a German agency for international trade on the eighteenth floor of the Whitehall Building at 17 Battery Place downtown. Nine people suffered minor injuries from shattered windows and splintered doors. The German consulate general on the floor above was unaffected.

The second bomb went off at 4:53 in the doorway of the storefront at 35 East 12th Street near University Place that had been well known for years for housing the headquarters of the CPUSA, the offices of the *Daily Worker*, and the Workers Book Shop. The bomb splintered the door and shattered the store's plate glass window. One person was slightly injured by flying glass. DA Thomas Dewey, FBI agents, and city police examined the sites. The police theorized that a single "crackpot" planted both bombs; the *Daily Worker*'s editor Clarence Hathaway thought it was "the work of some stupid, misled maniac." Some believed the dual bombing was a protest against the Nazi-Soviet pact of the previous summer. The police rounded up and released at least thirty suspects but no perpetrators were ever found.

The next day, someone called in a bomb threat to the Italian pavilion at the fair. The NYPD's Bomb and Forgery Squad searched the building and found nothing. The Bomb Squad got a call the next day, threatening to blow up the East River bridges. Again, searches turned up no bombs. A few days later, a passenger on a train that had just pulled into Penn Station from Washington found an 18-inch mortar shell in the luggage rack. The Bomb Squad, firemen, and the FBI all converged on the station and shut it down for a few hours. The next day, a munitions salesman sheepishly reported that he'd simply forgotten the shell when he got off the train and that it was a harmless sample.

On July 1 someone called in a bomb threat to the British pavilion at the fair. Police found nothing. Two days later, an electrician working in the fan room found a small canvas bag. It was ticking. Incredibly, he did nothing about it. It was still there, and still ticking, the next day—Thursday, the Fourth of July. He carried the bag to a supervisor, who carried it to another, who showed it to yet another, who finally alerted the police.

The two detectives who arrived carried the bag out a back door to a relatively remote spot behind the black-draped Polish pavilion. Two more detectives, Joseph Lynch and Fred Socha of the Bomb Squad, arrived. Kneeling on the ground over the bag, they cut away a small section of the canvas and saw sticks of dynamite inside.

And then it blew up. Lynch and Socha died instantly, horribly mangled by a blast that left a crater three feet deep and five wide. Five others were injured, two of them critically. The police commissioner Valentine, Grover Whalen, and Mayor La Guardia all arrived. The carnage shocked the latter two; the mayor looked shaken and Whalen blinked back tears when he spoke to reporters.

With virtually nothing to go on, Commissioner Valentine resorted to rounding up "agitators," including members of the Bund and the Christian Front. One of them was Richard Eichenlaub, a German immigrant who ran the Little Casino restaurant and bierstube in Yorktown, known to be a popular meeting place for both Bundists and Nazi spies. He was questioned and released, as were scores of other suspects. The city posted a reward that eventually reached $26,000, but weeks and then months went by with no break in the case.

It remains unsolved today. The number of bomb scares and bomb threats all over the city escalated for a few weeks, then died down.

The fair would quietly fold at the end of October. It had attracted some 19 million visitors in 1940, 7 million fewer than in 1939, and because of the cheaper tickets it generated only about half the turnstile revenues. The fair corporation would declare bankruptcy; bondholders got back about 40 cents on the dollar for their investment. On the other hand, an estimated seven million out-of-town visitors spent $280 million in the city over the two seasons—not the $1 billion originally projected but still a handsome sum. The Parachute Jump and some other amusements went to Steeplechase Park and Luna Park at Coney Island. Most of the rest was immediately torn down, including the iconic Trylon and Perisphere; useful material like steel girders and trusses was designated for reuse in new defense facilities. Eventually only the New York City pavilion would remain.

Making the world's fair happen was the peak of Grover Whalen's career, but he would continue serving as New York City's toastmaster through the rest of the 1940s and into the 1950s. He would die in 1962, shortly after Robert Moses named him honorary chair of the new world's fair he was planning for Flushing Meadows in 1964.

CHAPTER 20

The Last Time I Saw Paris

When France signed its armistice with Germany on June 22, the Nazis occupied the northern two-thirds of the country, including its Atlantic coast, leaving only a southern corner "free" yet firmly under the German thumb. Millions of refugees who had fled the Blitzkrieg were now bottled up there, hoping to cross the border into neutral Spain or Portugal, or to catch any sort of ship out of Marseilles or other Mediterranean ports. But as part of the armistice, the new French puppet government, centered in the drab spa town of Vichy, agreed to "surrender on demand" any refugees the Nazis named. The Gestapo had a very long list.

In July, Varian Fry and others in New York hastily formed a group they called the Emergency Rescue Committee, with the goal of helping targeted refugees in Vichy France escape the trap and come to the United States. He was especially worried for the many artists, writers, scientists, and other intellectuals who were likely to be on the Gestapo's list.

The problem was that between anti-Semitism, isolationism, and the fact that the Depression had made so many of its own citizens homeless, the United States was not at all welcoming to refugees fleeing from Europe. Congressman Dies summed up the extremist viewpoint in 1934: "We must ignore the tears of sobbing sentimentalists and internationalists, and we must permanently close, lock, and bar the gates of our country to new immigration waves and then throw the keys away."

Officially, the quota for European immigrants in the 1930s was 154,000 a year, of which 84,000 slots were earmarked for British and Irish evacuees. But in fact only a tenth of that number were allowed in. From Hitler's rise in 1933 to 1940, only about 105,000 people fleeing the Nazis got into the United States. Breckinridge Long, the assistant secretary of state most responsible for the department's immigration and refugee policies, agreed with the hard line of Congressman Dies. He sent out a memo: "We can delay and effectively stop for a temporary period of indefinite length the number of immigrants into the United States. We could do this by simply advising our consuls to put every obstacle in the way and to require additional evidence and to resort to various administrative devices which would postpone and postpone and postpone the granting of the visas." This would be the de facto U.S. policy for the duration of the war, when nine out of ten requests for visas from countries under German or Italian control were denied.

Even children who were orphaned and in danger of being exterminated themselves were kept out. After Kristallnacht, New York's progressive senator Robert Wagner cosponsored a bill that would allow twenty thousand Jewish children to be brought out of Nazi Germany in 1939 and 1940. (He was an immigrant himself. He had moved with his parents from Prussia to Yorkville as a boy in 1885.) Despite backing from newspapers around the country and such political figures as Fiorello La Guardia and Herbert Hoover it did not pass.

With Congress and the State Department so bent on keeping refugees out, a number of private organizations did what they could: the American Friends Service Committee, the Unitarian Service Committee, the Committee for Catholic Refugees, the German Jewish Children's Aid Society, and the U.S. Committee for the Care of European Children, or USCOM, which started out in Eleanor Roosevelt's Greenwich Village apartment in 1940. At first, USCOM, which eventually had offices on Fourth Avenue near Union Square, focused specifically on evacuating British children from London and other Luftwaffe-targeted cities and placing them for the duration with American families. Despite cheery press like a *Life* spread entitled "U.S. Opens Its Homes and Heart to Refugee Children of England," only a trickle crossed the Atlantic under the program. The first five hundred steamed into the harbor of New York in July, and the total was still only eight hundred by the fall. There were thousands more whose parents would send them if they could, and USCOM heard from some five hundred American families every day offering to put them up. Wealthy New Yorkers pitched in. Mrs. Daniel Guggenheim opened Hempstead House, her baronial Long Island estate, to eight children. Mrs. Nelson Doubleday took in Somerset Maugham's grandson Vincent. But because of the dangers presented by U-boats, England was loath to put children on convoy ships, while neutrality laws forbade American ships from helping out. The program languished. USCOM would turn its attention to Jewish refugee children in 1942 and help to get a meager few hundred into the country.

Official America was not much more welcoming to the sort of intellectuals and artists Fry wanted to help. Part of the reason given was that the Depression had impoverished thousands of homegrown scholars and artists who deserved to get help before any foreigners. But a bigger problem was that so many of the foreigners were Jews and/or leftists. Even Einstein had faced a grassroots movement to ban him from settling in Princeton in 1933 because he was said to be a "Jew Bolshevist."

Here again private institutions stepped in. Alvin Johnson was a cofounder and the director of the New School for Social Research in Greenwich Village. He traveled in Germany in 1932 and was very concerned about what he saw. The following year, Hitler was in power only a few months when he ordered the removal of hundreds of scholars from the faculties of German universities because they were Jewish, progressive, or in other ways not consonant with the Nazi ideal. In response, Johnson created the University in Exile, a graduate program initially in political and social sciences, to bring the best of Hitler's tossed-off scholars to New York. With the fall of France in 1940, Johnson expanded his scope. By the end of the war the New School would bring 183 exiled intellectuals to New York, more than any other institution in America. They represented many countries and disciplines. Among them were Hannah Arendt, Claude Lévi-Strauss, Wilhelm Reich, Hanns Eisler, Erwin Piscator, Bronislaw Malinowski, George Szell, Nino Levi, and Max Ascoli.

Johnson was also instrumental in the creation of the Emergency Committee in Aid of Displaced German (later Foreign) Scholars, which helped bring Thomas Mann, Herbert Marcuse, Paul Tillich, and others to America, many of them settling in New York City. Collectively, all these exiles, effectively the cream of European scholarly and cultural life, would accelerate New York's intellectual and artistic development through the war years and beyond. Meanwhile in Princeton, the Institute for Advanced Study became a similar refuge for Einstein, Kurt Gödel, Wolfgang Pauli, and others.

Operating from an office in the Chanin Building across 42nd Street from Grand Central, Fry's ERC easily won the support of luminaries including Dorothy Thompson, Thomas Mann's daughter Erika Mann, the theologian Reinhold Niebuhr, and Alvin Johnson. But the government was very reluctant to help. Again, Eleanor stepped in, forcefully twisting her husband's arm to get emergency visas.

Now someone had to go to Vichy France to negotiate or otherwise facilitate the refugees' release. The job fell to Fry. Eleanor finagled him a passport, but it was validated for only six months. He flew in a Pan Am Yankee Clipper from New York to Lisbon at the start of August 1940 and made his way to Marseilles. He was planning to stay only one month. He was still there in January 1941 when his passport expired, and he remained there till the following August.

In his 1945 memoir *Surrender on Demand*, Fry described how at first he and a few volunteers operated from his small room in a dowdy Marseilles hotel, with applicants lined up down the hall and massing in the lobby under the watchful eye of Vichy police. Later he would rent a large, tumbledown villa outside of the city; it was called Villa Air-Bel, but the refugees nicknamed it Château Espère-Visa (Hope-for-Visa). With little help from American diplomats, who considered him a dangerously provocative amateur, Fry and his staff used any means available to get people out. They bribed officials and border guards. They worked with forgers, black marketeers, and waterfront gangsters to get bogus visas and travel documents. They set up a sort of underground railroad to shuttle refugees across unguarded stretches of the border into Spain.

After Fry's visa ran out in January 1941, the American embassy began cooperating with the French to force him out of the country. Though increasingly harassed, he continued his work the best he could. In the spring of 1941 the Vichy government swept through Marseilles' hotels arresting all the Jewish refugees they found, including Marc Chagall. Fry got him out by threatening to inform the *New York Times* that the French were about to consign the world-famous artist to death at Nazi hands. Fry would hang on until the end of August 1941, when he was put on a boat for New York.

"When Varian Fry arrived in Marseilles in August 1940 he brought with him a list of two hundred people to be rescued. By the time he was expelled from France a year later he had, incredibly, arranged the escapes of nearly fifteen hundred people," Andy Marino wrote in his 1999 biography, *A Quiet American*. Among those he'd helped to escape were Chagall, André Breton, André Masson, Marcel Duchamp, *The Eternal Road*'s Franz Werfel, and Max Ernst.

Back in New York, Fry would continue to criticize U.S. policy toward refugees, writing articles and giving lectures with titles like "The Massacre of the Jews." France would award him the Legion of Honor in 1967, shortly before he died at the age of fifty-nine.

Many other New Yorkers, especially in the arts, nurtured strong bonds of affection for Paris and were deeply saddened by its fall that summer. One of them was Oscar Hammerstein II, son and grandson of great Broadway impresarios, who'd written the enormously successful *Showboat* (1927) with composer and friend Jerome Kern, also a New York native. On hearing of the city's occupation by the Nazis that June he sat down and immediately started on the lyrics for "The Last Time I Saw Paris," ending with, "No matter how they change her I'll remember her that way." Kern wrote the music, and by the end of 1940 half a dozen singers, including Kate Smith, had recorded it. Hastily added to the movie *Lady Be Good* and sung by Ann Sothern, it won the best song Academy Award for 1941 and went on to be an enduring classic.

Hammerstein and another composer, Richard Rodgers, would team up on two of the biggest Broadway musicals of the war years: *Oklahoma!*, which opened in 1943 and ran for five years, and *Carousel*, which opened in the spring of 1945. In the postwar years they'd create the war-themed *South Pacific* (1949), followed by *The King and I* (1951), and then return to the war as a theme in *The Sound of Music* in 1959.

Another pair of rather different New York artists watched with mounting anger in the summer of 1940 as Hitler devoured Europe while the United States remained neutral. Jack Kirby and Joe Simon decided to take matters in their own hands.

Kirby was born Jacob "Jakie" Kurtzberg on the Lower East Side in 1917, the older of two sons of garment workers who had emigrated from Austria. The constant fighting with other kids' street gangs—Jewish boys against Irish, Italian, and black—made him tough and pugnacious, and it also left him with the intimate understanding of hand-to-hand combat that would show up in his brawny drawings. "I hated the place," he would recall. "I wanted to get out of there!"

He escaped by walking up to the movies on 42nd Street and by reading newspaper comic strips. He said he found his first pulp magazine, *Wonder*

Stories, floating in a gutter. He saw the drawing of a rocket ship on the cover and was hooked. Except for one week as a student at the Pratt Institute in Brooklyn—his parents couldn't afford to have him stay, and he didn't fit in anyway—he was self-taught. By eighteen he was drawing editorial cartoons and comics for newspapers, signing them Jack Cortez, Jack Curtis, finally settling on Jack Kirby, which he made legal, to his parents' dismay. While still a teen he worked for a while in Max and Dave Fleischer's animation studio, helping to draw Popeye and Betty Boop cartoons.

His career took off with the rise of the comic book industry in the late 1930s. Comic strips had been appearing in newspapers since the turn of the century, but it wasn't until the Depression years that Max Gaines (born Max Ginzberg in the Bronx), a printer's salesman, racked his brain for some way to feed his kids and struck on the comic book format. The startling success of the first Superman comic book in 1938 set off a mad scramble of competitors and imitators. Characters, titles, and whole companies rose and fell at a phenomenal clip. Kirby worked for the legendary Will Eisner's studio, where he met Bob Kahn (who, as Bob Kane, would create Batman).

Joe Simon, born Hymie Simon upstate, took a room in an uptown Manhattan boardinghouse to start his career in this burgeoning new field. He and Kirby teamed up and created a series of characters who failed to impress readers, despite wonderful names like Master Mind Excello, the Fin, Flexo the Rubber Man, and the Phantom Bullet.

Then in 1940, inspired by watching Hitler rampage across Europe, they came up with one of the most popular comic book heroes ever: Captain America, the Sentinel of Liberty. His real name was Steve Rogers, a skinny art student from Brooklyn. Trying to enlist, he flunked the army physical but was accepted into a test program, taking Super Soldier Serum and Vita-Rays that transformed him to physical perfection.

Simon and Kirby put him in an American flag–themed outfit and started him off with a bang in the first issue (dated March 1941, but it actually came out in December 1940). The cover showed him socking Adolf Hitler on the jaw. It was a great success, selling a million copies. It also drew death threats for Simon and Kirby from the city's pro-Nazis. Mayor La Guardia called them and said not to worry, the city of New York would protect them.

With some money coming in, Kirby finally could move off the Lower East Side, to the Jewish neighborhood of Brighton Beach in Brooklyn, where he met and married Harriet Feldman, who remained his wife until his death in 1994. In 1943, Kirby would get the chance to fight the Nazis personally. Drafted into the army, he landed with the Eleventh Infantry at Omaha Beach two months after D-day. A lieutenant who recognized him as the Captain America cartoonist made him an advance scout, sending him in front of the unit to sketch the terrain. He would be hospitalized with a severe case of trench foot and thought for a while he might lose his legs. He was sent home in January 1945, his legs intact. He would go on to work for Stan Lee at Marvel Comics and cocreate the Fantastic Four, Black Panther, Thor, Iron Man, the Hulk, and many other characters.

CHAPTER 21

Wendell Willkie vs. the Third Termites

In an age of bullies, we cannot afford to be a sissy.

—*William Donovan*

All the new war equipment Roosevelt ordered up in the spring and summer of 1940 would be pointless without trained men and officers to use it. America's existing ground forces totaled around two hundred thousand regular troops, fewer than half of whom could be fielded quickly. Germany and Japan each had millions.

Some of FDR's advisers urged a peacetime draft, the first in the nation's history. But 1940 was an election year, and with isolationism still strong around the country and in Congress Roosevelt hesitated to ask for it.

It was in fact one of the odder election years on record to that point. The three men who emerged as the major presidential candidates all had New York City connections: Franklin Roosevelt, Thomas Dewey, and Wendell Willkie. For months no one even knew if Roosevelt was running; if he did, it would be for an unprecedented third term. The other two men were absolute wild cards. Although Dewey was a national folk hero, the highest elected office he had held was his present position as Manhattan district attorney. Willkie had never held any public office at all. He was a well-known figure on Wall Street but a complete political outsider whose candidacy was at first treated almost as a joke. Still, the two of them would far outshine the only traditional Republican in the running, Senator Robert Taft of Ohio, son of a president, conservative, strictly isolationist, and so lacking in color as to be practically transparent.

Roosevelt was never more effectively devious than in the way he stage-managed his nomination for a third term in 1940. As early as 1938 he had told Harry Hopkins that he was disinclined to run again, and that if Hopkins could get his health back he could win the Democratic nomination. To help position him, Roosevelt had Hopkins resign from his highly contentious directorship of the WPA, and then appointed him secretary of commerce the day before Christmas 1938. That this was pure political maneuvering—Hopkins had no qualifications for the job—stirred up Hopkins's enemies anyway. He would keep the position through the summer of 1940 but was so ill for much of that time that he was rarely seen behind the desk and the department ran itself.

Meanwhile, a large field of other Democrats were thinking about running in 1940 if the president did not. Secretly, he encouraged each and suggested that each would have his support. "Roosevelt cheerfully welcomed them all to the arena," the historian Susan Dunn writes. "Playing on their ambition and their vanity, flattering and manipulating them," Roosevelt whipped up what Frances Perkins called a "general melee" of lesser rivals, which only made his running for a third term seem not only feasible but imperative.

Hopkins began to do some exploratory campaigning and speechmaking. He was not a good campaigner, and as the operative most identified with the New Deal he had made too many political enemies. One afternoon he was enjoying a day at the Empire City Race Track (now Yonkers Raceway) with some of his New York friends, including the Broadway producer Max Gordon. According to Gordon, Hopkins crowed of the Democrats' program for the near future, "We shall tax and tax, and spend and spend, and elect and elect." It made hundreds of newspapers around the country and provoked an enormous uproar from Hopkins's enemies. He was grilled about it at length by the Senate Commerce Committee. He categorically denied saying it, and Gordon waffled, but the quote stuck, and Hopkins's presidential aspirations sank to nothing. Despite Roosevelt's having maneuvered him into sure failure, Hopkins remained faithful and played a large behind-the-scenes role in the movement for a third term—known to their enemies as "third termites."

Stiff and mechanical in public as a windup toy, Thomas Dewey was not a natural politician. He refused to kiss babies, wear silly hats for the photographers, or press the flesh in crowds. At thirty-eight he was too young to be taken seriously by older Taft-supporting Republicans. But his successful prosecutions of top New York gangsters—including mob boss Lucky Luciano, whom he put away for thirty to fifty years in 1936, and Louis "Lepke" Buchalter, sentenced to thirty years early in 1940—had earned him national celebrity. He was the Gangbuster, Public Hero No. 1, and his star power made him a candidate who could not be instantly dismissed.

The *New York Times* was the first paper to float Wendell Willkie as a potential Republican candidate, even though the February 1939 column by Arthur Krock was half-joking. After listing Dewey and a number of other more likely hopefuls, Krock wrote, "If he is a Republican—is he?—you can't wholly count out Willkie... But he'll have to go down as the darkest horse in the stable."

Wendell Willkie was born in 1892 in Indiana, where his father was a lawyer and his mother was the first woman admitted to the state bar. "Wen" taught high school, passed the bar, enlisted in the army during the Great War but got to France just as it was ending. He moved with wife and son to New York City in 1929, when he became general counsel for Commonwealth & Southern, a gigantic public utilities company then operating in eleven states. They took an apartment in the just-completed luxury high-rise at 1010 Fifth Avenue, across the street from the Metropolitan Museum of Art. They were still there when he became president of Commonwealth in 1933, using the subway or cabs to get to his office down at 20 Pine Street, a block from Wall; the family was still living there when he ran for president in 1940. That year he told a reporter for *Life* that the thing that had scared him most about New York City when he first arrived from Indiana was his building's uniformed doormen.

The New York media were unfailingly charmed by that down-home side of him. He was a friendly bear of a man with tousled hair and a loose tie; his education and intelligence emerged only when he spoke, often in droning detail, about economics and politics. His affect of the common man wasn't the only aspect that made him an unusual choice for a Republican presidential candidate. He had been a Socialist in his university days, and after that a Democrat. He voted for Al Smith in 1928, and he approved at first of Roosevelt and the New Deal—until 1935, when the Democrats passed legislation to break up and regulate multistate utility combines like Commonwealth, even as the federal government was creating its own massive, monopolistic Tennessee Valley Authority. To Willkie this was both antibusiness and undemocratic. He voted for Alf Landon in 1936 and spent the next few years in a highly publicized fight against the TVA. By the time he gave in and sold his company's Tennessee holdings to the feds in 1939, at which point he resigned, he was saying that he hadn't deserted the Democratic Party, it had deserted him. In fact his politics remained much closer to FDR's than to any of his Republican rivals. He basically still approved of the New Deal, he just thought it had gone too far. And where other Republicans spoke isolationism, Willkie said he believed Hitler needed to be "licked," the sooner the better.

It was Henry Luce's empire and the Reids' *Tribune* that pushed Willkie to the center of the stage. In the summer of 1939, participating in a *Fortune*-sponsored roundtable, Willkie met the magazine's managing editor Russell Davenport. Charmed and impressed, Davenport helped Willkie craft a manifesto, "We the People," in which Willkie attacked Roosevelt for his tyrannical domestic policies but also criticized isolationist Republicans. *Fortune* ran it with much fanfare in April 1940. Oren Root, a twenty-eight-year-old Wall Street lawyer and grandnephew of Elihu Root, was so inspired he left his job to start a grassroots "Willkie for President" mail campaign, which he ran at first from the midtown apartment he shared with his mother. The response was very encouraging: fans formed Willkie Clubs all around the country and circulated petitions that gathered more than three million signatures. Davenport left *Fortune* to start up and manage Willkie's campaign, with an office in the Grand Central building.

Henry Luce had been in Europe when the *Fortune* piece ran, but soon he and Willkie were having frequent get-togethers. Luce liked Willkie personally—most everyone did—as well as agreeing with his politics. *Life* ran a giant, eleven-page puff piece on Willkie that May. It opened with the line, "In the opinion of most of the nation's political pundits, Wendell Lewis Willkie is by far the ablest man the Republicans could nominate for President." And later: "A vote for Willkie is a vote for the best man to lead the country in a crisis." Luce ordered *Time* to support Willkie as well; when some editors grumbled about ethics, he fired back that this was no time for impartial journalism, the fate of the country and the world were at stake.

At the same time, the *Tribune*'s book review editor Irita Van Doren introduced Willkie to owners Ogden and Helen Reid, who decided to back him. Van Doren also helped Willkie write some of his best speeches and papers. They had been lovers since 1937, a fact known to Mrs. Willkie and to everyone in politics and the media, but not to the voting public. Just as they did for Roosevelt, the press kept Van Doren and Willkie's secret.

The *Tribune*'s stridently interventionist Dorothy Thompson naturally preferred Willkie over the isolationists Dewey and Taft, and she also liked him personally. But as western Europe's dominoes began to fall she harbored a concern that perhaps the experienced hand of FDR might be best for leading Americans into the fray. In the spring she hoisted the notion, not as outlandish in retrospect as both sides scoffed it was, that Willkie should leave the Republicans to be FDR's running mate. Sensing a powerful ally, Roosevelt twice invited Thompson to the White House to woo her to defect.

Willkie's campaign for the nomination, proudly run by political amateurs such as Davenport and others, played up his image as a rank outsider, a plainspoken, straight-shooting nonpolitician from the heartland who just happened to live on Fifth Avenue, a kind of Will Rogers of presidential politics. He entered no primaries, just barnstormed and worked his friends in the press.

When the Republicans went into their convention in June most party regulars were still for Dewey or Taft. But with the Blitzkrieg racing across Europe, the strict noninvolvement both those candidates espoused was starting to sound a bit weak and craven. While Willkie argued against sending American troops abroad, he was also for giving the Allies any material help they needed. Through six increasingly raucous ballots Dewey and Taft faded and Willkie emerged the candidate.

The Democrats' convention, held in Chicago in July, was far less dramatic. By keeping his intentions vague, Roosevelt had made it nearly impossible for anyone else to present himself as an alternative, so the convention started with no candidates. Pulling strings from a distance, Roosevelt allowed himself to be drafted; the delegates nominated him and went home.

⌢

Until his nomination was safely in hand, Roosevelt let some old friends and acquaintances in New York make the case for conscription for him. Grenville Clark and FDR had known each other growing up wealthy in New York, and at Harvard, and as law clerks on Wall Street. FDR called him Grennie. In 1915, two days after a U-boat sank the *Lusitania*, Clark had met with a small group of similarly wellborn young men at the Harvard Club on West 44th Street. Foreseeing America's entry in the world war, they formed the Military Training Camps Association to prepare themselves and others to serve as the army's officer corps. Because their first camp was in Plattsburgh, New York, they came to be known as the Plattsburgh Group. Some sixty-six thousand junior officers, four-fifths of American line officers in the Great War, got their training in these camps.

In May 1940, seeing Hitler devour Europe, Clark brought the Plattsburgh Group back together at the Harvard Club. At the meeting were Julius Ochs Adler, general manager of the *New York Times*; William Donovan; and another prominent Wall Street lawyer, who was also one of the most respected Republicans in America, the former secretary of war and secretary of state Henry L. Stimson. On May 23, Adler's *Times* ran a front page story headlined "Plattsburgh Group Asks Conscription." Clark's group issued a call for "universal compulsory military training and, in time of war, universal service." They also recommended "immediate and concrete measures, short of war" to help England resist Hitler.

Roosevelt could not have asked for a better front. The group included highly respected businessmen and decorated veterans of the Great War—and Republicans. But when Clark requested a meeting with him in the White House, Roosevelt cannily declined. He wasn't ready yet to go public with his support of conscription. Instead, with his private encouragement, the Plattsburgh Group drafted a bill, adopting the Great War euphemism of "selective" rather than "compulsory" service, and convinced the Democratic senator Edward Burke of Nebraska and the Republican congressman James Wadsworth of upstate New York to sponsor it.

Stimson took their argument to the public. At seventy-two, he had a long record of honorable public service. Born to the purple in Manhattan just two years after the Civil War ended, son of a wealthy physician, he had matriculated into the ruling elite at Phillips Academy, Yale, and Harvard Law School. In 1891 he joined Elihu Root's prestigious Wall Street law firm. In 1899, when Root went to Washington to be McKinley's secretary of war, he handed the firm to Stimson and another young partner. Among the younger lawyers they would bring in was Felix Frankfurter.

In 1911 Stimson became President Taft's secretary of war. He served as an artillery officer in the Great War, ensuring that he would ever after be known as the Colonel. Foreign service in Latin America and the

Philippines in the 1920s, followed by four years as Herbert Hoover's secretary of state, expanded his worldview and eroded his faith in gentlemanly diplomacy. When Hoover lost in 1932, Stimson went back to Wall Street. In early 1933 Frankfurter arranged for him to go up to Hyde Park and meet Roosevelt for the first time. Alone among former Hoover men, Stimson was willing to share what he knew about international affairs with the new Democratic president, and Roosevelt never forgot it.

Stimson spent the rest of the 1930s practicing corporate law with decreasing satisfaction. As political gangsters in Europe and Asia went from success to success, Stimson used speaking engagements, radio, and the *Times* and other newspapers to oppose the isolationists in his party.

In June, as Panzers rolled down Paris streets, Stimson gave addresses at Phillips, Yale, and on NBC radio, stressing the need for national preparedness, as well as for aid to England. Roosevelt saw an opening. He had been thinking for months about putting a couple of interventionist Republicans in his cabinet to help blunt the party's opposition to his defense and conscription plans. He called Stimson on June 19 and asked him to be his secretary of war. Roosevelt had been fighting with his current war secretary, the isolationist Democrat Harry Woodring, who said that a draft smacked of totalitarianism. On June 20 FDR fired Woodring and Stimson took the job. Roosevelt also appointed William Franklin "Frank" Knox his new secretary of the navy. Knox was a former Rough Rider, Alf Landon's running mate in 1936, publisher of the Republican *Chicago Daily News*, and as pro-defense as Stimson. Republicans denounced them both as Benedict Arnolds, but it was a great coup for FDR.

When Stimson went to Washington he brought a team with him from New York to be his assistant secretaries. His first assistant secretary and then undersecretary was the New York federal judge Robert Patterson. Wall Street lawyer John McCloy had fought in the Great War before attending Harvard Law. Robert Lovett was a Wall Street banker and bon vivant who partied with Robert Sherwood and the Algonquin crowd. He was also a friend of fellow Wall Street banker James Forrestal, Knox's undersecretary of the navy. (Forrestal would take over as secretary when Knox died of a heart attack in 1944.)

Knox's appointment was cheered by his friend and longtime supporter in New York William Donovan. Roosevelt and Donovan had come to appreciate each other better since 1932. From 1935 on Donovan had traveled extensively in Europe and Asia, his wealth and fame opening doors everywhere. He met Mussolini in Rome, toured the Italian front lines during Italy's conquest of Ethiopia, observed military maneuvers in Germany. It had all put him firmly on the side of FDR's plans for military preparedness.

At Knox's urging, Roosevelt called Donovan to the White House in July and gave him an assignment. Donovan took off that month from the seaplane basin at Municipal Airport in a Pan Am Clipper bound for England. According to Charles Sweeny, Roosevelt had not informed Joseph Kennedy, his ambassador to England, whom he mistrusted, about Donovan's mission, so at first the American embassy in London stonewalled him. Once Sweeny, who had high-level access in the British government, smoothed the way for him, Donovan was able to confer with Churchill and be briefed on classified British intelligence. Roosevelt wanted Donovan's opinion on whether England could withstand a German invasion. On his return in August Donovan made a full report to Knox and the president, then went on Mutual radio to call for the immediate passage of the conscription bill. In addition, he convinced Roosevelt to let the British have the Norden bombsight in a trade for Britain's superior sonar technology. That the Germans also had the Norden plans was still unknown to them at the time.

⁓

By the end of July, national polls—a relatively new and inexact science in 1940—indicated that two-thirds of Americans now favored a draft, though to most this would still be only for national defense, not for getting entangled in foreign wars. In August even Willkie spoke in favor of conscription.

FDR now felt comfortable publicly backing Burke-Wadsworth. As Congress started to debate the bill, however, there remained fierce opposition around the country. It came from all sides: Communists as well as Bundists, the labor movement and pacifists. Declaring that "to fight war we must fight conscription," Dorothy Day went to Washington to testify against the bill before the Senate Committee on Military Affairs. The FBI started a file on her, convinced that the Catholic Workers were a Communist front.

Norman Thomas was vociferously against Burke-Wadsworth as well. He had started an organization, the Keep America Out of War Congress, staging antiwar rallies in Carnegie Hall and Town Hall that attracted audiences the *Times* described as mostly college students. He accused both Roosevelt and Willkie of being willing to "gamble with the lives and fortunes" of all Americans. "Rarely has any people been so deliberately panicked into hysteria and fooled into possible wars of aggression in the name of defense." When he accused Roosevelt of "advocating steps in preparation for war as a means, not only of resolving the unemployment problem, but of enhancing his own power as well," Roosevelt fired off a hurt and angry letter asking him to "withdraw the grossly unfair suggestion."

In the halls of Congress the draft debate quickly descended to shouts, name-calling (liar, rat, traitor), and one fistfight. Finally, the bill squeaked through on September 16. It set the draft age at twenty-one to thirty-six (this would change) and gave college males a one-year deferment. Isolationists had packed it with two significant stipulations. Conscripts would serve for only one year, followed by a decade in the reserves, and they would be deployed only for national defense, not be sent overseas. In a nod to nonviolence activists like Day and the War Resisters League, the act allowed conscientious objectors to choose between noncombatant military service and a new Civilian Public Service agency (CPS), to be jointly administered by the government and traditional "peace churches" such as the Mennonites and Friends.

It also expanded the guidelines for who could apply for CO status. But as twenty-five-year-old Ralph DiGia from the Bronx found out, in practice most draft boards would refuse CO status to anyone not applying for religious reasons. DiGia had come to pacifism by a rather different route from Dorothy Day's. His father, an Italian immigrant barber, had raised him as a Socialist. "As a youngster I was taken to many meetings where I heard talk about the exploitation of the poor by the rich and how in war the rich got richer and the poor died," DiGia wrote years later. At CCNY in 1935, he signed the Oxford Oath along with some sixty thousand other college students nationwide, pledging never to take up arms in war.

When draft registration started in October 1940, DiGia applied for CO status and was denied. He wouldn't be called up until 1942, when he'd face some hard decisions.

CHAPTER 22

Hell No, They Won't Go

Four days after FDR signed selective service into law, two of the most influential civil rights leaders in the country sat across the desk from him in the Oval Office. Asa Philip Randolph and Walter White had come down from Harlem for the meeting.

In 1925 Randolph had been editing the *Messenger*, a Socialist magazine in Harlem, when Pullman porters asked him to be the first president of a new union, the Brotherhood of Sleeping Car Porters. The Chicago-based Pullman rail company employed only black men as porters; with some twelve thousand in the 1920s, it was the largest employer of African Americans in the country. It took until 1937, but when Randolph and the BSCP finally won formal recognition from the company, it was the first contract successfully negotiated by a black union with a major American corporation—an extraordinary achievement in the heart of the Depression.

Walter White grew up in Atlanta. Although his family was by all visible signs white—he had blond hair, blue eyes, and pink skin—they had a trace of Negro ancestry and were therefore, by the "one drop" rule of the day, black. In 1906 Atlanta whites rampaged, killing forty blacks. Walter and his father escaped harm because they looked white. In his autobiography *A Man Called White*, Walter wrote that this was the moment he decided he would always identify as black—that he would "infinitely rather be what I was" than "one of the race which had forced the decision upon me."

When America entered the Great War he tried to enlist in a segregated black army unit but was turned down by recruiters, who suspected he was a German agent sent to stir up revolt among Negro troops. After graduating from Atlanta University he helped organize a local chapter of the new NAACP, then moved to Harlem to work for the national headquarters.

His ease at passing for white made him the perfect undercover investigator in the South, where he gathered intelligence on lynchings that he presented at congressional hearings.

In Harlem, his looks gave him another advantage. By long tradition, lighter-skinned, more Caucasian-looking people rose to the top of black society, in Harlem as in other black communities. White and his family moved into the towering high-rise at 409 Edgecombe Avenue, considered one of the best addresses in Harlem. W. E. B. Du Bois, future Supreme Court justice Thurgood Marshall, bandleader Jimmie Lunceford, and other Harlem elites also lived there.

In 1931 White became the NAACP's executive secretary. He was considered one of the more moderate of black leaders, who believed that the way forward was to cooperate with right-thinking whites and gradually educate the rest. But by 1940 he was losing patience and collaborating with more aggressive younger leaders like Randolph.

Born and raised in princely isolation, Franklin Roosevelt could often express the WASP patrician's unthinking condescension toward blacks, Jews, the Irish, Italians. To him, blacks were "coloreds," Fiorello La Guardia was "the little wop," and so on. Still, in 1935 he had pushed through an executive order forbidding discrimination in WPA hiring. With prompting from Eleanor and Interior Secretary Harold Ickes, he had also seeded his administration with some of the most accomplished black professionals in America, including several Harvard-trained lawyers. They took high-level posts at Interior and most other departments. The press called them his "black brain trust" or the Black Cabinet.

Now Randolph and White had come to ask Roosevelt to end segregation in the armed forces. The Marine Corps and Army Air Corps were all white. There were only two black officers in the entire military. Blacks who were in the military were almost all in bottom-rung service positions—working in the mess hall, cleaning toilets, polishing brass.

Desegregating the military was just about the last issue FDR wanted to take on in September 1940 with an election coming up. He did not want to alienate voters in the South, or the Southern Democrat bloc in Congress, who a few years earlier had demonstrated how much they cared about civil rights by killing an antilynching bill that Senator Robert Wagner had cosponsored and Walter White had lobbied hard for. Roosevelt also didn't want to antagonize the military, where a large number of officers were southerners. Both Stimson and Knox were against integrating.

Stimson believed that black men "lacked the moral and mental qualifications" for combat and were ill equipped for "weapons of modern war." He liked to point out that his family had been abolitionists and fought for the Union in the Civil War, so he did not consider himself a racist but simply a realist.

At Eleanor's insistence, Roosevelt agreed to the meeting. He made sure Knox and an assistant to Stimson were there to help him explain to Randolph and White why now was not the time to bring the issue of integration before the people or Congress.

It's known exactly what was said at the meeting, because that August the White House had for the first time begun secretly recording Oval Office press conferences and meetings. White House staff hoped that keeping audio records might dispel some of the confusion Roosevelt's affable vagueness often caused. The recordings, created on an RCA experimental rig, were not made public until a researcher stumbled upon them in the FDR Presidential Library in 1978. (They are now online.)

Despite the poor audio quality, it's clear that FDR was at his worst in his meeting with the black leaders. White and Randolph are dignified and direct. White says that black Americans "feel they have earned their right to participate." Randolph points to formerly all-white labor unions that successfully integrated. Roosevelt interrupts them, talks over them, tells pointless jokes and stories to divert them. He even lies outright at one point, claiming that the new draft law stipulated that black conscripts would be placed in ground combat units, which in fact it did not; that would not happen until 1944. He refers to black men in the navy as "colored boys." Frank Knox flatly declares that having white and black sailors on the same ship "won't do," and he ruefully suggests that the only way to "integrate" the navy would be to have all-white and all-black ships. FDR suggests, "There's no reason why we shouldn't have a colored band on some of these ships, because they're darn good at it."

Randolph and White endured the humiliation, and it's a testament to FDR's ability to charm that they left the Oval Office actually believing they had won him over. They were stunned a couple of weeks later when the White House issued a press release saying that the tradition of keeping whites and blacks separated in the military was to continue. White's NAACP issued a statement denouncing the "trickery." Randolph wrote the president an enraged letter. FDR backtracked a few paces and released a new statement making vague promises that blacks would get "fair treatment" in the military.

Willkie and the Republicans capitalized on Roosevelt's gaffe with black America. Willkie's platform included calls for an antilynching law and universal black suffrage. He also got the most popular black man in America in 1940, Joe Louis, to stump for him. Privately, the champ admired Roosevelt, but in speeches he made in more than a dozen cities he noted, "Roosevelt has had two terms to do what he could do, but didn't give us an antilynching law...I am for Willkie because I think he will be good for my people." Gene Tunney, the extraordinarily well-read former world champion boxer from Greenwich Village, also came out for Willkie. Jack Dempsey, a staunch FDR man, excoriated them both.

⌒

Since June, Churchill had been imploring Roosevelt for American destroyers to help Britain fend off the German navy. William Donovan had lobbied Roosevelt on Churchill's behalf after his summer trip. Having already stirred up his opponents over selective service, FDR hesitated. In mid-July, Henry Luce went down to Washington for a White House dinner, ferrying a suggestion that the United States might swap England some old destroyers for military bases from Newfoundland to the Caribbean. The next issue of *Time* ran a large article on the need for Caribbean bases to guard the Panama Canal.

Still Roosevelt moved cautiously. Failing to marshal bipartisan support in Congress, he sent Grenville Clark to sound out Willkie. Though Willkie had backed selective service, he bowed to the isolationists this time and declined to support the deal. In early September Roosevelt closed the deal by executive fiat, without congressional approval. In exchange for eight island bases that would extend the country's defense lines into the Atlantic, the United States sent England fifty Great War–era destroyers. Several had been sitting mothballed at the Brooklyn Navy Yard. The navy slapped a new coat of paint on them and sent them off. Robert Sherwood called it the start of a "common law marriage" of U.S. and British interests. (In March 1942 the Royal Navy would pack explosives into one of those old destroyers—the USS *Buchanan*, renamed HMS *Campbeltown*—and ram it into the huge dry dock at Saint-Nazaire in France, destroying it. The only dry dock capable of servicing the giant German battleships *Bismarck* and *Tirpitz*, it had originally been built for the largest ocean liner in the world, the *Normandie*.)

The combination of selective service and the warships deal galvanized isolationists. That September, the America First Committee, the largest and most respectable of all isolationist organizations, was founded. Begun by a handful of law students at Yale, it quickly grew into a wide coalition of students and corporate leaders, mothers and sons, left and right, Republican and Democrat. Whatever their other differences, they all agreed on one fundamental: that while the United States should maintain "an impregnable defense" against any aggressors, "American democracy can be preserved only by keeping out of the European war." The heroes Charles Lindbergh and Eddie Rickenbacker, the anti-Semite Henry Ford, Kathleen Thompson Norris, Norman Thomas, and even Teddy Roosevelt's daughter Alice joined.

Norman Thomas was an uneasy bedfellow among the right-wingers, and it caused his already small Socialist Party to shed members until it nearly vanished, with fewer than one thousand followers by the end of 1941. At one America First rally in Madison Square Garden, Thomas looked distinctly ill at ease when the master of ceremonies asked the crowd to sing "God Bless America" and many booed, because it was written by a Jew.

⌒

Given all the enemies he'd made and all the criticism he'd attracted since coming to Washington, Harry Hopkins felt he'd be a liability to FDR's reelection campaign and should at least appear to distance himself until after the election. In September he resigned as secretary of commerce, where he'd been ineffectual anyway, and moved out of the White House, all the way back to Manhattan, where he and his daughter Diana moved into a small apartment in the Essex House on Central Park South. However, he remained very involved in the campaign behind the scenes. That month he and Robert Sherwood were at a party out on Long Island. Sherwood had first met Hopkins in 1938, and though he thought him "profoundly shrewd and faintly ominous" he had kept in touch. Now Hopkins buttonholed him and, referring to the CDAAA, cracked, "What are you warmongers up to?"

Hopkins was sounding Sherwood out. In October, he called Sherwood to the Essex House. The president was going to speak about Hitler on Columbus Day. Hopkins asked Sherwood what he thought the president should say. Sherwood, who said that he was "flabbergasted," spoke his piece. Satisfied, Hopkins walked him a few blocks to Sam Rosenman's apartment on Central Park West.

"We found him in his dining room, the table littered with papers including notes from the White House and material that Roosevelt had dictated," Sherwood later wrote. "At first, I did not know why I was there but I soon found out that I had been pressed into service as a 'ghost writer'...From that moment on, for the next five years, Hopkins, Rosenman and I worked closely together on all the major Roosevelt speeches until the President's death." Throughout that period Sherwood worked full time for the president and did not write another play.

Both Republicans and Democrats wooed La Guardia. Early on, it had been rumored that Willkie was considering La Guardia as a running mate. Roosevelt, cunning as always, headed off the Republicans by letting it be known that he was considering La Guardia for a cabinet post, perhaps secretary of the navy or even secretary of war—a job that would have pleased the mayor mightily. Roosevelt disappointed La Guardia with the appointments of Stimson and Knox in July, but won him back in August by appointing him to chair the American side of a U.S.-Canadian Permanent Joint Board on Defense. La Guardia campaigned for FDR that fall with all his characteristic vigor and intemperance, attacking Willkie so viciously some observers wondered if he hadn't gone a bit unhinged.

The massive shift to a wartime economy that FDR had started caused a fatal rift between CIO leaders John L. Lewis and Sidney Hillman. As the CIO's president, Lewis predicted that wartime inflation would run amok, while "labor will find itself increasingly restrained in its attempts to adjust wages to the cost of living. These restraints would be exercised in the name of national defense, while all restraints upon the rapacity of the profiteers and munition makers would be relaxed under the same excuse." Through the summer of 1940 he tried to steer the CIO to an isolationist, antiwar position and spoke out against the draft. Then in the fall he shocked the nation by endorsing Wendell Willkie. The potential consequences to the election were significant: by 1940 the CIO had grown to nearly two million dues-paying members.

Lewis's defection brought Roosevelt and Sidney Hillman closer together. With so many Jewish immigrants on their rolls, the garment district's unions stood solidly with the president in anything he said or did against Hitler. When Roosevelt created a federal bureaucracy to oversee defense production—reviving the World War I National Defense Advisory Commission, which was to become the Office of Production Management, then the War Production Board—he filled it with dollar-a-year men from some of the country's largest corporations, including GM and U.S. Steel. For the sole labor representative, he shunned Lewis and appointed Hillman.

~

For much of the campaign, Roosevelt was just as elusive with Willkie as he'd been with members of his own party. He declined to debate him, or even to mention his name, saying, "Why should I advertise him?" Willkie was left struggling to draw fine distinctions between his own ideas and his opponent's. What Republicans wanted to hear, *Time* opined, was "griddle-hot partisan talk." In October, with the election just a month away, Willkie finally gave it to them. He completely reversed himself on preparing for war, now accusing FDR of being a warmonger. "We do not want to send our boys over there again," he told cheering crowds. "If you elect me, I will not send them over."

His numbers rose. The *New York Times* joined the *Tribune* in endorsing him. But Dorothy Thompson was dismayed. In October she startled Republicans when she switched her allegiance to FDR in "On the Record," declaring that it was no time to change leadership. Ogden Reid roused himself from his cups sufficiently to be enraged. His wife felt betrayed as well. When Thompson submitted a long column explaining her reasoning they refused to run it. By the following spring she'd leave the *Trib* and was writing "On the Record" for the liberal *Post*. Roosevelt cheered her defection; she began assisting Sherwood with his speechwriting.

Clare Luce used Thompson's absence as the excuse to launch yet another career for herself as Willkie's star stump speaker. She debuted at a rally at the Manhattan Center on 34th Street a week after Thompson's column ran, lampooning Thompson as a dizzy and frightened old lady and declaring that Roosevelt's weak foreign policies had led to France's fall. Thompson fired back on her CBS radio show, marveling that Luce "has torn herself loose from the Stork Club to serve her country in this serious hour." The two continued to lob volleys at each other for the rest of the campaign, as Luce dazzled crowds at Carnegie Hall, Town Hall, and at a prestigious *Herald Tribune*–sponsored forum in the Waldorf-Astoria ballroom, where she held her own among a list of speakers that included Thompson, Eleanor Roosevelt, Fiorello La Guardia, William Donovan, Archibald MacLeish, Wendell Willkie, and the president himself. She would triumph at Willkie's last campaign rally in Madison Square Garden on November 2, wowing a packed house of twenty-two thousand and another fifty thousand out on the street.

Willkie's rising numbers forced Roosevelt to come out and fight. In the last two weeks before the election he spoke to large rallies in Boston, Philadelphia, Cleveland, and New York. In New York he spent the day motoring around the boroughs, including opening and groundbreaking ceremonies for the Queens–Midtown Tunnel and the Brooklyn–Battery Tunnel. The nominally Republican La Guardia rode by his side.

That evening the president spoke to a packed crowd at Madison Square Garden. His speechwriting team of Hopkins-Rosenman-Sherwood begged him to assure voters he would not get the country "entangled" in war. According to Sherwood, the president complained, "But how often do they expect me to say that? I've repeated it a hundred times." Sherwood replied, "I know it, Mr. President, but they don't seem to have heard you the first time. Evidently you've got to say it again—and again—and again." A few nights later in Boston, Roosevelt declared, "I have said this before, but I shall say it again and again and again. *Your boys are not going to be sent into any foreign wars.*" The crowd roared.

So in the last days of the campaigning both candidates dissembled to exploit voters' fears. Sherwood later wrote that he was ashamed of convincing Roosevelt to do it, and Willkie would apologize for going too far in the heat of battle.

On November 5 Willkie waited out the results in a suite at the Commodore Hotel near Grand Central, Roosevelt and his inner circle at Hyde Park. Early reports leaned toward Willkie and put Roosevelt in a testy mood, but as the evening wore on the tide turned his way. Willkie got a respectable 45 percent of the popular vote, better than Alf Landon had done in 1936, but carried only ten states, mostly in the Midwest (plus Vermont and Maine, the only two states that had gone for Landon in '36), giving him 82 electoral votes to FDR's 449.

FDR took New York's crucial 47 electoral votes, but by no great margin, only 51.5 percent of the popular vote to Willkie's 48 percent. In the city, where voters had given him landslides in 1932 and 1936, Roosevelt slid to just under 60 percent, losing the most in the Italian and German communities, where his interventionism remained unpopular. On the other hand, his standing with black Americans, despite his hemming and hawing on issues vital to them, held very strong: two-thirds of their votes went to him.

On election day, CIO workers repudiated John L. Lewis and voted overwhelmingly for Roosevelt. Two weeks later Lewis was out as CIO president.

CHAPTER 23

New Yorkers and the Blitz

It was like something out of the Book of Revelation.

—*Ben Robertson*

On June 18, four days after Nazi tanks had rolled into Paris, the first issue of Ralph Ingersoll's daily newspaper *PM* hit the streets of New York. From the outset, *PM* reflected Ingersoll's obsession with the war in Europe and his willingness to fly headlong into the face of isolationism. The first eight pages of the inaugural issue were all news from a Europe reeling under the onslaught of the Blitzkrieg. In an open letter to his readers, Ingersoll noted: "*PM* starts off at the most critical moment in the history of the modern world. The news is too big, too terrible, to seem for a second like a break for a newspaper coming into being. Instead, it dwarfs us. It pitches us, without preparation, into the midst of horror." On the opposite page was a letter from President Roosevelt that began, "Dear Ralph: This is to welcome *PM* to the New York and to the American scene." Through the rest of the summer Ingersoll wrote a series of editorials arguing that "Nazi expansion will go on as long as Hitler is able to feed his people the raw meat and butter of conquest." It was foolish, he wrote, to think the war wouldn't come to America if Hitler wasn't stopped soon. A July 9 item headlined "What Nazi Bombs Could Do to a Brooklyn Street" juxtaposed photos of a typical block of houses in Brooklyn and a bombed-out row in England.

With the help of his many friends, colleagues, and even some enemies in the press, Ingersoll had whipped up such a fever of expectation that people actually mobbed the delivery trucks the first day. More than 450,000 copies were sold that day, roughly as many as the *Times*. It was a height from which *PM*'s circulation would quickly and permanently tumble.

Ingersoll had been planning *PM* since leaving Time Inc. a year earlier. Although he characteristically churned out miles of vague and high-minded verbiage describing his vision, the basic idea was simple enough, if quite radical: he would try to adapt the hugely popular pictures-and-text format of *Life* to a daily newspaper. He would use new printing technology and high-quality paper so the photos would look cleaner and crisper than they ever had in newspapers—and the ink wouldn't rub off on your fingers. Unlike other papers it would be printed in two colors. It would be a tabloid, so you could one-hand it on the subway, and it would be stapled, like a magazine. (Norman Bel Geddes mocked up a more radical design: an accordion-folded tabloid that was a single sheet of paper 32 feet long. Ingersoll wisely turned it down.) Because the city's other tabloids hit the streets in the morning, Ingersoll's would come out in the afternoon, hence its name, *PM*. (Another explanation was that it stood for *Picture Magazine*.)

And it would run no advertising. It would derive its income entirely from subscriptions and a five-cent cover price on weekdays (the city's other dailies were two or three cents), ten cents for the Sunday *PM Weekly*. That way, Ingersoll reasoned, he and his writers would be completely free to express their opinions.

Pitching *PM* as a liberal, maverick alternative to the city's many other dailies, Ingersoll raised start-up capital from investors including the unthinkably wealthy playboy and philanthropist John Hay Whitney, chewing gum king Philip Wrigley, A&P heir George Huntington Hartford II, and most importantly the department store heir and liberal *Chicago Sun* publisher Marshall Field III. Ingersoll rented cheap office space in a dowdy three-story warehouse at the corner of Sixth Avenue and Pacific Street in downtown Brooklyn. He bought time on the presses at the *Brooklyn Eagle*'s building a few blocks away, near what is now Cadman Plaza.

Although it could never have lived up to Ingersoll's hype, *PM* often managed to be lively and interesting, and it was always handsome, with large-scale, crisply reproduced photo spreads, illustrations and maps, and the two-color scheme, black and red or blue, throughout. Being new and different, it attracted celebrity writers including Lillian Hellman, Dashiell Hammett, Ernest Hemingway, Dorothy Parker, Ben Hecht, Erskine Caldwell, and Walter Winchell. They often contributed anonymously and used *PM* as an outlet for opinions too radical for their regular venues. Heywood Hale Broun began his sportswriting career at *PM*. I. F. Stone, well established as a left-wing investigative journalist at the *Post* and the *Nation*, became *PM*'s Washington correspondent. The artist Ad Reinhardt drew comics. Mayor La Guardia was an admirer and sometime contributor.

Ingersoll hired some of the best photographers in the business. Margaret Bourke-White contributed photos early on, but she was by then too much the celebrity diva for the scrappy upstart and lasted less than a year before going back to the Luce empire. The less flamboyant but no less trailblazing Mary Morris was *PM*'s go-to photographer. Born into a straitlaced Republican household in Chicago, she had rebelled early and come to New York to attend Sarah Lawrence. In 1936 she was the first female photographer hired by the Associated Press, known for her stylish and insightful portraits of figures ranging from Aldous Huxley to Gypsy Rose Lee. When Ingersoll started *PM* she jumped at the chance to work for a paper where quality photography was a priority.

Photographer Marjory Collins, a native New Yorker and Greenwich Village bohemian, described herself as "a rebel looking for a cause." She found it at *PM* and then, during the war, at the Office of War Information, where she specialized in documenting America's multiethnic character in images that ran pointedly counter to racism and xenophobia.

Another photographer really flourished at *PM*: Weegee. Born Usher Fellig in 1899, in a Jewish shtetl in an eastern province of Austria, he had come with his family to the Lower East Side at age ten. Usher's name was Americanized to Arthur as he passed through Ellis Island. Raised in a Yiddish home, he struggled to learn English, and his lingering accent would later be an integral part of his legend (and imitated by Peter Sellers when he played Dr. Strangelove).

As a freelance news photographer from the mid-1930s on, Weegee was a ubiquitous and astonishingly prolific shooter of crime scenes and criminals. His iconic images defined the noir metropolis he indelibly dubbed the Naked City. By 1940 he was an industry legend, but his photos in the dailies were frequently uncredited. It was *PM* that made him a public star by giving him space for bylined photo-and-text pieces in which he got to branch out from strict news to more leisurely human interest stories. On hot summer nights, he would go up to the rooftops of Lower East Side tenement blocks, lean over the edge, and photograph families sleeping curled up together on the fire escapes below him, the only place they might catch a puff of air in that pre-air-conditioned age. He was a regular at the missions along the Bowery. He snuck into movie palaces costumed as an usher and used infrared film to capture the slack, mesmerized faces of the crowds.

PM's many business troubles started the day it appeared. None of the hundred and fifty thousand charter subscribers got their copies of the first issue, in what was either a giant screw-up or sabotage. (Ingersoll suspected infiltrators from the Communist Party, who saw the left-leaning *PM* as competition for the *Daily Worker*.) With a five-cent cover charge and no advertising, *PM* was going to have to sell a couple of hundred thousand copies a day to break even. But as the novelty quickly wore off, street sales soon plummeted disastrously to below forty thousand. Already by September, Ingersoll was telling his shocked investors that *PM* had at best six weeks to live. Marshall Field bought out all the other backers and became *PM*'s sole owner.

⌣

On Monday, September 9, *PM* ran an article by its London correspondent Ben Robertson, a South Carolinian who'd moved to New York in the late 1920s to write for various papers and wire services, then joined *PM* when it started up. His report, headlined "Hail of Nazi Bombs Turned London into Hell on Earth," began: "These last two days have been like the end of civilization. They have been filled with the utterest and most savage horror and I for one am somewhat surprised still to be alive."

The previous Saturday, Robertson had driven out of London along the Thames with two other American journalists. One was Vincent "Jimmy" Sheean, a newsman's newsman. He had moved from the Midwest to Greenwich Village and then Paris in the 1920s. He covered wars and revolutions in Europe and Asia for the *Herald Tribune* and the *Daily News*, and was now with the *Saturday Evening Post*. His memoir *Personal History* inspired the Hitchcock film *Foreign Correspondent*, which had just been released.

The other was Edward R. Murrow. Raised in North Carolina and the Pacific Northwest, Murrow had come to New York City as a college student in 1930, then ran the Emergency Committee in Aid of Displaced German Scholars for three years. In 1935, at twenty-seven, he was hired as "director of talks" at CBS Radio. Network radio was still young and growing in the mid-1930s. NBC and CBS had been formed only in the late 1920s, and in 1935 the smaller Mutual Broadcasting System was only a year old. Backed by RCA, NBC was the oldest and largest, with two national networks called NBC Red and Blue (which later became ABC). The ruthlessly competitive David Sarnoff, who had emigrated with his family from Belarus to New York City in 1900, ran the RCA/NBC empire. Because CBS was younger, smaller, and not so well heeled, its boss William S. Paley, son of Jewish immigrants from Ukraine, focused on quality programming, including news, to build its audience. Mutual was a cooperative run by member stations around the country.

In 1937 CBS sent Murrow and his wife, Janet, to London, where his job was to chip away at NBC's dominance in European coverage. CBS's headquarters in London was three rooms in a building across the way from the BBC's massive art deco Broadcast House. Murrow's initial staff consisted of a receptionist and two office boys. For help he hired the print journalist William L. Shirer, who was just a few years older but had far more experience after reporting from Europe and the Middle East since the mid-1920s. In Berlin Shirer had been covering the Nazis' rise since 1933 and would write *Berlin Diary* (published in 1941) and *The Rise and Fall of the Third Reich* (1960). This was the start of the team that came to be known as Murrow's Boys. It would expand to include Eric Sevareid, Howard K. Smith, Charles Collingwood, and others who would go on to be stars of radio and then television news for decades.

⁓

With France in Nazi hands by the middle of June, Göring had been able to mass nearly the full might of the Luftwaffe on the coast, where it was only a five-minute flight across the Channel to England. That July, the Luftwaffe began clearing the skies over the Channel of British warplanes to gain complete control before the launching of the invasion Hitler wanted for September. Göring orchestrated an intense program of bombing and strafing raids over coastal England, targeting military airfields, radar installations, docks, factories, and other strategic sites. The RAF, roughly half the size of the Luftwaffe's forces, engaged them in what came to be called the Battle of Britain.

Although the first Eagle Squadron would not be operational for a few more months, a handful of American volunteers were already flying with the RAF during the Battle of Britain. They included two Brooklynites, one of them the shortest pilot in the RAF, the other the oldest. The shortest was Vernon Keogh, who at four-foot-eleven was inevitably nicknamed Shorty. In the late 1930s he'd been a barnstorming flier and parachute jumper who performed at airfields all around the United States, calling Brooklyn's Floyd Bennett Field near Coney Island his home base. When not flying he lived with his mother, a secretary, in Crown Heights. He was her only child.

In the spring of 1940 he'd made his way to Canada, then sailed from there to France, where he volunteered with the French air force. When the Germans overran France a few months later he escaped to England and joined the RAF. He had to sit on two extra cushions to see out of his Spitfire. When the first Eagle Squadron went into service he'd be a charter member—and one of its earliest casualties, shot down over the English Channel on February 15, 1941, one of the first Americans to be killed in World War II, a full ten months before America officially entered the war.

At forty-seven, the Eagle Squadron's Paul Haaren of Bay Ridge was the oldest pilot in the RAF. He and fellow Brooklynite Quentin Reynolds would meet up in London during the Blitz. Their fathers had known each other as school superintendents; John Henry Haaren was highly respected in New York and had a high school in Manhattan named for him.

⌒

Late on the night of Friday, August 23, after a day and night of heavy raids on airdromes and radar stations outside London, a squadron of German bombers, driven off course by heavy flak, dropped a load of bombs on the city, smashing some homes and killing civilians. It was the first nighttime bombing of the city. At 11:30 the following night, Murrow stood in Trafalgar Square with a microphone. He had orchestrated a broadcast for that night, with correspondents reporting from various spots around the city, called *London After Dark*. Murrow intended for it to give American listeners an intimate feel for what life in wartime England was like—and so prod them into sending help. An estimated 30 million Americans were transfixed by the broadcast, which still has the eerie power to raise the hairs on the back of one's neck. It began with ghostly sirens wailing in the near distance as Murrow intoned, "This..." He paused dramatically, a trademark. "...is Trafalgar Square...The noise that you hear at this moment is the sound of the air-raid sirens...A searchlight just burst into action off in the distance, one single beam sweeping the sky above me now." He held his microphone to the pavement to catch the footfalls as Londoners passed "like ghosts" on the darkened street to enter the air raid shelter behind him, one man calmly stopping to light a cigarette.

Elsewhere in the city, Sevareid, a lanky twenty-seven-year-old originally from North Dakota, reported from the ballroom of the Hammersmith Palais as the orchestra played soothing tunes and couples danced, defying the bombers. Earlier in the summer, Sevareid had broadcast from Paris as bombs fell, then got out of France one step ahead of the invaders. Larry LeSueur reported from an air raid station. Born in New York City, the son of a *Tribune* foreign correspondent, he'd gone to NYU and worked at Macy's before becoming a United Press stringer and then joining Murrow's team in 1939. He'd also gotten out of France in the nick of time. Jimmy Sheean reported from Piccadilly Circus.

The *London After Dark* program was a triumph for Murrow. It was far from the first field reporting on radio, but Murrow was exploring new ways to use radio to paint vibrant, intimate pictures in sounds and words. Thousands of miles away, Americans were hearing the actual sounds of the war as it was happening, and it began to make Murrow a household name back home.

During the Battle of Britain, American journalists would drive out of London with picnic baskets, heading down the Thames toward the coast where the fighting was heaviest, hoping to see some dogfights to report on. That's what Murrow, Sheean, and Robertson did on Saturday, September 7.

"We knew the day was perfect for an air battle and we wanted to get somewhere outside the city in order to watch its progress," Robertson wrote in *PM*. They bought "three tin hatfuls of apples from a farmer for two shillings and, coming upon a haystack on the edge of a turnip field, we lay down to eat and sleep in the sun." Soon they were watching "36 German bombers with British and German fighters about them in desperate combat." They jumped into a ditch and listened as waves and waves of more bombers passed overhead and antiaircraft shrapnel fell all around them for the next twelve hours.

"When night came we watched the most appalling and depressing sight any of us had ever witnessed. An immense flame lit the entire west sky." London was burning. "From our haystack we watched Armageddon. We watched searchlights, fires, smoke, red flares, white flares, and for hours we heard German planes coming over in twos and threes...It was like something out of the Book of Revelation."

Hundreds of German bombers hit the city in that raid. London's East End took the hardest pounding; almost five hundred civilians were killed, thousands more injured and trapped in rubble. No one knew it yet, but it was the start of the Blitz, more than two straight months of German bombs raining down on London every night. As it continued, London life moved underground at night. Tube stations served as shelters. BBC and CBS reporters broadcast from tiny studios in a dank subbasement of Broadcast House. Correspondents for the *New York Times* and the *Herald Tribune* led an American colonization of the luxurious Savoy Hotel, which had not only one of the deepest shelters but an excellent restaurant and the American Bar, both below street level. So many American journalists congregated at the bar that the Ministry of Information made it its official briefing room.

By the end of September Murrow was doing his live *London After Dark* reports from the rooftop of Broadcast House, describing the glimpses of bombers caught in searchlights, the glow of fires, the broken windows in a building across the way against an aural backdrop of bombs exploding and antiaircraft guns booming. They made him a hero to American audiences.

In England, however, Quentin Reynolds was the best-known and admired of the Americans. After a harrowing escape from France he'd gotten to London in time for the Blitz. In October and November he kept a daily record of his experiences. Ostensibly to keep his father back in Brooklyn from worrying, he wrote with a plucky insouciance and gallows wit that made surviving the nightly raids sound like a game. The first entry was about a party: "I made some very bad martinis and then Bob made some very good martinis. The sirens of course had sounded by now, and soon we heard the German planes overhead...But we all talked loudly and drank martinis and made believe that everything was just dandy."

The British appreciated his defiance and humor, so like their own. Random House would publish the pieces the following spring as the best-selling *A London Diary*. Reynolds furthered his reputation with the British by writing and narrating a nine-minute propaganda film called *London Can Take It!* Warner Bros. flooded the United States with prints; it ran simultaneously in eight movie theaters in downtown Manhattan and ultimately in twelve thousand theaters nationwide, with proceeds going for British relief. In 1941 Reynolds would go on BBC radio to read a satirical open letter to Goebbels, "Dear Doctor." Staid BBC officials worried that his language was too rough and "rude," but listeners all over England cheered him—as did Churchill, who after all had been saying rude things about Goebbels for years by then. Reynolds returned by popular demand to deliver an address to Hitler, "Dear Mr. S" (as in Schicklgruber). Both would be released as 78 rpm records.

⌒

Despite having the very competent Ben Robertson in England, Ralph Ingersoll decided he simply had to see the Blitz and report on it himself. He flew to England by way of Lisbon and spent two weeks there in October 1940, then came back and churned out a series of articles, some of them quite long, that ran every day in *PM* from mid-November into early December. Simon & Schuster rushed them out as the book *Report on England, November 1940* before the year was out.

Robertson would continue through 1942 as a war correspondent for *PM* and write a book, *I Saw England*, published by Knopf in 1941. In February 1943 he would be heading from New York to London to start a new job running the *Herald Tribune*'s desk there when the Pan Am Yankee Clipper in which he was flying crashed in Portugal, killing him.

⌒

The Blitzkrieg and the Blitz politicized an illustrator in New York who'd previously been known only for wacky advertisements and surrealist children's books. He drew his first political cartoon in the fall of 1940, lampooning Italian Fascists. A mutual friend showed it to Ingersoll. By January 1941 *PM* had its first regular editorial cartoonist: Theodor Geisel.

Geisel was born in 1904 in Springfield, Massachusetts, where his family ran the prosperous Kuhlmbach & Geisel brewery, referred to by locals as Come Back & Guzzle. Between the anti-German sentiments that swept the country during World War I—something he'd never forget—and the Prohibition years, his family's fortunes faded, but they were still able to send him to Dartmouth and then Oxford. He hated it and left after a year. Returning to the United States, he sold his first cartoon to the *Saturday Evening Post* in 1927 and used the check to move to New York, taking a studio walk-up in Greenwich Village. He signed the work "Seuss," his mother's maiden name, which his family pronounced the German way, *Soyss*. He soon added the "Dr."—a winking reference to the Ph.D. he failed to get at

Oxford. During the Depression, when so many others struggled, Dr. Seuss made a comfortable living drawing humorous advertisements for Standard Oil and saw his first couple of children's books published, including 1940's *Horton Hatches the Egg.*

He wouldn't do another children's book until after the war. Through 1941 and 1942 Dr. Seuss drew at least three editorial cartoons a week for *PM*, freely mixing odd fantasy creatures like those in his children's books with caricatures of his favorite targets: Hitler, Mussolini, Lindbergh and the American isolationists, nameless "Japs." For those who know only his children's books, the rude caricatures and racist stereotypes can be startling, but they're entirely consistent with other propaganda and editorializing of the war years.

CHAPTER 24

Harry Who?

With the election behind him, one of FDR's first acts was to have Harry and daughter Diana Hopkins move back into the White House. Roosevelt and Hopkins spent the 1940 Christmas season working with Sherwood and Rosenman on the text for a December 29 fireside chat. FDR relished the opportunity to speak his mind openly to the American public for the first time in months, and the address contained some of the most direct and harshest language he'd used yet to describe the Nazi menace. "The Nazi masters of Germany have made it clear that they intend not only to dominate all life and thought in their own country, but also to enslave the whole of Europe, and then to use the resources of Europe to dominate the rest of the world," he intoned. "A nation can have peace with the Nazis only at the price of total surrender...No man can tame a tiger into a kitten by stroking it. There can be no appeasement with ruthlessness...We must be the great arsenal of democracy. For us this is an emergency as serious as war itself." According to Sherwood it was Hopkins who suggested "arsenal of democracy," a phrase that went back to the Great War.

Under the Neutrality Acts, England had been allowed to buy American war matériel with gold, but its reserves were now running out. FDR could not sell combatants arms on credit, or loan them money with which to buy arms. As a work-around, his administration developed what came to be known as the Lend-Lease program, a spinoff and expansion of the earlier destroyers-for-bases idea. The United States would "lend" the Allies (England, Russia, China, and the Free French) warships, airplanes, ammunition, fuel, and other essentials, in return for leases on army and naval bases. After a great deal of rancorous argument, Congress would approve it the following March.

In January 1941, two men from New York went on separate trips to

England and served as FDR's unofficial envoys there. One of them, oddly, was Wendell Willkie. Roosevelt and Willkie had come out of the fall election battle with respect for each other. Roosevelt said he was glad he won but sorry Willkie lost. Within a week, Willkie was exhorting all Americans to stand together behind the president in the crisis that seemed to be coming. "He is your president," he said. "He is my president."

Carrying a personal note from Roosevelt to Churchill, Willkie went to England that January to assess the situation there. Returning to the United States greatly impressed with the courage and resolve of the British people, he testified in the Senate in favor of Lend-Lease, had a friendly private dinner with Roosevelt in the White House, and headed back to New York to urge a black-tie gathering of Republicans at the Waldorf-Astoria to take the lead in aiding Britain. Virtually the entire party leadership rejected that. The one exception was Thomas Dewey. Originally against Lend-Lease, he now changed his mind.

Harry Hopkins had left for England a little before Willkie as FDR's "personal representative" to discuss Lend-Lease and get an idea of exactly what equipment and supplies England needed. Speaking to reporters—who, if they were from conservative papers, still expressed nothing but scorn for Hopkins as the worst of tax-and-spend New Dealers—Roosevelt stressed that it was not an official mission in any way. "He's just going over to say 'How do you do?' to a lot of my friends," he said through his customary grin.

In England, when Churchill heard Harry Hopkins was coming, he reputedly said, "Harry who?" That soon changed. Hopkins landed in Poole, on England's southern coast, ill and exhausted after a five-day, multileg trip. His train was nearly bombed on its way to London. After dropping his bags at Claridge's he went straight to 10 Downing Street. "Thus I met Harry Hopkins," Churchill would write in *The Grand Alliance*, "that extraordinary man, who played, and was to play, a sometimes decisive part in the whole movement of the war. His was a soul that flamed out of a frail and failing body. He was a crumbling lighthouse from which there shone the beams that led great fleets to harbour."

By the time Hopkins left England six weeks later, the grateful British had nicknamed him Hurry Upkins. He bustled all around the island and reported his findings to Washington in official cables, but he also sent Roosevelt more personal letters handwritten on Claridge's stationery. "The people here are amazing from Churchill down and if courage alone can win—the result will be inevitable," he wrote. "But they need our help desperately and I am sure you will permit nothing to stand in the way." He met up with Willkie in London and reported to Roosevelt that Willkie pledged his total support for Lend-Lease.

Churchill dragged the sickly Hopkins around England and Scotland, showing him off to crowds as proof that "the Americans are with us." Asked to speak in Glasgow, Hopkins quoted the Book of Ruth: "Whither thou goest, I will go; and where thou lodgest, I will lodge: thy people shall be my people, and thy God my God." It brought tears to Churchill's eyes.

German bombers raided every day Hopkins and Willkie were there. Hopkins was having lunch with the king and queen at Buckingham Palace when bombs started falling. The assembled rose from the table, went "down two or three flights of stairs, through a dark hallway, led by a guard, through several doors and finally landed in a small lighted room with a table and chairs," where they calmly resumed their conversation until the all clear sounded an hour later.

⌣

When Hopkins's seaplane landed in New York's harbor in February after his six-week trip to England, two prominent and wealthy New Yorkers were waiting to meet with him: John Gilbert Winant and W. Averell Harriman. In short order they'd both be going to London themselves.

Roosevelt had just appointed Winant his new ambassador to the Court of St. James's, to enormous relief in the UK. England had survived the Blitz and staved off invasion, but the Nazis dominated on land and sea and the Americans had still not "come in" with anything like the support Roosevelt had pledged to King George in 1939. After almost three years of Winant's predecessor Joseph Kennedy—the former bootlegger, Wall Street financier, and father of John and Robert—England was desperate for a positive attitude. Kennedy had spent his time there distressing the British and enraging Roosevelt by preaching appeasement, predicting that England could never hold out against the Nazis, and publicly lecturing the president that aiding the British was useless.

Roosevelt forced Kennedy's retirement in the fall of 1940 and replaced him with a man who seemed very much his opposite. Kennedy was a scrappy Irish Catholic from Boston who schemed and clawed his way to riches and influence. John Gilbert Winant was a shy, gentlemanly WASP who let his work speak for him. He was born in 1889 and grew up in an affluent home on the Upper East Side. He was schooled and then became a teacher at the elite preparatory academy St. Paul's in New Hampshire. In the Great War he was a pilot, then came home and married a New York socialite whose grandfather had been president of the National City Bank of New York (now Citibank). They kept a palatial apartment on Park Avenue, but he spent more time on the country estate he bought in New Hampshire. A Republican reformist, he ran for governor of New Hampshire in 1924; his rival in the primary was Frank Knox. Winant won, becoming the youngest governor in the country, and one of the most progressive. He was in office through 1934, spending the last years as an enthusiastic supporter of Roosevelt and the New Deal, which made him no friends in the GOP.

In 1935, when Congress enacted the Social Security Act over bitter opposition from the GOP minority, Roosevelt appointed Winant to run the program, making him an even greater pariah to his party. Then he sent Winant to Geneva to head the International Labor Organization, the only League of Nations program the United States ever joined. Winant wrote frequent reports to FDR as Europe tumbled into war. He was in Prague when the Nazis occupied Czechoslovakia in March 1939, in Paris in June 1940 until a few hours before the Panzers rolled in, then in London during the Battle of Britain. While Ambassador Kennedy was predicting England's defeat, Winant was arguing that the British could hold out with enough American support.

When Winant arrived to take up his post in March, King George made an unprecedented gesture and went to the Windsor rail station to welcome him personally. Normally a new ambassador presented his credentials to the court in a formal ceremony and could wait weeks before getting a private audience with the monarch. Here was the king warmly greeting Winant like an old friend, then driving with him to Windsor Castle, where they had tea with Queen Elizabeth and a long talk. Winant would remain ambassador to England throughout the war.

⌣

Hopkins and Averell Harriman were friends, to the extent that Harriman had friends, as a consequence of Harry's hobnobbing. Starting in the early 1930s he spent many weekends at Arden, the Harriman family's baronial Hudson Valley estate. When business leaders howled at Roosevelt's nominating Hopkins for secretary of commerce in 1938, the White House enlisted Harriman's aid in corralling them. In 1940 Harriman helped Hopkins with his aborted presidential campaign. Now Hopkins returned the favors by convincing a reticent FDR to send Harriman to London to facilitate Lend-Lease and "recommend everything short of war that we can do to keep the British Isles afloat."

Roosevelt and Harriman were both scions of New York's super-rich elite, but the similarities ended there. Harriman was born in 1891 in a brownstone on East 51st Street near Park Avenue and grew up there and on the huge Arden estate. His father, E. H. Harriman, was a self-made railroad tycoon notorious as one of the most cutthroat of all Gilded Age robber barons. E. H. died when Averell was seventeen and on his way to college. Averell inherited a hyperactive instinct for competitiveness and enough wealth that he never wrote his own checks and rarely carried spending money. A 1952 *New Yorker* profile related the tale of his having to borrow a nickel from an assistant to buy a candy bar from a vending machine, then a penny for a bag of peanuts. He studied at Groton and Yale, where he was invited into the Skull and Bones society. Henry Luce, Archibald MacLeish, and George W. Bush's grandfather Prescott Bush were also "Bonesmen."

As landed Hudson Valley gentry the Roosevelts and Harrimans knew each other, but Franklin's family looked down on the Harrimans as parvenus. The charming, outgoing FDR had little time for the stiff, cool Harriman, who was absolutely bereft of a sense of humor or, many said, any personal empathy at all. Roosevelt may also have been envious. Even before the polio, he had always been more a cheerleader than an athlete. Harriman, on the other hand, was a tall, square-jawed sportsman, expert—and extremely competitive—at polo and skiing (he developed Sun Valley). And with his combination of enormous wealth and good looks he took his pick of pretty young women, from Ziegfeld Follies girls to debutantes.

Roosevelt had other reasons to be circumspect about Harriman. There was something self-serving and amoral about Harriman's forays into public life. He approached it like a businessman. When the United States entered the Great War and many of Harriman's cohort enlisted to serve as officers—and FDR was an assistant to the secretary of the navy—Harriman chose to stay home and profit from the war by building the largest merchant fleet in America to supply the Allies. Between the wars, his Wall Street banks funneled millions of dollars into two growth markets: the industrialization of the new Soviet Union and the recovery of Germany.

Harriman backed Roosevelt's 1932 presidential bid, then showed little interest in the New Deal's social welfare programs. He was, however, disturbed enough by early New Deal rumblings about regulating business that he lobbied for and got the job heading the National Recovery Administration, where he could personally keep FDR's gang from going too far. In the 1940 election he hedged his bets, contributing equally to the Roosevelt and Willkie campaigns.

⁓

In *Citizens of London*, a chronicle of Americans in wartime England, Lynne Olson describes Winant and Harriman as opposites in almost every way. The almost pathologically self-effacing Winant eschewed the pomp and hobnobbing that normally went with his post. At black-tie functions he was more likely to be found talking with the help than with dignitaries. He declined to stay at the ambassador's traditional residence and took a humble flat a short walk from the embassy. He worked long days and nights and ate the same severely rationed foods that Londoners did. He took on the suffering and problems of the British people and, later, the American GIs stationed there as personal burdens, performing more like a social worker than an ambassador. He earned undying respect in England but exhausted himself—and his personal finances.

Harriman swept into London with a very wealthy man's sense of entitlement and was instantly dining and weekending with the top tier of British society. He took a ground-floor suite in the Dorchester, one of the most luxurious and expensive hotels in the city; Charles Sweeny was also staying there. Harriman set up a vast, opulent office that an assistant compared to Mussolini's. He was convinced that he was vastly more qualified to help save England than Winant was, and he was soon greatly exceeding his Lend-Lease role, shoving Winant aside and inserting himself into the highest-level meetings and negotiations between the United States and England. Harriman ingratiated himself with Churchill, who never felt quite comfortable around the shy Winant.

When Hitler shocked the world yet again by invading the Soviet Union in June 1941, Churchill would nominate Harriman to lead the joint U.S.-British delegation that went to Moscow to ask Stalin what help he needed from them. Roosevelt, at Hopkins's urging, concurred. Harriman would return to Moscow with Churchill for another conference with Stalin in 1942, and in October 1943 Roosevelt, with Churchill's blessings, would appoint Harriman the U.S. ambassador to the Soviet Union. He'd remain at that post until January 1946, then briefly replace Winant as ambassador to England.

Winant and Harriman did have one thing in common. They both had affairs with Churchill women. Harriman wasn't in London a month when he took up with Pamela Churchill, Winston's twenty-one-year-old daughter-in-law. She had married Randolph Churchill after a two-week courtship in 1939. Randolph wanted an heir, which she gave him; she, the daughter of a frayed-cuff Dorset aristocrat, wanted an entrée to London society, which he gave her. Otherwise they were a bad match, and soon after his regiment was posted to North Africa she set her sights on the wealthy American. Harriman was thirty years her senior and flattered by the attention; he also saw her as a useful go-between with the prime minister, who liked Pamela better than his son did.

Before long she was living in Harriman's suite at the Dorchester, where she hosted some of the most lavish parties in wartime London, stocked with champagne and caviar only a man like Harriman had the money and connections to bring into the city. Vivacious, fun, and sexually adept, she attracted men easily and had affairs with other New Yorkers in London during the war, including Ralph Ingersoll's financial backer Jock Whitney, and William Paley, who called her "the greatest courtesan of the century." When Harriman left for Moscow in 1943, she instantly took up with Ed Murrow, who came close to wrecking his marriage to be with her.

Winant's affair was characteristically quieter and far more discreet. It was with Sarah Churchill, the prime minister's favorite though somewhat wayward twenty-seven-year-old daughter. When she met Winant in 1941 she was married to another man but they had drifted apart.

After taking dance lessons to counter her girlhood clumsiness, in 1935 the twenty-year-old had distressed her parents by taking a part in the chorus line of a touring musical revue. She promptly fell in love with the show's star, the thirty-seven-year-old, twice-divorced Vic Oliver. Born Victor von Samek to a prosperous Jewish textile merchant in Vienna, he had studied music under Gustav Mahler before sailing in the 1920s to New York City, where he struggled for years in vaudeville and musical theater until developing a successful comedic persona as a classical musician with a funny German accent. When Vic returned to New York in

1936, Sarah waited for her twenty-first birthday to announce her plans to marry him. Her father pronounced him "common as dirt" and an "itinerant vagabond," so she ran away, sailing to New York City. Randolph sailed two days later in pursuit. Newspapers on both sides of the Atlantic ran front-page stories about the "runaway debutante," and a crowd of reporters was surrounding Vic when he came to the Hudson Street pier to meet her. She headed for the Waldorf, where Bernard Baruch took her in. Randolph went home to reconcile the parents with the inevitable. Vic and Sarah were married in a civil ceremony at City Hall on Christmas Eve 1936 and sailed for England the same day.

By the time Sarah met Winant she had developed her performing career, Vic had turned out to be a louse, and though they wouldn't divorce until after the war it was over between them. Winant and Sarah would manage to keep their relationship a secret to all but a few close friends for the duration of the war.

CHAPTER 25

Unlimited Emergency

On Tuesday, May 27, 1941, a paltry seventeen thousand fans trickled into the Polo Grounds for the Giants' first night game of the season. The lackluster attendance might have been partly due to the poor early season both the Giants and their opponents the Boston Braves were having. But the bigger reason was that earlier in the day the White House had announced that due to an "unlimited national emergency" the president would be addressing the nation by radio at 10:30 p.m. Most people, in New York and around the country, planned to be home around their radios.

The words "unlimited national emergency" came from Hopkins. According to Sherwood, the president was mildly shocked when he first read the words in a draft his speechwriting trio had prepared. Isolationists were still attacking him viciously. Roosevelt, as always, was reluctant to stir them up further; in fact, he had postponed this speech for two weeks, pretending to have a bad cold. But the interventionists in his inner circle, particularly Hopkins and Stimson, had been hounding him to speak boldly and definitively about an urgent need to support the Allies. Churchill was pleading with him to get into the fight now or all might be lost. In the end, Roosevelt opted to keep Hopkins's phrase in what was the grimmest, darkest speech he had yet made.

At the Polo Grounds, the game started at 8:40 and was tied 1–1 in the seventh inning when the umpires called a time-out. The players left the field, the lights dimmed eerily, and FDR's voice rolled out of eleven giant loudspeakers. Elsewhere around the city, waiters stopped serving at the Stork Club, the band at the El Morocco fell silent, barkeeps unplugged the jukeboxes.

At the start of a deeply sobering forty-five-minute talk the president said, "What we face is cold, hard fact. The first and fundamental fact is that what started as a European war has developed, as the Nazis always intended it should develop, into a world war for world domination." Outlining all the steps he'd been taking to both build up the nation's defenses and supply aid to England, he said, "Our whole program of aid for the democracies has been based on hard-headed concern for our own security and for the kind of safe and civilized world in which we wish to live. Every dollar of material that we send helps to keep the dictators away from our own hemisphere."

He went on to paint an apocalyptic picture of a world under Nazi domination, a world with no freedoms, in which all workers were reduced to slave labor, the only religion allowed would be the worship of Hitler, and "our children... wander off, goose-stepping in search of new gods." Then he declared, "We do not accept, we will not permit, this Nazi 'shape of things to come.' It will never be forced upon us, if we act in this present crisis with the wisdom and the courage which have distinguished our country in all the crises of the past."

In conclusion, he said: "I have tonight issued a proclamation that an unlimited national emergency exists and requires the strengthening of our defense to the extreme limit of our national power and authority. The nation will expect all individuals and all groups to play their full parts, without stint, and without selfishness, and without doubt that our democracy will triumphantly survive."

A little before midnight, Giants fans watched their team pull out a 2–1 win in the ninth inning, then everyone quietly filtered out of the stadium.

Irving Berlin was in the White House that night and sat with Sherwood in the East Room as the president delivered his speech. Afterward, as Eleanor and a few close friends gathered in the Monroe Room, Roosevelt insisted that the composer sit at the piano and bang out "Alexander's Ragtime Band" to cheer them all up.

⌣

At the same time, working a hunch that Germany would soon invade Russia, *Life's* photo editor Wilson Hicks sent Margaret Bourke-White back to the Soviet Union to be present if and when it happened. Her husband of two years, Erskine Caldwell, went along.

Margaret had made a point of meeting Caldwell back in 1936, when he was just about the most celebrated and controversial writer in America.

His novels *God's Little Acre* and *Tobacco Road*, with their depictions of brutish, cretinous, thoroughly debased sharecroppers, had scandalized the South, titillated the North, and been banned in both regions. A Broadway adaptation of *Tobacco Road* opened in December 1933 and ran an astonishing 3,182 performances, by two years the longest run on Broadway at the time, not closing until May 1941. To counter criticisms that his stories were wild exaggerations, Caldwell toured the South to gather material for a nonfiction book. Margaret convinced him she should go along. They were both famous, powerful in their spheres, and control freaks, and they fought fiercely until she smoothed things over by seducing him. The result of their collaboration was the 1937 book *You Have Seen Their Faces*, which combined his words and her photos to document the wretched poverty and hopelessness he'd fictionalized in his novels. Caldwell left his wife and married Margaret in 1939, after a couple of years of their shocking people by keeping a room together at the Mayflower on Central Park West.

Hicks's intuition proved correct. Hitler invaded the Soviet Union on June 22. In Moscow's opulent Hotel National, the Caldwells had rooms previously occupied by Leon Trotsky and the Lindberghs, with a balcony facing the Kremlin. They were the only American journalists in the city when German bombers, following Hitler's order to pound Moscow into rubble, began nightly raids. For twenty-two nights, with bombs dropping all around them, Margaret took stunning rooftop pictures of the searchlights and fires while Caldwell broadcast radio reports.

While this was going on, Harry Hopkins flew by B-17 and B-24 back to England, arriving pale and nauseous for meetings with Churchill at Downing Street and Chequers. He brought Churchill cheese, which was in short supply in England, and Cuban cigars. At Chequers, Clementine mothered Hopkins again, trying to make sure he ate, slipping a hot water bottle in his bed at night. One of the physicians assigned to Hopkins told Sherwood that he knew Hopkins often poured his prescribed medicines down the toilet. When FDR learned that Churchill and Hopkins had stayed up talking past 3 a.m., he sent a cable to General George Marshall, the U.S. Army chief of staff, who was also in England: *Please put Hopkins to bed and keep him there under 24-hour guard by Army or Marine Corps. Ask the King for additional assistance if required on this job.*

Quentin Reynolds drove out to Chequers to help Hopkins write an address he gave on the BBC, in which he cheered the British public again with lines such as, "The President is at one with your Prime Minister in his determination to break the ruthless power of that sinful psychopath in Berlin." Dorothy Thompson and Sinclair Lewis were also at Chequers. With German troops taking Smolensk and surrounding Leningrad, Hopkins met with the Soviet ambassador to England. They decided Harry should go to Moscow to convey personally to Stalin Roosevelt's assurances that if the Red Army could hold out a while, supplies would eventually be coming. Hopkins spent most of the grueling twenty-one-hour flight to Archangel crammed into the frigid tail gun blister of an RAF Catalina. From Archangel he took another flight to Moscow, seeing the widespread bomb damage from the air.

When Bourke-White heard that Hopkins had arrived, she sought him out and dogged him to get her an audience with Stalin. Hopkins arranged it, and she returned the favor by taking him shopping and helping him pick out Russian peasant dresses for Diana. She wore red shoes and a red ribbon in her hair to the Kremlin. Hopkins accompanied her and made the introductions.

She had seen "so many giant statues" of Stalin that "I had come to think of him as a man of superhuman size," she wrote in her memoir. "He was standing very stiff and straight in the center of the rug. His face was gray, his figure flat-chested. He stood so still he might have been carved out of granite. There was nothing superhuman about his size. My own height is five feet five, and Stalin was shorter than I am. My first reaction was 'What an insignificant-looking man!'...I went away thinking this was the most determined, the most ruthless personality I had ever encountered in my life." Hopkins left for Washington the next day with her film in his luggage, and *Life* ran her photos in its September 1 issue.

CHAPTER 26

Spies, Traitors, and a Flying Ace

In January 1941, New Yorkers had gotten their very own Nazi flying ace to gawk at, and in some cases fawn over. In June they witnessed an even bigger Nazi spectacle.

Oberleutnant Franz Baron von Werra was born into a noble but poor Swiss family in 1914. He joined the Luftwaffe in 1936. He was a dashing playboy, a showboat and braggart who delighted the Nazi press by keeping a lion cub at his squadron's aerodrome and telling heroic tales about the numbers of enemy planes he'd shot down. They dubbed him the Red Devil and the Terror of the RAF. He was also intelligent, resourceful, and physically tough, and as a POW he gave his captors endless headaches.

His remarkable exploits, dramatized in the mid-1950s book and movie *The One That Got Away*, began in September 1940 when a Spitfire pilot shot down his Me 109 onto a field in Kent, where an unarmed cook from a nearby searchlight battery apprehended him. He made his first escape attempt just days later. After a period of interrogation in London, he was sent to a POW camp in the Lancashire countryside. There he made a more successful try, slipping away from a group of prisoners who were taken out for exercise. Crossing moors and woods trying to reach the coast, living on apples he picked up from the ground, he evaded a manhunt for three cold, wet days and nights. In a new camp in Derbyshire, he and other Luftwaffe pilots managed a bold getaway straight out of *The Great Escape*, tunneling their way out, equipped with disguises and false papers created in the camp. Posing as a Dutch pilot with the RAF, von Werra bluffed his way to an airfield and was actually in the cockpit of a parked Hurricane trying to fire up the engine when an RAF officer stopped him at gunpoint.

In January 1941 the British shipped von Werra and other German prisoners to Canada, where even if they did escape they'd have to cross the Atlantic to get back into the fight. Von Werra jumped out a window of the train taking them from Montreal to the camp. He landed in a snowbank, then, despite the deep cold, he trekked on foot to the ice-clogged Saint Lawrence River. He stole a rowboat, dragged it across ice and snow to the river, and floated rudderless and without paddles until he reached the ice pack at the other shore. There he hitched a ride into the riverfront town of Ogdensburg, New York, and surrendered to the police.

By the next day the Ogdensburg police station was jammed with reporters and photographers who had raced up from New York City. Baron von Werra put on a grand show for them, strutting and bragging so outrageously that one reporter dubbed him Baron Munchausen. In his photo in the next day's *New York Times* he grinned broadly, the white bandages on his frostbitten ears sticking out comically. He was allowed to call the German consulate at 17 Battery Place in New York City, and his bail on a charge of entering the country without going through proper immigration procedures was quickly posted. He was whisked away one hour before Canadian authorities could serve him with a summons for stealing the rowboat. That charge carried only a $35 fine but would have required him to return to Canada to face a judge.

In New York City, the German consul general instructed von Werra to stop showing off for the press, but he couldn't keep the twenty-six-year-old out of the nightclubs and Broadway theaters, where the gossip columnists made a game of spotting him as he lived it up. The baron also accepted invitations to parties and dinners in Yorkville. As the London *Times* put it, "Escaped Hun Baron Women's Pet in U.S."

Meanwhile in Washington, the British, German, and Canadian governments were all lobbying to have von Werra handed over to them. Neutrality law prohibited the Americans from giving escaped prisoners back to their captors, but at the same time they were reluctant to send an experienced fighter pilot back to the Luftwaffe. His situation came to a head on March 22 when two other German POWs escaped and crossed the frozen Saint Lawrence on foot, entering Ogdensburg, chased by Canadian police. After a few hours they were handed over to the Canadians, and a Justice Department official suggested that von Werra might be sent back as well.

At that he disappeared from view. Nothing was seen or heard of him until a month later, April 23, when the papers announced that he had fled "in flagrant abuse of neutral hospitality" and was believed to be in Peru trying to arrange passage to Germany.

He was in fact already back in Germany. On instructions from Berlin, the consulate had helped him sneak out of New York two days after the other POWs were handed over. He traveled by train, alone and unnoticed, to El Paso. There, disguising himself as a Mexican worker, he walked across the bridge over the Rio Grande into Ciudad Juárez. He caught another train to Mexico City, where the German embassy gave him the false passport he used to take a series of international flights that brought him to Berlin on April 18. Hitler personally awarded him a Knight's Cross of the Iron Cross. Von Werra was back in a Messerschmitt by summer, posted briefly to the Russian front, then to coastal defense in Holland. In October his Me 109 developed engine trouble and crashed into the sea. His body was never found.

The embarrassment von Werra's escape caused Washington had serious repercussions for German nationals in the United States—and for one Brooklyn-born journalist in Berlin. The Justice Department announced in April that from then on the borders were closed to escaped prisoners. In May, hundreds of German merchant seamen who had been allowed to stay in the United States since the start of the war were arrested and deportation proceedings against them began.

In Manhattan, Manfred Zapp and Günther Tonn, who ran the German Trans-Ocean News Service on Madison Avenue, were arrested in May and jailed on Ellis Island. Zapp, whom *Time* described as a "small, dark, dapper man, with horn-rimmed glasses and big beak nose anchored by a full mustache," had been in New York since 1938, living well in the Waldorf-Astoria. He and Tonn had been indicted in March for failing to report that Trans-Ocean, supposedly established to promote international trade, was in fact a leading distributor of Nazi propaganda in the United States and Latin America. They'd been released on bail but were now detained, Justice explained, to prevent their fleeing the country the way von Werra had.

At the same time, the *Herald Tribune* reported that Kurt Rieth, a former German minister to Austria, had been in New York for two months, also staying at the Waldorf, in a $600-a-month suite. He was accused of providing covert support for American isolationist groups on the one hand, and on the other offering American oil companies twenty-five cents on the dollar for their holdings in Nazi-held eastern Europe, from which they weren't earning a penny. Justice officials, calling him "the No. 1 Nazi in the U.S.," had him arrested and taken to Ellis Island as well.

Four days after the arrest of Zapp and Tonn, in what was widely interpreted as a retaliatory act, the Gestapo arrested United Press reporter Richard C. Hottelet in Berlin on charges of "suspicion of espionage." Hottelet was born in Brooklyn to German immigrant parents; the family spoke German at home. After graduating from Brooklyn College in 1937 he went to study at the University of Berlin. When a philosophy professor walked into class wearing a brown shirt and gave the Nazi salute, Hottelet dropped out and became a stringer for United Press in Berlin, his disgust for the Nazis unconcealed.

After Hottelet's arrest the United States raised the stakes in June, ordering the German consulate and Trans-Ocean to close. That month in his Ellis Island cell, Günther Tonn cut his neck and one wrist with a razor, in what officials scoffed was "a bluff at suicide…He did not lose much blood and will soon be all right." They suggested it was "a play for publicity and sympathy."

In July it was announced that Hottelet and another American journalist taken by the Gestapo were to be released in exchange for three German prisoners in the United States: Zapp, Tonn, and Rieth. Hottelet arrived back home in New York on August 1. He had not been mistreated in captivity—Hitler was not yet ready to poke the sleeping American giant too vigorously. Hottelet would later return to Europe to cover the war as one of Murrow's Boys.

⁀

Six months after von Werra made his flamboyant entry into the city, FBI agents swooped down on Nikolaus Ritter's spy ring, making thirty-three arrests. The ring had been infiltrated and brought down by a German-American double agent, Wilhelm "William" Sebold.

Wilhelm Sebold was born in the heavily industrialized Ruhr Valley in 1899. His father, who drove a beer wagon, named him for Kaiser Wilhelm. As a soldier in the kaiser's army during the Great War Wilhelm survived a gas attack, but it left his health permanently damaged. Six-foot-three and bone thin, he would be in and out of hospitals the rest of his life, the pain and frustration of it making him nervous and irritable.

In the postwar years the Ruhr was its own kind of battlefield, first when workers' soviets and right-wing freikorps murdered each other on the streets, then when French troops occupied it for nonpayment of reparations, bringing more violence. Like many other Germans, Sebold fled the chaos in the 1920s, making his way as a merchant seaman first to South America, eventually landing in Yorkville in 1929. He settled in, became "William," married a neighborhood German girl who worked as a maid for a wealthy Park Avenue family, scrambled for odd jobs as the Depression worsened, and took U.S. citizenship in 1936.

Although his wife's family had some dealings with Yorkville's pro-Nazis, Sebold had seen enough in his life to be wary of politics. When he sailed back to Germany in 1939 it wasn't to support Hitler but to try and find steady work in the booming wartime economy there. The return of a German-born American citizen was unusual enough to pique the interest of the Abwehr, which had two agents meet him when his ship landed. Over the course of 1939 Abwehr representatives including Ritter used threats against Sebold and his family to coerce him into spying for them, and then trained him in how to build and use a shortwave radio.

Sebold only pretended to go along. Meanwhile he secretly sought help from the U.S. embassy in Cologne. When he returned to New York in February 1940, using his Abwehr cover name Harry Sawyer, FBI agents were waiting for him. They helped him set up an office as a consulting engineer in what was just becoming known as the Newsweek Building, at 152 West 42nd Street in Times Square. (It was originally built as the Knickerbocker Hotel by John Jacob Astor IV. His son Vincent, FDR's chum, inherited the Beaux Arts behemoth when John Jacob went down with the *Titanic*. Vincent redeveloped it as an office building and moved *Newsweek* there in 1940. Given his avid interest in espionage, Vincent gladly cooperated with the FBI in the Sebold case.)

The FBI bugged Sebold's office with audio recording equipment and took the room next to it so agents could film through a two-way mirror. Then they trailed him as he set out to meet Ritter's other spies in New York. One of them was Lilly Stein, a former Viennese prostitute whom one of the FBI men described as "a well-built, good-looking nymphomaniac with a good sense of humor." She was also Jewish, and when Hitler annexed Austria in 1938, the Abwehr used threats against her life to frighten her into spying. Arriving in New York City in the spring of 1939, she had opened a dress shop as a front and started mailing reports to Germany, mostly low-level information. The FBI was soon intercepting her mail and removing anything that might be useful to the Abwehr.

Sebold also contacted Fritz Duquesne, who preferred meeting in downtown Automats near the office he had rented in the Wall Street area for his front, Air Terminals Company. On company stationery Duquesne wrote breezy letters to aircraft manufacturers like Grumman asking for information on the latest technological developments, which was often naively provided.

Herman Lang was still living in Ridgewood and still working at Norden when Sebold met him. In June 1940 Sebold gave the FBI the startling news about the Norden bombsight. Hoover informed Roosevelt.

The member of Ritter's spy ring Sebold least liked meeting was an American of German heritage, Everett "Ed" Roeder. Born in the Bronx, son of a pianist who taught at Juilliard, Roeder was bright, undisciplined, and unscrupulous. After studying engineering at Cornell he worked, on and off, as an ideas man at Sperry Gyroscope Company in Brooklyn. Elmer Sperry pioneered the development of the gyroscope and founded the company in 1910. Gyroscopes revolutionized navigation for ships and aircraft, improved the aim of long-range artillery, and made possible the air-dropped torpedo, in effect the first cruise missile. In 1915, expecting windfall profits from the Great War, Sperry built the eleven-story concrete factory that still stands near the Brooklyn foot of the Manhattan Bridge. Staying on the cutting edge of innovation—a stereoscopic range finder, direction-finding radio, automatic guidance for antiaircraft guns, and its own version of an automated bombsight—the company kept expanding and diversifying after the war, becoming Sperry Corporation in 1933, with offices in Rockefeller Center. As World War II approached the company enjoyed more growth, its workforce blooming from sixteen hundred in 1938 to fifty-six hundred in 1941.

All of this made it a prime target for the Abwehr. Roeder came to Ritter's attention as an insider who could be bought in 1936. Ritter paid his passage for a visit to Germany, where the Abwehr wined and dined him. Roeder returned to the United States on the Abwehr's payroll at $200 a month, making him their highest-paid spy in the country.

When Sebold contacted Roeder he was living in the suburban town of Merrick on Long Island and a member of the top secret Sperry team developing an autopilot for bombers. Sebold would take the Long Island

Rail Road from Penn Station out to a stop where Roeder picked him up in his Buick, and then they conducted their business driving around. Roeder made Sebold nervous. He had a temper and always carried a pistol.

The FBI helped Sebold set up shortwave equipment in a secluded cabin near Centerport on Long Island's north shore. Every telegrapher has a distinctive "fist," or way of tapping the key. An FBI agent learned how to imitate Sebold's and carried on hundreds of conversations with Sebold's handlers in Hamburg, gathering valuable information on Abwehr activities and sending disinformation in return. While this went on, agents filmed Sebold's meetings with Duquesne and other agents through the two-way mirror in his office.

After eighteen months of collecting information and fattening dossiers, Hoover ordered his agents to spring the trap. On Sunday, June 29, they swept up twenty-three suspected Nazi spies in New York and New Jersey. More arrests followed in the next few days, bringing the total to thirty-three. They included Duquesne, Lang, Roeder, Lilly Stein, and Richard Eichenlaub, the Little Casino proprietor who'd been a suspect in the previous summer's bombing at the world's fair. It was, Hoover crowed, the largest roundup of spies in U.S. history, and the end of "one of the most active, extensive and vicious groups we have ever had to deal with." Winchell led his Sunday night broadcast with the news.

On Monday, twenty-five of them were marched in handcuffs into the medieval-looking Federal Building in downtown Brooklyn for arraignment. They were charged with failing to register as agents of a foreign government and the far more serious "conspiracy to transmit to a foreign government information vital to the national defense of the United States." Seven pleaded guilty right away. Duquesne, Lang, and the rest maintained their innocence. After bail was announced they were all jailed in Greenwich Village, the men in the Federal House of Detention on West Street and three females in the Women's House of Detention next to the Jefferson Market Courthouse, where other inmates taunted them out of "patriotic feeling."

Sixteen remaining defendants would be perp-walked before newsmen and a few hundred oglers outside the Brooklyn courthouse on the morning of September 8. With Duquesne setting the tone, the defendants acted defiantly jaunty and flashed the V sign for the cameras. Duquesne's self-inflated notoriety came back to bite him now. Prosecutors portrayed him as "one of the most dangerous criminals in the United States," and the mastermind of what the FBI and the press insisted on calling the "Duquesne Spy Ring." For stealing the secret of the Norden bombsight, Lang was the other star. The trial would grind on slowly through September, October, November. The FBI's films of conspirators in Sebold's office were screened, and Sebold shyly testified. Testifying in his own defense, Fritz Duquesne mugged and showboated, telling hours-long tales of his adventures, much of it lies, as though he were at a cocktail party, not a felony trial. The *Sun* described his performance as "bizarre" and wondered if he was preparing to cop an insanity plea.

—

That summer, yet another New York Nazi sympathizer was making news. In July Laura Ingalls went on a speaking tour for the America First Committee. She was now flagrantly pro-Hitler, citing passages from *Mein Kampf* and even giving the stiff-armed Nazi salute to her crowds. Although the AFC's moderates fretted about that, they couldn't deny she attracted enthusiastic audiences.

What they didn't know was that she was actually being paid by the Nazis as a publicity flack. Earlier in the year she had gone to the German embassy in Washington, D.C., to see Baron Ulrich von Gienanth, who ran the Gestapo in the United States. He was paying her $300 a month to spread Nazi propaganda. On the road, she corresponded with von Gienanth and the embassy's chargé d'affaires Hans Thomsen. When the Germans sank a British cruiser, she wrote, "I could tear the skies in triumph. Heil Hitler!"

Her crash landing would come soon.

CHAPTER 27

Civil Defense and Amateur Intelligence

In the spring of 1941 Roosevelt's aides completed plans for a new agency, the Office of Civilian Defense (OCD), to coordinate city and state preparedness programs in case of attack by, for instance, enemy bombers. The Midwest had little to worry about, but cities on the coasts could be vulnerable to carrier-based air attacks and, as events would soon prove, submarines. Secretary of War Stimson took the threat seriously, and Mayor La Guardia had been fretting about it for some time.

For his part, Roosevelt had been casting about for a way to reward the mayor for his campaign support the previous fall without letting him get too involved in the administration's business. He decided to offer La Guardia the job of running OCD. Most of his advisers were against it; they considered La Guardia a loose cannon best left rolling on the deck of New York City. But FDR insisted. On May 17, the day before he flew to Washington to accept, La Guardia hosted a giant "I Am an American Day" rally that drew an estimated three-quarters of a million New Yorkers to the Sheep Meadow in Central Park. Eddie Cantor joked with the crowd; Bill "Bojangles" Robinson warned Hitler he better stay out of Harlem; Kate Smith and Irving Berlin led the assembled in a rendition of "God Bless America." The entire crowd stood, raised their right hands, and recited a version of the pledge of allegiance with additional language about defending the flag "in the crisis that now confronts my country." Interior Secretary Ickes (who had been among those opposed to the mayor's OCD appointment) came to deliver the administration's message that "If we are to retain our own freedom, we must do everything in our power to aid Britain." No one enjoyed the day more than the mayor, its master of ceremonies. He warned "Adolf, Benito and Joe" that "We are not afraid to defend our institutions." Then he led a combined police and fire department band in a rousing Sousa march, swinging his baton so wildly he almost tumbled off the stage.

Roosevelt and La Guardia assured each other that he could run OCD and New York City at the same time. They were wrong. Racing around the country the way he bounced around his city, La Guardia soon ran himself to exhaustion and generated confusion and chaos in an already haphazard field of local programs. With criticism mounting, he asked Eleanor Roosevelt to help him run OCD, and she agreed, but found she could do little to rein him in.

A few other prominent New Yorkers pitched in for Roosevelt's defense buildup in a different way. During the Great War, organized efforts to give servicemen on leave things to do besides getting drunk and chasing whores had seen measured success. With the start of conscription in 1940, the War Department began looking into ways to build and expand on what had been learned. With one and a half million Americans in uniform by the end of 1940, FDR called for a private organization that would provide them clean, morale-building entertainment when on leave. The YMCA, YWCA, Salvation Army, and other groups got together and formed the United Service Organizations, the USO, in 1941. USO clubs were to be "a home away from home." They'd serve soft drinks and coffee, not alcohol, and instead of hookers there would be hand-picked young women for the purpose of chaperoned conversation and dancing only.

The USO opened an office in the Empire State Building. The government agreed to build the clubs, but the USO would have to raise its own funds for everything else. To that end, Arthur Sulzberger of the *New York Times* recruited Tom Dewey as the first national chairman. Dewey flew around the country in an army DC-3 and raised $16 million for the organization in a year. After him the Wall Street banker Prescott Bush took over the chair.

The USO turned out to be one of the greatest success stories of the war. More than a million volunteers would serve. In 1942, an average of 4.5 million military personnel would visit a USO club every month, and by 1944 it was more than 12 million a month.

⁀

In June, with William Stephenson's tutoring and Frank Knox's backing, William Donovan presented the president with a vague but persuasive plan for an intelligence "superagency," above and independent of all others, that would "collect, analyze, and correlate information and data which may bear upon national security," reporting its findings directly to the White House and Joint Chiefs. J. Edgar Hoover went apoplectic, as did all the other heads of the existing agencies. But Roosevelt loved the idea of having a spy organization of his own, a larger version of what Vincent Astor was doing for him in New York. In July he named Donovan his coordinator of information and gave him lavish, off-the-books White House funding to get started.

The COI started with two basic missions, which could be summed up as input and output: intelligence gathering and analysis on the one hand, and the dissemination of propaganda based on that intelligence on the other. While Donovan organized the input side in Washington, he enlisted Robert Sherwood to assemble the propaganda operations, called the Foreign Broadcast Information Service, in New York. Each of them hired his own staff. For COI Donovan recruited friends from Wall Street law firms, wealthy Ivy Leaguers, and interventionist Republicans. National pollster Elmo Roper helped think about how to gather and analyze data. Roosevelt's son Jimmy, now a captain in the Marine Corps, came on to be Donovan's liaison with the prickly military agencies. Felix Frankfurter's sister Estelle read and digested government reports.

Allen Dulles volunteered to coordinate COI intelligence gathering in New York City. Early in 1942 he rented offices on the thirty-sixth floor of the International Building at Rockefeller Center—by no coincidence, just down the hall from William Stephenson and the BSC. Information flowed freely in both directions along that hallway. He developed contacts with other foreign intelligence services headquartered in the city—Free French, Belgian, Czech, Polish, Dutch—and with the various American agencies as well. For instance, he passed along to the FBI any information he caught on Nazi spies in the city. That didn't stop him from placing a mole in the FBI office, or the FBI from tapping his phones. He sent agents out to interview refugees newly arrived in the city, and sailors coming into the port who might have useful information on port cities in Hitler's Europe. A Polish seaman drew them a sketch of Nazi fortifications at Genoa. Dulles mined information from New York–based corporations doing business in Europe as well. As he built his staff his operation expanded to three more floors, behind the cover name Statistical and Research Office for the Coordination of Information. Besides offices with encrypted phone lines there were vaults for secret documents, a laboratory for creating spy gear, and a printing plant forging agents' documents.

⁓

At the outset, Donovan reasoned that collecting and organizing data was only half of COI's job. Just as important was how to present the information in quickly digestible form to Roosevelt, a very busy man with a notoriously short attention span. Donovan had made good use of visual aids in the courtroom, and now he devoted nearly a quarter of his original budget to set up a Visual Presentation Branch. The unit was supposed to be secret, but Donovan's gregarious ego and his perceived need to one-up his rivals got the better of him. He spilled to *Times* Washington columnist Arthur Krock, who enthusiastically reported the plan that October. "The tired mind of the President or another high official, now burdened by a mountain of reports," he wrote, could get the same information in "easy, prompt visual presentation."

To develop what he was calling the Presidential Situation Room, Donovan sought experts on both coasts. From Hollywood he recruited director John Ford, the producer Merian C. Cooper, and a couple of Walt Disney's animators. In New York he hired four star industrial designers who were fresh from creating futuristic spectacles for the New York World's Fair: Raymond Loewy, Norman Bel Geddes, Henry Dreyfuss, and Walter Teague. Also from Loewy's firm came the NYU-trained architect Donal McLaughlin and the young Oliver Lundquist, whom Loewy had hired when he was still an architecture and design student at Columbia, and who had recently designed the Q-Tip box. Other New Yorkers on the team included the architects Eero Saarinen and Louis Kahn; the futurist Buckminster Fuller, who had been thinking Internet-like ideas about global information and communications for years by then; Queens-born urbanist and sociologist Lewis Mumford; veteran Broadway set designers Joseph Mielziner and Lee Simonson; and the Viking Press editor David Zablodowsky.

They brainstormed a facility that would be housed in its own windowless building, code-named Q-2 because the COI's building was code-named Q. It would contain a semicircular auditorium that could present "a panorama of concentrated information" using state-of-the-art film and projection screens, three-dimensional models, and a mammoth, translucent globe "on which could be projected everything from weather fronts and oil fields to the disposition of land, air, and naval forces" in bold symbols and colors.

It's likely that Buckminster Fuller's contribution to the plan was the concept he called Dymaxion World. Dymaxion was his often-used coinage—he designed Dymaxion homes and Dymaxion cars—that stood for dynamic + maximum + tension. His Dymaxion World was a globe made of flat triangular segments that resembled a cube with its corners lopped off, which displayed the relative dimensions of land masses and oceans more accurately than a traditional curved globe. Its flat planes would offer obvious advantages as projection surfaces.

In November Donovan showed a scale model of the situation room to Roosevelt, who was thrilled and instantly authorized a million dollars in funding. The Joint Chiefs saw the plans and were so interested themselves that they ordered two more situation rooms of their own.

For the propaganda side of the COI, Robert Sherwood hired a motley gang of journalists, other writers, and people from the theater, including the producer and director John Houseman, the poet Stephen Vincent Benét, and the surrealist André Breton, whom Varian Fry had gotten out of France along with other European exiles and expats. At first they all rubbed elbows in a crowded, half-finished space on the fourth floor of a large office building midtown at 270 Madison Avenue. Their major focus would be to create propaganda programs in multiple languages to broadcast the American point of view into Europe via shortwave radio—a project that would soon be called Voice of America.

Houseman would direct the broadcasts. Born Jacques Haussmann in Bucharest in 1902, he grew up in Paris and England, then came to the United States in 1925. In New York in the 1930s, now calling himself John Houseman, he produced and occasionally directed stellar productions on Broadway, codirected the FTP's Negro Theatre unit with the black actress Rose McClendon, and cofounded the Mercury Theatre with Orson Welles. Then he went to Hollywood, worked with David O. Selznick, and would be there when the Japanese attacked Pearl Harbor. The next night Sherwood would telegram, asking him to come back east. Houseman met with Sherwood and Donovan, and by January 1942 he would be shuttling between an apartment on West 9th Street in Greenwich Village and the FBIS offices on Madison Avenue.

He started out making daily fifteen-minute broadcasts in English, German, French, and Italian, combining propaganda messages with news that people listening in Nazi-held Europe would not have heard. The opening music was going to be the "Battle Hymn of the Republic," until someone noted a strong similarity to the Nazi marching song "Laura." The composer Virgil Thomson, a friend of Houseman, whipped up a new orchestration of "Yankee Doodle" instead.

⁓

Meanwhile, Roosevelt started yet *another* private spy ring, this one run by the journalist John Franklin Carter. Carter had gone to Yale with Henry Luce and Archibald MacLeish, then wrote for *Time*, the *New York Times*, and some magazines. In 1936, writing as Jay Franklin, he started a very pro–New Deal, inside-Washington syndicated column "We, the People," which earned him easy access to the Oval Office.

Carter agreed with Roosevelt that the intelligence community was "pretty well loused up and floundering around." Early in 1941 the president gave Carter discretionary funds to start his own small intelligence operation, independent of and secret from all the others, reporting only to him. Roosevelt used him like a private detective to gather dirt on political enemies, as well as on government officials whose loyalty Roosevelt doubted. Roosevelt even had Carter snoop on Vincent Astor.

CHAPTER 28

Bums and Bombers

The America First Committee held what turned out to be its last big rally at Madison Square Garden on September 11. It was a fiasco. Charles Lindbergh, already notoriously warm toward Hitler and the Nazis, flew full throttle to the lunatic fringe, expressing his opinion that a triumvirate of "war agitators"—Roosevelt, the British, and the Jews—were colluding "to involve us in the war, step by step." He called England's situation "desperate" and claimed that even with American help "it is improbable" that Britain could "overcome the Axis powers." Of the Jews he said, "Their greatest danger to this country lies in their large ownership and influence in our motion pictures, our press, our radio and our government." According to the *Times*, he was booed as often as cheered. In the days that followed he was roundly condemned as an anti-Semite and a defeatist, and the committee floundered in a public relations morass it could not escape. Norman Thomas finally ended his association with the group, though as late as December 6 he was still writing antiwar letters to the *Times*. The AFC would disband after December 7.

For the first week of October 1941, New Yorkers ignored the dire news from around the world and focused maniacally on what really mattered: the first ever World Series between the New York Yankees and the Brooklyn Dodgers. There were few echoes of international politics in baseball anyway. The ballpark was where everyone went to distract themselves from their troubles, and the world's.

Professional baseball had not immediately felt the effects of the Depression. Record-breaking crowds had filled the parks in 1930, when Americans needed something to cheer about. But over the next few years attendance plummeted, teams went bankrupt, and owners scrambled to invent new ways to get the fans back, including the introduction of night games—already old news in minor league parks—in 1935.

Professional black baseball, like black America generally, was hit especially hard by the Depression and effectively disappeared for a few years in the early 1930s. Then black entrepreneurs started the new Negro National League in 1933 and the Negro American League in 1937. Major league ball, however, would remain whites-only until Branch Rickey brought Jackie Robinson to the Brooklyn Dodgers in 1947.

In 1941, New Yorkers had three major league baseball teams to root for, and against: the heartbreaking Dodgers at Ebbets Field (named for a former owner, Charles Ebbets) near Prospect Park; the solid if not terribly exciting New York Giants at the Polo Grounds in Harlem; and, right across the Harlem River in the Bronx, the most successful, most hated team in America, the Yankees. Pretty much every New Yorker was devoted to one of these teams and despised the other two. (The National Football League also had a New York Giants and a Brooklyn Dodgers at the time.)

The Yankees and Giants ran on business models developed by their distinctive owners. Colonel Jacob Ruppert, inheritor of the Ruppert Brewery fortune and four-time congressman for the city's 15th and 16th districts—who earned his honorific colonelcy in the Seventh Regiment of the National Guard—bought the Yankees in 1915, brought on Babe Ruth in 1920, and built the magnificent Yankee Stadium in 1923. The Giants' owner was the notorious Charles Stoneham, a double-chinned, raccoon-eyed former Wall Street trader who was tried and acquitted on charges of fraud and perjury in the early 1920s. He was alleged to have business ties with Arnold Rothstein, owned a few racetracks, and was a whale of a gambler himself. He bought the Giants—or, according to one story, won them in a poker game—in 1919.

The Brooklyn team was less organized in most every way. They went through a variety of owners and couldn't even settle on a name for themselves. Officially they were the Brooklyn Base Ball Club; over the years they were called the Superbas, the Bridegrooms, the Robins, and stuck with the Dodgers, shortened from Trolley Dodgers, only in the early 1930s.

The Yankees dominated baseball through the second half of the 1930s, winning the World Series four years in a row, 1936 to 1939. It was in '36 that Daniel Daniels, the star sportswriter for the *World-Telegram*—who simply used "Daniel" as his byline so as not to attract anti-Semites—gave the team one of its enduring nicknames, the Bronx Bombers.

By 1940 fans mostly came to watch Joe DiMaggio hit home runs. Or boo him after he sat out some games trying to negotiate a raise from the Colonel. The twenty-one-year-old San Francisco native had never been east of the Rockies when he came to play for the Yankees in 1936. The New York sportswriters hailed him as the next Babe Ruth. (Ruth had retired in 1935 to prowl around his Riverside Drive apartment, play golf, and be in the celebrity crowd at younger men's events.) DiMaggio was kindly greeted by Yorkville-born slugger Lou Gehrig, the last of the Ruth-era stars. Batting third and fourth, they powered the team to its World Series victory over the Giants that year. Gehrig made MVP and DiMaggio made the cover of *Time*.

In 1937, DiMaggio had his first and only role in a feature film, the musical revue *Manhattan Merry-Go-Round*, shot at Biograph's studio in the Bronx. Shy and tight-lipped, he had three lines and it took twelve takes. He met a chorus girl, Dorothy Arnold, whom he married in 1939.

At the start of the '39 season, a cover story in *Life* took the trouble to note that he didn't use olive oil on his hair and "never reeks of garlic." When Gehrig, diagnosed with ALS, dropped from the roster that year, DiMaggio was now the Bombers' undisputed star, leading them to another World Series and earning an MVP for himself. He was the toast of New York, feted in the nightclubs, especially in Toots Shor's place on West 51st Street; he and Toots became personal friends. Joe was pursued everywhere by pretty women who didn't let his marriage to Dorothy that year deter them. Neither did he.

The Yankee machine didn't inspire the passion the scruffier Dodgers did, and in 1941 they were actually drawing larger crowds to Ebbets Field than DiMaggio brought into Yankee Stadium. After two decades of accident-prone losses that earned them the nicknames Dem Bums and the Daffiness Boys, the Dodgers had a new executive, Larry MacPhail, and a new manager, Leo Durocher, who stunned the sports world by whipping them into the best team in the National League in 1941. (Colonel Ruppert also did himself no favor by refusing to install lights at Yankee Stadium. Night games started at Ebbets Field in 1938 and proved a big success in a working-class borough where getting out to day games could be tough.)

When the Dodgers actually made it to the World Series, against the Yankees no less, all of Brooklyn was on tenterhooks. The first two games were at Yankee Stadium. The Yankees won the first, the Dodgers the second. The third game, in a jam-packed and tumultuous Ebbets Field, went scoreless for seven innings, then the Bombers won it 2–1. In the infamous Game 4, the Dodgers were up 4–3 in the ninth and one pitch from tying the series. The crowd was uncannily hushed, holding their breath, as Dodger relief pitcher Hugh Casey wound up and threw a curve—which bounced off the glove of catcher Mickey Owen, keeping Yankee hopes alive. "Upon the stricken multitude grim melancholy perched," the *Times*' Meyer Berger wrote in a parody of "Casey at the Bat." The Yankees went on to win it, then take Game 5 from the demoralized and deflated Bums.

"It could only happen in Brooklyn," sportswriter Red Smith opined. "WAIT TILL NEXT YEAR," the *Brooklyn Eagle* cried. America was at war the next year, and Dodger fans would wait until 1955 to see them finally win a World Series—against the Yankees.

⌣

Along with Lou Gehrig, two other native New Yorkers had interesting major league careers in the years leading up to the war. Hyman "Hank" Greenberg was born in Greenwich Village to Romanian Jewish immigrants. A rangy first baseman and power hitter in college, he was courted by the Yankees but signed instead with the Detroit Tigers in 1929. He went on to be the first Jewish star in major league ball. It wasn't easy being the most visible Jew in Detroit in the 1930s. Besides being home base to Henry Ford, Father Coughlin, and the Midwest chapter of the Friends of the New Germany, Detroit also hosted thriving contingents of the Klan and the Black Legion, a Klan splinter group.

In his 1989 memoirs, Greenberg remembered how hard it was to go up to bat "and have some son of a bitch call you a Jew bastard and a kike and a sheenie and get on your ass…If the ballplayers weren't doing it, the fans were. Sometimes I wanted to go up in the stands and beat the shit out of them." When the time came to fight the Nazis, not surprisingly, Greenberg would be one of the first major leaguers to sign up.

And then there was Morris "Moe" Berg, one of the oddest oddballs in major league history. There was more than a little Zelig in the way Berg managed to appear in a strange variety of settings and capacities, interacting with some of the most important figures of his time, yet always remaining something of a blur. For all his celebrity, Berg was a loner whose personality and motivations eluded both his associates and his future biographers.

He was born to immigrant parents in 1902 in "a cold-water tenement not far from the Polo Grounds on 121st Street in Harlem," Nicholas Dawidoff wrote in his 1994 biography, *The Catcher Was a Spy*. Berg's father later shifted the family across the Hudson to Newark, where he opened a drugstore. The Bergs were nonpracticing and strove so hard to assimilate that as a boy Moe gave himself a pseudonym, Runt Wolfe, that he thought sounded less Jewish. A very bright and voracious student, he managed after a year at New York University to get into Princeton, where he was the rare "Hebrew," as his senior yearbook noted. He excelled, graduating magna cum laude in philology, proficient in at least seven languages, including Sanskrit.

Princeton invited him to stay and teach, and there was some talk of his going on to the Sorbonne. But he had another love, baseball, and the Brooklyn Robins made him an offer. He joined the team as a shortstop in 1923. He was a weak hitter and prone to errors in the field yet he would remain in the game for fifteen seasons, wandering from team to team, switching from shortstop to catcher and eventually coach, while spending most of his time on the bench. Off-season he studied at Columbia Law School, passed the bar, and joined a Wall Street firm. He would never practice law full time, preferring the diamond. Exactly why a man who might have accomplished so much chose a career in which he did so little confounded all who knew him. "I call him the mystery catcher," Casey Stengel once said. "Strangest fella who ever put on a uniform."

Sportswriters loved him. He was such a freak of nature to them—an extremely bright, widely read Jewish lawyer in the dugout, the egghead in a world of jocks and hicks. If nothing was happening in the game, they could always get him to spout some Latin, French, or Greek. John Kieran, who wrote the daily "Sports of the Times" column from the late 1920s to 1942 for the *New York Times*—the paper's first signed column—built a humorous, long-running legend around "Professor Moe," in which Berg discussed higher math with Einstein, lived in a house completely lined with books in all languages, and went on the road with a trunk stuffed with international newspapers and massive scholarly tomes. The thing was, much of it was true.

In 1932 and 1934, Berg traveled to Japan with groups of "baseball ambassadors." Most of his traveling companions were stars, including Babe Ruth and Lou Gehrig, and how the benchwarmer got in with them was another mystery. But Berg loved Japan and the Japanese loved him back, marveling at how quickly he learned to get by in their language. By the second trip, political relations between Japan and America were souring, however, and Japanese authorities were on guard for American spies with cameras posing as tourists. Berg put on a Japanese robe and geta (wooden sandals), slicked back his hair, and wandered around in this disguise shooting 16mm film footage. He was caught doing it in Japanese-held Korea, where police confiscated some of his film and briefly detained him. From there he took the Trans-Siberian railroad to Moscow, where officers in Red Square relieved him of some more film, and again as he crossed into Poland. There was much speculation on what he'd been up to.

Berg's time in baseball ended with the 1941 season. But his life of international intrigue was just getting started.

CHAPTER 29

The Mayor and Murder Inc.

In the fall of 1941, Mayor La Guardia ran for his own unprecedented third consecutive term in office. His opponent was William O'Dwyer, the Brooklyn district attorney. O'Dwyer was surfing a tsunami of publicity that stemmed from his pursuit of the mafiosi who ran Brooklyn's waterfront. Soon enough his actions would yield as many questions as convictions, but for now he was a strong contender for La Guardia's job.

New York owed its growth and wealth to its magnificent waterfront. It was situated on one of the finest deepwater harbors in the world, with easy access to the sea and, once the Erie Canal was opened in the 1820s, to the vast resources of the Midwest as well. Over time it grew into the busiest port in the world.

Though the shorelines of Manhattan, Brooklyn, and New Jersey bristled with hundreds of piers, the enormous volume of shipping in and out created crowding. Crafts of all sizes and purposes choked the Hudson and East Rivers every day, from large ocean liners and globe-crossing cargo vessels to fishing boats, ferries, garbage scows, and tugboats. Fishing vessels and cargo ships carrying perishables like fruit and vegetables jockeyed for dock space. Exploiting these conditions, gangsters began muscling onto the waterfront in the nineteenth century, extorting both the shipping companies and the truckers for tribute before they'd allow cargo to be unloaded and hauled away. Pilferage was also rife. Some percentage of nearly every cargo unloaded simply melted away. Waterfront cops and the city's crooked politicians padded their earnings in return for letting it all go on.

Working on the docks was hard, dangerous, unskilled labor. Like migrant farm workers, longshoremen were what is known as "casual labor," meaning they were perpetual temp workers, hired only for short-term jobs when there was work to be done. Early in the morning they'd gather for a "shape-up," when union hiring bosses picked workers as needed that day. It was work for men on the lowest rungs of the social ladder. In the early 1800s that was mostly black men. The poor Irish immigrants who flooded into the city in the mid-1800s took the work away from them, especially on Manhattan's Hudson piers. The poor southern Italians who poured into the city in the later 1800s became the predominant labor force on the East River docks. The gangsters on the waterfront reflected these ethnic patterns: Manhattan's west side waterfront was run by Irish gangsters, while the Italian Mafia ran the East River waterfront.

Dockworkers could not look to their union, the International Longshoremen's Association, for much help. It was in effect the waterfront arm of organized crime, deep in the pockets of the Manhattan Irish gangsters and the Brooklyn Mafia. From 1927 to 1955, the president of the ILA was Joseph "King Joe" Ryan, a product of the Chelsea waterfront. He left the exploitation of the East River to the Italians: chiefly his vice president Emil Camarda; Joe "Socks" Lanza, who dominated the Fulton Fish Market; and Brooklyn Mafia dons Vincent Mangano and Albert Anastasia.

The shape-up was key to the systematic exploitation of the dockworkers. The Irish and Italian longshoremen were overwhelmingly Catholic. Families of eight, ten, a dozen kids were not unusual. They desperately needed the work. If you were not picked at the shape-up your kids might go hungry. If you *were* picked, you had to kick back as much as half your pay to the union hiring boss, who in turn gave a percentage to the gangsters. The gangsters surrounded the workers with many other ways to siphon off their pay. They lined the waterfront with bars, gambling dens, bookies, whores, and loan sharks. Mangano threw an annual ball at the mammoth, swanky Hotel St. George on Henry and Clark Streets in Brooklyn Heights, a hangout for celebrities and celebrity watchers, with famous amenities including the Colorama Ballroom and the largest indoor saltwater pool in the world. As many as ten thousand longshoremen were forced to buy tickets, though the ballroom held only five hundred and the workers were definitely not expected to attend.

Brooklyn longshoreman could expect no support from the borough's politicians or legal system. Brooklyn's version of Tammany, the Democratic Machine, was thoroughly corrupt and in bed with the Mafia and the Mafia's ILA locals. Everyone from beat cops to judges was on the take. The leaders of the Mafia, the ILA, and the Machine all met and talked mutual business interests over pinochle at the innocuous-sounding City Democratic Club, located at Clinton and Degraw Streets in the Italian neighborhood Carroll Gardens. Mangano owned the building.

In the mid-1930s, encouraged by FDR's pro-labor gestures and backed by the CPUSA, longshoremen began to organize their own rank-and-file committees to protest the system. In the spring of 1939, twenty-eight-year-old longshoreman Pete Panto emerged as a popular speaker for the rank and file on Brooklyn's waterfront. Addressing gatherings of hundreds of workers, he called for an end to the shape-up and kickbacks. When casual threats from the gangsters didn't stop Panto, Camarda called him in for a formal meeting at the ILA office in Carroll Gardens. He told Panto he liked him personally, but "some of the boys" wanted him to shut up now. Panto continued to speak. On the evening of July 14 Panto left his rooming house at 11 North Elliott Place, just across Flushing Avenue from the Brooklyn Navy Yard, summoned to yet another meeting with Camarda. He was never seen in public again.

Within days of his disappearance, the graffito *Dov'é Panto?* ("Where is Panto?") began to appear scrawled on waterfront warehouses, freight cars, subway walls. As the summer turned to fall, the *Brooklyn Eagle* and then Manhattan papers picked up the story, as did Winchell: "Coppers are worried about Pete Panto, a courageous dockworker who was bothering Brooklyn banditi. Police fear Pete is wearing a cement suit at the bottom of the East River."

A few years earlier, the Panto story might have ended there. But in 1939 there were two prosecutors in Brooklyn investigating crime and corruption on the waterfront. One was an incorruptible outsider. The other was very much an insider, a product of the Machine, and apparently dirty up to his eyeballs.

The outsider was John Harlan Amen (pronounced Ay-men), appointed as special prosecutor by Governor Lehman in response to complaints, raised by Mayor La Guardia and other Republicans, of widespread corruption in the Democratic stronghold. Amen was born in Exeter, New Hampshire, where his father was the principal at the elite Phillips Exeter Academy, and came to New York to join a white-shoe law firm near Wall

Street. He married Grover Cleveland's daughter Marion and they lived at 812 Park Avenue, one of the finer buildings on the Upper East Side. In the early 1930s he became an assistant U.S. district attorney in Manhattan and specialized in using antitrust laws to get convictions of racketeers. From 1938 into 1942, Amen would conduct a painstaking investigation that exposed everyone from cops to judges to the DA's staff in Brooklyn taking bribes from hoodlums, bookies, abortionists, and the waterfront racketeers. It yielded dozens of convictions, guilty pleas, resignations, and even a couple of suicides.

The insider was O'Dwyer. Raised in Ireland, a son of schoolteachers, O'Dwyer was twenty when he sailed for New York City in 1910. Sturdy, friendly, and likable, he worked on the Brooklyn docks, then was a hod carrier and plasterer's apprentice on the construction of the Woolworth Building, then tended bar at some of Manhattan's finest hotels. In 1917 he joined the police force in Brooklyn and walked a waterfront beat, while studying law at Fordham at night. In 1925 he passed the bar and quit the force, hanging out his shingle in Brooklyn. With the Machine's backing he became a city magistrate in 1932, a judge in 1937, and then DA.

He entered office in January 1940 vowing to crack down on organized crime on the waterfront. But he had larger political aspirations: he was planning to run for mayor against La Guardia.

As a Machine-made man in Brooklyn in the 1930s, O'Dwyer had to walk a wobbling line between pursuing the gangsters and protecting them. In March 1940, Amen began looking into the Panto case by issuing a subpoena for ILA locals' books and records. The ILA resisted, through its lawyer, who happened to be Paul O'Dwyer, William's younger brother. When the Supreme Court upheld Amen's subpoena in April, DA O'Dwyer announced he was starting his own investigation. He collected the ILA records, thereby securing them from Amen. The records were "filed." Paul O'Dwyer soon moved out of Brooklyn, presumably to avoid any further appearance of conflict of interest.

At the same time, a gangster who wanted to turn state's witness offered O'Dwyer a golden ticket to career-making headlines. Abe Reles, aka Kid Twist, was born in the Brooklyn neighborhood Brownsville to Jewish immigrants from Austria and was a hoodlum from early on. By 1940 the thirty-three-year-old had been arrested dozens of times, six on murder charges. Now, with the pressure on from federal and local prosecutors, he felt his luck was running out and offered to sing for a deal.

O'Dwyer stashed Reles in the luxurious Hotel Bossert ("the Waldorf-Astoria of Brooklyn") in Brooklyn Heights, where for twelve days and nights he unspooled incredible stories about more than two hundred unsolved murders in New York and around the country, all conducted by the crew of Brooklyn hit men he belonged to, run by the thugs Lepke Buchalter and Jacob "Gurrah" Shapiro for Albert Anastasia. The press had a field day, dubbing Reles's crew Murder Inc. and Anastasia the Lord High Executioner. (O'Dwyer's Brooklyn-born assistant DA Burton Turkus would title his 1951 memoir and exposé *Murder Inc.*) Anastasia went into hiding.

Among the twenty-five notebooks' worth of stories Reles told, two were of particular interest. One was what he'd heard about the night Pete Panto disappeared. According to Reles, after his meeting with Emil Camarda, Panto was driven out to a chicken farm in Lyndhurst, New Jersey, where Anastasia and some of his thugs were waiting. One of them strangled Panto to death, then his body was dumped in a lime-filled pit in nearby marshland. In December 1940 O'Dwyer had a steam shovel dig in the area. Panto's corpse, badly decomposed, was pulled out of the bog that January. With other stool pigeons corroborating Reles's story, O'Dwyer announced he had a "perfect" case against Anastasia—if he could be found. A few months later Emil Camarda was bumped off.

Reles's other story linked Lepke Buchalter to the 1936 murder of a garment industry trucker in Brownsville. O'Dwyer had Lepke brought from Leavenworth, where he was already serving time, to stand trial in Brooklyn in the summer of 1941. Meanwhile O'Dwyer moved Reles to a ninth-floor wing of the massive Half Moon Hotel in Coney Island, with cops guarding him around the clock.

Then, lifted aloft by all the great Murder Inc. press he'd been receiving, O'Dwyer removed himself from the case while he campaigned for mayor. He was backed by Tammany, the Brooklyn Machine, and Governor Lehman. La Guardia came out swinging as usual. One day, strolling past a vegetable stand trailing reporters, he picked up a cabbage, grinned, and said, "My opponent's head." He lashed out at Governor Lehman for backing O'Dwyer, using personal invective that shocked and saddened most observers. La Guardia won reelection by his smallest margin yet, roughly 53 percent to O'Dwyer's 47 percent.

O'Dwyer went back to DA work that November. The Lepke trial had proceeded by inches. Just finding fourteen Brooklynites brave enough to sit on the jury took five weeks. Then, on November 12, as O'Dwyer was preparing to bring his star witness into the courtroom, Reles—still with six cops guarding him night and day—somehow managed to fall to his death out the window of his Coney Island hotel room. The official story that he had died trying to escape was fairly preposterous. It was widely assumed that Anastasia and/or Lepke had reached out to the cops and/or O'Dwyer. In *Murder Inc.*, Turkus would stop just short of accusing O'Dwyer of being involved.

Lepke was convicted anyway, and he was sentenced to death on December 2, five days before Pearl Harbor. After appeals and delays, he would die in the electric chair in 1944. That same year, the navy would lease the Half Moon Hotel for a hospital and rehabilitation center serving sailors and marines. After the war it would house a Jewish nursing home until it was razed in the mid-1990s.

Without the key figures Reles and Camarda, O'Dwyer claimed that his investigation of Anastasia could not proceed. Anastasia came out of hiding. The country went to war, and gangsterism on the Brooklyn waterfront would not capture much public attention for the next four years. But after the war, when O'Dwyer revived his political career, his apparent collusion with Anastasia and other mobsters would come back to haunt him.

PART THREE

Boom Town

My friends, we must toughen up. We have our homes and our lands to defend now.

—*Fiorello La Guardia (December 7, 1941)*

Whatever is asked of us I am sure we can accomplish it. We are the free and unconquerable people of the United States of America.

—*Eleanor Roosevelt (December 7, 1941)*

CHAPTER 30

Day of Infamy

On the evening of Saturday, December 6, 1941, Franklin Roosevelt and Harry Hopkins sat quietly in the Oval Room study on the second floor, reading through a long communiqué from Tokyo to the Japanese embassy in Washington. It had been intercepted and decoded by Magic, the U.S. military's cryptanalysis unit. The Japanese government was instructing its diplomats to reject Roosevelt's recent offer to ease economic sanctions if Japan withdrew its forces from China and Indochina.

There was no question that the Japanese were preparing to go to war. The question was how and where they would strike. William Donovan's new agency was just getting up and running, so Roosevelt still depended on half a dozen competing services for intelligence. What they fed him was murky at best. They knew that a Japanese attack fleet had steamed out of Tokyo but not where it was heading. At a cabinet meeting on December 5, Knox had told the president it was most likely going south toward British Malaya, but Roosevelt wasn't so sure.

The next day, Sunday, December 7, the Japanese aerial attack on Pearl Harbor began a few minutes before 8 a.m. there, which was 1 p.m. in Washington. Roosevelt was in his Oval study again that afternoon, fiddling with his stamp collection and munching an apple, while Hopkins lounged on a couch. "We were talking about things far removed from war," Hopkins would write, when Knox called around 1:45 p.m. with the first confused news from Hawaii. "I expressed the belief that there must be some mistake and that surely Japan would not attack in Honolulu." The president replied that "it was just the kind of unexpected thing the Japanese would do." Outwardly calm, Roosevelt called his press secretary Steve Early and dictated the statement Early gave to the White House press corps a little before 2:30, sending them stampeding to the phones.

Eleanor came up to the second floor after hosting a luncheon. From the bustle of secretaries in and out of FDR's study she knew something big had happened. When she found out what it was, she went down to her end of the hall and reworked some of the text for her regular Sunday evening radio program on NBC. (She'd been hosting her own programs since 1932, making her the first paid radio host to reside in the White House.)

Janet Murrow called from a Washington hotel. In November, she and Ed had reluctantly left battered London for New York City, where he was to begin a three-month lecture tour. They hadn't been back in New York since 1938. Stepping out of a Pan Am Clipper at La Guardia, they were startled by the clamoring crowd of print and newsreel reporters who treated Murrow like an arriving movie star. It was only the first shock. Over the next few days, as he strolled Fifth and Madison Avenues where the expensive shops and restaurants did business as usual, Murrow found himself "spending most of my time trying to keep my temper in check" at the sight of "so many well-dressed, well-fed, complacent-looking people." On December 2, William Paley held a black-tie dinner at the Waldorf-Astoria to honor him. Murrow threw a bit of a pall on the evening when he grimly told the thousand or so guests that "unless the United States enters this war Britain may perish or at best secure a stalemate peace—a delayed action defeat."

The Roosevelts had invited him and Janet for an informal dinner on December 7. Eleanor usually scrambled eggs on Sundays because it was the White House cooks' night off. Hearing the news from Pearl Harbor, the Murrows figured dinner was canceled. "We all have to eat," Eleanor told Janet. "Come anyway."

In England, Averell Harriman and Ambassador Winant were at Chequers, sitting down to a quiet dinner with Churchill and Pamela at a little before 9 p.m.—4 p.m. in Washington. Churchill, brooding and depressed, had his valet tune a portable radio, a gift from Harry Hopkins, to the 9 p.m. BBC news. At the very end of the program the announcer read one deadpan sentence about the Pearl Harbor attack, stunning them all. Winant called the White House and put Churchill on the line with Roosevelt. "We are all in the same boat now," the president famously told the prime minister. Churchill and his New York guests were ecstatic. The long wait was over. America was finally going to "come in." By the end of the week Churchill would be steaming across the Atlantic on the battleship *Duke of York* to meet with Roosevelt.

At the Polo Grounds that afternoon, fifty-five thousand New Yorkers were braving a cold wind to watch the last game of the NFL regular season, the New York Giants versus the Brooklyn Dodgers. William Donovan was in the stands. He had taken a train up from Washington as usual on Friday afternoon. An announcement came out of the stadium's loudspeakers: "Here is an urgent message. Will Colonel William J. Donovan call operator nineteen in Washington immediately." Donovan found a phone box under the stands. Jimmy Roosevelt told him of the attack and said the president wanted him at the White House right away. He flew out of La Guardia at 5:15 p.m.

J. Edgar Hoover was also in New York City for the weekend. An FBI agent called him from Honolulu with the news; he stuck the phone out his window so Hoover could hear the faint sound of bombs detonating. Hoover flew back to the capital that afternoon as well.

In an office at the headquarters of the Third Naval District at 90 Church Street, a young ensign named Sargent Shriver had been at his desk since 9 a.m. Born into an old German Catholic family in Maryland in 1915, he moved to Manhattan with his family in 1929. He first met Jack Kennedy when they were students at the Canterbury School, an elite Catholic prep school in Connecticut. While a student at Yale and then Yale Law School Shriver went on summer trips to Europe in 1936 and 1939 and witnessed Nazism in full malignant flower. Deeply concerned, he was among the group at Yale Law who founded the America First Committee in 1940. But like others who believed America should not get involved in Europe's war, he also thought it should build up its defenses against potential attack, so he enlisted in the U.S. Naval Reserve. He dropped out of America First, convinced that U.S. involvement in the war was inevitable.

He went on active service in the navy in September 1941, hoping for duty at sea, and was disappointed to be stuck behind a desk in Manhattan. His chore that Sunday afternoon was to monitor radio dispatches and, in the highly unlikely event of an attack, sound general alarm. Bored, he switched his desk radio to the Mutual Broadcasting System for the Giants-Dodgers game. At a little before 2:30, announcer Len Sterling cut into the broadcast to read a United Press bulletin: "Flash: Washington—White House says Japs attack Pearl Harbor." Spinning the dial, Shriver heard CBS newsman John Daly and NBC's Robert Eisenbach reporting the same.

At first he thought it might be a *War of the Worlds* hoax. He called his brother Herbert, on duty at the Brooklyn Navy Yard, who confirmed that it was real. Shriver flipped a switch that sounded general alarm, which alerted a small army of switchboard operators who got busy calling officers all up and down the eastern seaboard, wherever they might be enjoying a Sunday afternoon.

Ensign Shriver would later get the combat duty he craved, serving on the battleship *South Dakota* and earning a Purple Heart at Guadalcanal. Returning to Manhattan after the war, he'd get an editorial job at *Newsweek* and marry Jack Kennedy's sister Eunice in St. Patrick's Cathedral in 1953.

Vice Admiral Adolphus Andrews was lunching with his wife and friends in Syosset on Long Island when he heard the radio reports. He raced into the city, the siren on his car wailing, and was at 90 Church Street by 3:45. As commander of the North Atlantic Naval Coastal Frontier, Andrews, a former battleship commander from Galveston who was affectionately known as Dolly, had been planning for coastal defense all along the Atlantic seaboard since March. He spoke to newsmen that evening. Calling the city "a possible but not a probable danger zone," he reassured citizens that "Every possible step has been taken to protect the New York area from such an attack as surprised Pearl Harbor."

A few blocks away in the financial district, the editorial staff of the *Wall Street Journal* had reported for work on a Sunday for the first time in the paper's fifty-two-year history. Until this day, the copy for the Monday morning edition was compiled on Saturday, and the staff took Sunday off. The *Journal* had barely survived the Depression and was still struggling in 1941; the paper made the schedule switch so that the Monday news would be as fresh and timely as possible. The editorial team was quietly compiling business news for the next morning's edition when the bells on all the newswire machines started clanging with the first reports from Pearl Harbor. The editors scrapped most of the front page, and when the *Journal* came out on Monday it was full of hastily jotted articles about the attack.

⌒

Mayor La Guardia was at the studios of city-owned WNYC radio that afternoon. He and other civic leaders were going to present the station with a plaque in recognition of its public service. They were waiting to go on the air when a United Press teletype machine chattered out the news.

La Guardia instantly sent his civil defense volunteers out to guard bridges and tunnels, docks and airfields, and he put his auxiliary firemen on alert.

At 5 p.m. he went on the air. Speaking as both the mayor and the national civil defense director, he gravely began with, "I want to warn the people of this city that we are in an extreme crisis." On his own authority, he said, "All Japanese subjects" in the city were ordered to "remain in their homes until their status is determined by our federal government." At the time there were fewer than one hundred thousand Japanese in the entire nation registered under the alien registration law, and only about two thousand in New York City—eleven hundred issei born in Japan and their American-born children, called nisei.

After blaming "the thugs and gangsters now controlling the Nazi government" for inciting the Japanese, La Guardia went on to "warn the people of this city and on the Atlantic coast that we must not and cannot feel secure or assured because we are on the Atlantic coast, and the activities this afternoon have taken place in the Pacific. We must be prepared for anything at any time...There is no need of being excited or unduly alarmed, but we are not out of the danger zone by any means. It is necessary that we be on the alert at all times.

"My friends, we must toughen up. We have our homes and our lands to defend now. We must remain cool and yet determined. We are aware of the danger ahead, but unafraid. In the meantime, know that your city government is on the job and looking after your welfare and comfort and safety."

At Carnegie Hall, the New York Philharmonic began a concert of Shostakovich's *Symphony No. 1* and Brahms's *Concerto for Piano and Orchestra in B-flat Major* at a little past 3 p.m. After the Shostakovich there was an intermission. On the radio, John Daly in the CBS newsroom in New York came on at that point, 3:35, and announced the news from Pearl Harbor. In the hall, backstage workers listening to the radio generated a bit of a confused stir, but the concert proceeded. Radio listeners heard Daly interrupt the Brahms three times with brief updates. Meanwhile the audience in the hall knew nothing until the concert ended. Conductor Artur Rodzinski and pianist Artur Rubinstein—both born in Poland—stood together, receiving the audience's applause. CBS's in-theater concert announcer Warren Sweeney, who usually just gave a brief introduction and wrap-up, crossed the stage and asked Rodzinski to read a message. The conductor handed it back to Sweeney, shaking his head.

It was up to Sweeney to inform the audience that Pearl Harbor had been attacked. Rodzinski led the orchestra in "The Star-Spangled Banner," and the audience sang along.

On NBC Red at about the same time, H. V. Kaltenborn, the man with the fancy diction who had predicted the bright future of Democracity at the world's fair, now gave his analysis of the dark present. He began, "Good afternoon, everybody. Japan has made war against the United States without declaring it." After summarizing what little was known, he ended with, "The United States has been attacked, and the United States will know how to answer that attack."

Because it was the only New York newspaper that came out on Sunday afternoons, the weekly *New York Enquirer* was the first with the Pearl Harbor story. New Yorkers mobbed newsstands to snap up the issue, which bore a giant three-deck headline:

JAPS ATTACK U.S.
HAWAII, PHILIPPINES
BOMBED BY AIRMEN!

The irony was that the *Enquirer* had always been virulently anti-Roosevelt, anti–New Deal, and hysterically isolationist. William Griffin, a protégé of William Randolph Hearst, had started the paper with Hearst's backing in 1926. Hearst used it as a place to air articles and opinions that might be too extremely conservative for his conservative dailies. The result was a broadsheet that read like a tabloid, so sensationalist that one observer called it the Sunday Scream.

In 1936, Griffin wrote that on a recent trip to London he'd had a private conversation about the Great War with First Lord of the Admiralty Churchill, and Churchill had in effect agreed that America never should have gotten into that war and should stay out of any future European war. Churchill evidently wasn't an *Enquirer* reader and issued no response to the article. Then in the summer of 1939, when Hitler had annexed Austria and was threatening Poland, isolationists exhumed Churchill's remarks in their arguments against America's getting involved. When the *New York Times* questioned Churchill about Griffin's story, he called it "a vicious lie." Griffin lashed back with a million-dollar libel suit and they began fighting it out in print. Churchill was forced to back away from an initial insistence that he'd never met Griffin, but remained adamant that Griffin's version of their conversation was "a palpable travesty and distortion of anything I have ever said or thought." The lawsuit was still working its way through the court system on December 7. (It would be dropped when Griffin failed to make a court date in 1942. Accused of sedition—along with George Sylvester Viereck, Joe McWilliams, Peter Stahrenberg, and some two dozen others—he had suffered a heart attack. After the war his widow sold the newspaper and it would morph into the supermarket tabloid *National Enquirer.*)

⌣

Eight ships built at the Brooklyn Navy Yard were at Pearl Harbor that Sunday. Of them, the cruiser *Helena*, launched in 1938, was seriously damaged, but the worst news was the complete destruction of the "superdreadnought" *Arizona* (launched in 1915) and the deaths of 1,177 of her crew. "Remember the *Arizona*" would become a familiar slogan at the yard. The Brooklyn-built repair ship *Vestal*, moored alongside the *Arizona*, was heavily damaged as well. Rear Admiral Edward Marquart, commandant of the yard, had once skippered the minelayer *Oglala*, also sunk. Marquart would soon ask for volunteers from the yard's skilled civilian workers to go to Pearl and help with repairs. More than a thousand signed up, and several hundred were sent in January. Workers also pledged to produce new ships as quickly as humanly possible. In August 1942 they would launch a new battleship, the *Iowa*, which was completed a full seven months ahead of schedule. Already working a six-day week, many would put in as much as twenty days at a stretch to meet accelerated production schedules. They were proud to call the Navy Yard the "Can Do" Yard.

⌣

At Admiral Andrews's request, New York's police commissioner Lewis Valentine instructed his cops to tell any men in uniform they encountered that Sunday afternoon and evening to report to their ships and posts. Soldiers and sailors tossed down a last few drinks bought for them by grateful civilians in the bars, then crammed onto buses and subways, and into Penn Station and Grand Central. The blue-uniformed American Women's Voluntary Services, founded by Upper East Side socialites in 1940 and the butt of a lot of male haw-hawing ever since, leapt into action Sunday afternoon, offering to drive to their posts any servicemen who showed up at AWVS headquarters on East 58th Street. Most of the young men requested rides out to Mitchel Field or down to Fort Monmouth or Fort Hancock in New Jersey. One soldier got a ride all the way out to Camp Upton a good sixty miles away, "in a comfortably heated Airflow Chrysler," the *New Yorker* reported.

"There was some grumbling about broken furloughs," the *Times* reported the next day, "but in the main the men seemed eager to get back." In the *Brooklyn Daily Eagle*, "Gotham Grapevine" columnist Harold Conrad reported that Jack Dempsey's bar in the Brill Building, so popular with sailors on leave that it was nicknamed Broadway's Singapore, "was strangely deserted. There wasn't a sailor in the place, every man having been ordered to his base."

In nightclubs, the music and dancing went on, if a bit subdued. In the Broadway theaters, audiences laughed at performances of *Arsenic and Old Lace* and *My Sister Eileen*, Danny Kaye in *Let's Face It!* and Sophie Tucker in *High Kickers*. Two dramas seriously addressed the war in Europe: Maxwell Anderson's *Candle in the Wind*, about Nazi-occupied France, at the Shubert, and Lillian Hellman's *Watch on the Rhine*, about an anti-Nazi German and his American wife, at the Martin Beck. (Both had sets designed by Joseph Mielziner.) In the nearby movie palaces—the State, the Broadway, the Rivoli, the Strand—folks enjoyed *Dumbo*, *The Maltese Falcon*, *How Green Was My Valley*, and Abbott and Costello's *Keep 'Em Flying*, about a couple of foul balls who join the Army Air Corps, advertised as "America's favorite comics with a bombload of belly-laughs!"

Leaving the theaters, many joined the large crowd in chilly Times Square watching updates crawl across the *Times*'s electronic bulletin board, officially the Motograph but commonly known as the Zipper. *PM* writer John Hennessy Walker described the mood there as one of "hard boiled gallantry. There wasn't a glum face to be seen, but neither was there any hysteria or false enthusiasm." As they watched the Zipper's "twinkling electronic news" people "looked thoughtful, calm and not too surprised."

As usual, tens of millions of listeners around the country tuned in to Walter Winchell's regular Sunday night show. "The importance of the Japanese attack is that war between the United States and Hitler is imminent," he (or probably Cuneo) editorialized. "The national emergency is no longer a phrase. Persons who arouse suspicion by their conduct, speech or deeds are inviting microscopic examination, perhaps prison. Nothing matters anymore now except national security." A telephone poll put the show's ratings at 29.9 percent—his highest ever at that point, though it would continue to climb over the next few months, cresting at one-third of all listeners in his time slot.

FBI agents and police fanned out around the city to Japanese homes and businesses Sunday night. A half dozen cops went to the Japanese consulate offices in Rockefeller Center and found the consul general and his staff "preparing to leave." The consul general was escorted to his home and told he couldn't set foot outside without police escort. At the same time his wife and some twenty other Japanese nationals who arrived at Municipal Airport with tickets for flights out were sent back to their homes under a federal no-fly order. Two months later, Allen Dulles would rent the consul's hastily vacated offices, just down the hall from William Stephenson's BSC, for his secret COI operations.

Cops went into Japanese restaurants in the five boroughs and, after allowing patrons to finish their meals, shut them down. They also shut down the Nippon Club, a social organization on West 93rd Street founded in 1905.

Around the country and in Hawaii, the FBI had been keeping dossiers on issei considered "dangerous." Agents and detectives now went into the homes of up to two hundred in New York City and on Long Island (the December 8 *Brooklyn Daily Eagle* put it at 118), told them to pack their bags with "traveling essentials," and took them to the nearest precinct houses, where they booked them as "prisoners of the federal authorities." Then paddy wagons carried them to the Federal Building in Foley Square, where FBI agents interrogated them. From there they were taken to the Battery, and from there by ferry to Ellis Island to be held without formal charges. Most would remain in custody for the rest of the war. One was a fifty-year-old physician who had left Japan in 1917, graduated from NYU, and lived on Park Avenue. "This is an unfortunate situation," he told the press.

FBI and Treasury agents went into Japanese offices in the city on Monday, including Japanese news bureaus, the Japanese Institute and Japanese Chamber of Commerce in Rockefeller Center, and the Mitsui bank offices on the seventh floor of the Empire State Building. Most of these offices closed for the duration.

PM's Tom O'Connor interviewed some nisei in the city, "whose short stature and slant eyes and light-brown skin label them Japanese, but whose every thought and every word and every aspiration label them American. They heard the news of the war with anger, and with disgust." At the Japanese Methodist Church on West 108th Street, the Reverend Alfred Akamatsu told O'Connor, "What gripes me is that the innocent bystander is always the one to suffer." A group of young nisei in his office were composing a telegram to Roosevelt, "condemning Japanese aggression against our country."

Only a few acts of violence or vandalism against Japanese were reported in the city. A trio of young thugs beat a Japanese man on the West Side of Manhattan, fracturing his skull; stones were thrown through the windows of a few Japanese shops. Still, O'Connor's tolerant attitude was rare, even in the ultra-liberal *PM*. Dr. Seuss's December 9 illustration had a bunch of slit-eyed, bucktoothed Japanese rudely waking the American eagle from his "nap." In February *PM* would run a Seuss cartoon depicting thousands of Japanese lining up to receive packages of TNT from a booth labeled "Honorable Fifth Column," with the legend "Waiting for the Signal from Home..."

⌣

On the radio Sunday evening, Eleanor sounded resolute and unruffled. "We must go about our daily business more determined than ever to do the ordinary things as well as we can," she said, "and when we find a way to do anything more in our communities to help others, to build morale, to give a feeling of security, we must do it. Whatever is asked of us I am sure we can accomplish it. We are the free and unconquerable people of the United States of America."

She dined as planned with the Murrows, while the president met with his cabinet and congressional leaders, arranging to address both houses of Congress the next afternoon at 12:30. Then he and Hopkins sat up over sandwiches and beers until midnight writing the historic "date which will live in infamy" address.

When William Donovan reached the White House after midnight, he found Roosevelt sitting up with Ed Murrow, talking about the day's events in much more detail than had been released to other newsmen. Murrow understood the conversation to be off the record and kept it to himself. It was dawn when he walked out of the White House.

⌣

The White House and the military moved instantly to limit the public's knowledge of what a fiasco the Pearl Harbor attack had been. Most Americans wouldn't really know until the war was over that in a single morning the Japanese had all but demolished the U.S. Pacific fleet, while going almost unscathed themselves.

One newsman who tried to counter the White House's cooked figures was John O'Donnell, the Washington bureau chief of the *New York Daily News* and writer of the syndicated column "Capitol Stuff." The *Daily News* had supported Roosevelt through his first two terms and endorsed his candidacy for a third term. Both O'Donnell and his publisher, Joseph Medill Patterson, were personally friendly with the president. But the paper turned fiercely hostile soon after Roosevelt's reelection in November 1940. Patterson's Great War experiences had left him a confirmed isolationist. As Roosevelt pushed the country into more involvement with the war in Europe, the attacks against him in the *Daily News* grew increasingly vicious. Through the war, the only papers in the country as critical of Roosevelt and the War Department were the *Washington Times-Herald,* published by Patterson's sister Cissy; and his cousin Robert McCormick's *Chicago Tribune.*

Patterson sent O'Donnell to Pearl Harbor, where he could clearly see that the damage was far worse than the White House had let on. But the country was now at war, and it was standard practice for the military to censor all news and mail from war zones. O'Donnell submitted what he'd written to the censors, who cut out everything that conflicted with the official story. Still, he was far from through being Patterson's attack dog.

CHAPTER 31

The City Mobilizes

Thousands of volunteers started lining up Sunday night, December 7, outside the city's recruiting stations—the Federal Office Building at 90 Church Street (the navy and marines), the Army Building at 39 Whitehall Street, the Coast Guard center at 1 State Street, as well as the Federal Building in downtown Brooklyn. Some centers opened an hour early Monday morning to begin interviews. "The lines were filled with boys not old enough to fight, with men too old to fight, but also with many men young enough and healthy enough to get their wish for a 'crack at the Japs,'" the *Times* reported. "There were students with books under their arms, truck drivers, store owners, salesmen, bakers, clerks and professional men..." They were still lining up by midweek, and the army put its centers on a twenty-four-hour, seven-day schedule. Some volunteers were answering the call of duty, some signed up for the steady paycheck or the heady adventure, while still others calculated that it was preferable to enlist in the service they wanted rather than be drafted and take potluck. As often happens in wartime, after this early rush enlistment would markedly decline.

Among the volunteers that Monday was the future novelist Herman Wouk, who crossed a gangplank to board an old, mothballed battleship moored at the foot of West 135th Street and signed up for the naval reserve. At twenty-six, Wouk's qualifications as a naval officer were a bit dubious. He'd never been a sailor and had spent the previous five years writing gags for comedian Fred Allen's weekly radio show. But the navy was ravenous for midshipmen and took him.

Wouk was born in the Bronx in 1915 to Russian immigrants. As he was growing up his father built a successful laundry business and moved the family to the Upper West Side. Herman studied the Talmud under a grandfather, a Hasidic rabbi from Minsk, and would grow devoutly Orthodox and Zionist. He went to Townsend Harris High, the city's free prep school for gifted students, then graduated with honors from Columbia in 1934. Starting in 1936 he made a comfortable living through the last years of the Depression writing for Allen's show, broadcast from Radio City. In his 2016 memoirs *Sailor and Fiddler*, published on his one hundredth birthday, Wouk remembers this period as "a long dream in a featherbed." When Hitler devoured Europe in the summer of 1940, Wouk and his friends "chattered quite a bit" about it, yet "remained as oblivious—so now it seems to me—as well-fed apes in the zoo."

That nonchalant attitude had changed by the summer of 1941, when he started writing for *The Treasury Hour*, a government show promoting defense bonds. On the morning after Pearl Harbor he saw a small ad in the back of the *New Yorker* in which the U.S. Navy sought applicants for its V-7 program, an accelerated course that trained college men and grads to be midshipmen in three months—"90-day wonders" as they came to be known. The navy had started V-7 in the fall of 1940, when it was obvious that a whole new generation of young officers would be needed to run all the new warships FDR had ordered up. Besides its own campus in Annapolis, it launched the program at Northwestern University and in twelve buildings it leased on the Columbia campus, by far its largest V-7 center. The old battleship Wouk stepped onto at West 135th Street, a few blocks from the Columbia campus, was the USS *Prairie State*, formerly the *Illinois*, which dated back to 1898 and had been converted into a training facility.

Columbia's V-7 program would churn out twenty-three thousand ensigns by the end of the war—ten times the number produced at the Annapolis program. The great majority of them would see active duty in the Pacific. Wouk would serve on two minesweepers, the *Southard* and the *Zane*. In off-hours he'd write his first novel, the satire *Aurora Dawn*; Simon & Schuster sent him the contract for it when he was stationed off Okinawa and it would be published to nice reviews in 1947. He'd later meet Kurt Weill and they'd seriously discuss turning it into a Broadway musical, but Weill died before they could get to it. Wouk would write one of his most successful novels based on his experiences on the *Southard* and *Zane*—*The Caine Mutiny*, published by Doubleday in 1951.

Not long after Wouk joined the navy, another young Jewish New Yorker who'd later be famous did the same. Bernie Schwartz was born in 1925 to poor Hungarian immigrants. He grew up in ethnic neighborhoods all around upper Manhattan and the Bronx, as his parents kept skipping out on their landlords. Bernie would write in his autobiography that they weren't a happy household. His father, a tailor, was already poor when the Depression hit. His mother was a sad soul who'd later be diagnosed as schizophrenic. At one point they put Bernie and his younger brother in an orphanage for a few weeks because they simply couldn't feed them. Bernie worked odd jobs from the time he was twelve, played hooky, ducked anti-Semitic bullies, and went to the movies as often as he could for escape. Picturing himself on the silver screen someday, he started in his teens to do some acting on stage with the 92nd Street Young Men's Hebrew Association.

When his family moved near Yorkville in the later 1930s, he and other Jewish boys would climb up on rooftops to watch Kuhn and the Bund march on First Avenue. They'd fill condoms or stockings with "water or piss or colored dye or dog food" and bomb the Bundists "marching in those stinking Nazi uniforms," then get chased across the rooftops.

Early in 1942 he'd take the subway down to Whitehall Street to enlist in the navy. Because he was sixteen he needed a parent's signature; he took the form outside and forged his mother's. He'd be trained as a signalman and a submariner, then sent to Pearl Harbor, which "looked like a massive naval junkyard" when he arrived, oil still leaking up to the surface from the sunken *Arizona* (as it still does). He was posted to a sub tender, the *Proteus*. On September 2, 1945, the *Proteus* would be in Tokyo Bay, and he'd watch through binoculars as MacArthur accepted the Japanese surrender on the deck of the *Missouri*. In 1948 he would fly to Hollywood and be billed as Anthony—later Tony—Curtis.

⌒

Mario Puzo, author of *The Godfather*, would recall, "When World War II broke out, I was delighted. There is no other word, terrible as it may sound."

America's entry into the war exacerbated rifts between older Italian immigrants and their American children. Despite Mussolini's fall from grace in the second half of the 1930s, he had remained a symbol of pride to many immigrants. Both La Guardia and Roosevelt found that criticizing Il Duce even after Pearl Harbor cost them Italian votes. Four out of five Italian-American voters in New York City had voted for Roosevelt in 1932 and again in 1936. Roosevelt had in turn soft-pedaled his criticisms of Mussolini through this period. He finally lashed out when Italy declared war on France and England on June 10, 1940. That day, delivering a commencement address at the University of Virginia (Franklin Jr. was in the graduating class), Roosevelt had extemporized that "the hand that held the dagger has struck it in the back of its neighbor."

In an election year it was an impolitic choice of words, evoking old stereotypes of Italians as sneaky and stiletto wielding. Many in New York's Italian community were outraged. That fall, "Democratic Party workers needed police escort to campaign in New York City's Italian-American neighborhoods." Roosevelt's numbers among the city's Italians that November plunged from 80 percent to 42. Because La Guardia was now speaking out against Mussolini as well, his numbers also fell in Italian neighborhoods, though not as drastically.

After Pearl Harbor, the government classified the nation's six hundred thousand nonnaturalized Italians as enemy aliens. Though only four thousand were detained, and of them only some two hundred hard-core Fascists would be held for the duration, New York's older Italians were insulted. Roosevelt would get the message and lift the enemy alien status in time for the 1942 midterm elections. People would party in the streets of Little Italy, but there was still enough residual resentment that Democratic tallies among the city's Italian voters dropped 40 percent below prewar highs. Their support for FDR and his war would remain lukewarm at best.

For their American children, the war represented something very different: escape. Young men went off to war to see the world and get away from the restrictions of family life in an Italian household. Mario Puzo was born in 1920 to illiterate immigrants and grew up with six siblings on Tenth Avenue in Hell's Kitchen, looking out, he wrote decades later in *The Godfather Papers*, on "the vast black iron gardens of the New York Central Railroad," whose tracks ran down the west side, "absolutely blooming with stinking boxcars freshly unloaded of cattle and pigs for the slaughterhouse." Puzo's father and all four of his sons would work for the New York Central, the daughters in the garment district. Mario worked after school and on weekends in the railroad freight office and hated it. When he was twelve his father abandoned the family, and his mother—who he said would be the model for Don Corleone—moved them to the Bronx.

"In my youth I was contemptuous of my elders," he writes, "a grim lot; always shouting, always angry, quicker to quarrel than embrace." He dreamed of getting out, of becoming either "a great artist" or "a great criminal."

That's why he was delighted when the war started and he went into the army. It was his way out. "I was delivered from my mother, my family, the girl I was loving passionately but did not love. And delivered WITHOUT GUILT...And what an escape it was. The war made all my dreams come true. I drove a jeep, toured Europe, had love affairs, found a wife, and lived the material for my first novel."

Other future stars who would don uniforms during the war included Astoria-born Tony Bennett, who was drafted into the army and saw combat in France and Germany; Brooklyn's Melvin Kaminsky—later Mel Brooks—who enlisted at seventeen and also saw combat in Europe; and Leonard Schneider from Long Island, who joined the navy at eighteen, saw two years of action in the Atlantic, and would start his performing career in Greenwich Village in 1947 under the stage name Lenny Bruce.

⌒

Stocks on Wall Street took a predictable tumble Monday morning, except for basic commodities such as wool, steel, and beef, which all rose. At noon, trading paused as everyone on the Street, along with most everyone in the country, listened to the president declare war.

That morning, Mayor La Guardia ordered the distribution of 4 million copies of a civil defense leaflet called "If It Comes" to banks, department stores, and other places where New Yorkers could pick them up. It noted that an air attack was unlikely but "not impossible," given the city's role as "the nerve center of the nation." It advised citizens that in the event of an air raid they should "keep cool. Don't be alarmed. Just use common sense!"

Antiaircraft batteries of the army's 62nd Coast Artillery, stationed at Fort Totten at the north entrance to the East River, were wheeled out to various points around the city. For the next four years, New Yorkers would be either comforted or alarmed by the sight of these guns and their armed pickets in Bryant Park behind the New York Public Library, near the Brooklyn Bridge, in Prospect Park, Greenpoint, and elsewhere. Periodically their spotlights scissored the night sky over the city as they drilled.

The city had its first air raid alert the very next afternoon. A junior officer monitoring coastal radar spotted ten unidentified aircraft out to sea, ten minutes from the city. Mitchel Field scrambled fighters. Firehouse sirens wailed all over the city. WNYC broadcast an emergency alert, instructing residents to stay off the streets and away from windows and to keep telephone lines clear. Police, fire, and civil defense workers raced to their posts. Yet most New Yorkers were more perplexed than alarmed. "A million delighted school kids were sent home and a few frightened elevator girls ran their cars down to the basement and refused to come up again," *Life* reported. Otherwise, "Nothing stopped—traffic, business, lunch, conversation." When the unidentified planes failed to materialize, an all clear was sounded. That didn't stop that evening's *Brooklyn Eagle* from shouting, "N.Y.-BOUND ENEMY PLANES ALARM ENTIRE NORTHEAST."

Mayor La Guardia was not in the city to dispel the confusion. He had flown to Washington on Monday. Then he and Eleanor, as codirectors of OCD, flew to the West Coast to inspect civil defense preparations there. He was in Seattle Tuesday afternoon. Asked about the false alarms in his hometown, he barked, "Am I embarrassed? Am I humiliated? And won't somebody catch hell about this when I get home!" Yet there were two more false alarms that week—one at rush hour on Wednesday morning prompted by misidentified navy seaplanes. And in another case of mistaken identity the following week, a B-17 patrolling out of Mitchel Field dropped four bombs at a U.S. destroyer steaming past Montauk.

All the New York papers howled for the mayor to come home and take care of his own city before showing off in anyone else's. The *World-Telegram* blasted him as "a dizzy show off...juggling multiple jobs." The *Herald Tribune* called his absence a "tragic absurdity." The *Times* and other papers all insisted that La Guardia give up the OCD job.

Harry Hopkins suggested that FDR take the OCD away from the mayor and give it to Willkie. Roosevelt would characteristically dither for a few weeks, hoping to finesse the situation, but in mid-January he would persuade La Guardia to resign. It would be a blow to both La Guardia's ego and his reputation, and not the last.

Though Nazi bombers would never pose an actual threat to the city, German U-boats certainly did. On Wednesday, December 10, Admiral Andrews's Coastal Frontier office announced: "A mined area covering the approaches to New York Harbor has been established. Incoming vessels will secure directions for safe navigation from patrol vessel stationed off Ambrose Channel Entrance." The navy also stretched a steel antisubmarine net across the entrance to the New York harbor from Norton Point near Coney Island to Hoffman Island near Staten Island. From now to the end of the war, some fifteen thousand ships leaving New York with munitions or other war matériel would be sent up the East River and out to Long Island Sound, a more protected route than the Lower Bay where U-boats prowled.

Out to sea, Andrews deployed some light Coast Guard vessels as observers, while three army spotter planes from Mitchel Field started to make two flights daily farther out over the Atlantic, hoping to sight periscopes breaking the surface—although, Andrews noted in a fretful report, "should enemy submarines operate off this coast, this command has no forces available to take adequate action against them, either offensive or defensive." His complaint would very shortly prove prophetic.

⁀

In a cold twist of fate, the defense lawyers for the Duquesne Spy Ring in Brooklyn began summations on Monday. They pleaded futilely with the stone-faced jury not to let Sunday's attack on Pearl Harbor prejudice their decisions. At midnight on Saturday, December 13, the jury found them all guilty. The judge would hand down sentences on January 2. Herman Lang and Fritz Duquesne drew the longest—they each got eighteen years. The rest got a year up to sixteen. Lang would be shorn of his citizenship and deported in 1950. Duquesne was taken to Leavenworth. He was a frail seventy-seven when finally released in 1954. Back in New York City, placed in a nursing home by his parole officer, he would die of a stroke in 1956.

Wilhelm Sebold, the double agent who had sunk Duquesne et al., entered a witness protection program and moved to California. He did not enjoy a hero's life. He worried about the safety of his family back in Germany until the war was over. Plagued by ill health, he would drift from job to job through the postwar years and 1950s and suffer bouts of depression that saw him committed to a state mental institution, where he died in 1970.

⁀

In a fireside chat in the spring of 1940, Roosevelt had warned Americans, "Today's threat to our national security is not a matter of military weapons alone. We know of new methods of attack—the Trojan Horse, the Fifth Column that betrays a nation unprepared for treachery. Spies, saboteurs and traitors are the actors in this new strategy. With all of these we must and will deal vigorously."

A month later, in June 1940, he had signed the Alien Registration Act, aka the Smith Act. It made it a crime punishable by up to twenty years imprisonment to advocate the overthrow of the federal or local governments. Now he directed Attorney General Francis Biddle to use the Smith Act to begin rounding up and putting away some of the country's more vocal and visible Nazi sympathizers.

Laura Ingalls was the first woman arrested. Unable to post bail, she would sit behind bars until her trial the following February. Witnesses would remember her wearing a swastika pendant and calling Hitler "a marvelous man." The prosecutor called her a "missionary for the Nazi cause." Ingalls claimed that it was all a ruse. She said she'd gone to Hoover and offered to spy on the Nazis for the FBI; when he turned her down she went ahead on her own, ingratiating herself at the embassy so that she could gather intelligence on Nazi activities in the United States. She admitted that she'd said and written much praise of Hitler, but only to maintain her cover. Questioned about why she'd never passed any information to the FBI, she said she'd been arrested before her investigations were complete.

The jury didn't buy it. It took them only an hour to convict. She gave a grand prepared speech at her sentencing hearing. "My motives were born of a burning patriotism and a high idealism," she said. She declared herself "a truer patriot than those who convicted me," and concluded with, "I salute the Republic of the United States." ("Republic" was right-wing code. They liked to say that they honored the republican virtues of the founding fathers but not the mongrel, rabble democracy of modern times.)

The judge gave her eight months to two years behind bars and sent her to the District of Columbia prison. According to the *Daily Mirror*, when denied parole in October 1942 she would begin to "act up. She continually praised Hitler as a great man and expounded on 'what a wonderful place this will be' when Hitler takes over." She was placed in solitary confinement "because her ranting and screaming so disrupted prison routine." When she tried to organize white women inmates against black ones, the white women beat her up, reportedly breaking her nose and a few ribs. She would be removed to the West Virginia federal women's reformatory in July 1943 and serve the remainder of her sentence there before being released that October.

She would emerge unrepentant. Her response to D-day would be that it was “a power lust, blood drunk orgy” and that the Germans were fighting for “the independence of Europe—independence from the Jews. Bravo!” The following month, she was stopped in El Paso trying to cross into Mexico; government agents found her suitcase stuffed with pro-Nazi and pro-Japanese literature. She was turned back. After that she would settle in Burbank, California, fade into obscurity, and die quietly in 1967.

CHAPTER 32

You're a Sap, Mr. Jap

While Mayor La Guardia's civil defense operation was looking a bit chaotic in the first days of the war, another group of New Yorkers got themselves organized and responded with amazing alacrity: the songwriters of Tin Pan Alley. On the evening of December 7, according to "Gotham Grapevine" columnist Harold Conrad, Lindy's deli and restaurant, a favorite hangout of Tin Pan Alley and Broadway types, was already crowded with "song-pluggers, hoofers, comedians, tragedians and press agents" who were "mapping a battle plan for our Pacific fleet."

Conrad was joking. But in fact Tin Pan Alley's songwriters reacted to Pearl Harbor with instant fury and patriotic zeal, churning out hundreds of war songs at a ferocious clip. Amateurs jumped into the fray as well. By December 20, just two weeks later, New York's *Billboard* (renamed *Billboard Music Weekly* in 1961) was already reporting that music publishers had received more than *one thousand* war song submissions. Only a fraction were ever published and recorded, but even that amounted to a lot of records, and a few would have big impacts on American morale early in the war.

The hive of most of that activity was the Brill Building on the west side of Broadway between 49th and 50th Streets. At the start of the century, when the term "Tin Pan Alley" was coined, the music business was concentrated on West 28th Street between Fifth and Sixth Avenues, with Broadway cutting diagonally through. Its nickname referred to the constant racket of cheap upright pianos where guys stacked five stories high toiled long into the night banging out a cacophony of competing tunes. By 1941 most of the publishers had migrated uptown to the eleven-story Brill Building, opened in 1931. Lindy's, immortalized by Damon Runyon as Mindy's, was across Broadway.

The first two Tin Pan Alley songs reacting to Pearl Harbor—"We'll Knock the Japs Right into the Laps of the Nazis" and "We Did It Before (and We Can Do It Again)"—were allegedly written that very day, December 7. Hearing the news from Hawaii, composer Lew Pollack and lyricist Ned Washington whipped out "We'll Knock the Japs" on Sunday afternoon and rushed it to Bert Wheeler, of the vaudeville and Broadway comedy duo Wheeler & Woolsey. (Woolsey had died in 1938.) Wheeler apparently introduced the song that night as part of his club act in Los Angeles. In part the chorus went:

Oh, we didn't want to do it but they're asking for it now
So we'll knock the Japs right into the laps of the Nazis.

Also on Sunday, another pair of Tin Pan Alley stalwarts, Charles Tobias and Cliff Friend, knocked out "We Did It Before," a rousing George M. Cohan–style march. Friend, a Cincinnati-born composer who had moved to New York at Al Jolson's urging in the 1920s, is best known now for having written the theme song for *Looney Tunes* ("The Merry-Go-Round Broke Down") in 1937. New York–born Tobias's long list of credits includes "Those Lazy-Hazy-Crazy Days of Summer," "Merrily We Roll Along"—which he cowrote with his brother-in-law Eddie Cantor, and which Warner Bros. adapted for its Merrie Melodies theme song—as well as one that became a huge hit during the war, "Don't Sit Under the Apple Tree (With Anyone Else but Me)."

Cantor (born Israel Iskowitz on the Lower East Side) introduced "We Did It Before" on his popular weekly radio show *Time to Smile* that Wednesday, December 10. Dinah Shore sang it on her radio show the following Sunday, and Cantor went on to interpolate it into his stage revue *Banjo Eyes*, which opened on Broadway on Christmas Day and ran into April 1942. The sheet music was a top ten seller for a couple of months. Bringing things full circle, in 1943 Warner Bros. would use the song in a Merrie Melodies cartoon, *Fifth Column Mouse*, in which the mice mobilize for war against a dictatorial cat.

By Monday morning, December 8, the Tin Pan Alley trio of lyricist James Cavanaugh (best known for "You're Nobody till Somebody Loves You"), John Redmond, and Nat Simon had written the upbeat "You're a Sap, Mr. Jap":

You're a sap, Mr. Jap, you make a Yankee cranky,
You're a sap, Mr. Jap, Uncle Sam is gonna spanky

It was released as a single before the month was out. In 1942 it also found its way into a cartoon, the first Popeye cartoon of the war, with caricatures of Japanese that were so extreme it was removed from circulation after the war—along with a number of other patriotically racist cartoons—and rarely seen again until the birth of the Internet.

By the week of January 11 *Billboard* counted twenty-four war singles released since December 7. There was the catchy "Goodbye Mama, I'm Off to Yokohama," written by Brooklyn-born J. Fred Coots, better known for writing "Santa Claus Is Coming to Town" in 1934. The singer of this song was going to "teach all those Japs / The Yanks are no saps."

Kate Smith weighed in with the spritely "They Started Somethin' (But We're Gonna End It)" and the sentimental ballad "Dear Mom," a soldier's letter home. She would follow them in February with "This Time," a not particularly memorable Irving Berlin number. ("We'll fight to the finish this time / Then we'll never have to do it again.") *Billboard* listed three different recordings of the inevitable "Remember Pearl Harbor," plus the clever "Let's Put the Axe to the Axis" and the swinging "The Sun Will Soon Be Setting (For the Land of the Rising Sun)."

The list also included two interesting "hillbilly" songs, as country music was then called. They emanated not from Nashville but the Brill Building. Tin Pan Alley had been exploring the relatively small markets for hillbilly and folk music since the 1920s. Then the genres got a boost in popularity in 1941 from an unlikely source. In January, ASCAP (American Society of Composers, Authors and Publishers), the professional organization that licensed music to the radio broadcasters, demanded a doubling in fees. Broadcasters responded by pulling all ASCAP music from the airwaves and plugged the gap with music by non-ASCAP members, especially hillbilly and folk. By October, when ASCAP and the broadcasters came to new terms, hillbilly and folk had expanded their niche in the market, and the Tin Pan Alley pros cashed in.

One of those pros was Fred Rose, whose "Cowards Over Pearl Harbor" was a mournful, guitar-strumming folk ballad recorded by Denver Darling. Two of the most prolific were Memphis-born Bob Miller and Kansas-born Carson Robison, who both came to Tin Pan Alley in the

1920s. Miller worked for a while as Irving Berlin's arranger, while Robison specialized in country and cowboy songs that humorously treated topical themes. Their response to Pearl Harbor was the outrageous "We're Gonna Have to Slap the Dirty Little Jap," sung to a silly, quick-time oompah melody.

Robison went on to record several more humorous war songs, including "Mussolini's Letter to Hitler" and its flip side "Hitler's Reply to Mussolini," "Get Your Gun and Come Along (We're Fixin to Kill a Skunk)," and "Who's Gonna Bury Hitler (When the Ornery Cuss Is Dead)?"

Far and away the most successful song responding to Pearl Harbor was Frank Loesser's "Praise the Lord and Pass the Ammunition," one of the biggest hits of 1942. Within his family, Loesser was a sort of class traitor. He was born in 1910 and raised on the Upper West Side in a refined, cultured German Jewish household, the kind of Jews that Lower East Side Jews called a *yekke*, a Yiddish word that connoted a finicky mania for punctuality and *Ordnung* they saw as more German than the Germans. The Loessers spoke German in the home and knew no Yiddish, which they considered a gutter dialect. They read Goethe and played Beethoven on the Victrola. Frank's father and older half brother Arthur were classical concert pianists and teachers. No form of popular culture, especially pop music, was allowed in the home.

Frank dismayed the family when he went first to Tin Pan Alley and then to Hollywood, where he wrote the lyrics for such standards as "Heart and Soul," "Baby, It's Cold Outside," and "Two Sleepy People." Along the way, he spent so much time working with the Lower East Side Jews who ran the music and movie businesses that he came to talk, dress, and act like them, and new people who met him just assumed that's what he was. His daughter would later write that he seemed to believe it himself.

"Praise the Lord" was inspired by a Pearl Harbor legend concerning the fleet chaplain ("sky pilot" in the song) Father William A. Maguire, who helped carry ammo to the guns firing at the attacking planes and supposedly cried out the song's title. Father Maguire told *Life* he didn't remember saying the line and it would not have been heard in all the uproar even if he did, but you can't stop a legend. In some versions—including Loesser's—Maguire actually manned a gun himself.

Loesser wrote both the music and the words, which was unusual for him at the time. First recorded by the vocal quartet the Merry Macs, then by Kay Kyser and others, "Praise the Lord" sold huge numbers in both disc and sheet music, nearly matching Irving Berlin's giant "White Christmas" in sales and jukebox plays for a time. No doubt much of its popularity stemmed from its easy-to-sing simplicity, with lyrics that weren't much more than the title repeated over and over to a strolling melody that sounded like an old-time spiritual. Loesser donated his proceeds from the song to the U.S. Navy Relief Fund.

⌒

New York's comic book publishers also jumped straight into the war effort. Within a few weeks of Pearl Harbor, a very unusual hero joined Captain America in the fight against Nazis and fascists.

Wonder Woman was the creation of William Moulton Marston, a feminist and psychologist with a strong interest, both personally and professionally, in nontraditional sexuality, including polygamy, bondage, and dominant, "Amazonian" females. Brilliant, eccentric, and self-promoting, he invented the lie detector when he was still a junior at Harvard, though an assistant later beat him to the patent office with it. As a psychology professor he was inspiring to students, but a whiff of the unsavory about him made it hard for him to hold on to faculty positions, and he bounced from school to school, including Columbia, NYU, and the New School.

As a child he'd been doted on by his mother and a gaggle of aunts, and he would always surround himself with strong, somewhat androgynous women. His wife, Sadie, was "a whip-smart tomboy," Jill Lepore writes in *The Secret History of Wonder Woman*. The other love of his life, Olive Byrne, was also a tomboy—a "boyette" in 1920s slang—a denizen of Greenwich Village and niece of Planned Parenthood's Margaret Sanger. She started out one of Marston's students, then joined him and Sadie in a permanent threesome. He had children with both of them and they all raised them together in a big, boisterously unconventional household in the New York suburbs. Lepore finds elements of both Sadie and Olive in Wonder Woman, including the heroine's cry of "Suffering Sappho!," which was suggested by Sadie; and her magic bracelets, modeled on ones Olive wore.

In 1937, Marston held a press conference at the Harvard Club near Grand Central and announced that within the next millennium women would come to rule the world. The *Times*, the *Washington Post*, and other papers around the country reported it. Three years later, as the Blitzkrieg raced through Europe in 1940, critics began to fret that comic book superheroes like Superman and Captain America came a little too close to the Nazis' ideal of Aryan masculinity. *Time* came right out and asked, "Are Comics Fascist?" Marston approached Max Gaines with a partial solution: a female superhero, who would embody his ideas about feminine superiority. He called her Suprema, the Wonder Woman.

Gaines dropped the "Suprema" but kept all of Marston's other ideas. Wonder Woman debuted in *All Star Comics* in October 1941 (cover dated December), and was on the cover of *Sensation Comics* the following January. As the war progressed she would fight not only Nazis and the Japanese—her nemesis Doctor Psycho was said to be the mastermind behind Hitler, Mussolini, and Tojo—but male chauvinists on the home front as well. At the same time, Wonder Woman rather openly revealed Marston's interests in alternative sexual activities. "Not a comic book in which Wonder Woman appeared, and hardly a page, lacked a scene of bondage," Lepore notes. "In episode after episode, Wonder Woman is chained, bound, gagged, lassoed, tied, fettered, and manacled." This did not go unnoticed at the time, but despite fretful critics Wonder Woman was as big a success as Superman—not only with adolescents but with adults. Marston got fan mail from men sharing his interest in erotic bondage, and Wonder Woman went on to be as popular a pinup for lonely GIs as Betty Grable was.

During the war, many other comic book, radio, and movie serial heroes would join the fight against the Axis. Hop Harrigan, "America's Ace of the Airways," started as another Max Gaines comic book hero, then went on to radio and serials. Gaines's competition at Fawcett Comics created Captain Marvel and his nemesis Captain Nazi as well as Spy Smasher. Flying ace Captain Midnight, who originated on Chicago radio in the late 1930s before coming to Mutual in New York in 1940, also fought Nazis and Japs around the world. Kids who became honorary members of his Secret Squadron swore an oath "to save my country from the dire peril it faces or perish in the attempt." And of course Superman and Batman did their parts as well—though Superman's creators had to keep him from participating directly in the war, because it would have ended in a few days if he did.

CHAPTER 33

Lights Out

When it went into service in 1935, the French-owned SS *Normandie* was the world's largest passenger liner. Like the special dock built to accommodate it at Saint-Nazaire on the French coast, Pier 88 on the midtown Manhattan waterfront had to be lengthened to receive it. It was also the fastest ocean liner ever, shuttling passengers across the Atlantic in four days of art deco luxury.

It made its last run to New York in August 1939; when the war started the following month, the French government decided it was too big and juicy a target for U-boats and kept it safely berthed at Pier 88. When the United States entered the war in December 1941, Roosevelt had the U.S. Navy seize the giant ship as property of the enemy Vichy government. The navy renamed it the USS *Lafayette* and began hastily converting it into a troopship, painting it regulation gray and stripping it of its opulent furnishings.

That work was proceeding on February 9, 1942, a few weeks before it was to carry its first ten thousand troops to England. At 2:30 in the afternoon a spark from a welder's torch ignited a stack of kapok life preservers in the main saloon. As the fire and smoke spread quickly, some three thousand sailors, Coast Guard men, and civilian workers on the ship rushed around in confusion. Almost three hundred sustained injuries, and one worker from Brooklyn was killed. Acrid smoke billowed over midtown, and it seemed that all of Manhattan rushed to the scene. Fire boats, fire trucks, and ambulances, air raid wardens and Red Cross volunteers, Mayor La Guardia, navy officials, and the police swarmed in what the *Tribune* called the city's first major test of wartime preparedness. Onlookers braved the blustery cold to mass along the elevated West Side Highway.

The blaze was brought under control in six hours, but so much water had been poured on it that the ship began to list to port, away from the pier. At 2:45 a.m. it went over on its side and settled in the mud, its stacks barely out of the water.

Inevitably there were rumors that the fire was the work of Nazi saboteurs. Vincent Astor was on the scene in minutes, personally conducting as much of an investigation as was possible in the chaos. He would tell Roosevelt that he agreed with the consensus that the fire was accidental. It was his last report. A week later, the *Journal-American* ran a small article blowing Astor's cover. Astor was forced to retire from the spy game.

The *Normandie* would lie on its side into 1943, looking forlorn and, many thought, ominous. The navy and civilian salvagers eventually refloated it and towed it first to the Brooklyn Navy Yard, then to a Red Hook dry dock. The navy would sell it for scrap after the war.

⌒

After Pearl Harbor, much of the navy's Atlantic fleet was sent to the Pacific, leaving only a handful of warships. Most of those were assigned to guard convoys in the mid-Atlantic, so that in early 1942 Admiral Andrews was left guarding the entire eastern seaboard with only his handful of Coast Guard vessels and a few spotter-plane pilots.

Fortunately for him, Admiral Karl Dönitz, head of the U-boat fleet, was at first similarly hamstrung. In January 1942 he had only five U-boats to deploy in a line from Canada to the Carolinas to attack coastal shipping, a project code-named Operation Drumbeat. Still, they did significant damage. Drumbeat began on the evening of January 11 when the submarine *U-123* sank a British freighter approaching the port of Halifax. Three nights later *U-123* was about a hundred miles off Montauk at the tip of Long Island when another tanker strayed into its sights and was sunk. The next night, *U-123* was gliding past Coney Island, so close that its crew was enchanted by the twinkling lights of the Ferris wheel and Parachute Jump, with the bright haze of Manhattan beyond. Silhouetted by those lights, the British tanker *Coimbra*, just emerging from the New York harbor with its belly full of lubricating oil bound for England, was an easy target. A single torpedo amidships ignited that oil in a giant fireball; the *Coimbra* broke in half and sank instantly. The captain and thirty-five crewmen died.

In February, Dönitz was able to put two dozen U-boats along the coastline, with spectacular results. That month U-boats sank thirty-six ships along the eastern seaboard. Among them was the World War I–era destroyer *Jacob Jones*, which left the Brooklyn Navy Yard on February 27 to patrol off Cape May. On this day it encountered the burning wreckage of a tanker torpedoed by *U-578*. Just before dawn the next day, *U-578* struck the *Jones* with two torpedoes. The destroyer's depth charges exploded, sending it to the bottom. It was the first navy warship sunk in coastal waters. Only eleven men of a crew of 149 survived.

U-boats sank another fifty vessels in March. By the end of June, the total would be 226 vessels sunk in Atlantic coastal waters, plus more in the Caribbean and Gulf of Mexico. U-boat men would remember the first six months of 1942 as a glorious time when they had virtually free reign to hunt and kill as they pleased just off America's shores. Oil, life rafts, and other detritus from sunken vessels washed up on Long Island's beaches, where people gazed at the black smoke of ships burning out at sea.

As the sinkings continued through the spring, a frantic Admiral Andrews scraped together what he called a "bucket brigade," in which the few warships at his disposal shepherded small convoys of merchant vessels making zigzag daylight hops from one port to the next to the next along the eastern seaboard. The waters off New York were so U-boat infested that shipping was temporarily routed around the port, causing thousands of workers in New York's harbor to be laid off.

Andrews also wanted a blackout of the coastal lights that were silhouetting merchant ships like targets in a shooting gallery every night. Mayor La Guardia, the mayor of Atlantic City, and seaside businessmen all argued that a blackout would be ruinous to their local economies. A compromise was struck, and the army imposed a "dimout" of the entire eastern seaboard, which went into effect the night of April 28. Total blackout drills would occasionally be conducted.

The effects of the dimout in New York City were dramatic enough. As though a giant switch had been thrown, the city went dark at nights, and stayed that way until the end of the war. Along the shoreline, no lights that could be seen more than a mile out to sea were allowed. Coney Island stayed open but went gloomy, lit only by weak night-lights in vendors' stalls and dim lamps, their sides painted black, barely illuminating the boardwalk—where you weren't supposed to smoke now, because it was thought lurking U-boats might spot the glow. The Statue of Liberty went dark, except for two small aircraft warning lights in the torch. The torch would be relit later in the war as the threat of U-boats faded.

All over the city, streetlamps and traffic lights were dimmed, and vehicle headlights were painted over to emit just thin strips of light, low-beam only, or drivers crept along using their parking lights. Outdoor floodlights at parks, parking lots, stockyards, and shipyards were shut off or dimmed to a wan glow as night fell. Night games at the Polo Grounds and Ebbets Field ended. Lights inside office and apartment towers from the fifteenth floor up were switched off or hidden behind blackout shades. Homes were also supposed to be darkened. Compliance with this was never fully achieved, as night photos of the city's wartime skyline show. The volunteer air raid warden's cry of "*Hey, turn out that light! Don't you know there's a war on?*" would be so familiar it became a cliché.

Without their external floodlights, people said, landmarks such as the Empire State and Chrysler buildings, Rockefeller Center, and St. Patrick's Cathedral looked like giant mausoleums. Times Square was a somewhat different story. The truth was, long before the dimout Times Square had already lost much of its luster. From the Great War through the Prohibition 1920s, Times Square had been the dazzling, racing heart of Manhattan, and the whole world pulsed through its theaters, movie palaces, bars, restaurants, and nightclubs. Then the Depression shut down most of its theaters and other legitimate businesses. The area took on a sleazier, seedier reputation through the 1930s as a lower class of nightlife flowed into the empty spaces—burlesque houses (until La Guardia went on a campaign to shut them down), movie grind houses, dime-a-dance halls, amusement arcades. The toffs in their top hats and gowns were replaced by hoodlums and gamblers, drug dealers and their customers, and prostitutes male and female strolling 42nd Street in increasing numbers.

Still, if it was a sinkhole of vice, at least it was a dazzlingly lit-up one, and now even that ended. The multicolored neon signs that flashed and shimmied and sparkled all over the area and gave it its hectic year-round carnival atmosphere now went black. The Wrigley's fish blowing neon bubbles, the neon peanuts cascading out of the Planters bag, the Four Roses bouquet blooming above it, the neon Bromo-Seltzer fizz, and all the others. The Wrigley's sign would be pulled down and donated to a scrap metal drive. The Camel cigarette man, who began blowing perfect five-foot smoke rings (actually steam) every four seconds day and night from the facade of the Hotel Claridge at Broadway and West 44th Street in 1941, kept puffing, but those rings floating silently over the darkened street now looked strange and spooky. Originally a civilian, the Camel man would become a soldier, sailor, and marine during the war years. The *Times* Zipper stopped zipping after dark. Movie and theater marquees went out, with only weak lights underneath. Because of the dimout, in 1942 and '43 the dropping of the ball on New Year's Eve in Times Square, begun by *Times* owner Adolph Ochs in 1907, was replaced by a moment of silence.

The start of the dimout significantly hampered the U-boats' effectiveness at night. Andrews also accepted offers of help from two groups of civilians. Formed a week before Pearl Harbor by La Guardia's OCD, the Civilian Air Patrol (CAP) was put at Andrews's service to augment his handful of military spotter planes. The second offer came from New York businessman Alfred Stanford, commodore of the Cruising Club of America, an organization of yachting and sailing enthusiasts. Arguing that wooden ships under sail could approach U-boats undetected, he proposed organizing a fleet of them to patrol coastal waters and spot, report, even attack the enemy. Despite skepticism in the upper echelons of the navy, Congress approved Stanford's plan in June, placing his citizen navy under the auspices of the Coast Guard Reserve. It was officially known as the Coastal Picket Patrol, colloquially as the Corsair Fleet or, as some in the navy scoffed, the Hooligan Navy. Rufus Smith, editor of the magazine *Yachting*, came on to run it, operating out of the deepwater harbor at Greenport, a sailing village on the eastern tip of Long Island that had previously sheltered pirates and bootleggers. A dockside tavern named Claudio's became the corsairs' favorite hangout.

The Corsair Fleet very quickly put to sea in more than four hundred private ships, from luxury yachts to humble fishing schooners, forming a picket line all down the coast. They were manned by some twenty-five hundred volunteers who ranged from millionaires to college boys, sport fishermen, former rumrunners, and one member of the Glenn Miller Orchestra, all too young or too old for the military or otherwise undraftable. The ships' hulls were painted Coast Guard gray. Walt Disney drew their insignia: Donald Duck in a pirate outfit. They were outfitted with ship-to-shore radios, primitive hydrophones, and surplus guns, including mounted 50-caliber machine guns dating back to the Spanish-American War. Some carried small depth charges, not much bigger than paint cans, that the crews could toss over the side. Volunteers brought their own rifles and tommy guns as well.

Actual combat with a U-boat, in which the sailing vessel would be at a suicidal disadvantage, was not encouraged. The Hooligan Navy's best service was to spot and report. In daylight the U-boats stayed submerged, with at most a periscope breaking the surface. In the dark of night they surfaced for fresh air and to recharge their batteries, and it was then that the pickets might hear or smell their diesel surface engines. Encounters were rare. The crew of one yacht drifting just outside the New York harbor thought that their hydrophone was picking up the electric motors of a submerged U-boat. Two navy destroyers charged to the spot and dropped depth charges. It turned out the crew had been hearing the motor of the refrigerator in their own galley. The Hooligan Navy served into the autumn of 1943, and although it never sank any U-boats its presence helped to keep them running and hiding.

Between the burning of the *Normandie* and the U-boats running rampant off the coast, the New York Office of Naval Intelligence was deeply concerned about "possible sabotage by enemy agents" in New York's harbor, and "subversive activities among those who worked as longshoremen, stevedores and other similar workers." The ONI also wanted to know if informants at the shipping companies were feeding the Germans intelligence about convoy movements, and if commercial fishing fleets, or maybe the Mafia's former rumrunners, were sneaking out to sell the U-boats fuel and supplies.

ONI agents who infiltrated the waterfront were stonewalled by tight-lipped longshoremen. So on March 7, one month after the *Normandie* fire, ONI officers met with Manhattan's district attorney Frank Hogan and Murray Gurfein, who ran Hogan's Rackets Bureau and had been one of Dewey's top investigators. They asked if the gangsters who ran the waterfront might be persuaded to do their patriotic duty and help out. Gurfein thought they might, and Operation Underworld commenced.

A native New Yorker, Gurfein had graduated Phi Beta Kappa from Columbia and second in his class at Harvard Law. He was stocky and street smart, and the gangsters knew to respect him. He went to see Joe "Socks" Lanza, the mobster who dominated the Fulton Fish Market. No fisherman pulled into the market and no trucker pulled away without paying Lanza his cut. In fact, Hogan was preparing to indict him for racketeering. Lanza agreed to cooperate. With his help, the ONI put undercover agents on fishing boats all along the eastern seaboard to watch for U-boats and other suspicious activities. Despite this patriotic service, Hogan would have Lanza arrested early in 1943 and convicted of racketeering.

As a midlevel mobster, Lanza had no pull with either Albert Anastasia's Brooklyn operations or Joe Ryan's Irish West Side waterfront. To get to them, Gurfein contacted Meyer Lansky. Lansky was considered one of the big brains in the mob. As a Russian Jewish immigrant, he was also fiercely anti-Nazi and had, allegedly with Rabbi Stephen Wise's blessing and tips from Walter Winchell, sent Jewish toughs to disrupt a few Bund events in Fritz Kuhn's heyday. Lansky quickly agreed to assist Gurfein, and he suggested another partner in the operation: Lucky Luciano, who was only a few years into the thirty-to-fifty-year prison term that Dewey, with Gurfein's help, had won against him.

In May, the feds moved Luciano from the grim Dannemora prison to the more amenable Great Meadow Correctional Facility. Lansky met with him there and explained that if he helped the navy his sentence might be reduced. Luciano quickly agreed. Lansky acted as Luciano's contact with Ryan and Anastasia, and he reported regularly to the ONI. The ILA agreed not to strike for the duration. Dockworkers were instructed to report any suspicious activities or shipments, and to keep their mouths shut (a practice they were well used to) about any movement of troops or war supplies they witnessed. John "Cockeye" Dunn, one of Ryan's more vicious goons, enforced wartime D&D (Deaf & Dumb) on the West Side. (In 1947, Dunn would be convicted for the murder of a recalcitrant longshoreman who, when police asked him who had shot him five times, allegedly uttered the immortal last words, "Dunn. He done well too." Dunn would be executed in Sing Sing in 1949, the beginning of the end of the Irish gangsters' waterfront rule.)

In 1943, as the Allies prepared to invade Sicily, Lansky would bring numerous Sicilian-born New Yorkers to the ONI to be interviewed on any details they remembered about ports, the coastline, and other useful details of the landscape. At the same time, Luciano asked his Mafia contacts in Sicily to cooperate with the invading forces when they arrived.

Historians still debate how much help Luciano actually was to the war effort. But the arrangement was certainly helpful to the Mafia. The feds let Lansky, Frank Costello, and other of the city's top gangsters make numerous visits to Green Meadow during the war. After discussing the war effort, they'd lean their heads together and conduct their own business in whispers. Whatever the value of Luciano's assistance, the bargain with him would be kept; Governor Thomas Dewey would commute his sentence in 1946 and he'd be deported to Italy.

Anastasia would do his part for the war effort as well. In 1942 he went into the U.S. Army, even though he was not a citizen. There's still some mystery about how and why this happened. He was made a technical sergeant and sent to the base at Fort Indiantown Gap in central Pennsylvania. Although it was far from any waterfront, his job was to train GIs as longshoremen. His reward would be citizenship papers in 1943. He was honorably discharged in 1944 and moved with his family to New Jersey, picking up his mob activities where he'd left off. In the 1950s, government attempts to revoke his citizenship and deport him would be blocked in the courts. In 1957 he'd be shot to death in a mob hit while sitting in a barber chair in the lobby of the Park Sheraton Hotel at Seventh Avenue and West 55th Street.

⌒

One small group of Nazi saboteurs did actually infiltrate New York City in June 1942.

Shortly after midnight on the morning of Saturday, June 13, a twenty-one-year-old Coast Guardsman from the Bronx, John Cullen, started walking a lonely beat along the beach near Amagansett, on the eastern tip of Long Island. A red-faced Irishman with wavy hair and blue eyes, he'd been delivering furniture for Macy's when the war started and he signed up. Now he was patrolling the beach for Nazis, though if he did run into any his only defense was his flashlight. And even that wasn't much good as a thick fog rolled in off the surf, making the moonless night even darker. He had left the Coast Guard's wood-framed lifeboat station to walk three miles along the beach and back, a two-hour tour. To keep himself company in the misty dark he sang hit tunes, including Glenn Miller's "I've Got a Gal in Kalamazoo" and Jimmy Dorsey's "Tangerine."

He'd been out fifteen minutes when his flashlight suddenly picked out a group of three or four men struggling to haul some boxes out of the low-tide waves. Startled, he called out, and one of them strolled over. He was a hatchet-faced man in his thirties with a distinctive gray streak in his slicked-back hair. Acting both friendly and edgy, and speaking with a slight accent Cullen couldn't place, he told Cullen they were fishermen out of East Hampton whose boat had run aground. In soggy, wrinkled street clothes, they didn't look like fishermen. When Cullen invited them to come wait out the night at his Coast Guard station the man turned hostile. Cullen heard one of the others growl what sounded like German, and knew he was in trouble.

"I wouldn't want to kill you," the hatchet-faced man said. "You don't know what this is all about." Then he produced a pouch, pulled $300 from it, and pressed the money into Cullen's hands. He asked Cullen if he'd recognize him if he saw him again. Cullen said no. Satisfied that they had an understanding, the man watched as Cullen backed away into the fog.

As Cullen ran back toward the Coast Guard station, the men on the beach dragged four wooden crates up from the surf and hastily covered them with sand. Then they crawled inland across low dunes and scrub. Eventually they came to the tracks of the Long Island Rail Road and followed them to the small station at Amagansett. They hid in bushes, waiting for dawn. When the station opened, the hatchet-faced man went in and bought four one-way tickets to Jamaica, Queens, from the sleepy stationmaster. When the train left Amagansett at 6:59 a.m. the four men in their wrinkled clothes were the only passengers.

They were all German. Cullen had stumbled across Operation Pastorius, a plan for infiltrating saboteurs into the United States to strike industrial plants and other sites. It was organized by Walter Kappe, the man who had returned to Germany from New York in 1937 after Fritz Kuhn pushed him out of the Bund. He was now an Abwehr officer.

When the United States was neutral, Hitler and his Abwehr chief Admiral Wilhelm Canaris had agreed that sabotage could only provoke the sleeping giant. Now that the Japanese had aroused the beast, Hitler approved of any program that might cripple America's awesome industrial might. Canaris remained skeptical, as did Admiral Dönitz, who'd have to lend some of his precious U-boats to sneak saboteurs onto the American continent. But Hitler wanted it, so Operation Pastorius was a go.

Born weak and halfhearted, the operation was doomed from the start. Kappe handpicked Germans who had lived in America. The Abwehr hastily trained them in bomb making and other sabotage skills, and they were provided with false papers and fantastic amounts of American cash to buy whatever and whomever they might need to complete their mission. Eight men were selected for the first wave. The submarine *U-202* set off for

Long Island with four of them, while another U-boat carried four more to Florida.

The hatchet-faced man was George Dasch. In 1922, at the age of nineteen, he had stowed away on a German liner and jumped ship in Philadelphia, where his first American meal was coffee and pie at a Horn & Hardart Automat. He made his way to New York, where he lived on and off until 1941, waiting tables at various restaurants in the city and out on Long Island in the Hamptons. He liked America, took citizenship, and even spent a year in the U.S. Army Air Corps. When the war started in Europe he felt drawn back home even though he'd never much cared for the Nazis. Kappe got him a job with the Abwehr translating overseas radio broadcasts, then recruited him for Pastorius.

Ernst Burger, Dasch's sidekick, had joined the Nazi Party at seventeen and fled to America when the movement was struggling in the mid-1920s. He went back to Germany when Hitler assumed power in 1933, but for his allegiance to SA leader Ernst Röhm, whom Hitler had executed in 1934, he spent seventeen months in a Gestapo prison.

Richard Quirin was a mechanic who had lived in Schenectady from 1927 to 1939, joined the Bund, then returned to Germany and a good job assembling Volkswagens. The fourth man, Heinrich Heinck, was another mechanic at Volkswagen. He had jumped ship in New York in 1926, also joined the Bund, and returned to Germany in 1939.

The four of them made a rather pathetic team of saboteurs. They'd received sketchy training and had only the vaguest plans for carrying out their grandiose mission to blow up hydroelectric dams, Alcoa plants, bridges, railroad lines—anything to spread fear and disrupt America's war industry. They'd just left all their sabotage gear in a shallow pit on the beach. They were bedraggled and nervous. Quirin and Heinck believed in the mission, but Dasch and Burger were far from committed to it.

When they reached Jamaica they split into two pairs, and each pair went on a shopping spree, buying themselves spiffy new American outfits. Then they proceeded into Manhattan. It's indicative of how hapless their operation was that, when they got there, they found Manhattan in the midst of what the *Times* would call "the greatest spectacle of its kind New York has ever seen"—a massive, all-day "New York at War" parade, organized by Mayor La Guardia's Committee for Mobilization.

As bombers and fighters from Mitchel Field roared in the blue sky over the would-be saboteurs' heads, some half a million "soldiers, sailors, marines, industrial workers, air raid wardens and others, including just plain 'little people' of the home front," were marching up Fifth Avenue from Washington Square to 79th Street, accompanied by rumbling tanks and artillery fresh off the assembly lines and hundreds of floats. An estimated two and a half million spectators lined the avenue and tossed tons of confetti out of windows, and nearly ten thousand cops kept order. It started at 10 a.m. and went on and on until ending with a torchlit procession at 9 p.m. Several floats featured comical and grotesque caricatures of Hitler and Mussolini. The crowd cheered a German-American trade union contingent carrying "an outsized figure of a worker aiming a sledgehammer at a swastika." There were more cheers for a hundred and fifty merchant marine survivors of U-boat attacks and their banner, "The Axis Subs Don't Scare Us." Between the clanking war machinery, the blaring brass bands, and the cheering of millions, no one could hear the day's scheduled testing of the city's air raid sirens.

The *Times* reported only one untoward incident. A woman holding a homemade "Stop Hitler" sign laughed as a float caricaturing Der Führer rolled by. A man standing near her "appeared annoyed." Later, he followed her to a subway station, where he punched and kicked her. He was quickly arrested and identified as Patrick Gill, possibly one of the city's pro-Nazi Irishmen. He pleaded guilty to assault.

Dasch and Burger skipped the festivities and ducked into Macy's, where they went on another shopping spree. They bought themselves so many clothes they had to buy suitcases to haul it all back to their hotel, the thirty-two-story Governor Clinton across Seventh Avenue from Penn Station. Then they treated themselves to a big dinner in one of the hotel's restaurants. After two and a half years at war, life for most Germans on the home front was severely straitened. To the saboteurs, their purses and money belts bulging with Kappe's cash, New York seemed a cornucopia of luxuries.

Back out at Amagansett, Cullen had raced to the lifeboat house and reported his suspicious encounter with Dasch and his cohorts. The officer on duty handed Springfield rifles to Cullen and six other men, none of whom had ever fired one before. When they reached the beach, the strange men were long gone but had left a trail of footprints in the sand that led to the spot where they'd buried the four boxes. These turned out to contain their explosives and other equipment, some clearly marked in German. The Guardsmen smelled diesel fumes. Peering out at the dark, fog-banked surf, they were astonished to make out the long, low shape of a submarine lying very close to shore. It was *U-202*, which had run aground on a sandbar while dropping off the saboteurs. They watched and listened, transfixed, as the U-boat captain revved his engines, trying to rock the boat free. Finally, around 3 a.m., the incoming tide lifted it. *U-202* quickly showed them its tail and bustled out to sea. It would remain in service for another year before being sunk by a British warship.

On Sunday evening a man with a slight accent called the FBI field office in Manhattan. Identifying himself as Franz Daniel Pastorius, he said he had a story so big he could tell it only to J. Edgar Hoover himself. When the FBI man said the director was busy, the caller huffed that he'd call Washington instead. It was filed as a crank call. The FBI was hearing from a lot of overheated imaginations now that the country was at war.

The caller was Dasch. He and Burger had revealed to each other that they had no intention of carrying out their mission. Burger, still seething over his rough treatment by the Gestapo, had signed on only as a way to return to the States. Dasch had grown thoroughly disaffected with the Nazis himself and said he'd been planning to scuttle the mission from the first time Kappe had told him about it.

For the next few days, while Quirin and Heinck fumed, Dasch dithered, showing Burger the sights of the city and playing pinochle with waiter friends from his New York years. Then on Thursday he vanished. The next day he was in FBI headquarters in Washington, D.C. He spent the next week telling his life story in numbing detail as stenographers worked in shifts.

Burger expressed relief when agents barged into his room at the Governor Clinton on that Saturday. Quirin and Heinck were nabbed coming out of a deli on Amsterdam Avenue. Meanwhile, the other quartet of saboteurs, who had landed in Florida, by then had split up. Two went to Chicago, while the other pair took a train to Grand Central, booked rooms in the Commodore, and spent the next few days getting in touch with old girlfriends and Bund pals. The FBI arrested them in a midtown bar on Tuesday, June 23. The Chicago pair were soon in custody as well.

Operation Pastorius was over after two weeks, having accomplished nothing. The eight saboteurs faced a closed-door military tribunal in August. By turning themselves in and cooperating with the FBI, Dasch and Burger evaded death sentences. Dasch drew thirty years, Burger life; both would be deported to West Germany after the war. The other six were immediately executed and buried in unmarked graves.

The Coast Guard gave John Cullen a medal and would use him for publicity for the duration of the war, showing him off at parades, ship launchings, and war bond drives. He would die in 2011 at the age of ninety.

CHAPTER 34

You're in the Army Now

At the swearing in for his third term on January 1, 1942, La Guardia warned that "the war will come right to our streets and residential districts." Through the OCD he already had more than sixty thousand volunteer air raid wardens and auxiliary emergency firemen; now he asked Washington for armed troops to guard the city's waterfront, bridges, tunnels, and other potential targets against invaders, spies, and saboteurs. When the War Department turned him down, believing the city at minimal risk, he asked Governor Lehman to send National Guardsmen. But in running for reelection the previous fall the mayor had in one of his excitable moments railed that the governor was "a thief, a double-crosser and a fixer," and now the governor took pleasure in turning him down too.

Undaunted, La Guardia announced he would organize his own City Guard. Albany informed him that state law prevented municipalities from having "private armies," and that calling it a "Guard" was also prohibited. La Guardia countered that they would be "auxiliary police," not an army, and named them the City Patrol Corps. New Yorkers called it La Guardia's Army.

To command it La Guardia enlisted Major General Robert M. Danford, a West Pointer and distinguished cavalryman who had just retired at sixty-two as the army's last commander of horse-drawn artillery. On April 1 Danford moved into his headquarters at 300 Mulberry Street just above Houston Street. The mayor asked the city's employers and administrators of public agencies to encourage their workers to volunteer. The VFW and American Legion proved rich sources of volunteers as well. A recruitment office appeared in Pershing Square, across from Grand Central.

The mayor also eyed the approximately one and a half million men in the city who had been granted deferments by their draft boards. In June he sent a letter to thousands of them through Manhattan and Staten Island draft offices, effectively demanding that they sign up for patrol duty. Any man who refused, he growled to the press, was "a contemptible fifth columnist." But many did refuse, and the Selective Service administrator for the city was quick to point out that there was no law requiring them to serve. General Danford followed up with a more polite letter.

The CPC quickly assembled some four thousand volunteers, a motley collection of 4Fs, college students, and older men, some of them too fat to fit the khaki uniforms the army provided. By the fall enrollment would peak at nearly eight thousand. The army would not give them weapons, so Danford and La Guardia pressured the police commissioner Valentine into passing along some handguns confiscated from city hoodlums. In Brooklyn, the private Metropolitan Rod and Gun Club in Cobble Hill offered its indoor shooting range for CPC target practice. Most CPC troops made do, however, with nightsticks made from the legs of illegal pinball machines the mayor had warehoused as part of his crime-busting efforts in the 1930s. The CPC also had mounted troops, who had to rent their own horses and saddles, and rowboat "navies" who paddled around the lakes of Central and Prospect parks at night watching the shorelines for suspicious activities. According to the *Brooklyn Eagle*, they were instructed "not to disturb couples unless they go beyond the common laws of decency."

Corps duty was very light: two four-hour night patrols every eight weeks. As increasing numbers of policemen went into military service, and the fear of invading Nazis faded, corpsmen did routine beat cop duty, on guard more for purse snatchers and street gangs than subs and saboteurs. In Brooklyn, CPC patrolmen escorted young women to the subway after nights of dancing with military men at USO clubhouses because they were "fearful of muggings on wartime-dimmed streets." After walking the streets through the winter of 1942–43, CPC morale would decline and no-shows became rampant, yet La Guardia kept the program running for the rest of the war.

By the end of 1942 La Guardia would be finding his third term in the mayor's office less satisfying than the previous eight years. Many of his top aides had left him to do war work—and to get away from his increasingly frequent tantrums. Where running the city had once been his fondest ambition, he now had the frustrating sense that the big events of his lifetime were passing him by. He itched for a larger role in the Big Show. Running his own little army of potbellied and nearsighted volunteers was not enough.

In a White House meeting late in 1942 he told President Roosevelt that he was "dying" to get back into a uniform. Roosevelt deflected with humor, replying that the mayor was "too old and too fat." As usual, La Guardia persisted. A couple of months later he sent FDR a handwritten note that included the sentiment, "I still believe the General Eisenhower can not [*sic*] get along without me and am awaiting your order (but as a soldier)...Let me know how and when I can help." As usual, Roosevelt gave in; in March 1943 he would propose that La Guardia be commissioned a brigadier general and sent first to North Africa, then on to Italy once it was occupied, to direct civil affairs. Ecstatic, La Guardia crowed about his appointment to the City Hall press corps, started choosing his aides, and even had himself fitted for a uniform.

But Secretary of War Stimson and the army's chief of staff George Marshall found the idea ludicrous. They offered La Guardia a colonelcy, one grade up from his Great War rank, and a much smaller role in the war. Hurt and insulted, La Guardia rejected the offer and went over their heads to the president. The two of them would volley the idea back and forth until the war was nearly over, their relationship frosting along the way.

Possibly the worst insult of all to the mayor was that his nemesis William O'Dwyer got the wartime honors that he had sought. After the fiascos of the autumn of 1941—losing his mayoral bid, losing his prime Murder Inc. witness, and suspending his investigation of Anastasia—O'Dwyer did a wise thing: early in 1942, at fifty-one, he volunteered for the army. He was given a major's rank and posted to Wright Field in Ohio, assigned to a team investigating fraud by U.S. contractors supplying the Army Air Forces. In 1944 he would be promoted to brigadier general and sent to run civilian affairs in Italy—the rank and job La Guardia had lobbied for so intently and futilely.

Stars from Broadway and the ballparks, singers and songwriters, poets, journalists, artists, and filmmakers entered the armed services in sizable numbers during the war. Few ever saw combat, although one who did earned a Medal of Honor. For the most part, they served behind the lines or on the home front, where the brass thought they could do the most good, entertaining the troops and boosting civilian morale.

Professional sports figures were by definition fit for military service. Already by the start of the 1942 season major league baseball had lost more than sixty players, either drafted or through enlistment, and many more would go—about five hundred of them by the end of the war. The Yankees lost Yogi Berra, Phil Rizzuto, Bob Lemon, and Ralph Houk for the duration, and the Dodgers lost Pee Wee Reese. Some managers and executives, including the Dodgers' Larry MacPhail, also signed up. Branch Rickey came over from the Cardinals after the 1942 season to general manage the team. The minor leagues were virtually cleaned out, losing more than four thousand young players to the military during the war.

With flashbulbs popping, Hank Greenberg had been among the first major league players to sign up for Roosevelt's peacetime draft in October 1940. Then, at the start of the 1941 season, his draft board declared him 4-F because of flat feet. Razzed about that by the fans, Greenberg asked to be reclassified. He went into the army that May but was mustered out on December 5 with other older draftees (he was going on thirty-one). After the Japanese attacked Pearl Harbor two days later, he reenlisted and joined the army's air corps.

As they did with other celebrities, the brass kept him well away from the shooting war, directing physical fitness programs at bases in the United States. In 1944, he would finally be posted to the Pacific theater; though he begged to fly combat missions, he was instead given command of a bomber squadron in China, still well out of harm's way. He would complete his service in 1945 and return to the Tigers that July, hitting a home run in his first game back and helping them win the pennant.

Joe DiMaggio, on the other hand, did not rush to trade in his pinstripes for a more patriotic uniform, and the longer he held out, the angrier New Yorkers got with him. As a father of a small child he was classified 3-A. He was also disgruntled that his parents, who had lived in San Francisco for forty years but had never taken citizenship, were classified as enemy aliens. Their movements were restricted to a five-mile radius of their home, and his father's beloved fishing boat was impounded.

Joe sat out the start of the 1942 season, demanding a raise. When he finally showed up to play, Yankee fans, many of them in uniform now, booed him. "Doesn't he know there's a war on?" was a recurrent gripe. Rattled and brooding, he had the worst season of his career to then. He still led the Yankees to a pennant, but they lost the World Series to the Cardinals four games to one.

With his wife and baby son on West End Avenue, Joe whiled away long nights at Toots Shor's, the only place he seemed to feel comfortable now. Shor always kept his corner table for him, where DiMaggio sat with his back to the wall, and only his invited guests—who included Ernest Hemingway and Jim Braddock—were allowed to approach. DiMaggio, not much of a drinker, stuck to coffee and chain-smoking cigarettes.

Pressured by the press, the public, and his wife, DiMaggio would finally enlist in February 1943. He was stationed in California and Hawaii and spent his time in the army playing exhibition games and giving physical fitness training. He'd win few friends among his bunkmates with his constant grousing about how much money and time he was losing. Dorothy divorced him in 1944.

After Pearl Harbor, Moe Berg quit baseball and prowled around Washington offering his services where he thought he'd be of most use—intelligence. For William Donovan he recorded a personal message to be broadcast in Japan, telling the Japanese people that by attacking Pearl Harbor "you have lost face and are committing national seppuku." He read it in Japanese. Berg spent the last months of 1942 touring U.S. military and naval bases scattered throughout Central and South America for the Office for Inter-American Affairs. He was mostly looking into morale, but also doing a little amateur-spy nosing around. Meanwhile he kept lobbying Donovan for a real spy job, which he'd get in 1943.

The National Football League gave up many players as well. Jack Lummus, who'd been a star player at Baylor in Texas, was a rookie end with the Giants in 1941. He played nine games with them—including the one Bill Donovan attended on December 7—before enlisting in the U.S. Marines. He would get a first lieutenant's bars. In the assault on Iwo Jima in 1945 he was wounded by a grenade but continued leading his platoon, taking out three Japanese gun emplacements. Then he stepped on a land mine that blew off his legs. He died shortly after and was posthumously awarded the Medal of Honor.

World champion boxers Gene Tunney, Jack Dempsey, and Joe Louis all went into uniform. Tunney, an Irish longshoreman's son from Greenwich Village, had enlisted in the marines and served in France during the Great War. He was in his midforties by the start of World War II, unlikely to be called up, but he enlisted in the navy's reserve and was given a commander's rank. For the duration he taught recruits fitness and calisthenics (grueling, some complained) and traveled to the war zones on morale-boosting tours.

Dempsey, whom Tunney had famously beaten twice for the world title in the 1920s, was a few years too old to be drafted. He enlisted, joining the New York State National Guard and then the Coast Guard Reserve. At the Coast Guard's training station at Brooklyn's Manhattan Beach near Coney Island he also taught fitness, then went on his own goodwill tours. Dempsey got closer to the action than many sports celebrities, serving as an officer on a transport ship that unloaded men and matériel during the invasion of Okinawa in 1945. He would remain in the Coast Guard Reserve until 1952.

Joe Louis enlisted early in 1942 and reported to Camp Upton. Although he was posted, like all other black soldiers, to a segregated "colored" unit, he was as stoic as always and never expressed doubt that it was his patriotic duty to serve his country. That March he was one of the celebrities at a fund-raiser for the Navy Relief Fund that filled Madison Square Garden. Jimmy Walker, Wendell Willkie, Tom Dewey, and Walter Winchell all appeared, as did Tyrone Power, Bette Davis, Tallulah Bankhead, Myrna Loy, Jimmy Durante, Sophie Tucker, Vincent Price, Boris Karloff, and a small galaxy of other stars. But everyone agreed it was Private Louis, in his quiet way, who stole the show when he stood shyly at the mic and said, "I'm only doing what any red-blooded American would. We're gonna do our part, and we'll win because we're on God's side." The whole country cheered him for it, and "We're on God's side" was a ubiquitous slogan for the rest of the war.

⌒

Frank Loesser enlisted in the army as a private and was assigned to the unit called the Special Services branch, created by the army as a place where writers, entertainers, and others from the arts could serve their country in noncombatant roles. It was nothing like the regular army. Special Services troops worked in offices around Times Square and Grand Central. Using their military per diems, they took rooms in nearby hotels, ate their meals in midtown restaurants, drank in the midtown bars. They never saw the inside of barracks, never did KP or guard duty, and got the bare minimum in any kind of training as soldiers. Except for their ranks and uniforms, they lived very much as they always had, sometimes better. A wealthy man, Loesser had his private's uniforms tailored. He lived in a suite at the Hotel Navarro at 59th Street and Sixth Avenue and spent his evenings at the Stork Club.

For Special Services he worked on a few of the morale-building musical revues known as "Blueprint Specials," which soldiers could perform themselves. They were sent out to far-flung bases as pamphlets that included the script, song charts, and instructions for constructing simple sets and costumes using materials soldiers could find around the base. Loesser collaborated on these with other impressive Special Services talents. Composer Alex North would go on to a long career in Hollywood. The songwriter Jerry Livingston had a big hit on the charts at the same time he was working with Loesser: the silly novelty ditty "Mairzy Doats." He later wrote the score for Disney's *Cinderella*. Famed cartoonist Al Hirschfeld drew cover art for the pamphlets.

⌒

Irving Berlin was in his fifties, too old to be put back in khakis, but he did organize hundreds of soldiers in one of the largest theatrical spectacles of the war years. At the start of 1941 he, like many Americans—up to 80 percent in the polls—had still wished America could stay out of the European war, but he no longer believed that would be possible. He released six songs with war themes that year. He wrote "Any Bonds Today?" at the request of Treasury Secretary Morgenthau to promote the defense bond drive; Bugs Bunny sang it in a 1942 cartoon. He backed FDR's defense buildup with a rousing march called "Arms for the Love of America." Then there was the weirdly jolly "When That Man Is Dead and Gone"—that man being Hitler, whom Berlin calls "Satan with a small mustache"—and the wistful "When This Crazy World Is Sane Again."

After Pearl Harbor, Berlin got General George Marshall on the phone. The writer of "God Bless America" could do that. He said he wanted to do a new *Yip! Yip! Yaphank!* type of revue he'd call *This Is the Army*. Marshall okayed it, and in 1942 Berlin was back at Camp Upton, organizing a crew of Broadway professionals—some already in uniform, others he convinced to enlist specifically to join the project—and a cast of 359 GIs. He insisted on including black soldiers, making his cast the only integrated unit in the army. At the same time, though, he had to be talked out of one grand number that would feature 110 of the white performers doing a blackface minstrel routine. The black soldiers never appeared on stage at the same time as the white ones; Berlin wrote "the colored guys," as he called them, a separate number about military uniforms called "That's What the Well-Dressed Man in Harlem Will Wear."

This Is the Army opened at the Broadway Theatre on the Fourth of July 1942. Berlin had booked the theater for only four weeks, but it was such a success the run went to the end of September. Eleanor Roosevelt saw it three times, then arranged a command performance for Franklin in Washington. Afterward the entire cast and crew went to the White House, where FDR shook all 359 cast members' hands.

At the army's request the show toured around the country, raising $2 million for the Army Emergency Relief Fund. Then for the rest of the war *This Is the Army* played to frontline troops throughout the European and Pacific theaters. Warner Bros. made it into a Technicolor movie in 1943, with a cast that included Joe Louis—now a sergeant—and Lieutenant Ronald Reagan.

In August 1942, while *This Is the Army* was still packing the Broadway Theatre, Berlin's latest film, *Holiday Inn*, premiered at the Paramount movie palace down Broadway. It was a lightweight revue built to showcase more than a dozen of his songs, along with the talents of two stars he chose himself, Bing Crosby and Fred Astaire. Audiences and critics liked *Holiday Inn* well enough, but nobody had any inkling that one of its songs was about to become the biggest of Berlin's career. As the 1942 Christmas season approached, American servicemen wherever they were started flooding the Armed Forces Radio Service with requests for "White Christmas," the Crosby single from the movie. Without intending to, Berlin had written the perfect expression of their loneliness and nostalgia. Crosby said that when he toured the front with the USO, "They'd holler for it. They'd demand it. When I'd sing it, they'd all cry." It won the Oscar for best song of 1942 and came back into circulation at Christmastime in 1943, and again in 1944.

By war's end it would be a permanent fixture in American culture. The flip side was another inherently melancholy holiday number, "I'll Be Home for Christmas," written in 1943 by composer Walter Kent, who'd cowritten "The White Cliffs of Dover," and Brooklyn-born lyricist Kim Gannon. Though Gannon also said he wasn't thinking of a lonely soldier or sailor when he wrote it, everyone who heard it did.

⌒

Hundreds of New York entertainers who didn't go into uniform did their bit in another way. Rachel Crothers had been writing, and often directing, popular Broadway plays since 1906. During the Great War she founded the Stage Women's War Relief fund. After Germany invaded Poland in 1939 she revived it as the American Theatre Wing, which opened the

Stage Door Canteen in March 1942. It was in the basement of the 44th Street Theatre between Seventh and Eighth Avenues in the heart of the Times Square district and just behind the New York Times Building. The basement space was previously known as the Little Club, a famous speakeasy during Prohibition. The *Times* had bought the building in 1940 and leased it to impresario Lee Shubert, who donated the club to Crothers's group for the duration. Broadway stage designers and crews spruced up the old spot, which could fit three hundred at small tables (later expanded to five hundred); set designer Joseph Mielziner painted murals.

Irving Berlin donated a piano and, later, all his profits from Sammy Kaye's hit recording of his song "I Left My Heart at the Stage Door Canteen," which he wrote for *This Is the Army.* The Canteen was rather like a USO, only staffed with stars. Hundreds of performers of stage, screen, and popular music volunteered to entertain, wait tables, make sandwiches, dance, or just sit and chat with boys in uniform. On any given night Tallulah Bankhead, Judy Garland, Guy Lombardo, or Count Basie might perform. Katharine Hepburn might be serving hot dogs and milk (no alcohol), Alfred Lunt bussed your table, and you might jitterbug with an aspiring teenage actress from Flatbush named Lauren Bacall.

The Canteen was open seven nights a week, six to midnight. It was free to enlisted men of all Allied services, but no officers were admitted, and no servicewomen—the latter, the Wing explained, because it wanted to devote the small space to "men who were headed to or returning from combat," Richard Goldstein writes in *Helluva Town.* The Wing did sponsor "a weekly Sunday afternoon tea and dance at the Roosevelt Hotel, where men and women in the armed forces could meet."

On the other hand, it was one of the very few venues anywhere, including anywhere in New York City, that welcomed black servicemen as well as white; even more rare, they danced with white hostesses, and black hostesses danced with white servicemen. Hostesses of either race who felt uncomfortable with this were instructed to get over it or leave. A few southern politicians complained; the rabidly racist senator Theodore Bilbo of Mississippi cried that the Canteen's racial policies "could only be designed to promote the mongrelization of this country." It's said that only two racial scuffles ever broke out in the place, and on both occasions the band brought calm by striking up "The Star-Spangled Banner." No doubt the no-alcohol policy also helped.

The American Theatre Wing would open six other Canteens around the country, and ones in London and Paris late in the war, that served an estimated total of eleven million servicemen. The Wing also sponsored the 1943 Hollywood movie *Stage Door Canteen*, which raised more than a million dollars to keep the venues running.

⌒

One of the Blueprint Specials Frank Loesser et al. created was called *Hi, Yank!* It was inspired by *Yank* magazine.

A month after Pearl Harbor, Egbert White, vice president of the giant Madison Avenue advertising firm BBDO, wrote to General Frederick Osborn, head of Special Services. White had served with the servicemen's newspaper *Stars and Stripes* as an enlisted man during the First World War. He now proposed starting a new magazine, called *Yank*, that would be written and illustrated entirely by soldiers, for soldiers. He had already rounded up an impressive list of other former enlisted men to help him plan it, including Harold Ross and Alexander Woollcott of the *New Yorker*, Adolph Shelby Ochs of the *Times* Ochses, the popular sportswriter Grantland Rice, and the witty *Herald Tribune* columnist Franklin Pierce Addams, known as FPA. They decided *Yank* should be a weekly, with a five-cent cover price, half the price of most commercial weeklies. It should be available to all soldiers everywhere, and only to soldiers. Osborn took the idea to Secretary Stimson and General Marshall, who approved it by the end of April 1942.

The notion that *Yank* would be produced by soldiers for soldiers was a bit of a conceit. While it was true that the initial twenty writers, editors, photographers, and illustrators held ranks from private to sergeant, they weren't GI Joes. Most were professional newsmen who'd been hastily tossed into uniform specifically to work on the magazine. As Special Services personnel, they experienced nearly no army training or discipline. They reported for duty in the Bartholomew Building, a twenty-one-story office tower a block from Grand Central, which the Special Service staff dubbed Fort Bartholomew. They took lodging in nearby hotels; a $6 per diem easily covered their rooms, meals, drinks, and smokes.

Before long it was clear that a magazine that spoke to and for fighting troops couldn't possibly be generated solely from East 42nd Street. The *Yank* editorial board added a rule that reporters, photographers, and illustrators had to spend at least six months in the field. As they fanned out to cover the fighting in North Africa and the Pacific in 1942, *Yank* staffers were still not quite regular army. They reported only to Manhattan, not to any field commanders, could go anywhere they chose, and, though they were issued weapons and combat gear, operated as war correspondents first, as soldiers only under duress. Their anomalous status was approved by the Pentagon but would cause friction with some officers in the war zones, especially Douglas MacArthur's general staff, who'd go beyond the bounds of customary military censorship attempting to mold how *Yank* portrayed the progress of General MacArthur's war in the Pacific.

Yank pulled a major blooper with its inaugural June 1942 issue. Congress had just approved a hefty pay raise for privates, from $21 to $50 a month. The cover of the first *Yank* was a photo of a soldier clutching bills and grinning broadly, above the tagline, "$50 A MONTH RIGHT NOW." Unfortunately, *above* the photo was another headline referring to a different story—"FDR: WHY WE FIGHT." It looked like *Yank*—or, worse, the commander in chief—was saying American soldiers were a bunch of mercenaries who would fight only for the money. Fifty thousand copies were printed before anyone noticed the gaffe; they had to be scrapped while a new cover was hastily composed.

Yank recovered from early mistakes to become the most widely read publication in U.S. military history at more than two million copies a week, printed in twenty-one regional editions, from Alaska to North Africa to the South Pacific, to get around the logistics of global distribution. (*Stars and Stripes*, the U.S. Army's daily newspaper, did the same.) The staff grew to more than a hundred and twenty. It carried stories from all the front lines, giving the GI a broader sense of the war beyond his own unit. From their start as dilettantes in uniform, the field reporters developed into seasoned war correspondents who were credited with accurately capturing the average soldier's experiences better than most of the press did. The "Mail Call" and "Poets Cornered" sections carried writing by regular GIs. *Yank*'s most popular features were the *Sad Sack* cartoon strip and the full-page pinups in the back, wholesome yet alluring images of actresses and models such as Lauren Bacall, Lucille Ball, Ava Gardner, and Rita Hayworth. *Yank* would run from 1942 through VE and VJ days, the last issue coming out in December 1945.

⌒

Also in 1942, the army came to Astoria, Queens, to begin making military training films. It took over a facility with a storied movie past. In

1920 Paramount's Adolph Zukor, a Hungarian Jew who'd immigrated to the Lower East Side as a youth, built the large, state-of-the-art studio in Astoria; nicknamed the "subway studio," it was the best in the world for a time.

Commercial filmmaking in New York had dwindled in the 1930s. When the United States entered the war, the old Paramount studio was being used to shoot industrial and educational films and record the sound for newsreels. At the end of January 1942 the army acquired it for the Signal Corps Photographic Center (SCPC). Over the next three years the studio was bustling with film crews, if not movie stars. The staff of more than two thousand was roughly half civilian, half in uniform. They worked around-the-clock, churning out more than a thousand mostly short (two-reel) films a year—training and entertainment films for men and women in uniform and instructional/propaganda films for the public. The center also trained combat photographers and film crews.

Close by, another well-known Astoria institution was making its own changeover for the war effort. Steinway & Sons, the world-famous piano company, had always promised that it would make its instruments using "the best and thoroughly seasoned material." Within days of December 7, seeing what was coming, the company changed that to "best material available."

Steinway had a long and venerable history in New York City. Patriarch Heinrich Steinweg, later anglicized to Henry Steinway, built his first grand piano in his kitchen in the town of Seesen near Hanover in 1836. He brought his family to New York City and began crafting pianos in a small loft on Varick Street in lower Manhattan in 1853. In the 1860s Steinway & Sons built a larger factory on Park Avenue at 53rd Street and the grand Steinway Hall concert space on East 14th Street.

In 1870 Henry's son William, hoping to isolate the workers from the growing labor movement in the city, bought four hundred acres of farmland in Astoria and constructed Steinway Village, a complete company town with a factory, housing, a school, a hospital, a church, a post office. Nearby, at North Beach, the company built an amusement park and beer garden.

In 1938 Steinway shipped a new grand piano to FDR's White House, where it was installed in the East Room, replacing the one the company had sent to Teddy Roosevelt in 1908. The following year, La Guardia's Municipal Airport opened on the former site of the North Beach amusement park.

In the summer of 1942 the War Production Board ordered Steinway (and Baldwin in Cincinnati) to halt production of grand pianos so that the materials and skills could be turned to military use. At first the army contracted Steinway to build "Victory Verticals"—"small, sturdy uprights, painted olive drab and shipped by cargo vessels and transport planes to military theaters around the world." Then the company kept one thousand of its expert craftspeople in jobs constructing the wings and tail sections for the army's wood-and-fabric gliders—CG4As, also known as Wacos. Steinway would work on more than a thousand of the thirteen thousand gliders the army had contracted by D-day.

As it happened, the army used only about three thousand of those. Gliders proved such a dangerous way of transporting men and matériel to the front that their pilots were nicknamed suicide jockeys and the troops they carried called themselves flak bait. The army canceled its contract with Steinway after D-day. The company struggled financially for the balance of the war, then went back to building grand pianos, which it still produces today.

CHAPTER 35

Boom and Gloom

Within a year, the massive war production Roosevelt had summoned in the summer of 1940 was in full swing. *Time* would call it a "miracle," and it was certainly astounding. In 1939 U.S. production of military matériel had been practically nil. Two years later America was producing more than all the Axis nations combined. After Pearl Harbor, Roosevelt directed all defense plants to go on an around-the-clock, seven-day workweek. Production surged. By VJ Day 1945, U.S. workers would have churned out close to 88,000 warships, landing craft, and other vessels; nearly 300,000 warplanes; some 100,000 tanks; 370,000 pieces of artillery; 44 billion bullets; and 47 million tons of artillery shells. By war's end the federal government would have spent some $350 billion on the war, more than double the accumulated federal expenditures in all the years prior to the war.

During the same period, more than 12 million American men and women went into the military, while some 18 million women found jobs in every sector of the galloping economy. The last vestiges of the Depression vanished in much of the country. National unemployment plummeted from nearly 15 percent in 1940 to 1 percent by 1944.

Yet the benefits of the wartime boom hardly came uniformly to all areas of the country or the economy. A handful of giant corporations and cartels gorged on tens of billions in defense funds, while thousands of small businesses in New York and around the country struggled and starved.

In the summer of 1942, there were an estimated four hundred thousand New Yorkers out of work, actually *more* than in 1939. New York lagged far behind other major cities in attracting defense spending during the first two years of the buildup. Where New York had been the model candidate for New Deal projects, it was at a fundamental disadvantage in the new warfare economy. Ostensibly for speed and efficiency, the government let the bulk of its defense contracts go to the country's largest corporations and cartels—six of them held a third of all the contracts in 1941—operating giant facilities in heavy industries like steel and aluminum, the automotive and aircraft industries. The defense bureaucracy was stuffed with dollar-a-year men from these giant corporations who "assiduously lobbied to protect the industrial status quo ante, encouraged the further cartelization of the economy, and resisted pressure for regulatory controls," the labor historian Steven Fraser explains. "The commingling of industrial, financial, and military elites, the linkages of interest and belief that gave them a unity of purpose, rapidly converted the defense mobilization apparatus into a branch of corporate America." It was the start of the military-industrial complex.

In cities where giant aviation, steel, or automotive plants were located—from Seattle to Detroit, Boston to Newark to Baltimore—the boom was on, unemployment plunged, and in some places there were even manpower shortages. In 1942 agents from a giant shipyard in Oregon swooped into New York, hired four thousand unemployed waterfront workers in three days, and moved them all out west.

New York City, however, was singularly lacking in the heavy industries. Although it was in fact the largest factory town in the world, its industrial base was made up of many very small manufacturers, averaging twenty employees (half the national average), and they mostly produced "nondurable consumer goods" such as clothing, printed materials, and food items. Raw materials they needed for their products were being directed to the giant corporations, choking them off. On top of that, wartime rationing and restrictions on consumer goods across the board meant that without contracts for government war work many small manufacturers in the city faced almost guaranteed bankruptcy.

Even contracts that one might have expected to come to the city, those for military uniforms, for instance, went elsewhere. The city's garment industry was the largest in the country, but although it produced 40 percent of the men's pants worn in America, in the first two years of the war it took in contracts for only 3 percent of military trousers.

The boom was skipping over the metropolitan region. La Guardia put his customary full-court press on Roosevelt and his administration, constantly shuttling from New York to Washington and back, but found he couldn't wheedle his way around the city's structural deficiencies. He argued that the greatest metropolis in the world was bursting with skilled workers—many of them still idled—who could contribute tremendously to the war effort in other ways than entering the military. He complained in a letter to Roosevelt that it was "most discouraging to keep on writing and phoning, appealing, begging and pleading" with little result.

It took until the summer of 1942 for his cajoling to wear down his old friend in the White House. At FDR's prompting, the War Production Board announced that it would begin ordering nearly a quarter of its military trousers from the garment district, the navy accelerated hiring at the Brooklyn Navy Yard, and contracts began to be funneled to the city's smaller businesses that had the capacity for some kind of defense-related production. Defense spending in the city shot up from $77 million in the spring of 1942 to $1.5 billion at the end of the year. Industrial hires increased 40 percent that year. Unemployment in the city was cut in half.

The wartime boom had finally come to New York City, and it spread out through the entire town. For the first time in a decade, New Yorkers had spending money in their pockets. So did the millions of soldiers and sailors, of all the Allied nations, who passed through the city during the war. Given severe wartime restrictions on virtually every type of consumer good, they all spent it on entertainment. Nightclubs, restaurants, and cafés, effectively dormant during the Depression, soared again. Movie theaters were packed, as were music and dance halls, where audiences enjoyed everything from classical to boogie-woogie. Broadway theaters, which had also barely survived the Depression, were reborn. In the 1943–44 season alone they would stage forty-one comedies, thirty dramas, and twenty-five musicals. *On the Town*, *Oklahoma!*, and *Carousel* all debuted during the war, and all outlived it. *Oklahoma!* enjoyed a spectacular run, from March 1943 to May 1948; *On the Town* ran from 1944 into 1946; *Carousel* from the spring of 1945 to the spring of 1947. Their successes inaugurated the golden age of the Broadway musical. The city's museums, the ballet, and modern dance thrived as well.

Even without its bright lights, Times Square was mobbed most every night. Something like three million servicemen from all the Allied nations would surge through it during the war, drawn by precisely the sort of illicit enticements that La Guardia had tried to clear out. Around them swirled New Yorkers who wanted to drink with them, dance with them, sleep with them, and/or pick their pockets.

Many other New Yorkers avoided it. In a May 1944 *New Yorker* piece titled "Big Night," the magazine's art critic Robert M. Coates wrote that he found Saturday night in crowded, dimmed-out Times Square "sinister" and "depressing."

Born in New Haven in 1897, Coates was a student at Yale when America entered the Great War, part of a literary clique with Henry Luce, Thornton Wilder, and Stephen Vincent Benét. Like many Yale men he interrupted his studies to sign up for the grand adventure, but the war ended before he made it to the front. In 1921 he followed the crowd of expats to Paris; his writing would reflect his time soaking up the avant-garde there. On his return in 1927 he moved to Greenwich Village, married an artist, and was hired by the new *New Yorker*, joining his neighbors E. B. White and James Thurber as a defining voice of the "Talk of the Town" section. He went on to write numerous short stories published in the magazine, as well as book reviews that championed generally misunderstood modernists including Gertrude Stein, whom he'd known in Paris. In 1937 he started writing about art for the magazine, which he would do for thirty years; in a March 1946 review, he would casually coin the term "abstract expressionism."

Shy but not aloof, with a slight stutter, Coates gathered material for "Talk" by endlessly walking the streets of the city, a solitary observer hovering near the city's diverse crowds, eavesdropping and watching without ever quite joining them. The same approach is evident in "Big Night."

"Times Square and its bars, on a Saturday night, are places I would normally stay away from," he began. "However, some friends of mine who had been inadvertently drawn into the maelstrom there were so impressed by their experience that they urged me to go take a look. If I wanted to see wartime crowds, they said, if I wanted to see New York at its boom-town boomingest, that was the place to do it."

The area was, as usual, thick with milling crowds of civilians and guys in various uniforms, motivated by what Coates assessed as "a kind of nervous restlessness." On the murkily lit streets, they "look, somehow, as if they didn't belong there, and the effect created is curiously sinister… It was somewhat as if, well past midnight in a suburban community, the streets had been invaded by a mob—fairly well behaved and orderly, but still a mob. The effect was depressing."

Everywhere around him were small knots of soldiers and sailors who "wanted to have a good time, but they were painfully uncertain how to go about it." Moving among them were small groups of young women and teenage girls, "and I was surprised to see how casually pickups were made...For the most part, a fellow would simply pull up alongside a girl and glance at her. If she smiled, he took her arm. If she didn't, he just walked on."

Military brass, health officials, law enforcement, and society's moral watchdogs all worried about these women and girls who flocked around men in uniform wherever they were. They called them victory girls, khaki-wackies, even "patriotutes." By the time of Coates's article, New York City courts were reporting large increases in arrests for prostitution, other "offenses against common decency," and female juvenile delinquency. There was also a noticeable increase in births out of wedlock.

The military was particularly concerned that both professional prostitutes and amateur patriotutes were spreading venereal diseases that could seriously weaken the nation's capacity to fight. "A diseased prostitute," it was argued, "can do far more damage than a 500-pound bomb dropped squarely in the middle of an army camp." Syphilis was still a great scourge at the start of the war. Six percent of draftees were rejected when it showed up in their blood tests. Available treatments were drawn-out and not guaranteed effective. The country would be three years into the war before limited supplies of the new miracle cure penicillin—discovered in England, developed for large-scale distribution by Pfizer in Brooklyn—were available.

Military brass conceded that if you segregated hordes of healthy young males on army bases and ships for long periods of time, when you let them loose they were going to race off to do what young men do. You couldn't punish them for that without seriously damaging morale. They also worried that if you denied them female company, they'd turn to homosexuality, described as "a blight...known to ravage European armies." So they showed them instructional films on the horrors of VD, postered the walls of bases with messages the likes of "She may look clean—but pick-ups, 'good time girls,' prostitutes spread SYPHILIS and GONORRHEA," and handed out condoms.

Because the men in uniform apparently couldn't be restrained, the authorities—federal, state, and local—focused on the females. Former gangbuster Eliot Ness, who ran a federal agency called the Social Protection Division, gave serious thought to rounding up women and girls accused of prostitution and "promiscuity"—the two were generally equated—and quarantining them for the duration in former Civilian Conservation Corps camps out in the boonies. New York City considered a midnight curfew for girls (but not boys) sixteen and younger. Newspapers and magazines fretted endlessly about these wanton and potentially diseased females. There were even a couple of Broadway plays addressing what seemed to be a grave threat to, as J. Edgar Hoover put it, America's "moral fibers." The hysteria about sexualized females spreading physical and moral corruption would play a large hand in the country's wholesale retreat to "traditional," desexualized feminine ideals after the war.

Coates prowled Times Square until 2 a.m. that night, a middle-aged aesthete in a sea of glandular youth, and little of it seemed joyful to him. He entered a couple of bars so crowded he had to shout and reach over shoulders to get a drink. A bartender at the Hotel Astor disapprovingly described for him how one party, at midnight, had just downed martinis, whiskey sours, and double scotches, followed by more martinis. "I don't know how their stomachs can stand it." Harry James and his swing band were playing dinner-and-dance sets that week up in the Astor's open roof garden, where, because of the dimout, couples might actually be dining under a few visible stars, which nobody had seen from Times Square in years.

After two in the morning "the street was left chiefly to the drunks—the youthfully, pitifully drunk drunks," and the military policemen who picked them up and moved them along. Coates straggled home to Greenwich Village, demoralized by his brief sojourn on the dark side of boom town. He'd evoke the spring of 1944 again in a slim, melancholic 1946 novel, *The Bitter Season*, in which he writes that the vast dislocations of the war had produced "a sort of global loneliness" that drove people into places like Times Square and its overstuffed bars, instinctively seeking some kind of human contact and life in a world given over entirely to death. "Death was all around us in those days, in the newspapers, the newsreels, the radio...But it was a death that was curiously impersonal, and that had little individual feeling behind it." The war made death anonymous, "mass-produced," and "except in the most generalized way it was wholly unmotivated."

⌒

Characteristically, blacks had to fight for their own jobs themselves. The massive increase in defense spending reduced unemployment among whites by 13 percent nationally by the end of 1940, but not at all among blacks. HELP WANTED, WHITE signs hung outside many defense plants. Of some twenty-nine thousand jobs in defense work in the New York region early on, black workers held only 142—at a time when there were almost half a million black New Yorkers.

On returning to Harlem after the demoralizing meeting with Roosevelt in September 1940, A. Philip Randolph shifted his focus from segregation in the military to discrimination in defense plants and the federal government. Randolph had wanted Roosevelt to issue an executive order ending the discrimination. This time he decided not to go begging in a private meeting, but to prod the president in public. He announced a mass march on Washington for July 1, 1941. Pullman union members posted flyers everywhere blacks lived and shopped. Sales of "March on Washington" buttons, and collections in black churches raised funds to hire buses. Walter White and the NAACP joined the movement.

By June of '41 black leaders were threatening to bring a hundred thousand marchers to Washington. Alarmed, Roosevelt asked "the missus," La Guardia, and others to speak to Randolph and "get it stopped." Randolph would not be dissuaded, but he and White did agree to another Oval Office meeting, which took place on June 18. There was little of the false bonhomie of their previous meeting. Roosevelt was testy and querulous; Randolph and White stood firm. One week later, June 25, Roosevelt signed Executive Order 8802, prohibiting discrimination in defense plants and in all branches of the federal government. He also set up the Fair Employment Practice Committee to see that 8802 was carried out. When the FEPC encountered resistance from defense contractors, especially but not only in the South, FDR would issue further orders giving it more teeth.

The terrible unemployment in Harlem would ease somewhat in the war years. Bellevue and other hospitals gave in to pressures to hire more black women as nurses. A bus boycott organized by Adam Clayton Powell Jr. opened up jobs for Harlem men as drivers and conductors. The Brooklyn Navy Yard hired more blacks.

Still, Harlem and black communities around the country harbored deep doubts about participating in the war effort. Walter White wrote:

> How can a Negro believe in democracy when the Army and the Navy of his government say to him: "You can fight and die for democracy but you can't experience it in the Army and Navy?" How

> can a Negro believe wholeheartedly that the cause he is asked to die for is worth dying for when daily he is confronted by insult discrimination and segregation? Prove to us...that you are not hypocrites when you say this is a war for freedom. Prove it to us and we will show you that we can and will fight like fury for that freedom. But we want—and we intend to have—our share of that freedom.

That June, Randolph drew twenty thousand people to a rally at Madison Square Garden with a flyer that exhorted: "WAKE UP NEGRO AMERICA! Do you want work? Do you want equal rights? Do you want justice? Then prepare now to fight for it! STORM MADISON SQUARE GARDEN." The rally included the singing of new songs, including Eubie Blake's "We Are Americans Too," and a performance of an agitprop play by Harlem's Rose McClendon Players, in which a young black man told his draft board, "Yes sir, I am against them Japs. I'm against them Germans, them Italians—and I'm also against them Negro-hating crackers down South." The crowd applauded wildly. As the rally was happening, Harlem went into a self-imposed blackout, symbolizing, Randolph said, "the economic and political blackout through which our people still stumble and fall."

CHAPTER 36

Rosie, and Not So

She's making history, working for victory
Rosie the riveter

The Todd Shipyards company had roots on the Brooklyn waterfront that went back to the construction of the ironclad *Monitor* during the Civil War. Besides its main shipyard and dry dock complex at the man-made Erie Basin in Red Hook, it had large shipbuilding and repair facilities in Hoboken and in Seattle. In the fall of 1942, Elinore Morehouse Herrick, the personnel director, announced that Todd was seeking female applicants to be trained in welding, operating machinery, and other shipbuilding and repair jobs. Within days Herrick, who had served as the New York regional director of the National Labor Relations Board since 1935, received letters from some thirty-five hundred women. Among them were recent college graduates and Broadway actresses; women who had "worked on assembly lines in small industries snuffed out by the war program," according to the *Times*; and mothers in their fifties and sixties who wrote that they had sons in uniform and wanted to do their part. "I have learned a lot in my years," one of these older applicants wrote, "and I can handle myself just as well as anyone 20 years old. And I can swing a mean, mean hammer."

Herrick selected seventy-five for interviews; of these, twenty-six would be hired as "shipyardettes." Todd would hire more women during the war, a tiny but widely noted percentage of its nearly sixty thousand workers who would build more than one thousand ships, including three hundred fifty landing craft, and repair another twenty-three thousand.

Herrick was a leader in the push to get women into wartime work. The ratcheting up of the country's war industries, at the same time that working men were being siphoned off into uniform, created new job opportunities for millions of women, including black women. But getting women into those jobs meant bucking long-held traditions, beliefs, and attitudes. "There are many deterrents—largely psychological—to the increased employment of women in industry," Herrick would write in the *Times* in January 1943. "Many of them arise from prejudice, lack of information, and fear of change." From the start of the buildup in 1940 through most of 1942, employers staunchly refused to hire women to do "a man's job." In heavy industry especially—the shipyards and steel mills and airplane factories—employers argued that women simply were not physically or emotionally capable of handling the work. They further believed that women workers would distract and upset male workers. There were conflicting concerns that the industrial work environment might either hypersexualize or defeminize women workers.

For married women to take work outside the home had always been considered shameful to the man of the house, because it indicated to the world that he was not a good provider. It was fine for single women, but only in traditional woman's work, behind a sewing machine, a typewriter, or a shop counter. Even for them, wage labor was seen as temporary, something they did until they got married and had children.

These ideas pervaded American society. Well before Pearl Harbor, administrators in Roosevelt's government recognized that switching the entire nation to war footing would require millions of women taking nontraditional jobs, but it would mean a giant shift in how employers, husbands, and women themselves thought. As early as December 1941, the Office for Emergency Management released a ten-minute film, *Women in Defense.* The text, written by Eleanor Roosevelt and read by Katharine Hepburn, declared that with "total war" on the horizon, "Every woman has an important place in the national defense program, in science, in industry, and in the home." The footage showed women working in munitions factories and scientific laboratories, volunteering with the Red Cross, and of course a lot of women running sewing machines, "bringing a natural skill to an important job."

The federal government could do little at first to compel employers to see the situation Eleanor's way. Most New Deal experiments in regulating big business had ended in failure. Employers were free to resist hiring women, and they did. For the better part of a year after Pearl Harbor, many employers filled the increasing gaps in their manpower by hiring older males, teenage males, disabled males, even convicts—anything to avoid having to hire females.

The government could lead by example. A million women flooded into Washington to staff the offices of the burgeoning wartime federal bureaucracy. At the Brooklyn Navy Yard, only about a hundred women were employed before Pearl Harbor, all doing traditional woman's work in the flag loft, stitching flags, pennants, and the tablecloths for the officers' mess. In 1942, the navy announced it would hire six hundred female trainees, or "mechanic learners." *Twenty thousand* women applied. Of the first hundred and twenty-five hired, twelve were black.

That year, in addition to widening the draft eligibility age bracket, the government announced that it would begin phasing out deferments for men doing semiskilled work. Employers like Todd—which had hired Herrick to be its new personnel director that year—bowed to the inevitable and began hiring females. The floodgates opened. By 1944, the War Manpower Commission would report that more than 18 million women were working—some 35 percent of the nation's workforce.

By midwar the sea change in the American workforce was quite evident. The cover of the August 9, 1943, *Life* carried one of Margaret Bourke-White's typically striking images of American industry at work. But this particular image was one that few Americans could have pictured just a few years before. A young woman in blue jeans and a flannel shirt, wearing round goggles and workman's big gloves, squats on a pad of steel. She's operating an arc welder, burning a hole through the steel, a fountain of sparks jetting below.

Inside the issue was an eight-page spread, "Women in Steel," with equally remarkable Bourke-White photos taken at a giant steel plant in Gary, Indiana. Almost five thousand women were working there in 1943, in every phase of pouring, rolling, stamping, cutting, welding, and riveting. They were middle-aged moms and young singles, black, white, and Hispanic, and they were all holding down jobs they never could have gotten before the war. "Although the concept of the weaker sex sweating near blast furnaces, directing giant ladles of molten iron, or pouring red-hot ingots is accepted in England and Russia," the accompanying text noted, "it has always been foreign to American tradition. Only the rising need for labor and the diminishing supply of manpower has forced this revolutionary adjustment."

That same August, *Newsweek* ran a similar report. Women were working in "shipyards, lumber mills, steel mills, foundries. They are welders, electricians, mechanics, and even boilermakers. They operate streetcars, buses, cranes, and tractors. Women engineers are working in the drafting rooms and women physicists and chemists in the great industrial laboratories."

Government propaganda would portray women war workers as young, white, and middle class—homemakers and their daughters who had never worked outside the home before, who signed up because it was their patriotic duty to help win the war, and who looked forward to the war ending so that they could get back to their "real" job of starting and raising families. This image, the historian Maureen Honey wrote in her landmark study *Creating Rosie the Riveter*, was "almost completely false. Contrary to popular belief, the women who entered war production were not primarily middle-class housewives but working-class wives, widows, divorcées, and students who needed the money to achieve a reasonable standard of living." Many of them had held jobs in the past but lost them during the Depression. Others were working in the sorts of low-paid, nonunion jobs generally available to women when the war started—on the farm, in restaurants, in laundries, shops, hotels, wealthy homes—and grabbed the opportunity to switch to better-paying, unionized ones on the factory floor. By 1944 women held nearly half of the jobs in the durable goods industries, up from 15 percent in 1939; they held a quarter of the jobs in aircraft, shipping, and ammunition manufacture, up from less than 10 percent previously. At their new, union jobs, they earned as much as 40 percent more than they previously had.

"For professional women, the war provided a chance to become newspaper editors, personnel managers, pilots, engineers," Honey continued. "The emergency opened new vistas for black women too as many left domestic service and farm work to take jobs previously performed by whites. The proportion of black females in industrial occupations rose from 6.5 percent to 18 percent from 1940 to 1944, although they were confined to the lowest paying sectors of manufacturing. They were also employed as white-collar workers in federal agencies for the first time."

Jewish women, however, found that despite Executive Order 8802 some defense contractors, like Sperry Gyroscope, refused to hire them. This was especially disheartening because many Jewish leaders, including Rabbi Stephen Wise, had wholeheartedly supported 8802. Jewish women had no such trouble getting hired at government facilities such as the Navy Yard and Army Terminal.

In her 1943 *Times* article, Herrick ticked off some of the challenges industrial employers faced hiring women for the first time. Todd had to build new restrooms and showers for the women. The presence of females raised general issues of sanitation and safety that employers had often not taken very seriously when their factories and shipyards were all male. They scoured the country to procure work boots and other safety equipment in sizes small enough, and applied new dress codes that, as another *Times* article noted, barred "skirts, loose sleeves, frills, shoes with high heels or open toes, pendant earrings, necklaces, bracelets, and finger rings." Women operating machinery were expected to wear "caps, hats, or turbans" to keep their hair out of the way. Tight sweaters were banned as another kind of safety hazard: they might distract the men.

Many states limited women's hours and mandated rest periods employers weren't used to. This caused resentment among male coworkers. Hiring mothers with children raised issues of day care that were never fully addressed during the war. In 1943 Mayor La Guardia set up some nurseries and after-school programs; some settlement houses, churches, and synagogues started their own. Failing that, mothers relied on kindly neighbors to watch their kids or, in a pinch, parked them in movie theaters for hours at a time, to the chagrin of theater managers. Having children to deal with contributed to higher absentee rates for women than for male workers.

For all that, by 1943 women working in formerly male-only jobs throughout the home front were becoming accepted, even cheered. That year they got an affectionate nickname, Rosie the Riveter. Since the 1970s, the image most often called Rosie is an illustration of a pretty young woman in a red bandanna flexing her biceps, bragging, "We Can Do It!" But she was never called Rosie the Riveter during the war. She was the nameless image on a Westinghouse poster aimed at boosting workers' production.

Rosie the Riveter was first mentioned in a hit song by that name, which came out in February 1943. It was written by a Tin Pan Alley duo, Redd Evans and John Jacob Loeb, and first recorded in a marvelously snappy rendition by a black vocal group, the Four Vagabonds. Imitations would come along soon, including one called "Sweethearts in Overalls," but none matched this song's popularity.

Rosie's status as an icon was quickly confirmed. That May, Norman Rockwell drew her for the cover of the *Saturday Evening Post*. Rockwell's

Rosie was a big-boned, freckled tomboy in denim overalls, eating a ham sandwich, with her rivet gun on her lap like a weapon and one of her scuffed penny loafers (evidently she couldn't find work boots) crushing a copy of *Mein Kampf.* The Westinghouse woman is striking a "manly" pose, but she's pretty, sexy, and wearing makeup. Rockwell's Rosie is plain, and her fleshy body sprawls across traditional gender lines. The Westinghouse Rosie is a young woman whom men might rush to meet; Rockwell's Rosie is a gal that men—certainly Nazi and Japanese men—should fear to cross.

As widely recognized as Rockwell's Rosie was, the Westinghouse image was actually more representative in one way. Though the woman worker was expected to handle a man's job, she was constantly reminded not to sacrifice her femininity doing it. No matter how loud, grimy, dirty the job was, she was supposed to maintain what one advertisement called her FQ: her femininity quotient. Images like Rockwell's tomboyish plain Jane were actually rare. Whatever she did on the job, the ideal female continued to look a lot more like the glamour girls and pinups in *Yank.*

A full-page ad for Woodbury facial soap that ran in the "Women in Steel" issue of *Life* summed up the notion well. It purported to feature an actual defense worker, a pretty young woman named Marguerite, who "looks trim and feminine" in her factory outfit.

> She turned her back on the Social Scene and is finding Romance at work!
>
> She's thrown in her lot for Victory, wiring panel boards for Flying Fortresses in the Boeing plant, Seattle. Says Marguerite: "My job is worth every broken finger nail and dirty oil smudge a million times over!
>
> "Besides," continues Marguerite, "with famous Woodbury Soap to help freshen my complexion, coarse pores and a dingy, dirt-clouded skin are no beauty problems of mine."
>
> Busier lives—but beauty as usual. Keep *your* complexion clear, smooth. Use Woodbury, the soap made for the *skin* alone. Get it today.

The image of the glamour girl who was happy to dirty her hands or break a nail to support the boys on the front was repeated endlessly, in magazine articles and ads, in newsreels and Hollywood films, on posters like the Westinghouse one. Women weren't the only intended audience.

America wanted the boys off fighting the war to know that even if their wives and sweethearts were doing man's work they weren't sacrificing any FQ and would clean up nicely when the time came. As late as 1945, *Yank* ran a photo of a pretty nineteen-year-old brunette, Norma Jean Baker Dougherty, looking glamorous in tight overalls as she supposedly did her job at a defense plant. After the war she'd go blonde and change her name to Marilyn Monroe.

⌒

The Brooklyn Navy Yard continued to hire prodigiously through the war years, going from fewer than ten thousand workers before the war to a peak of almost seventy-two thousand during. In 1942 alone, some thirty-two thousand new workers were hired. They ate at eight cafeterias and twenty-eight outdoor canteens, and they had their own weekly newsletter, the *Shipworker*. The massive influx of workers brought boom times to the restaurants, corner stores, and gas stations in the surrounding neighborhoods of Fort Greene, Williamsburg, and today's Dumbo.

In the waning months of the war, of a total Navy Yard workforce of about seventy thousand, more than forty-six hundred were women. Like the men, they put in ten-hour shifts, six days a week. As newly trained and semiskilled labor, most worked in two areas: building gunsights, gauges, and other small precision instruments, because they were thought to be more dexterous than men; and in the shipfitters shop, where they mostly worked as welders' assistants. A few worked as crane operators, electricians, pipe fitters, and drivers ("chauffeurettes"). But very few received the advanced training needed to take on the most highly paid, highly skilled jobs, which were still reserved for men. No women were allowed to work on the ships themselves until the summer of 1944, when the few hundred of them who had earned advance ratings in the welding, sheet metal, and electrical trades began to do so. Women and the roughly five thousand black workers at the Navy Yard were paid less than white males until 1944, when women successfully lobbied for a pay hike. It made them the highest paid of any women wartime workers.

⌒

There was no question that the war created a vast new field of opportunities for millions of women, and for black Americans as well. It was not unlimited or unfettered progress, but they made gains that otherwise might have taken many more years—not just new and better jobs but new skills, new self-reliance, new self-esteem.

Yet there was a catch, and it was a big one. None of it was ever meant to be permanent. When the war ended, everything was supposed to go back to the way it was—women back to their families and shop counters, blacks back to domestic service and menial labor. This wasn't just an expectation, it was backed by federal legislation. Both the Selective Training and Service Act of 1940 and the Veterans' Preference Act of 1944 mandated that nonveterans would have to give up their jobs to returning vets when the time came.

Surveys conducted in 1944 indicated that only one in five of the Rosies in new and better jobs was okay with that. The rest liked their new jobs, new pay, new lives. They intended, or at least hoped, to keep them after the war was won. Many of them were going to be disappointed.

CHAPTER 37

No-Good Thieving, Chiseling Tinhorns

Just as Americans were getting back to work and had money to spend for the first time in a decade, their government asked them—and then forced them—to scrimp and sacrifice. Just about any product they might have spent their money on was either strictly rationed or completely unavailable for the duration. Rationing, though it reached into every corner of life on the home front, was more inconvenience than hardship. Americans were very well aware that scrimping on red meat and silk stockings was not remotely like what millions of other people around the world were suffering. This didn't stop them from scamming and scheming their way around wartime restrictions and price controls, in ways large and small, from relatively innocent finagling to outright criminal fraud.

Well before declaring war, FDR and his advisers saw that severe shortages in rubber were on the horizon. The United States consumed half the world's natural rubber, most of which came from Asia. As Japan expanded its empire in the 1930s it came to control virtually the entire supply. In 1940, Bernard Baruch proposed to FDR that someone should form a committee to determine just how extreme the U.S. rubber shortage could get and figure out what to do about it. FDR said Baruch was just the man for the job. The Rubber Reserve Company, formed in June of that year, was Baruch's signal contribution to war planning. The RRC began buying and stockpiling existing reserves of rubber in the United States. In addition, Americans were asked to donate anything rubber, from old tires to garden hoses to galoshes, and by 1942 it was announced that no new rubber items were to be produced or sold for the duration. There was one exception: women protested so vigorously that the government backed down on rubber girdles.

The strict gas rationing that went into effect in 1942 and bedeviled

Americans through the war years wasn't actually to save on gasoline but to reduce wear and tear on tires. Designated "essential drivers," who included doctors and nurses, police and firefighters, and military contractors, were allotted the most fuel. Everyone else grumbled, especially as the war ground on and the tires on their cars went bald. Constant blowouts and tires that were more patches than rubber became the source of much aggravation and many rueful jokes during the war.

The government also set a "Victory Speed" of 35 mph, with the slogan "Keep it under 40!," and encouraged carpooling. The last new car rolled off the assembly line in February 1942. For the remainder of the war, the government allowed dealers to sell off cars from the existing stock of more than half a million to those designated drivers. There were still more than three hundred thousand "new" cars warehoused at the end of the war.

At first Roosevelt tried to get Americans to reduce their consumption voluntarily. After the hunger and hardships of the Depression years few were enthusiastic. By the end of 1941 increasing shortages drove consumer prices up 10 percent. In an April 1942 fireside chat, Roosevelt informed Americans that a time of "self-denial" was upon them. To ward off inflation, he proposed to raise taxes; put ceilings on prices, rents, and wages; stop installment-plan buying; and "ration all essential commodities, which are scarce."

The Office of Price Administration proceeded to cap prices on virtually anything civilians could spend money on, as well as mandating rationing. Rationing worked on a "two-price system." The government issued all citizens monthly ration books containing ration stamps. To buy a rationed item such as a dozen eggs or a pound of sugar, you paid the cash price plus a certain number of stamps as prescribed by the OPA. If you ran out of stamps before the end of the month, you couldn't legally buy any more eggs or sugar until you got your next ration book.

Besides gasoline and rubber, sugar and eggs, the government rationed bicycles, kerosene, toasters, waffle irons, shoes, meat, fish, dairy, coffee and tea, the chicle for chewing gum, stoves, and even typewriters. The purchase of razor blades was restricted to one a week. Kids' lunch boxes, now called victory kits, were made out of cardboard, and their toys went back to being made of wood.

Restrictions on material for clothes had an immediate impact on fashions. "Skirts got shorter, dickeys replaced blouses, and a piece of jewelry had to substitute for now-banned ruffles on collars and cuffs," Lorraine

B. Diehl notes. "Designers faced with no metal for zippers or buttons replaced both with bows and stressed durable fabrics that would last for several years." Men's lapels got narrower and their trousers lost their pleats.

All citizens were also exhorted to participate in scrap drives. They collected newspapers; tin cans, aluminum, pots and pans, and other metals; silk and nylon stockings (for parachutes); even grease and fat, which contained glycerin for making gunpowder. City College students collected the tin foil from cigarette packs and chewing gum.

And everyone, even in crowded, gritty New York City, started to grow their own vegetables. The war was barely under way when tin cans, and the fruits and vegetables and sardines and beer they packaged, disappeared. To keep Americans eating their greens, the OCD started the Victory Garden Program early in 1942. It proved to be one of the most wildly popular and successful exercises in home front social engineering of the war years. Some four hundred thousand Victory Gardens sprouted all over New York City, in all five boroughs, in backyards, in public parks, on the lawns of uptown mansions, on tenement rooftops and fire escape landings. A plaza at Rockefeller Center turned lush with greens. Macy's created an indoor "Victory Barnyard" on its fifth floor and offered New Yorkers, few of whom had ever touched a rake or a hoe, farming lessons. The Brooklyn Botanic Garden and Bryant Park were transformed into virtual farms. Everyone pitched in. Ladies joined Garden Clubs, pensioners lovingly tended the pea vines curling up their fire escape railings, and schoolkids throughout the city got their own gardens. New York City's Victory Gardens are said to have yielded 200 million pounds of vegetables during the war. The community gardens all around the city today are their direct descendants.

Food rationing was a boon, curiously, for the city's restaurants. When people ran out of stamps, they ate in restaurants, whose business increased almost threefold.

⌣

As dutifully as they weeded their cabbage patches and stored bacon grease, New Yorkers, and Americans generally, expended at least an equal level of energy in figuring out ways to get around wartime restrictions and shortages. As early as May 1942, *Time* announced, "Wartime price and priority controls have already brought back an old U.S. institution:

bootlegging...The U.S. bootleg business is already more diversified, if not bigger, than it was in Prohibition's peephole days." The article listed tires as the most-bootlegged commodity, followed by "scarce metals, chemicals, textiles, typewriters—even stockings."

In January 1942, Mayor La Guardia, sitting at his desk at City Hall, started going on WNYC at 1 o'clock every Sunday afternoon in a program called *Talk to the People*. He would continue it until a farewell address on December 30, 1945, his penultimate day in office. The show often had a couple of million listeners, making it the highest-rated broadcast in the city. It always began with the NYPD Orchestra playing the "Marines' Hymn," followed by the mayor uttering his longtime slogan "Patience and Fortitude"—qualities he'd said would get New Yorkers through the Depression, and now through the war. (He also named the two famous stone lions at the entrance to the main branch of the New York Public Library Patience and Fortitude.) He'd start with a review and commentary on the week's news from the front and what impact it might have on the city. After that he'd entertain his listeners with a chatty mix of other news and opinion, pep talk, holiday cheer, cooking and budgeting advice.

The most entertaining parts of the show were the tongue-lashings he administered to any New Yorkers he felt were not giving their all to the war effort, especially regarding rationing and price controls. Some of the infractions he addressed were minor. When he heard that drivers were topping up their cars' tanks to keep ahead of projected gas shortages, he told them, "Nothing could be more disastrous to the welfare, health, and safety of our city than that." He advised homemakers to buy more fish, which was cheaper than meat, and not throw out stale bread—"There is such a thing as bread pudding."

His message to barbers who were charging boys in uniform too much for haircuts, landlords who were evading rent control, and others he saw as war profiteers was more severe. "No-good thieving, chiseling tinhorns, cut it out right now! I'm not fooling. No more monkey business!"

The mayor could scold, but the fact was that black markets for just about every rationed and restricted commodity on the government's long list thrived throughout the home front for the duration. "During the war at least a million cases of black market violations were dealt with by the government. Illegal profits ran into billions of dollars," the sociologist Marshall B. Clinard wrote in 1952. "Such extensive conniving in the black market in illegal prices and rationed commodities took place among so many businessmen, ordinary criminals, and even average citizens that serious questions might be raised as to the strength of the moral fiber of the American people." There could be no question, he wrote, that black market activities "extended throughout the entire nation, among all classes of society, from the thief and counterfeiter to the businessman, at all levels of our economic structure, from consumer to large manufacturer, and in numerous commodities."

Clinard had been in the enforcement division of the Office of Price Administration throughout the war. He knew what he was writing about.

The government estimated that at least one in five businesses, and probably very many more, violated regulations. To the extent it had the manpower, the government brought legal actions that resulted in thousands of fines and sanctions but conceded that these barely scratched the surface.

One of the first and largest black markets dealt in illegal gasoline, which came to be called "black gas." OPA administrator Chester Bowles (another New York dollar-a-year man, from the Madison Avenue ad firm Benton & Bowles) estimated that 2.5 million gallons of "black gas" were sold every day nationwide. Drivers either used authentic ration stamps that had been stolen or ones counterfeited by mobsters. Or they surreptitiously slipped the station guy some cash to top up their tank. This would have been hard to combat even at the best of times, but with the ranks of investigators and legal teams severely depleted by the war, there was little Bowles could do but implore Americans not to participate.

In New York City, when Brooklyn mobster Carlo Gambino "saw the profits that could be made from being the supplier of [gas] stamps, several break-ins occurred at OPA administrative offices; safes were broken into and stamps stolen," the historian Allan R. May relates. "Gambino realized that continuing this practice could be risky. Before he could contemplate his next move, OPA officials handed him the solution on a silver platter. These government jobs were mostly low-pay or no-pay positions, many staffed by volunteers. The previous theft of the stamps opened a few greedy eyes within the offices, and these unscrupulous officials quickly figured out how they could make money, too. The ration stamps were soon being sold directly to the mob."

When the government made the stamps harder to steal, the mob started printing counterfeits. It was much easier than counterfeiting money, and just as lucrative. Besides fake gas stamps, they counterfeited millions of stamps for meat, sugar, even shoes.

Obviously, the bootlegging and black marketeering wouldn't have worked if only the gangsters, butchers, and shoe salesmen were involved. Consumers from every stratum of society knowingly bought and used forged stamps when they felt the occasion warranted it, to get an extra few ounces of beef, some extra sugar for a birthday cake, a tankful for a family outing. Slipping the butcher or baker some cash when your stamps ran out could work too.

⌣

Meanwhile, La Guardia railed, and he developed his own strategies to compel New Yorkers to play along. In a January 1945 radio show he announced that "meat is short... and it will continue to be very short for several months. Our army needs meat and the army is getting it. I am very glad that they are. But I believe that here in New York City where we have seven and one-half million people, with a consuming public of about ten or eleven million people, I think we should set the example for the rest of the country... If we can reduce consumption, we will do a great deal to beat the black market."

So he started meatless Tuesdays and Fridays. He asked all New Yorkers to go along in their homes, ordered butcher shops to close on Mondays, and warned hotels and restaurants that he would enforce their compliance. When restaurants asked for a compromise—just meatless Fridays—he replied, "Friday is a traditional fish day, and to make Friday your official meatless day smacks of the slicker, doesn't it? We don't want to be hypocritical about this. Let's give the example to the rest of the country."

Because coal was short that winter as well, he issued orders "to all dealers of coal not to deliver or sell any coal to the following: they are not to sell or deliver any coal to places of amusements, such as theaters, moving picture houses, bowling alleys, nightclubs, libraries, museums, colleges, universities, except of course dental and medical colleges."

In New York, a city of renters, controlling rent hikes was of vital interest, especially to lower-income households, and to families where the traditional wage-earning dad was away in the military and the checks from the government trailed behind wartime inflation. Compared to today, rents in wartime New York sound fantastically low. They ranged from below $30 to $150 a month, with the average $50. But in 1941 the average monthly wage in America was $145, so $50 or more for rent was a very significant outlay, and any increase could mean a family having to forgo other necessities. Federal rent controls would remain in effect through the war, and New York State would later add its own regulations.

La Guardia denounced landlords he suspected were gouging tenants. Some landlords simply took their buildings off the regulated rental market by offering them for sale. The reduction in rental units would play a hand in the severe housing crisis that hit New York City when all the men in uniform flooded home after the war.

CHAPTER 38

Women at War

A few months after Pearl Harbor, *Life* and the U.S. Army Air Forces had struck an arrangement making Margaret Bourke-White America's first official female war correspondent. She entered the AAF with the rank of lieutenant and would be a lieutenant colonel by war's end. The Army War College designed her a stylish uniform, which Abercrombie & Fitch executed. She went to England to photograph the first squadron of American B-17s stationed there. All the crews flirted with her and got her to name one of the bombers—she dubbed it *Flying Flitgun*—but the brass kept turning down her requests to fly on a bombing raid. While she was in England Erskine Caldwell shocked her with a cable telling her he was getting a divorce. Like Sinclair Lewis, he'd grown increasingly moody and jealous as her fame soared while he felt his career was foundering. As soon as the divorce came through he would marry a twenty-year-old college student.

In the fall of 1942, when the Allies invaded North Africa, she left England in a naval convoy headed there. She was on a luxury liner transformed into a troopship and stuffed with six thousand soldiers, some WACs and nurses, and her. The convoy had just passed Gibraltar when a U-boat struck her ship with a torpedo in the middle of the night, tossing her out of her bunk. She was impressed by the calm and courage as everyone abandoned the listing ship. Scattered on the night sea in lifeboats and on floating wreckage, someone started to sing "You Are My Sunshine" and everyone joined in. They were picked up the next morning and taken to Algiers. When Alfred Hitchcock's *Lifeboat* came out in 1944 it was widely assumed to be inspired by Bourke-White's experience, with the glamorous journalist played by Tallulah Bankhead based on her.

In North Africa Bourke-White finally got her chance to fly in a B-17 bombing raid. According to her biographer Vicki Goldberg she did it by sleeping with the commander of the squadron, the first of several wartime affairs. She flew in a raid on a Luftwaffe airfield. Her lover was the pilot. (The copilot was a young man from Illinois named Paul Tibbets, later the pilot of the *Enola Gay*.) *Life* ballyhooed the resulting piece as "LIFE'S BOURKE-WHITE GOES BOMBING." A photo of her in her flight suit, leather helmet in one hand and camera in the other, became, Goldberg writes, "the most dressed pinup in the history of the war."

Clare Luce also got to do some war reporting for *Life*, traveling to North Africa and Burma. Wherever she went, she wrote about herself as much as the military and political leaders she met. Her photo spreads always managed to include a shot or two of her looking impossibly, almost ridiculously cool and elegant no matter where she went, on a battlefield, in a jungle. It made her an easy target for sniping that she wasn't a serious journalist, just Henry Luce's "glamour girl" wife.

By mid-1942 she was ready for yet another career move anyway. She had done so well in her speeches for Wendell Willkie that Republicans convinced her to run for a congressional seat in Connecticut that fall. When the other five Republican contenders, all men, heard she had agreed, they dropped out. She beat the Democratic incumbent in a tight race and went off to Washington.

When she took her seat in January 1943, six other women sat in Congress, five of them fellow Republicans, including New York's Winifred Stanley, a Bronx-born lawyer and women's rights advocate who would serve only one term because her seat would be lost to reapportionment. Haughty as ever and trailing a perpetual cloud of news photographers, Luce raised a lot of hackles in D.C. Still, there was semiserious talk for a while of her running for vice president with Thomas Dewey in 1944. She did not, but she would stump for him, trading barbs with Roosevelt: he called her a "sharp-tongued glamour girl of 40," while she damned him as "the only American president who ever lied us into a war because he did not have the political courage to lead us into it." Dewey would lose, but Luce would be reelected by a slim margin. The Associated Press named her its Woman of the Year. Eleanor Roosevelt came in a distant second and Dorothy Thompson third.

Eleanor would make one trip each to the European and Pacific theaters during the war. In October 1942 she secretly flew to England for a goodwill visit, her seaplane at one point gliding over a zigzagging convoy in the U-boat-infested mid-Atlantic. Harry Hopkins told her not to bother with John Winant—Harriman was the American power broker in London. Eleanor was very fond of Winant and disliked Harriman, whom she'd known since he was a boy. She looked up Winant the moment she arrived in London and avoided Harriman the entire trip. The king and queen had her stay with them at Buckingham Palace, apologizing that the windows in her room were boarded up because the glass had been shattered by a bomb. At a Red Cross club in London, grinning GIs mobbed her, some calling out, "Hi, Eleanor!" Trailing exhausted reporters, she bustled around to many British and U.S. military bases in England, Scotland, and Ulster. She was particularly impressed by how much important work was getting done by British women in defense plants and in "auxiliary" military units.

On a visit to Chequers, she brought Churchill a gift of ham and honey from Franklin. She and the PM were too different in both personality and politics ever to warm to each other. At one dinner they argued about Spain. She insisted that the rest of the world should have come to the loyalists' aid. He angrily replied that if the Communists had been allowed to stay in power there, they would have toppled the U.S. and British governments next, then he abruptly stalked away from the table.

In the autumn of 1943 she flew to the South Pacific in a B-24, visiting Australia, New Zealand, and seventeen islands where Americans were based. She would log more than twenty thousand miles in this one trip and once again, at fifty-nine, exhaust the entourage struggling to keep pace. They nicknamed her Public Energy No. 1. By the end of it she had lost thirty pounds.

Officers from Admiral Halsey and General MacArthur down resented her visit as a distraction and a drain on their resources and gave her minimum cooperation. But soldiers and sailors reacted as though she were their own mother visiting them in their camps and hospital beds. Halsey, worried for her safety, tried and failed to keep her from going to Guadalcanal. Though the Allies had taken the island the previous February, it was still subject to frequent Japanese bombing raids. In fact, bombs fell the night before she arrived.

⌒

Margaret, Clare, and Eleanor were among the handful of American women who got around the prevailing attitude that a war zone was no place for a lady—one because she was the first lady and could largely make her own rules, the other two because they were pretty, sexy, and adept at getting men to bend the rules for them. For the many thousands of American women who sought a more direct role in the wartime military the going was tougher.

When Selective Service began in 1940, women's organizations lobbied for the opportunity to support the fighting men in a more direct way than knitting them sweaters and keeping the home fires burning. In May 1941, Congresswoman Edith Nourse Rogers of Massachusetts, who had served with the Red Cross in France during the Great War, introduced a bill to create a Women's Army Auxiliary Corps. She had Eleanor's support but very little from Congress, the military brass, or the general public. The bill was kicked around and finally passed in May 1942. The first eight hundred WAACs started their training that June. Within a year there were sixty thousand.

Meanwhile, again with prompting from Rogers and Eleanor, Congress passed separate bills creating the U.S. Navy's Women Accepted for Volunteer Emergency Service, or WAVES; the Coast Guard's SPARS; and the Marine Corps Women's Reserve. And while Laura Ingalls was being tried for her heil-hitlering, another star flier and familiar figure at New York's airfields, Jackie Cochran, helped found the Women Airforce Service Pilots (WASP).

To develop the WAVES training program, the navy turned to a native New Yorker, Virginia Gildersleeve, a friend of Eleanor and Frances Perkins and dean of Barnard College since before the Great War. She'd been fighting all that time to expand opportunities for women in higher education; for instance, she convinced Columbia Law to admit its first female students in 1926. After Pearl Harbor she argued that a nation at war, with its men siphoned off to the front, was going to need "trained brains," and women were ready. Barnard women would contribute to the war effort as physicists, chemists, mathematicians, and cryptologists.

Barnard English professor Elizabeth Reynard, a close friend and companion, helped Gildersleeve design the navy's program and suggested the name WAVES. Early in 1943, the navy took over the Bronx campus of Hunter College (established in the 1930s as an expansion of Hunter's main Upper East Side campus) for enlisted WAVES' six weeks of basic training. It also commandeered adjacent apartment buildings for barracks. Officers were trained separately at Smith College, and advanced training in specific skills took place on other campuses around the country. Soon six thousand WAVES at a time were going through boot camp in the Bronx. At the start, enlisted WAVES were trained for three jobs: bookkeeping, secretarial work, and radio operation. By the end of 1943 they were serving in more than two hundred fifty capacities, from running flight simulation programs to assisting with aircraft maintenance to training carrier pigeons.

Hollywood did its part to bolster public support with the 1944 Paramount movie *Here Come the Waves*. It was a light musical comedy starring Betty Hutton and Bing Crosby, coming off his hugely successful *Going My Way*. It produced one of the most popular and upbeat songs of the war years, "Ac-Cent-Tchu-Ate the Positive," sung by Crosby and Sonny Tufts.

They sang it in blackface. Meanwhile, mirroring the navy's general bias against blacks, the WAVES would refuse to admit black women until nearly the end of that year. The tortured rationale was that women were enlisted to free up navy men for combat duty, and since black men in the navy almost entirely served in mess halls and laundries at port, not at sea, black WAVES were not needed. At the end of the war, only about one hundred black women had served in the WAVES (out of a total of nearly a hundred thousand), and only five as SPARS.

⌒

After their initial reticence about the WAAC program, army planners turned enthusiastic. By the end of 1942 they decided that there were potentially more than a million slots in the rapidly expanding ranks that women could fill as well as men—not combat or heavy labor but just about anything else in the administrative offices, in transport and supply depots, in radio operations. To bring that many women into the army, one option seriously considered was to expand the draft to include females. Another solution was to entice more enlistees by shifting the WAAC from an auxiliary service to full military status (from WAAC to WAC), offering all the benefits soldiers got—health insurance, financial allotments for dependents, veterans' benefits, and so on.

Congress started discussing the appropriate legislation for it early in 1943. That's when the army discovered how deeply resistant soldiers and many civilians were to the idea of women in the army. A concerted effort to scuttle the program, which came to be known as the Slander Campaign, evidently started with men in uniform who felt that WAACs were actually harmful to their health. They were soldiers in rearguard, noncombat posts, who dreaded the idea that a million women in uniform would "free" them to go to the front to fight and maybe die. They began planting rumors—among themselves, to hostesses at the USO, in letters home to wives and girlfriends—that the majority of WAACs were either lesbians or whores. The idea spread. Soon it was alleged that thousands of WAACs had gotten pregnant or caught venereal diseases. Soldiers began writing their wives and sweethearts that they'd leave them if they signed up. They warned their sisters that no decent man would have them if they donned a uniform. These women in turn spread the rumors in the civilian population. Civilian men joined in, warning the women in their lives that they'd ruin their reputations if they enlisted.

Studies demonstrated that exactly the opposite of the rumors was true. WAACs, the WAVES, and the rest were carefully screened on recruitment, then trained to the highest levels of pride and proper deportment. Levels of VD and pregnancy among them were in fact far lower than among civilian women. The WAAC even banned contraceptives, except for use by married couples. On the whole, women in uniform were, as one historian has put it, "remarkably chaste."

That didn't stop the *Daily News*'s John O'Donnell from playing the gadfly and circulating the slurs. He had already irked Roosevelt toward the end of 1942. Still in the Pacific, he had joked in his column that his fellow war correspondents were playing "flutes and piccolos just to keep their fingers nimble for a time when censorship lets them beat the keys of their portable typewriters" and tell the real story of how badly the fight was going against the Japanese. The Pacific war had not gone very well for the Allies through much of 1942, and the government had in fact censored the worst of the news from there. But by the time O'Donnell was writing the tide had begun to shift. FDR was enraged. At a White House press conference on December 18, 1942, he shocked the assembled reporters by handing one of them a German Iron Cross and asking him to pass it along to O'Donnell, sneering that it was a reward for his service to the enemy.

O'Donnell was deeply insulted, and in his column for June 8, 1943, he sought revenge, writing, "Contraceptives and prophylactic equipment will be furnished to members of the WAAC, according to a super-secret agreement reached by high-ranking officers of the War Department" and the WAAC director. He quoted "a lady lawmaker" as saying that if the army was supplying prophylactics to male soldiers, it was only fitting that women in uniform had the same right "to indulge their affections and emotions, whether married or single."

Newspapers around the country picked up the story. The army, the WAAC, and the White House fired off hot denials. Henry Stimson denounced it as slander against not only WAACs but all American women. Eleanor went so far as to brand his report "Axis-inspired propaganda."

O'Donnell later apologized but the damage was done. WAAC/WAC enlistment plunged in the summer of 1943 from a peak of more than twelve thousand a month to around nine hundred. The WAC fought back with its own propaganda, including a 1944 short film called *Ladies, It's Your War Too* that directly attacked the male chauvinism of "armchair generals" who insisted, "This is a man's war." Generals Eisenhower and Marshall issued strong statements endorsing the WAC. Still, WAC rolls never reached anywhere near the projected million members; its peak strength was around one hundred thousand.

Resistance to the air forces' WASPs was equally strong. During the war, the 1,102 WASP pilots would log more than 60 million miles in the air, mostly ferrying thousands of new combat planes from factories to airfields across the United States. Yet they apparently faced actual injury and even death at the hands of unhappy males working with them. Sugar, which could cause an engine to seize, was found in the fuel tank of one of their planes, and there were other mysterious mechanical failures that might have been sabotage. It's possible that some of the thirty-eight WASPs who were killed in accidents were victims.

WASPs were ill-treated in another way. Although WASP was administered by the U.S. Army Air Forces, it was classified as a civilian program. Those thirty-eight WASPs who died in the line of duty were thus denied military honors. The situation wouldn't be redressed until 1977.

CHAPTER 39

Buffaloed Soldiers and Conscientious Objectors

I DON'T WANT TO STARTLE YOU but they are going to kill most of us

—*Kenneth Patchen*

Despite reservations about the war in their communities, more than two and a half million black men registered for the draft. Roughly a million black draftees and volunteers would serve during the war, in all branches. More than eight hundred thousand of them served in the army—in segregated units. The Red Cross even segregated black and white blood plasma, under directions from Stimson; the War Department feared that wounded white soldiers would refuse black plasma, and there can be no doubt that some would have.

The majority of the black men in the army never left the States. Only a handful who went overseas ever got near the front lines, and only one ground division, the Buffalo Soldiers of the 92nd Infantry Division, saw extensive combat. Another 145,000 blacks served in the army's Air Corps. Even the resistant navy and Marine Corps were forced to admit some black men, though the numbers were far lower.

For most blacks in uniform, life tended to be at least as demoralizing and degrading as it was as a civilian. They were penned up in de facto ghetto bases around the country, routinely insulted and harassed by white officers and soldiers, relegated to the same sorts of "service" jobs available to them in the civilian world. They received little combat training; one black soldier who was issued only one bullet for his carbine later joked, "I guess that was to kill yourself." They were far less likely to be injured in battle than in violent clashes with whites, both soldiers and civilians, on the home front. Writing a letter home to Harlem from Europe in 1942, Private Sal Thomas wondered why white Americans and Nazi Germans both believed in doctrines of "false superiority and yet are opposed on the battlefield of this war? Is it that the crackers don't want Hitler to tell them how to run their Negroes?"

The ill treatment extended even to the most feted and decorated black unit in the army, New York City's 369th Infantry Regiment, the Harlem Hellfighters, who had been cheered after World War I. As America ramped up for the next war, the 369th was reorganized as an antiaircraft unit and sent to Hawaii. They were on duty at Pearl Harbor when the Japanese attacked. Transferred back to the States in 1943, they passed through Harlem and went from there to the notorious Camp Stewart in Georgia, which one described as a "concentration camp." They were soon inundating the *Amsterdam News* and Walter White's NAACP offices with letters complaining about their deplorable treatment there.

Some draft-age males in Harlem heard those stories and decided the last thing they wanted was to be put into uniform. Malcolm Little, the future Malcolm X, was sixteen years old when the Japanese attacked Pearl Harbor. From the start he thought, "Whitey owns everything. He wants me to go bleed for him? Let him fight." He was working as a dining-car dishwasher for the New York, New Haven and Hartford Railroad, which brought him to Harlem for the first time. "I was into my zoot suit before the first passenger got off," he recalls in his autobiography. "New York was Heaven to me. And Harlem was Seventh Heaven!"

Within a year he was living in Harlem, waiting tables at the elegant basement nightclub Smalls Paradise on Seventh Avenue at 135th Street. A year after that he had become Detroit Red, a small-time but flashy hustler and dope peddler. That's when the draft board came calling. "In those days only three things in the world scared me: jail, a job, and the Army." He did everything he could think of to appear unfit to serve. He showed up at the draft office in his wildest zoot suit, with "yellow knob-toed shoes" and his hair piled up in "a reddish bush." Spouting jive, calling everyone Daddy-o, he said he was happy to join...the Japanese army. Failing that, he wanted to "get sent down South. Organize them nigger soldiers, you dig? Steal us some guns, and kill us crackers!" He was declared 4-F and never called up again.

Harlem's star Lindy hopper Frankie Manning didn't want to serve either. "My reason was simple," he recalled in his memoirs. "I wouldn't be able to dance anymore."

Born in Florida in 1914, Manning came to Harlem with his mom when he was three. He was a teen when dancers at the Renaissance Ballroom and the Savoy Ballroom merged the Charleston and other dances into the Lindy hop. Swing music, the Lindy, and Frankie grew up together during the 1930s. Frankie and other young people developed the Lindy into a wildly acrobatic, sexy-but-innocent display, with the boys swinging the girls high in the air, flipping them over their backs, sliding them between their legs—the latter two moves his inventions.

The Savoy Ballroom was their home base. Stretching along Lenox Avenue from 140th to 141st Street, it was the largest, grandest dance hall in Harlem. The block-long space had a bandstand at each end, where Cab Calloway, Louis Armstrong, Chick Webb, and other greats played, and booths lining the side walls so you could sit and study dancers' moves. Everyone dressed well, only ginger ale was served, and rowdiness was strictly forbidden. It attracted not only all of Harlem but a fair number of white patrons as well. Owner Moe Gale, a Jewish businessman, and manager Charles Buchanan, who was black, maintained a relaxed policy about whites and blacks mingling, a very rare attitude in the city at the time.

In the mid-1930s Frankie and a small troupe graduated from the Savoy to touring professionally with Duke Ellington and Cab Calloway, giving Lindy demonstrations. They sailed to France in 1937 for a monthlong gig at the Moulin Rouge, then went to London and gave a command performance for King George and Queen Elizabeth. In the next few years they brought the Lindy to Australia and New Zealand, to the New York World's Fair, to Broadway, and to the screen in the 1941 film adaptation of *Hellzapoppin'*.

When the army called him up in 1943, Manning was in his late twenties and hoping to be let off as unfit to serve. At Camp Upton he tried to get assigned to Special Services with other artists and performers, but the army apparently didn't know from the Lindy hop. He still tried for a discharge, playing sick, playing dumb, marching on the wrong foot. It didn't work. He was assigned to a black tank corps with white officers and sent to Camp Hood near Waco, Texas. In 1944 the corps would ship out and participate in the taking of New Guinea and the Philippines, then go to

Japan with the occupying forces in the fall of 1945. Manning would serve well and bravely enough to earn a few medals but notes in his memoirs: "I'm sorry to have to say this, but I experienced more prejudice, and worse prejudice, in the military than at any other time of my life."

Ralph DiGia's draft board called him up in the spring of 1942. He discussed his options with his parents. "My father, who had supported me up to this point, now advised me to report for induction," DiGia later wrote. "He was afraid that going to jail would ruin my future and believed that, as a college graduate, I could get a good job in the army."

Ralph decided he had to refuse.

Some forty-three thousand other conscientious objectors refused to bear arms during the war. The majority were Jehovah's Witnesses and Friends who refused on religious grounds. Twenty-five thousand COs agreed to serve in the military in noncombatant roles. Another twelve thousand lived and worked at 151 Civilian Public Service camps, mostly at former Civilian Conservation Corps sites in the countryside, which kept them and their ideas away from the general population. About six thousand conscientious objectors and war resisters, who declined to serve in either the military or the CPS camps, went to jail during the war, on sentences generally from two to five years. They came to represent a sixth of the total prison population.

DiGia was in the last category. When he decided not to report to the military, he went to consult with the city's War Resisters League. On December 8, 1941, the league's Jessie Hughan had telegraphed Roosevelt: "Do not let Japan lead us into disastrous war. We urge peace in spite of the Pearl Harbor events." Although the league would argue throughout the war that all sides bore responsibility for the conflict, and that peaceful resistance would be more effective against the military aggressors than military might, it also "recognized that Pearl Harbor, along with the subsequent declarations of war by Germany and Italy, 'left no choice for those who believe in military defense.'" For the duration of the war, the historian Scott H. Bennett writes, the War Resisters League and other pacifist organizations "sponsored public meetings; organized study groups; circulated petitions; provided financial support to COs; staged simulated draft board tribunals to give COs the opportunity to rehearse their responses; and distributed pacifist literature, newspapers, and periodicals."

The league put DiGia in touch with a Quaker lawyer who handled conscientious objector cases. Because DiGia's refusal to serve was not on religious grounds, they lost their case, and in early 1943 DiGia would be sentenced to three years in prison. He spent the month of March 1943 in the gloomy Federal House of Detention on West Street in Greenwich Village (commonly known as the West Street jail), largely used as a holding pen for inmates who were to be shipped out to other penitentiaries for longer stays. As it happened, Lepke Buchalter was there too, appealing his Brooklyn murder conviction of 1941, still hoping not to be sent to Sing Sing and the electric chair.

When the twenty-six-year-old poet Robert Lowell arrived at West Street some eight months after DiGia, Lepke was *still* there, still trying to fend off a trip to Sing Sing. Born into a Boston Brahmin family, Lowell would carom through his life suffering from severe manic depression, prone to fits of blackest gloom and abrupt bursts of towering rage for which his prep schoolmates nicknamed him Cal for Caligula. When America entered the war he tried to enlist but was rejected (for his poor eyesight, not his unbalanced mind). By the time the draft board called him up in 1943 he refused to serve, claiming, in what he later characterized as a "manic statement," that the Allies were just as brutal and savage as the enemy. Convicted of draft evasion, he spent a few months in the House of Detention, which in the 1950s inspired one of his more celebrated poems, "Memories of West Street and Lepke." ("Flabby, bald, lobotomized,/ he drifted in a sheepish calm...")

Lowell was transferred to the low-security Federal Correctional Institution in Danbury, Connecticut, where DiGia had already been sent. It housed many conscientious objectors and draft resisters, along with "butchers and gas station owners (convicted of violating wartime rationing laws), numbers runners, bootleggers, and bad check artists," DiGia later recalled. DiGia would serve his full three years there and in the federal pen at Lewisburg, Pennsylvania, not released until June 1945.

⌒

In 1943, Kenneth Patchen attended a meeting of one of New York's peace groups. A young man who'd already spent a year in federal prison for refusing to register for the draft stood up and started to recite a poem he said had inspired him, but he stumbled after a few lines. Patchen stood and recited the rest. It was one of his poems.

Patchen was a bit of an anomaly—a fierce, angry, two-fisted pacifist. He was also a writer of some of the most visionary American prose and poetry since Walt Whitman. Born a poor steelworker's son in Ohio in 1911, he began writing poetry in high school. His first published poem, a sonnet, appeared in the *New York Times* when he was in college (the first in his family to go). Hoboing around the country and doing migrant labor during the first few years of the Depression left him with a sense of social injustice that infused, among other things, his opposition to war.

He moved to Greenwich Village with his wife in 1934 and remained there, off and on, through the war years. The Patchens were leftists, like most everyone around them in the Village of the 1930s, but not doctrinaire Stalinists, as many were before 1939. Hoping to catch the wave of "rebel poets," Bennett Cerf of Random House published Patchen's first poetry collection, *Before the Brave*, in 1936. Given the eclectic fireworks of his mature writing it was rather formal and tentative, and it pleased neither the mainstream critics nor the Stalinists.

He found his voice in his next book, *First Will & Testament*, published by James Laughlin's three-year-old New Directions late in 1939. His indignation was now more focused: "...then let them/ Bring on their cannon and iron sugar, brother, for all the flags/ In all the world won't make a fatherland out of a butcher shop." It got a much more enthusiastic reception. Mainstream reviewers compared him to T. S. Eliot and E. E. Cummings, a Village neighbor who became a close friend.

Another friend, Henry Miller, was one of Patchen's greatest champions at a time when he needed one. Responding to the grim news of the Blitzkrieg in the summer of 1940, Patchen was moved to churn out the highly experimental antiwar novel—or antiwar antinovel—*The Journal of Albion Moonlight*, completing it by November. Beginning with a searing image of an angel lying in a ditch with its throat cut, *Moonlight* was ostensibly the story of a ragtag group of pilgrims making their way across a phantasmagorical war-torn America. But it was nothing like traditional storytelling. A surrealistic scrapbook bulging with characters, stories, dreams, jokes, diary entries, harangues, and assorted "interruptions," it was one of the most idiosyncratic, unruly works of American literature since *Leaves of Grass*. Laughlin declined it, telling Patchen he found it a "hopeless mess." Still, Laughlin joined Miller and a small group of Patchen's other writer friends in raising the funds for Patchen to publish it himself in a small edition, celebrated in a July 1941 party at the legendary Gotham Book Mart. The *New York Times* refused to run an ad for *Moonlight*, declaring its antiwar stance anti-American. But the edition sold well and earned some strong reviews. Its reputation would grow over the years—and New Directions would eventually reprint it.

The young man who stumbled over one of Patchen's poems in 1943 was the conscientious objector David Dellinger, who had developed a commitment to Gandhian nonviolence as a student at Yale. During the Spanish Civil War he drove an ambulance for the loyalists but refused to touch a weapon. He was studying at the Union Theological Seminary near Columbia when the draft started.

He and Patchen became good friends. Dellinger was rearrested later in 1943 and sentenced to two years at Lewisburg for his continuing resistance to the draft. He was in Lewisburg when his first son was born; he and his wife named him Evan Patchen Dellinger. Released near the end of the war, he'd continue advocating peace. He's best known today as one of the "Chicago Seven" Vietnam War protesters arrested at the 1968 Democratic National Convention.

⌒

While never explicitly advocating that any man refuse the draft—she said it was up to each to decide—Dorothy Day continued to preach pacifism and support Quakers and other conscientious objectors throughout the war. In December 1942, when "Remember Pearl Harbor" was a refrain heard around the country, she put out an issue of the *Catholic Worker* with the headline "Forget Pearl Harbor." Her extremely unpopular stance precipitated a sharp decline in circulation through the war years, from nearly two hundred thousand in 1940 to below twenty-five thousand at war's end. Even some of Day's disciples decided that they had to join up and fight. But she never abandoned her conviction that pacifism was a cornerstone of Christian morality.

In the spring of 1941, J. Edgar Hoover personally added her name to a long list of suspected subversives he thought should be rounded up and interned if the United States ever entered the war. The Justice Department would fatten its files on her through much of the war before officials finally decided that, although she was a radical with seditious ideas, she was harmless.

CHAPTER 40

Selling the War

In June 1942, President Roosevelt sat William Donovan and Robert Sherwood down like a pair of squabbling schoolboys and tried to broker a peace between them. It hadn't taken long for operational and philosophical conflicts to surface between the two of them and their two very different operations. Donovan's side of COI was largely conservative and Republican and emulated a military model. He saw propaganda as just another weapon in the military's arsenal, softening up the enemy for attack—"black propaganda." Sherwood's bohemian gaggle of creative people, New Dealers, and foreigners—not a few of them with Communist involvement or sympathies in their backgrounds—appalled Donovan. So did Sherwood's benign vision of propaganda not as a military tool but as a way to spread pro-American ideals of peace and democracy around a troubled world ("white propaganda," which Sherwood preferred to call simply "truth"). To make things worse, both of them were neophytes, making it up as they went, and sloppy administrators.

As usual, Roosevelt solved the problem by creating more agencies. COI was split in two. Donovan's intelligence and espionage operation, including Allen Dulles's unit in New York City, was put under military jurisdiction and renamed the Office of Strategic Services (OSS). Rather than reporting directly to Roosevelt, Donovan was now under the authority of the Joint Chiefs of Staff. For the rest of the war, the job of the OSS was to support operations of the army and navy.

Sherwood's FIS became the Office of War Information (OWI). Roosevelt asked Elmer Davis to replace Sherwood at the top. Davis was a midwesterner and Rhodes scholar who'd gone to New York City in 1914 to write for the *Times*. In 1939 he became a CBS news commentator, well liked around the country for his plainspoken horse sense. Sherwood stayed on to run OWI's overseas branch, including Voice of America. That suited Davis, who was more interested in domestic propaganda, explaining to the American people why they were at war.

Donovan's OSS rapidly grew to eclipse anything his rivals Astor or Carter had run. He was expert at coaxing ever larger staff and budgets from the president. In two years he was up to a staff of fifteen thousand and a budget of $60 million, including operations in England and elsewhere in Europe. He did that partly by keeping Roosevelt entertained, barraging him with intelligence, some good and some not, and ideas, some more harebrained than others, that appealed to Roosevelt's own boyish spy fantasies. He presented a plan to put female hormones in Hitler's food, causing his mustache to drop off. Just after Pearl Harbor he suggested a commando strike on the Japanese home island, which was absolutely impossible. He reported that the Japanese were going to bomb Los Angeles and the Germans were about to invade New York City. He assured the president that the Japanese were incapable of invading Singapore, which they did two days later. A man wrote to the president claiming that the Japanese were terrified of bats and suggesting that bombers drop large numbers of them over the home island. Roosevelt had Donovan look into it. The scheme got as far as test flights, during which the bats froze to death inside the planes at high altitudes.

Donovan's staff was a mixed bag. On the one hand, the OSS earned a somewhat dicey reputation as a safe haven for draft-dodging toffs as Donovan hired a DuPont, a Mellon, an Armour, and two Morgans. One Washington gossip columnist sniped that the OSS was a nest of "ex–polo players, millionaires, Russian princes, society gambol boys, scientists, and dilettante detectives," aided by "the prettiest, best-born, snappiest girls who used to graduate from debutantedom to boredom." It was joked that OSS stood for Oh So Social.

On the other hand, the OSS trained a generation who would go on to lifetime careers in intelligence. Four of Donovan's hires would become directors of the CIA in the Cold War decades: Allen Dulles, William Casey, William Colby, and Richard Helms. Dulles left his New York operation late in 1942 to start up an OSS outpost in Bern. Neutral and centrally situated, Switzerland was, as he remembered it from his Great War days, a buzzing hive of international finance and intrigue, crowded with intelligence services and spies of all nations.

William Casey was a native New Yorker, born in 1913 into an Irish

Catholic household in Elmhurst, Queens. The first Casey to go to college, he graduated from Fordham in 1934. After trying his hand at social work, he studied law at St. John's in Brooklyn, passed the bar in 1937, and went to Washington to work for an outfit called the Research Institute of America. Run by another young New York lawyer, Leo Cherne, the RIA hacked through the thickets of New Deal legislation and explained it all in publications for businessmen. The instinctively conservative Casey's exposure to the New Deal made him wary of it as creeping socialism. As a good Catholic, he also favored the fascists over the loyalists in Spain.

In 1939, Cherne and Casey switched the focus of their analyses to the growing defense industry; they published a volume called *The Business and Defense Coordinator* on September 1, the day Hitler invaded Poland. In 1943, a junior officer bored behind a desk at the Office of Naval Procurement, Casey heard about the OSS. He knew a young lawyer who worked at Donovan's Wall Street firm—they'd parked cars together at Jones Beach one summer—through whom he got an appointment. In a matter of weeks Casey was at the OSS London office.

One impact of bringing Donovan's outfit under the aegis of the Joint Chiefs was that his Visual Presentation Branch's elaborate plans for the Q-2 Presidential Situation Room were permanently shelved. The Joint Chiefs were already building their own less grandiose but still state-of-the-art situation rooms and did not see the point of constructing one just for the president. Roosevelt would make do with a more conventional map room in a converted ladies' lavatory near the Oval Office. He did get one of six very large traditional globes the War Department ordered, the biggest (more than four feet in diameter) and most finely detailed in the world. Churchill and the Joint Chiefs got their own. They were mounted on ball bearings to be easily spun in any direction. As for Buckminster Fuller's Dymaxion World, in 1943 *Life* would run an extraordinary feature introducing the idea to the public, complete with a full-color center spread readers could cut out and paste together to make their own Dymaxion Worlds. Although the Q-2 project was shut down, the design team survived the transition from COI to OSS and would operate throughout the war.

Sherwood's overseas branch of the OWI grew prodigiously as well. From their cramped Madison Avenue space they moved to General Motors' roomy Argonaut Building at West 57th Street and Broadway, with eight floors over what had been a street-level Cadillac showroom. Along with offices and conference rooms, it housed radio studios and the hub of the worldwide shortwave broadcasting system that came to be known as the Bronze Network. By the end of 1942 Voice of America, its dominant project, had three thousand people churning out more than two hundred fifty fifteen-minute programs a day in twenty-two languages. Besides news, they produced programs aimed at helping the English and other Europeans get to know—and like—the Americans who were coming to save them.

For one series, people in England submitted questions about American life, which were answered by luminaries such as Eleanor Roosevelt, Margaret Mead, and Walter Huston. Another series on American music ranged from orchestral (including the composers Henry Cowell and Samuel Barber) to folk and popular, the latter curated by Nicholas Ray, best known today as the director of *Rebel Without a Cause* and *Johnny Guitar.* The unit also produced propaganda films, and as the war progressed bombers dropped millions of OWI leaflets on Germany and Japan. ("The high leaders of the Japanese Army and Navy have bragged that the homeland of Japan will never be violated. This pamphlet which has been dropped from an American heavy bomber...is proof to you that they have lied.")

Separating the OSS and OWI did not end Sherwood's woes. An autonomous, ad hoc, basically amateur operation, his overseas branch sometimes went rogue and invented its own foreign policy, making as much trouble for the military and the State Department as for the enemy. In 1942, when official U.S. policy was to treat the Vichy government with a light touch and hope for the best, Sherwood's French exiles were sending out scurrilous messages calling Vichy leaders traitors, murderers, and "detested gangsters." Eisenhower, commanding the Allied invasion of Vichy-held North Africa that autumn, was trying to negotiate their peaceful surrender. He complained, as the *New York Post* put it, that "our propagandists were giving him almost as much of a headache as the Germans." In 1943, when Mussolini fled Rome, the Allies hoped for a negotiated peace with King Victor Emmanuel III. Meanwhile, the OWI was broadcasting a statement denouncing "the moronic little king" who'd acquiesced to Fascists for two decades.

That would be the beginning of the end for Sherwood at the Office of War Information. With Washington's backing, Elmer Davis tightened the reins and forced several of Sherwood's top people to resign. Then Roosevelt had Harry Hopkins explain to Sherwood that with the 1944 elections approaching he was needed more as a speechwriter than as a propagandist. Sherwood would take the hint and voluntarily resign.

⁀

There were internal squabbles at Elmer Davis's domestic branch of OWI as well. In April 1943, fourteen writers, editors, and graphic artists quit, telling the press that the agency's methods and agenda had been perverted by a pernicious outside influence: Madison Avenue.

As soon as Roosevelt shifted American industry from making washing machines to making war machines, Madison Avenue's advertising agencies knew they were facing a deadly crisis. Without new products to pitch, most of their clients would have no obvious need to advertise. Ad agencies could lose a crushing four-fifths of their revenues for the duration of the war.

In 1941, the city's leading ad agencies developed a plan to stave off this disaster. If they couldn't sell new cars and refrigerators, they'd sell the war instead. A month before Pearl Harbor, they formed what they called the War Advertising Council and offered their services to Washington to help design and execute home-front propaganda that would guide Americans in thinking and acting the way Washington wanted them to. As James Young of Young & Rubicam put it, "We have within our hands the greatest aggregate means of mass education and persuasion the world has ever seen." Chester La Roche, who chaired both Young & Rubicam and the WAC, saw it in terms of psychological warfare, and wrote, "We have the brains, the experience, the coast-to-coast polling machines; we know the people, know how to make them read; know how to plan huge informational efforts; and know how to coordinate every form of media."

Roosevelt was convinced. In 1942, when he split the COI into the OSS and OWI, he directed OWI's domestic propaganda branch to work closely with the advertisers. The Mad men quickly infiltrated the OWI and convinced Davis to shift its output from dull, earnest, government-style pamphlets and films to flashier advertisements and advertorials in all the leading magazines. A number of Davis's original hires—most of them from New York book publishing, and most of them progressives—were highly suspicious of the advertising men and their motives. When the fourteen of them quit in 1943, Mad men replaced them.

From then to the end of the war, the OWI's domestic propaganda was run like a massive advertising campaign, blanketing the home front with its messages, promoting American participation at every level of the war effort—and, not coincidentally, portraying corporate America as fighting for victory right alongside GI Joe and Rosie the Riveter. It churned out print advertising and print advertorials, produced radio programs, and worked with Hollywood on pro-war films. It recruited Boy Scouts to deliver posters to stores and other public spots.

All the most popular magazines—*Life*, *Look*, *Time*, the *Saturday Evening Post*, *Ladies' Home Journal*, and others—were packed with war-themed, propagandistic advertising, jointly paid for by the government and Madison Avenue's corporate accounts. Because those clients had few consumer goods to sell, the ads sold image—patriotic images of big business as a partner with all Americans in winning the war. The agencies' long-term goal was that when the war ended and the consumer economy got cranked up again, consumers would not only remember their clients as good corporate citizens, but identify their products with victory over the enemies of the American Way.

Thus an ad for Philco featured a drawing of three snowmen—Hitler, Mussolini, and Hirohito—melting under the blazing sun of "U.S. War Production." An ad for Florida grapefruit growers suggested, "Just ask a Jap what it feels like to be up against men who are fortified with Victory Vitamin C." Swift Premium meats showed a Rosie in a factory: "No sissy sandwiches for her *now*!" BVD promoted Freedom Shirts. ("Trim, almost-military lines. Ideal to slip on when he dashes out for civilian defense duties.") The Metropolitan Life Insurance Company declared, "Life Insurance Is as American as Free Speech and Apple Pie." A Coke ad similarly proclaimed, "As American as Independence Day—the soda fountain is the very expression of the democracy that is America." Stetson warned that "Loose talk can cost lives" and added, "Keep it under your Stetson." Studebaker crowed, "In this great, seething combat, the automobile industry is playing an important role, and Studebaker is proud of its assignments in arming our United States." (Studebaker made army trucks and engines for bombers.)

Oil companies, tire companies, steel companies, airplane manufacturers, and the railroads all touted their contributions to the war effort. So did—a bit less plausibly—Lifebuoy and Life Savers, liquor distillers, beer brewers, tobacco companies, ChapStick, Parker pens, Bell Telephone, Cannon towels, Nestlé's chocolates, and makers of toilet paper, hand cream, lipstick, and shredded wheat.

Sometimes subtly and sometimes not so, Madison Avenue spent the war years telling Americans that one of the basic freedoms they were fighting and sacrificing for was "the freedom of choice," which included the freedom to buy the brands and products of their choice. The selection might be limited in the present, but even that was quintessentially American—after all, a Budweiser ad explained, "rationing came over on the *Mayflower*." Besides, the sacrifice was temporary. When victory over the enemies of democracy and the free market was won, many ads promised, Americans would find themselves in a consumer paradise, a World of Tomorrow as bright and happy as the one the world's fair had depicted, where all Americans would exercise their hard-won right to a fully modern kitchen with all the appliances. "After total war," one ad promised, "total living."

It worked. The ad agencies not only averted bankruptcy but actually saw their revenues increase a little during the war. Their corporate clients kept their names in front of the American people in the best possible light. The government got propaganda created by experts, rather than Sherwood's and Davis's well-meaning dilettantes. When the war ended, the American consumer was well primed to go on a shopping spree the likes of which hadn't been seen since the boom years of the 1920s. And the Mad men who'd come up with it all would bask in a postwar golden age.

CHAPTER 41

Zoot Suit Killers and a Bobby Sox Riot

On November 20, 1942, a Brooklyn jury returned guilty verdicts on a pair of Williamsburg teens, sixteen-year-old Neil Simonelli and eighteen-year-old Joseph Annunziata, for the murder of Irwin Goodman, their math teacher at William J. Gaynor High School. The two of them had never much liked Goodman, a thirty-six-year-old father of two from the Jewish Midwood neighborhood. When he reported them to the principal for smoking in the boys' room, they walked eight blocks to Simonelli's home, where they picked up a pistol, then back to the school. They confronted Goodman and got into a scuffle with him. The gun, which Annunziata was holding, went off, perhaps accidentally, fatally shooting Goodman through the back. Because the jury entertained a doubt that the shooting was premeditated, they convicted the boys of murder in the second degree. The pair went off to Sing Sing together to begin sentences of twenty years to life. Had the verdict been first-degree murder, they could have been the youngest New Yorkers ever executed.

The city's newspapers, from the *Times* to the *Brooklyn Eagle*, provided extensive coverage of the case, and there was commentary in national magazines. What fascinated them all, beyond the crime itself, was the boys' lifestyle and attire: uniformly, the press described Simonelli and Annunziata as "jitterbugs," "Zoot Suit Youths," and "Zoot Suit Killers."

Whether or not anyone in the press had actually seen Simonelli and Annunziata wearing zoot suits was a moot point. By 1942 "zoot suit" was a metonym for "juvenile delinquent." What the black leather jacket and the hoodie were to later generations, the zoot suit was to the war years.

When the zoot suit first appeared it was associated mostly with black youths and the jitterbug in neighborhoods such as Harlem. It consisted of an outrageously outsized jacket, with superwide padded shoulders, that hung down to the knees and the fingertips. The pants were exaggerated as well, ballooning and deeply pleated, then pegged tight at the ankles. A broad-brimmed or porkpie hat, pointed or platform shoes, a long watch chain, and a variety of tie styles completed the ensemble.

At first it was seen as a rather comical and harmless style, just another example of young people going to silly sartorial extremes. It began to look more sinister amid increasing worries about what life in wartime was doing to America's families and children.

The Depression and Dust Bowl 1930s had already wreaked havoc on the American family, turning millions into homeless migrants, splitting off husbands who went on the bum seeking any work they could find, forcing some mothers and daughters into prostitution, and enticing some young men into lives of crime and gangsterism. The defense buildup and war brought new dislocations and disorder. Many millions of Americans were uprooted again, trekking across the country seeking defense work. Many moved more than once during the war, and few returned to their point of origin after it.

From 1940 well into 1943, the Selective Service exempted fathers with dependent children. As the war progressed, the draft age was lowered, as were the physical and mental fitness requirements, in attempts to keep filling the ranks with unmarried men. But with the military's ever expanding need for manpower, fathers began to be drafted in the fall of 1943. By the end of the war roughly a million had served. Others volunteered, often only after big arguments with their wives. Of course, some of them never came back. At war's end the government estimated that 183,000 children had lost their fathers in the fighting.

The government started sending monthly checks to servicemen's families in 1942, but in expensive cities like New York it often wasn't enough to run a household. By 1944 more than a million servicemen's wives nationwide had taken jobs.

Kids were working too. In the Depression years, new legislation against child labor had been enacted, largely to prevent kids from taking scarce jobs away from adult males. Now, as labor shortages grew more severe, many states and localities rolled back those restrictions. As a result, by 1944 high school enrollment had fallen 25 percent, while the employment of youths fourteen to eighteen had more than doubled. An estimated two million high schoolers had dropped out to take jobs, and many planned not to go back.

The impact of all this on kids' lives could be profound. They might lose their father for years, or forever. They might follow their parents from one defense job to another, always the new kids in the neighborhood and at school. If they stayed in school, whether dad was gone and mom worked or both parents worked, kids now found themselves with lots of free, unsupervised time. If they dropped out and took jobs, they had cash in their pockets to spend any way they wanted.

There was another, less definable but impossible to miss factor: they were growing up in wartime. Coates's culture of death, nihilism, and restless joy seeking was all around them. Teenage boys too young to be sent to fight knew that in a year or two or three they might well be. In the meantime they wanted to look and feel as manly as their fathers and older brothers in uniform. According to law enforcement, teenage gang activity and street fighting escalated, and the violence grew more serious; where teen gangs had formerly used fists and clubs, they now wielded zip guns and flick knives, sometimes inflicting deadly harm. Teenage girls as well as boys took to drinking, smoking, and sexual pickups, in full eat-drink-and-be-merry mode. Adults labeled it "war degeneracy." It's no coincidence that the terms "youth culture" and "teenager" (or "teen-ager") were also coined in this period. They were something new, a generation of latchkey kids, army brats, war orphans.

When the dimout began, New Yorkers feared that dark and lonely streets would be an open invitation to rapists, murderers, and muggers. In fact, except for muggings and robberies in the jam-packed Times Square area, major crimes actually decreased, and stayed down for the duration. Arrests of juveniles, however, climbed. The story of Simonelli and Annunziata neatly and frighteningly encapsulated what was seen as a broader trend. Youth crime figures in the first full year of the war were so disturbing, J. Edgar Hoover said, that a "counteroffensive" was necessary to prevent "a breakdown on our home front." He told a graduating class at the FBI Academy, "Something has happened to our moral fibers when the nation's youths under voting age accounted for 15 per cent of all murders, 35 per cent of all robberies, 58 per cent of all car thefts and 50 per cent of all burglaries." Later studies showed that nationwide juvenile delinquency arrests rose 72 percent during the war. In Brooklyn, it was 100 percent.

By 1942, the year of Simonelli and Annunziata, the zoot was identified as much with this behavior as with Lindy hopping and jitterbugging. That year, the War Production Board actually declared the zoot suit unpatriotic, because it was a waste of material in a time of rationing. The wide, pleated skirts girls wore for jitterbugging (and showing off their underwear) were denounced on the same grounds.

In 1943, one in five arrests was of someone under eighteen. But that year offered evidence that at least some of those arrests were the result of harassment and bias as much as bad behavior. In June, white sailors and soldiers in Los Angeles went on a rampage, attacking Mexican-American teens all over the city. The *pachucos* fought back, and a week of rioting followed. The national press, against all evidence that it was white servicemen who had instigated a race riot, chose to call it a "zoot suit riot."

A new raft of stories followed, as journalists competed to define what the zoot was, what it meant, who wore it, and who invented it. Claimants to the latter ranged from a busboy in Atlanta to tailors in Memphis, Chicago, and LA. The *New Yorker*, not surprisingly, decided that it started in Gotham. "With some friendly cooperation from the editors of the *Amsterdam News*, an uptown newspaper published by and for colored people, we got in touch with Lew Eisenstein, proprietor of Lew's Pants Store, on 125th Street," a "Talk of the Town" piece called "Zoot Lore" explained that June. Supposedly Lew's wife first pegged some loose pants in 1934, and the rest of the zoot suit followed in due course. Lew took credit for adding the long watch chain. Their claims were, of course, disputed by others.

The zoot suit would live on past the war, mostly worn by black and Hispanic men, though the influence of its wide shoulders and voluminous pants could be discerned in all men's suits in the early 1950s. Concerns about juvenile delinquency also continued after the war, rising to a level of national panic in the 1950s.

The story of the zoot suit killers lived on in its own way. In 1947, Irving Shulman's pulp novel *The Amboy Dukes*, set in wartime Brooklyn, was a shock sensation, selling five million copies even as it was banned in some locales for its sex and violence. Shulman, who was from Brooklyn himself and spent the war years writing for the War Department in Washington, obviously used Simonelli and Annunziata as the models for his lead characters Frank Goldfarb and Benny Semmel. They're a pair of juvenile delinquents in Jewish Brownsville, products of its "ugly gray and red tenements, tombstones of disease, unrest and smoldering violence...It was as if nothing bright would ever shine on Amboy Street." While their parents do defense work, Frank and Benny hook school almost constantly to hang out with their gang, the Amboy Dukes. They make money selling counterfeit gas ration coupons on the black market and spend it on liquor, marijuana, zip guns, and whores. They, too, accidentally shoot and kill a teacher in a scuffle, but they come to a worse end for it than their real-life models.

Lurid yet relentlessly downbeat, *The Amboy Dukes* looked both back to the worst of wartime New York and ahead to 1950s juvenile delinquent tales including *Blackboard Jungle* and Shulman's own screen adaptation of *Rebel Without a Cause*. (He would also write a novelization of *West Side Story*.) After the scandal kicked up by its first appearance, later editions of *Dukes* dialed back the sex and violence and, interestingly, deracinated the two antiheroes by giving them less Jewish-sounding surnames. In 1949, when it was adapted for the film *City Across the River*, it featured Bernie Schwartz, or Anthony Curtis, in his second film role.

⁓

A little more than a month after Simonelli and Annunziata's trial ended, Frank Sinatra sang his debut solo concert at the Paramount Theatre movie palace in Times Square. Since his first hit record in 1940, the skinny Hoboken crooner with the velveteen voice had been amassing a passionate following among adolescent and teenage girls. When he walked up to the microphone on the Paramount stage on December 30, 1942, the packed house, estimated at five thousand girls (in a space with an official capacity of thirty-five hundred), exploded in deafening shrieks and screams. Sinatra and his bandleader Benny Goodman were shocked and petrified. Although Goodman's swing music had been motivating high schoolers to jitterbug in the aisles of the Paramount and other venues since the late 1930s, he'd never provoked such a bacchantic frenzy as this. The girls drowned out the entire concert. Many wept and several fainted. The cacophony and pandemonium were as great as at any Elvis or Beatles concert in later years. Afterward the girls mobbed the stage door, hoping for an autograph, or at least a glimpse. The crowd surged out onto Broadway and 43rd Street, causing a traffic jam as frustrated and bewildered cops fought to maintain order.

The girls were known as bobby soxers for the rolled-down white socks they wore with saddle shoes, wide pleated skirts, and sweaters, a uniform as identifiable as the boys' zoots. Like those boys, they seemed a wild and alien species to their parents and other adults. They were mad for swing music, for the jitterbug and the Lindy. They salted their language with mysterious hepcat jive. They seemed to spend far more time and money collecting platters, starting fan clubs, and following their favorite bands and singers than they did on serious matters like schooling. In a time of war, of patriotic duty and sacrifice, these girls just wanted to have fun.

Scholars point out that although they appeared at the same time and shared some interests with the zoot suiters, bobby soxers tended to come from higher social strata; they were middle- or upper-class white girls with the leeway, and the expendable time and income, to devote a few years to pop culture fanaticism and fads before going on to college and marriage. This was not lost on Madison Avenue's ad men, who for the first time began targeting campaigns at teen females with disposable income as a distinct consumer market. The girls got their own magazine, *Seventeen*, in September 1944.

In October of '44, Sinatra returned for his third run of concerts at the Paramount, and the bobby soxers demonstrated that even if they were of a different class than the zoot suiters they could cause a "riot" of their own. The Paramount had announced that Sinatra would begin a three-week engagement, five shows a day, on Thursday, October 12—Columbus Day, a school holiday. The night before, bobby soxers had descended on Times Square, defying curfew to line up outside the theater. Many of them wore bow ties, in imitation of their "Frankie," or had photos of him pinned to their chests. By Thursday the crowd was up to "30,000 frenzied juvenile enigmas in bobby socks," as the *Tribune* put it. Security guards and two hundred cops hastily redeployed from the Columbus Day parade route struggled in vain to keep them out of the street and in some semblance of order. When the box office opened the girls rushed it with such vigor they broke its windows and stove in its sides.

Inside, the *Tribune* reported, the bobby soxers created their usual "bedlam" and "demonstrations of a peculiar, clannish hysteria incomprehensible to the adult world." Not even Sinatra's threat that he'd leave the stage if they didn't calm down helped. Weegee was there with his camera. After the first show, most of the girls refused to leave their seats to make room for the next show's audience. This caused a near-stampede outside, a maelstrom of shoving, tears, fainting. Though there was no real violence, the bemused press chose to call it the Columbus Day Riot.

This 1938 editorial cartoon forecast the World of Tomorrow more accurately than did the actual 1939 World's Fair. (1)

Harry Hopkins (*center*), FDR's "Deputy President," looking frail and sickly as always, with Stalin at the Tehran Conference, 1943. (2)

The giant airship *Hindenburg*, pride of Nazi Germany, sails past lower Manhattan in April 1936, a year before it crashed. (3)

American Führer Fritz Kuhn salutes a youth parade at Camp Siegfried on Long Island. (4)

Dorothy Thompson, the pioneering journalist who heckled both Adolf Hitler and Fritz Kuhn. (5)

Brooklynite Vernon Keogh, a volunteer with the Eagle Squadrons, was the shortest pilot in the RAF and one of the first Americans killed in the war. (6)

Manhattan's muted skyline during the wartime dimout. (7)

The *U.S.S. Lafayette*, formerly the *S.S. Normandie*, lies on its side after a fire at Pier 88 in February 1942. (8)

Inside the mammoth Brooklyn Army Terminal, where three million troops went off to war. (9)

Joe Louis pummeled Hitler's Superman Max Schmeling in Yankee Stadium, then enlisted to fight Hitler in another way. (10)

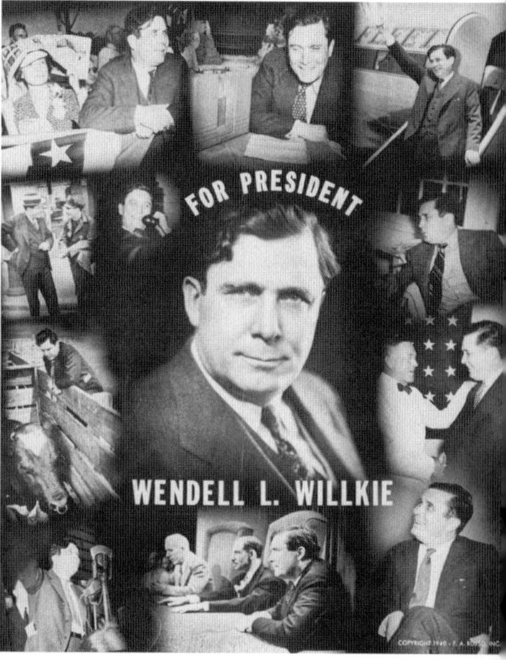

New York businessman Wendell Willkie opposed FDR in the 1940 presidential election but became his ally during the war years. (11)

Gertrude Lawrence and Vincent Price with servicemen at the Stage Door Canteen. (12)

Riveting Rosies at Todd Shipyard in Brooklyn. (13)

New Yorkers tended some 400,000 Victory Gardens, like this one on First Avenue. (14)

Life photographer Margaret Bourke-White after making a bombing run in a B-17. (15)

William "Wild Bill" Donovan, founder of the wartime OSS, precursor to the CIA. (16)

Mayor La Guardia, looking harried and exhausted, after a Harlem riot in 1943. (17)

On June 20, 1945, the *Queen Mary*, painted wartime gray, steamed into New York harbor, bringing the first 14,526 men and women in uniform home from Europe. (18)

An estimated two million revelers jammed Times Square on VJ Day, 1945. (19)

After the biggest spy trial of the century, Ethel and Julius Rosenberg were executed at Sing Sing in 1953. (20)

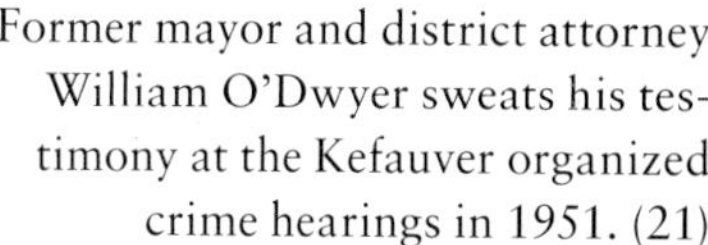

Former mayor and district attorney William O'Dwyer sweats his testimony at the Kefauver organized crime hearings in 1951. (21)

The cornerstone for the new UN complex in Turtle Bay was laid in 1949. New York City had truly become the capital of the world. (22)

CHAPTER 42

Banking on Hitler

In October 1942, the federal government froze the assets of Wall Street's Union Banking Corporation under the Great War–era Trading with the Enemy Act. Investigators charged that UBC was not so much a bank as a money-laundering front for Fritz Thyssen, an extremely wealthy German industrialist who had been one of Hitler's crucial financial supporters. The founder of UBC was Averell Harriman. Prescott Bush, father and grandfather to two future U.S. presidents, was on the UBC board.

The government took no direct action against Harriman or Bush. In 1942, after all, Harriman was Churchill and Roosevelt's point man with the Soviets; Bush had taken over from Tom Dewey as head of the USO, through which he would raise millions of dollars for the government's National War Fund.

The seizing of UBC funds was in fact a relatively rare example of the government moving against Wall Street banks or giant New York corporations that traded with the enemy and played both sides in the war. The impulse to prosecute them as traitors for their financial dealings with the Nazis and Japanese was countered by a simple, inescapable reality: the United States needed their backing as well.

At the same time that he was leading Wall Street's support for Mussolini, J. P. Morgan's Thomas W. Lamont played key roles in helping Germany rebuild financially after World War I. At Versailles, Lamont was on the American team, with Bernard Baruch and John Foster Dulles, that argued without much success against forcing Germany to pay the punitive reparations demanded by the other victors. In political and financial chaos, Germany was failing to keep up the payments within a year, and in

1923 France and Belgium occupied Germany's industrial Ruhr as a way to extract the funds directly. Lamont led the renegotiation of the reparation payment schedule, and he organized other giant Wall Street banks to bail Germany out with loans.

He also participated, with other New York bankers, in setting up the Bank for International Settlements (BIS) in Basel, Switzerland, in 1930, ostensibly to facilitate the reparation payments. The BIS was the brainchild of Hjalmar Horace Greeley Schacht, who in a few years would become Hitler's president of the Reichsbank and economics minister. Schacht came into his unusual middle name because his father, as a German immigrant to New York City shortly after the Civil War, idolized the liberal newspaperman Greeley. Hjalmar was conceived in New York but born in Germany.

The BIS was so low profile as to be nearly invisible, the Swiss bank to end all Swiss banks, without even a sign on its nondescript building in Basel. Its partners included the Reichsbank, the Bank of England and other European central banks, Japan's central bank, and three Morgan banks: J. P. Morgan and the Morgan-affiliated First National Bank of New York and First National Bank of Chicago. When Schacht stopped Germany's reparation payments in 1932, citing the world depression, the BIS sailed on, pursuing its intended goal: to be a safe and discreet clearinghouse that would allow all those banks to continue doing business together, despite whatever their respective nations were doing, even if that included war. Via the BIS, the American and British bankers would maintain a mostly secret friendship with their Nazi and Japanese counterparts straight through World War II, while thousands and thousands of American and British men in uniform were being killed and maimed in the fight to defeat the Nazis and Japanese.

When Germany annexed Austria in March 1938, the nation's gold reserves were looted and shipped via the BIS to the Reichsbank. When Germany absorbed Czechoslovakia, the SS actually held the directors of the Czech National Bank at gunpoint and demanded all their gold as well. The Czech bankers had just shifted millions to the BIS, thinking it was safe there; the BIS sent it along to Berlin.

Throughout the war, the BIS would shelter hundreds of millions of dollars in Nazi gold, stolen from conquered nations and from slaughtered Jews (including dental fillings, jewelry, and such). It also secretly facilitated exchanges between the Nazis and supposedly neutral nations like Sweden, which sold wartime Germany most of the iron ore for its steel in exchange for looted gold. Dag Hammarskjöld, who would come to New York after the war to be secretary-general of the United Nations, was directly involved as chairman of Sweden's central bank.

The American banks not only continued to participate in BIS activities as this was going on; the director of the BIS throughout the war was in fact a Wall Streeter, Thomas McKittrick. He traveled freely in Nazi territory and in Mussolini's Italy during the war. In 1943, U-boats received orders not to meddle with the ship that carried him back to New York for high-level meetings to discuss BIS business, after which he traveled to Berlin for a debriefing at the Reichsbank.

McKittrick returned to New York when the war ended and was made vice president at the Rockefellers' Chase National Bank. That's not surprising. During the 1930s and the war, the Rockefeller empire, through various of its entities, maintained extensive business relations with Nazi Germany. In 1939, for example, six months before Hitler invaded Poland, Chase sent him $25 million for his war machine. The funds came from the bank's sale of *Rückswanderer* (returnee) marks to Germans in America. RMs were another of Hjalmar Schacht's ideas, conceived as a way to flow much-needed U.S. currency to Germany. In theory, Germans who were living abroad but intended to return to the Fatherland would buy RMs. The RMs' value was to be credited to their personal accounts in German banks and available when they moved back. In practice, some German nationals and even Americans, never intending to move to Germany, bought RMs as a patriotic gesture of support for Der Führer—Nazi war bonds, in effect. Many people in Yorkville, in the Bund, and at Camp Siegfried invested in RMs. Chase was a major broker, earning a percentage on every dollar it sent to the Nazis. The German consulate in New York, naturally, did its banking with Chase.

When Germany occupied France in 1940, most American businesses there left. Chase and J. P. Morgan kept their banks in France open for the duration. They did business with and for the Nazi occupiers, from seizing the accounts of Jewish customers to funding the Gestapo's brutal activities against the French people.

⁀

Chase's collaborations with Nazi Germany look rather insignificant when compared to those of the Rockefellers' largest business, the wellspring of their vast family wealth, Standard Oil.

The gigantic Standard Oil monopoly that John D. Rockefeller had built in the late nineteenth century was broken up in the trust-busting 1910s into regional constituents, huge in their own right: Standard Oil of New Jersey, which became Exxon, and Standard Oil of New York, which became Mobil, and so on. In the years leading up to the war, Standard Oil of New Jersey was the largest petroleum company in the world, with roughly four-fifths of the U.S. market. Despite its name, its headquarters were in Manhattan, first in the monolithic Standard Oil Building at 26 Broadway, then at 30 Rockefeller Plaza. It did its banking, of course, with the Rockefellers' Chase.

The two largest shareholders in Standard Oil of New Jersey were the Rockefellers themselves and the colossal German chemical cartel I.G. Farben. Farben started out at the turn of the century as a group of companies that produced most of the world's synthetic dyes (*farben* is German for "dye"). Germany's great weakness as a world power was its lack of the domestic raw materials needed by a modern industrial society—petroleum, rubber, iron for making steel, and other resources. The chemists at Farben solved this to a degree by developing synthetic oil and gasoline, a synthetic rubber called buna, plastics, and synthetic fibers such as nylon and rayon. In other areas of applied chemistry, Farben also developed Bayer aspirin and various pharmaceuticals, Agfa film, explosives, armaments, and poison gases, including the Zyklon B that would be used in Nazi gas chambers. Several Farben chemists won Nobels.

Farben metastasized through the 1920s into the largest corporate entity in Europe, and then spread around the world. It established its first outpost in the United States in 1929, opening the offices of I.G. Chemical Corporation at 230 Park Avenue (then the New York Central Building, now the Helmsley Building). Soon its board of directors included Edsel Ford; Standard Oil president Walter Teagle; and Charles Mitchell, president of the Morgan-affiliated National City Bank of New York (now Citibank). As it expanded in the United States, Farben would also forge alliances with DuPont, Dow, Alcoa, and other American corporations. In the mid-1930s, when federal investigators began to probe this mysterious foreign company's growing presence and influence, I.G. Chemical shut down, only to reappear as American I.G., now operating through a Swiss dummy corporation.

By the time Hitler came to power, Farben was a phantasmagorically complex and secretive global hydra of a few thousand partnerships and cartel agreements, interlocking boards, and hundreds of subsidiary and shell corporations, a conspiracy theorist's dream. (It plays a role in Thomas Pynchon's *Gravity's Rainbow*.) Besides its factories and research labs, it ran its own power plants, mines, banks, patent offices, and a huge private intelligence-gathering operation that rivaled any nation's.

All this was put at Hitler's service in 1933. Farben was the industrial foundation on which Hitler built his war machine. Its president sat in the Reichstag; its production plants, scientists, technicians, and intelligence operatives prepped and equipped the Wehrmacht for conquest. During the war, hundreds of thousands of people from occupied countries were given over to Farben as slave labor. Farben used Auschwitz captives—and worked some twenty-five thousand of them to death—to build one of its synthetic fuel and rubber plants next door to the death camp, where its chemicals were used to massacre hundreds of thousands more.

At the end of the war, the U.S. Army colonel Bernard Bernstein, who'd been a New York lawyer in civilian life, would be tasked with investigating Farben's "far-flung and carefully concealed external assets." In his report he would write that "without I.G.'s immense productive facilities, its intensive research, and vast international affiliations, Germany's prosecution of the war would have been unthinkable and impossible."

⌣

There was one substance Farben could not produce or synthesize in the 1930s: high-octane leaded aviation fuel. Without it, Göring's Luftwaffe would be grounded. Only three corporations produced it. Luckily for Herr Göring, all three had close relations with Farben—Standard Oil, DuPont, and General Motors. Especially Standard, where Walter Teagle, president of the company from 1917 to 1937, then chairman of the board to 1942, as well as a director of American I.G., was a good friend of Farben CEO Hermann Schmitz. Teagle, who'd been born into Standard Oil aristocracy—his maternal grandfather was John D.'s first partner in the oil business—was a six-foot-two, 230-pound man's man who liked to dominate every conversation he had and fill every room with the clouds from his cigars. He was very conservative, very anticommunist, and a great supporter of Germany's recovery in the 1920s and '30s. He entertained Schmitz at the Cloud Club in the Chrysler Building when the German visited New York, and on some of Teagle's frequent trips to Germany the two of them went shooting game fowl with Göring. With Teagle and

Schmitz at the helms, Standard invested heavily in Farben and Farben in Standard.

In 1938, Teagle helped Schmitz get supplies of aviation fuel from a British subsidiary of Standard. The Luftwaffe planes that bombed London in 1940 were flying on this fuel. When the British government complained about American companies selling supplies to the people who were murdering its citizens, Standard switched all its tankers to Panamanian registry. They sailed to the island of Teneriffe, where their fuel was offloaded into waiting German tankers. The planes that bombed Pearl Harbor in 1941 also flew on fuel sold to Japan by Standard Oil.

Standard and Farben also colluded on synthetic rubber. The measures taken by Baruch's Rubber Reserve Company to stockpile and conserve natural rubber weren't nearly enough to cover projected shortfalls. Synthetic rubber was the answer. Farben had exclusive world rights to its form of synthetic rubber, buna, while Standard was developing its own version, butyl. In a series of cartel arrangements, Standard agreed to help Farben produce butyl, and Farben granted Standard exclusive U.S. rights to produce buna—*but only if and when Farben allowed it to*. In short, Standard Oil agreed to help the Wehrmacht get all the synthetic tires it needed for its planes, trucks, and other vehicles, while withholding the same from the U.S. military.

In FDR's cabinet, Treasury Secretary Morgenthau and Interior's Harold Ickes were incensed by all this, but Roosevelt kept them under tight rein. He was in a ticklish spot. He needed the mighty Rockefellers and Standard Oil and the Wall Street bankers for his own war efforts. Standard supplied most of the fuel used by the American military. Roosevelt had appointed Teagle to chair his National War Labor Board, and Teagle's right-hand man William Farish to the wartime Petroleum Board. (When Teagle moved from the Standard president's office to chairing its board, Farish became its president. He was as ultraconservative and pro-German as Teagle.) Within a week of the attack on Pearl Harbor, Roosevelt signed an executive order amending the 1917 Trading with the Enemy Act so that Morgenthau (meaning Roosevelt) could allow certain transactions to continue. Morgenthau fumed and Ickes threatened to resign more than once.

Roosevelt had less control over a previously unremarkable Missouri Democrat, Senator Harry Truman. On his own initiative, in the spring of 1941 Truman formed the Senate Special Committee to Investigate the National Defense Program. The committee probed waste, fraud, and other problems in the defense industry and, in 1942, turned its spotlight on Standard Oil. Called to testify, Farish put on a great show of belligerence and indignation for the stoic Truman, who told the press he believed Standard's activities amounted to treason. Roosevelt stepped in and blocked antitrust actions against Standard. When Teagle offered to resign from the NWLB, Roosevelt asked him to stay. Teagle did, however, resign from his chairmanship of Standard Oil's board. Although there were other probes of its activities, Standard Oil continued doing business, through various circuitous routes, with both Germany and Japan throughout the war.

When William Stephenson came to New York in the spring of 1940, he didn't have to look far or hard to find Nazi agents there. The month Stephenson arrived in the city, a Gerhard Westrick hosted a soiree for New York's corporate elite in the suite he was renting at the Plaza.

Westrick was a top corporate lawyer in Germany. He was fifty-one, stocky, with merry green eyes and silvery hair and mustache. He spoke fluent though guttural English, and he walked with a pronounced limp, having lost a leg to a British shell in the Great War. He had highest-level contacts in Hitler's regime. Stephenson alerted a reporter at the *Herald Tribune* about a Hitler crony living the high life at the Plaza. The reporter was intrigued enough to go interview Westrick yet found him genial and hard not to like.

Through the 1930s, Westrick had acted as a go-between for American companies doing business with the Nazis, including Standard Oil, Ford, General Motors, and ITT. In that capacity he had often shuttled between New York and Berlin, but the coming of war made this latest trip far more arduous for a man with close ties to Hitler's regime. The Royal Navy was now boarding passenger ships out of European ports, looking for Nazi agents. Westrick had to trek across Siberia, then sail from there to Japan and on to San Francisco before reaching New York. His wife and two young sons sailed on an Italian liner, undeterred by the British navy, to join him in New York, where he rented a house for them in suburban Scarsdale.

Westrick's role as a mediator between corporate America and the Nazis had gotten tougher as well. Since 1937 the German government had stipulated that all profits the American corporations made in Germany had to stay in Germany. Westrick's purpose in coming to New York now, he told the *Tribune*, was to reassure businessmen that their investments in Germany were secure, that the war would be over soon, and that when it was relations would normalize and profits would flow freely again. What Westrick did not tell the reporter was that in private meetings with his corporate clients he urged them to cut off any supplies they were selling to England, to help bring a hasty end to the war.

As a neutral, the American government tolerated Westrick's presence. New Yorkers, as always, were happy to host another party-throwing, fun-loving European. But then Westrick overstepped. On June 26 he put on a soiree at the Waldorf-Astoria to celebrate Germany's conquest of France. It did not sit well. Winchell lit into him. Grumbling crowds began gathering outside the Westricks' rented Scarsdale house, unhappy to have a Nazi stooge in their neighborhood. The owner got the police to post a guard. Under increasing pressure, the Westricks moved out in August. Their whereabouts were unknown for several days. On August 19 they turned up in Los Angeles, where they boarded a Japanese vessel and sailed away.

Of all the New York corporate leaders with whom Westrick worked, none had closer ties to him than Sosthenes Behn, the lordly founder of ITT. It was Behn who paid for Westrick's suite at the Plaza. For Westrick's help in managing ITT's extensive operations in Germany, Behn had put him on ITT's board. Like the Rockefeller and Morgan empires, ITT played both sides of the fence all through World War II. Behn styled himself a patriotic American, but his first allegiance was to his personal empire, and he showed no qualms about taking his profits anywhere he could find them.

He was born in the Virgin Islands in 1884, when they were still Danish. He became an American citizen after the United States acquired the islands in 1917, and he earned a Distinguished Service Medal as a colonel in the signal corps in the Great War. The telephone was still a new gadget when he and a brother acquired small companies in Puerto Rico and Cuba (which Fidel Castro would nationalize, to the great ire of the Behns' successors, in the 1960s). The Behns named their small company International Telephone & Telegraph so that it sounded like the larger, established American Telephone & Telegraph.

ITT didn't stay small for long. Backed by Morgan banking, it expanded in the 1920s into a multinational conglomerate of telephone companies (including the telephone systems for whole nations), cable companies, and electronics manufacturers. By 1928 Behn had built the fortresslike skyscraper at 75 Broad Street in the financial district, with an ornate Louis XIV office for himself and an elegant dining room where his French chef served lavish banquets. A tall, trim man with a regal bearing and the sharp eyes and beak of a hawk, Behn alternately charmed and chilled. He ruled over his empire as an autocrat. As a conservative Catholic he backed Franco in Spain's civil war—and, not coincidentally, had the exclusive rights to run Spain's national telephone system. He met with Hitler in 1933, at Berchtesgaden, and established a relationship with Göring as well. Also by no coincidence, ITT quickly expanded its interests in Nazi Germany, including a major stake in the Focke-Wulf aircraft company whose fighters and bombers were mainstays of the Luftwaffe during the war. When Hitler annexed Austria in 1938, top Nazis wanted to oust ITT's subsidiary there because of its American ties. Behn rushed to Berchtesgaden again and Hitler ordered his underlings to back off. A year later, Hitler similarly protected ITT's operations in Poland after the invasion.

Through the war, in addition to ITT's part ownership of Focke-Wulf, its German subsidiaries supplied the military with telecommunications, radar, electronic fuses for bombs, and electronics for V-2 rockets. At the same time, ITT was selling the U.S. military telecommunications equipment and the all-important high frequency direction finders that allowed naval ships to zero in on lurking U-boats.

Roosevelt's administration was of two minds about Behn. The Federal Communications Commission and State Department harbored extreme suspicions about his loyalty, but "Colonel Behn" was sheltered by powerful friends at the Pentagon, who needed the equipment he sold. They would see to it that he was protected throughout the war and, after the war, even awarded a Medal for Merit, then the highest decoration given to civilians.

CHAPTER 43

Murder and Massacre

At half past nine on the night of Monday, January 11, 1943, Carlo Tresca and an associate stepped out of the dowdy building (no longer standing) at the southwest corner of West 15th Street and Fifth Avenue where the *Il Martello* and IWW offices were located. At sixty-three Tresca was, if stouter and more gray, still an impressive figure, wearing a long black cape and a wide-brimmed hat. He and his friend crossed arm in arm to the north side of 15th Street. The lights were dimmed for wartime and there was little traffic.

A short man in dark clothes stepped out of the shadows and fired two bullets into Tresca, one in the back and the other in the face. As Tresca toppled backward to the street, his killer ran to a nearby car, which sped off. *PM*'s Weegee arrived in minutes to snap grisly photos of the anarchist lying on his back, his feet toward the curb, a pool of blood around his head.

It had all the earmarks of a gangster-style execution. But who killed Tresca? He had made no end of enemies on both the left and the right. Just as he had railed against Mussolini and the Fascists since the 1920s, he had bitterly denounced Stalin in the 1930s. He was enraged when the Soviets purged and murdered anarchists in Spain during the Civil War, and continued to condemn Stalin when he murdered Trotsky and other perceived enemies later. Tresca successfully fought to keep Communists out of the Mazzini Society. The day he was killed, he was considering boycotting an "Italian-American Victory Council" the OWI was organizing to advise on the makeup of a postwar, post-Mussolini government for Italy. The American government favored a sort of Popular Front strategy that would include both Communists and reformed Fascists in the government, which Tresca angrily opposed.

Following a few leads, the police arrested a minor mafioso, Carmine Galante. They held him for almost a year and grilled him over and over, but Galante never cracked. He was freed at the end of 1944.

No charges were ever brought for the murder of Carlo Tresca and it was never solved. Numerous conspiracy theories have circulated ever since. Most make Galante the trigger man, but who ordered the hit is contested. Some thought Stalin had reached out to silence Tresca. Another popular theory, still widely circulated, posits that Benito Mussolini asked Vito Genovese to silence Tresca, and the job went through Genovese to Galante.

But Stalin and Mussolini both had much more pressing matters to deal with in 1943 than a pesky anarchist in New York City. The historian Nunzio Pernicone offered a more plausible explanation in his 2005 biography *Carlo Tresca: Portrait of a Rebel*. He argued that Tresca was murdered simply for causing a local mafioso to lose face.

Frank Garofalo was a suave and handsome man, called the Cary Grant of mobsters. He owned a cheese and olive oil importing company on Avenue A, and even dated an assistant U.S. attorney for New York, Dolores Faconti. Behind that facade of respectability he had assisted Luciano in his bootlegging operations, was Joseph Bonanno's right-hand man, and provided muscle for Tresca's nemesis Generoso Pope, intimidating competitors and union officials for him. As early as 1934, Garofalo had visited *Il Martello*'s offices and threatened violence if Tresca continued his rants against Pope. True to form, Tresca responded by writing that Pope was trying "to exercise censorship over the Italian-language press by means of gangsters."

In September 1942, Tresca was at an Italian-American war bonds banquet at the Manhattan Center when Pope, Garofalo, and Faconti arrived. "Not only the Fascist Pope, but even his gangster is here!" Tresca loudly complained before storming out. Garofalo growled that Tresca would pay for the insult. The next day, Faconti visited Tresca and tearfully begged him not to write about the incident, for his own sake and hers. When she told Garofalo that she'd seen Tresca he beat her.

Four months later, Tresca lay dead on the street. It's likely that Garofalo hired Galante to avenge his and Pope's honor. Without naming names, Winchell implicated them in his column. But between Pope's chummy relationships at City Hall and the White House, and the embarrassment to the DA's office if Faconti's affair with a mobster were to go public, there was little follow-up.

⁓

In a roundabout way, the investigation of Tresca's murder put another mobster in a bad light, and a city magistrate along with him. Thomas Aurelio was an Italian-American success story, a kid from the East Side who fought in the Great War, got his law degree at NYU, was made a magistrate by Jimmy Walker, and was enthusiastically reappointed by La Guardia. In the summer after Tresca's murder, Tammany, state Democrats, and state Republicans all backed his candidacy for a place on the State Supreme Court. Then the front page of the Sunday *New York Times* for August 29 dropped a bomb: "Gangster Backed Aurelio for Bench, Prosecutor Avers."

The gangster was Frank Costello. Costello cut a highly unusual figure among the mobsters of the time. Born Francesco Castiglia in Italy in 1891, he came to New York in steerage with his mother when he was four, supposedly sleeping nights in a large cast iron pot, one of the family's few possessions. They settled in Italian East Harlem, where his father ran a small grocery store. Francesco joined a street gang after dropping out of the fifth grade. He participated in some robberies and provided muscle for a ghetto landlord, adopting the alias Frank Costello to get along with the Irish gangsters around him. But unlike most of his peers he had no taste for violence and gave it up as a young man. For the rest of his criminal career he would be known as a conciliator, a peacemaker and smooth deal maker, dubbed the "prime minister." When Dewey put Luciano away in 1936, Costello managed his operations for him.

For protection, Costello never surrounded himself with bodyguards, the way other mob bosses did. His form of protection was to camouflage himself as a legitimate, upstanding businessman who fit right in with the other toffs who lived at the lordly Majestic on Central Park West. And he bought himself a high level of influence with the Tammany Democrats as a bulwark against his Republican nemeses Dewey and La Guardia (who routinely referred to him as "the bum"). Tammany leaders breakfasted with him, lined up to lunch with him, joined him for cocktails at the Copacabana.

While investigating Tresca's murder, DA Frank Hogan had gotten permission to tap Costello's home phone. "We really didn't think Costello had anything to do with the murder of Tresca, but we thought we might pick up some information as to the identity of the killer," he would explain. The morning after the Democrats nominated Aurelio, detectives heard Costello pick up his phone. It was Aurelio calling to say "thanks for everything." "Congratulations," Costello replied. "It went over perfect. When I tell you something's in the bag, you can rest assured." "I want to assure you of my loyalty for all you have done. It's undying," Aurelio said.

Both Democrats and Republicans were mortified. It was too late to remove Aurelio's name from the ballot, and he refused to drop out. At a disbarment hearing that fall, Costello boasted about his political clout, while Aurelio wept and claimed he'd had no knowledge of Costello's criminal past. In the end, Aurelio was not only not disbarred, but he won the election and served until the early 1970s.

It was not the last time that having Costello's support would cause trouble for a New York political figure.

⌢

In the spring of 1943, Kurt Weill composed the music for another giant Jewish spectacle staged in New York, called *We Will Never Die*. By then the whole world knew of the Nazis' program to exterminate all the Jews under their dominion. In that horrifying—and politically polarizing—context, *We Will Never Die* had a far larger impact than *The Eternal Road* had.

In June 1942 a report smuggled out of Poland to London had detailed the massacre of seven hundred thousand Jews at the hands of the Nazis. In response, the American Jewish Congress organized another mass rally at Madison Square Garden that July. Roosevelt, Willkie, and Churchill sent messages of support. La Guardia spoke and was in fine form, denouncing the "schwein Hitler," "the little dog Mussolini," and "the yellow rat, the Mikado." He pointed out that those forces wouldn't be stopped by rallies and speeches, only by blood and bullets.

On the following August 8, a World Jewish Congress representative in Geneva informed the British Foreign Office and the U.S. State Department about an "alarming report" of a Nazi plan in which "all Jews in countries occupied or controlled by Germany... should, after deportation and concentration in the East, be at one blow exterminated... Action is reported to be planned for the autumn." It was the Final Solution, which Putzi Hanfstaengl had told Varian Fry was being discussed as early as 1935, and on which the Nazi hierarchy had finally agreed at their Wannsee conference in January.

State Department officials expressed skepticism and decided neither to go public with the report nor to inform Rabbi Wise and other American Jewish leaders. Wise got the news from British sources three weeks later. He rushed to Washington and met with undersecretary Sumner Welles, who asked him to keep the story private until the government could confirm its veracity. Wise agreed, sitting on the news for ten weeks, until Welles summoned him back to Washington on November 24 and said he could now "confirm and justify your deepest fears."

Wise called a press conference. The next day, the Wednesday before Thanksgiving, newspapers reported his statement that an estimated two million Jews—half of all those in Nazified Europe—had already been exterminated. In the *Times*, the story earned a small space on page 10, crammed above a large Thanksgiving ad for Seagram's whiskey. The *Tribune* ran a small piece at the bottom of page 1. The *Washington Post* also buried it. Americans went on with their holiday.

For agreeing to suppress the story as long as he did, Wise was soundly condemned by other Jews, especially but not only in the Orthodox community. They argued that during those almost three months that he said and did nothing, hundreds of thousands of Jews in Poland were massacred. His defenders pointed out that given the obvious indifference of the government and the press, it's not clear that anything he might have done or said would have saved a single life.

He should have tried anyway, his detractors countered. One of them was Peter Bergson. Bergson would later recall that when he saw the small item on November 25 blandly reporting the slaughter of two million Jews he'd had to read it several times before it sank in.

The news also shocked a star writer who now joined Bergson's public awareness efforts. Ben Hecht had grown up in New York City, the son of garment district workers, then moved to Chicago. A prolific journalist, playwright, novelist, and screenwriter, his credits included *The Front Page*, *The Great Magoo*, *Twentieth Century*, *Notorious*, *Scarface*, and *Gunga Din*. He felt no particular interest in Jewish affairs before "the German mass murder of the Jews, recently begun, had brought my Jewishness to the surface," he later wrote. "I felt no grief or vicarious pain. I felt only a violence toward the German killers." In a column he wrote for *PM* he excoriated "Americanized Jews" for not crying out more loudly about the massacres. Bergson wrote Hecht after reading the column, and when Hecht was next in Manhattan he invited Bergson to drinks at "21."

Hecht liked the twenty-seven-year-old's passion; Bergson found Hecht, who was in his forties, worldly and accomplished.

Hecht became the Bergson Group's chief propaganda writer. On December 7, 1942, the first anniversary of Pearl Harbor, the *Times* ran an ad across two full pages, paid for by Bergson's Committee for a Jewish Army of Stateless and Palestinian Jews, which had an office on Fifth Avenue at East 45th Street. The first page featured an illustration of a soldier with a Star of David on his helmet, a machine gun in one hand, cradling a wounded rabbi in his arm. It bore the text of a proclamation that "we shall no longer witness with pity alone, and with passive sympathy, the calculated extermination of the ancient Jewish people by the barbarous Nazis." It ended with a call for an "Army of the Fighting Jew... marching shoulder to shoulder with the Legions of the United Nations to ultimate victory!" Most remarkable was the second page, filled from top to bottom with the names of hundreds of signatories: twenty-seven senators, including Harry Truman; seventy-four representatives; other public and political figures such as Herbert Hoover and Grover Whalen; thirty-one generals and admirals; twenty-seven labor leaders, including Sidney Hillman and A. Philip Randolph; scores of governors, mayors, and judges; scores more of Christian and Jewish clergy; and dozens of doctors, lawyers, industrialists, and journalists. Through Hecht and another supporter, the actress and acting teacher Stella Adler, came assorted celebrities and leaders in the arts, including Clare Luce, Humphrey Bogart, Aaron Copland, Langston Hughes, Jimmy Durante, Eugene O'Neill, Cecil B. DeMille, Ira Gershwin, Arturo Toscanini, and Claude Rains.

Angry and envious at being so provocatively upstaged, Rabbi Wise wrote to FDR that week, requesting a meeting. His note began, "Dear Chief: I do not wish to add an atom to the awful burden which you are bearing..." He and a small group of mainstream Jewish leaders met with Roosevelt the day after Bergson's ad ran. They handed the president a memorandum detailing Nazi atrocities in eastern Europe but were careful not to push him for any specific action. He responded with equal vagueness, assuring them he would do what he could "to save those who may yet be saved." It was a phrase he would repeat during the war as the numbers of those who might yet be saved dwindled.

On February 13, 1943, the *Times* ran a small item that the government of Romania was willing to transfer seventy thousand Jews to Palestine, or anywhere else the Allies designated, for $50 per refugee. Morgenthau's

Treasury would release the funds if the State Department found the proposal to be credible. But the State Department meant Breckinridge Long, and he showed no interest in pursuing the offer. Frustrated, Hecht dashed off a three-quarter-page ad that ran in the *Times*, with the startling three-deck headline:

FOR SALE to Humanity
70,000 Jews
Guaranteed Human Beings at $50 a Piece

"Roumania is tired of killing Jews," Hecht went on. "It has killed one hundred thousand of them in two years. Roumania will now give Jews away practically for nothing." At the bottom was a coupon one could send with a donation. Wise and other mainstream leaders complained that Hecht and Bergson were just trying to con money from the public.

Hecht was already at work on a much larger project: the script for a pageant to memorialize the two million dead, *We Will Never Die.* Weill wrote the music and Moss Hart directed. Billy Rose came on as producer. They booked Madison Square Garden for two performances on the night of Tuesday, March 9, and spent a hectic month putting the huge spectacle together.

When Rabbi Wise and the American Jewish Congress heard of it, they booked the Garden for their own rally the week before, Tuesday, March 2. Called *Stop Hitler Now*, it was cosponsored by Christian organizations, the AFL, and the CIO. A packed house of twenty-one thousand, with an estimated ten thousand more out on 49th Street, heard Rabbi Wise, Mayor La Guardia, Governor Dewey by radio from Albany, and Supreme Court Justice William O. Douglas by radio from Washington urge the Allied nations to "save as many as possible of the five million Jews threatened with extermination by Adolf Hitler." Among the proposals raised was to increase the number of refugees allowed into the United States and Palestine. "Two million Jews have already been exterminated," Dr. Chaim Weizmann of the Jewish Agency for Palestine said. "The world can no longer plead that the ghastly facts are unknown and unconfirmed. At this moment expressions of sympathy, without accompanying attempts to launch acts of rescue, become a hollow mockery in the ears of the dying."

A week later, forty thousand people filled the Garden again for two sold-out performances of *We Will Never Die.* Giant tablets bearing the Ten Commandments stood against the backdrop curtain, which hid a large chorus. Four hundred actors, two hundred cantors, and two hundred rabbis filled the stage. Fifty members of the NBC Orchestra were in the pit to play Weill's somber, soaring score. The cast included some of the great Jewish stars of the time: Stella Adler; Sylvia Sidney; Edward G. Robinson and Paul Muni, both of whom had emigrated from eastern Europe to the Lower East Side in their youths; and Jacob Ben-Ami, a longtime star of New York's Yiddish theaters. They lent dignity to Hecht's melodramatic script about "a great and ancient people... crying like a single child." Toward the end, actors playing the ghosts of the massacred shuffled onto the dimmed stage, as one of the narrators intoned, "The corpse of a people lies on the steps of civilization."

Billy Rose had asked his mentor Bernard Baruch to get a message of support from the president that could be read on stage. FDR remained silent. Rose did talk Governor Dewey into declaring March 9 a day of prayer for Europe's Jews.

Asked afterward what he thought the impact might be, Weill replied, "All we have done is make a lot of Jews cry, which is not a unique accomplishment."

We Will Never Die was performed in six other cities in the following weeks, from Boston to Los Angeles, where the performance at the Hollywood Bowl was aired nationally by NBC Radio. Eleanor saw it in Washington and wrote about it in her column. She got Franklin to meet with Bergson and his group.

Pressured to show at least a modicum of concern, Roosevelt told Breckinridge Long to arrange a conference with the British to discuss the refugee issue. It was held that April in Bermuda, to keep the bulk of the American press away. The seventy-three-year-old New York City congressman Sol Bloom represented Jewish interests. Bloom had started out a theatrical impresario and Tin Pan Alley music producer. He was involved in the 1893 World's Columbian Exposition in Chicago, where he introduced the belly dance to America, and helped Grover Whalen put together the 1939 New York World's Fair. He was reputed to have coined the motto "His Master's Voice" for the Victor Talking Machine, and he helped build the Apollo Theater in Harlem. By 1943 he'd been in Congress twenty years, was a stalwart supporter of FDR, and was chairman of the House Foreign Affairs Committee, a position for which even his friend Rabbi Wise considered him uninformed and intellectually ill-equipped.

The conference made no practical recommendations, and its report was kept confidential anyway, supposedly for military security. It was widely condemned as a sham. Even Wise called it a "sad and sordid affair." Bergson and Hecht ran another large ad in the *Times* (May 4, 1943, page 17), which declared, "To 5,000,000 in the Nazi Death-Trap Bermuda Was a 'Cruel Mockery.'" Speaking at a Waldorf-Astoria luncheon for women of the Hebrew Immigrant Aid Society, Bloom declared that "as a Jew I am perfectly satisfied with the results of Bermuda."

Bergson's people convened their own weeklong Emergency Conference to Save the Jews of Europe, held at the Hotel Commodore that July. Rabbi Wise was largely successful in convincing Jewish and Christian leaders to stay away. But La Guardia attended, as did Dorothy Parker, Samuel Dickstein, IBM's Thomas Watson, and Herbert Hoover. Wendell Willkie and Eleanor Roosevelt, who turned down invitations to attend, sent letters of polite encouragement, and the president had Secretary of State Hull send a message that was meticulously noncommittal.

Still, Bergson's committee was winning some influential supporters. Interior Secretary Ickes, uncomfortable with State's stonewalling on refugee issues, agreed to be the honorary chair of the Washington, D.C., branch. More cautiously, Treasury Secretary Morgenthau told the committee that if they could develop credible rescue plans he'd review them. The most controversial support came from the conference's honorary chairman: William Randolph Hearst. Kristallnacht had disabused Hearst of his infatuation with Hitler. Never plagued with consistency, he turned anti-Nazi and pro-war, as well as calling for "a homeland for dispossessed or persecuted Jews." Hearst's thirty-four papers gave prominent placement to holocaust stories downplayed elsewhere. Hearst offered the Bergson Group free space for ads and wrote his own editorials in support. Bergson shrugged off criticism that accepting Hearst's support made him a fascist.

Bergson and his group would spend the rest of 1943 pressing Roosevelt to create an official agency charged with saving as many as possible of the remaining Jews in Europe. By the time they goaded him into a response it would be far too little and too late.

CHAPTER 44

A Spy on Staten Island; a Riot in Harlem

Around 9 a.m. on Sunday, June 27, 1943, a pair of dark sedans motored uphill into Tompkinsville, a neighborhood on Staten Island high above the St. George ferry terminal and Staten Island's north shore waterfront. They proceeded up Oxford Place and stopped at 123, a modest brick house behind a neatly trimmed box hedge. The street was quiet. Many of the neighbors were at church.

Five young men in dark suits got out of the cars and walked up to the house. Two positioned themselves outside in the already hot morning sun, one at the front door and one at the back. The one at the back probably noted the neat rows of healthy vegetables in the meticulously tended Victory Garden out there.

The other three went in. They spent three hours inside, most of it up in the attic under the pitched roof, where two quarter-moon windows flanking a brick chimney offered spectacular views of the wartime bustle in New York's harbor. Below and to the left, Port Richmond was busy with war work around the clock. The Bethlehem Shipbuilding Corporation launched destroyers and other warships and produced the giant propellers for larger oceangoing vessels. At Port Richmond's piers, giant cranes swung brand-new tanks, artillery pieces, and warplanes into the holds of cargo ships bound for the front. Across the steel-gray waters of the Upper Bay, the towers of lower Manhattan rose. Ferries beetled back and forth from there over to St. George below. To the right was the long swoop of the south Brooklyn waterfront with its giant Army Terminal and the Todd shipyard, spiny with crowded docks and more swinging cranes. In effect the entire New York Port of Embarkation and all the troopships, cargo ships, and warships entering and leaving it were on view.

At noon the three young men came out the front door. Two carried armloads of paperwork; the third led the home's owner by the elbow down the walk, through the box hedge, and out to one of the cars. Then they drove off as unobtrusively as they'd arrived.

The next day, the man from Oxford Place, Ernest Lehmitz, stood in a Brooklyn federal courtroom, blinking passively at a judge through round steel-rimmed glasses. Lehmitz was a wan fifty-seven years old, balding, a bit stooped, in a cheap suit. The young men who'd taken him out of his home were FBI agents. He was charged with spying on activities in the harbor for the Abwehr. Under the Espionage Act, the penalty was from thirty years in prison to death in the electric chair. When the judge asked how he pleaded, Lehmitz placidly replied, "Guilty." Unable to make bail, he was taken to the West Street jail, while the city's newspapers ran the story on their front pages.

Mrs. Lehmitz (described in the *Times* as "a rather ample hausfrau") and all their neighbors declared themselves shocked. Mr. Lehmitz had given no clue that he was anything but a solid, even model citizen.

Born in Hamburg in 1886, Lehmitz had come to New York in 1908 and lived on Staten Island ever since. He took U.S. citizenship in 1924, and he bought 123 Oxford Place in 1926. He worked as a porter, pushing a broom and mop around in Cuff's restaurant down in Port Richmond. He seemed patriotic to a fault. He was one of Mayor La Guardia's first and most dedicated volunteer air raid wardens, and his Victory Garden was said to be the best on the block. Through the USO, he and his wife rented a few furnished rooms in their home to merchant marine and army officers. Otherwise neighbors described him as quiet and shy, a bit hang-dog, a nearly invisible guy who shuffled off to his job every workday, then whiled away evening hours in some of Port Richmond's waterfront taverns, saying little, just hovering on the edges of conversations among the seamen and defense workers.

It was all a carefully crafted front. The feds discovered a curious and damning gap in Lehmitz's time as a Staten Island resident. He had returned to Germany in 1938 and lived there into 1941. During that period, the Abwehr trained him as a spy. Back on Oxford Place when the United States entered the war, his job was to observe and report on activities in the harbor. He spent long hours up in the attic, watching ship movements.

He gathered numerous other scraps of information by eavesdropping on the conversations in his home, at Cuff's, and in the bars—proving that the government signs warning that "loose lips sink ships" were no joke. He sent what he learned to German intelligence using an age-old trick, writing in invisible ink between the lines of seemingly harmless typewritten letters mailed to "friends" in Portugal, Spain, and Switzerland. In addition to what he saw and heard about convoy routes and troopship movements, the often quite detailed lists of the military equipment going out in cargo ships, he used up some invisible ink complaining. In one message he called the mayor's air raid precautions "indescribably confused," which was not wholly inaccurate.

There was a fatal flaw in Lehmitz's system. British postal censors in Bermuda, inspecting mail bags en route to Europe, became suspicious. Lehmitz's letters never reached the Abwehr after that. British intelligence alerted the FBI, leading over time to his downfall.

On Monday evening, as Lehmitz sat quietly as ever in the West Street jail, Harry De Spretter, a fellow Staten Island air raid warden of German descent, "seemed inordinately distressed" as he hurried toward his home in the Dongan Hills neighborhood. "Perspiration matted his graying beard and his fringe of graying brown hair," the *Times* would report, "while his heavy shell-rimmed spectacles were bedimmed a bit." He had "an enormous bundle of newspapers under one arm," all of them shouting the news about Lehmitz on their front pages.

De Spretter, a slight, balding man of professorial mien, had good reason to be alarmed. The next morning, FBI agents arrested him as a coconspirator with Lehmitz. Born in Uruguay in 1891, De Spretter had served as an officer in the German army in the Great War before coming to New York in the 1920s. He was an engineer who consulted with military contractors, but with four children he was often strapped for cash. He told interrogators he was not pro-Nazi but had colluded with Lehmitz in return for small cash payments.

Investigators turned up hints that the pair were part of a larger spy ring but nothing that led to other arrests. The two men would be tried that September and each sentenced to thirty years in prison.

⌣

Through the spring into the summer of 1943, racial tensions and violence boiled over on army bases, in communities near them, and in cities with large black populations. On May 2, Eleanor came to Harlem and addressed the issue before a crowd of five thousand in the Golden Gate Ballroom at Lenox Avenue and 142nd Street. According to the *Amsterdam News*, she "declared that if the race problem is not remedied, there can be no real peace." The *News* praised her as one of a handful of "honest, courageous persons," including Wendell Willkie and Pearl S. Buck, who were "sincere believers in and practitioners of honesty and fairness."

Words were not sufficient. Riots broke out around the country that June. Black soldiers at Camp Stewart, enraged by their treatment, rose up in revolt, killing one MP and wounding four others. Detroit exploded in a terrible riot that left thirty-four people dead and hundreds wounded. And just across the river in Newark, gangs of white and black youths fought on the streets for three days.

Harlem was a "cauldron of brooding misery and frustration," in Walter White's words, and the large black communities in Brooklyn's Bedford-Stuyvesant and Brownsville were also simmering with anger. La Guardia, troubled by the uprisings elsewhere, cast an anxious eye on these neighborhoods. After a black man in Harlem attacked two white cops with a knife, the mayor instructed Police Academy graduates to "shoot first and be quick on the trigger."

The mayor himself was responsible for at least some of the resentment in the neighborhood. In April, he had misguidedly ordered the Savoy Ballroom shut, acting on charges from the NYPD and the military that the place was a sin pit, and that more than a hundred and fifty servicemen in the past year had contracted venereal diseases from women they met there. All Harlem was insulted and outraged. Walter White, Adam Clayton Powell Jr., and other leaders in the neighborhood countered that in fact the Savoy was safer and more wholesome than many, many other spots below 110th Street. The actual reason for closing it, they charged, was that the racist NYPD had always hated it as a place where whites and blacks mingled. In *The People's Voice*, Powell declared that "Hitler has scored a jim crow victory in New York."

Black New York remained quiet, if sullen, through June and July. Then, on the evening of Sunday, August 1, Harlem erupted. It had been a hot day, and the whole neighborhood was out on the streets, strolling in their Sunday best. Around 7:30 p.m., a black private on leave, Robert Bandy, walked his mother into the lobby of the run-down Braddock Hotel at Eighth Avenue and 126th Street, where she was staying for the weekend.

They came upon an irate and probably drunk black woman screaming at the white policeman who was posted to the Braddock lobby, supposedly because it was a hangout for pimps and prostitutes. When Robert Bandy intervened, he and the cop scuffled. Bandy knocked the cop down, and then the cop pulled his service revolver and shot Bandy in the shoulder.

By the time the cop walked Bandy out of the hotel a crowd had formed. A rumor raced around Harlem that a white cop had shot and killed a black soldier. By 10 p.m. mobs were rushing along 125th Street and the avenues, smashing storefronts, setting fires, overturning parked cars. Soon the crackle of gunfire added grisly grace notes to the roars of the crowd. There was little looting at first; this was pure rage, with no other motive. The looting came later.

La Guardia ordered all available cops, some five thousand of them, to the neighborhood; called Governors Island for MPs to clear servicemen out; then called black leaders to meet him and Commissioner Valentine at the 28th Precinct on West 123rd Street. Walter White rushed there in a cab with his assistant Roy Wilkins. The fair-skinned White would later say it was good he had the darker-skinned Wilkins with him, because rioters were attacking any vehicle with white faces in it. La Guardia directed Valentine's men to use force only as a last resort. He bundled White with him into a patrol car and toured the littered streets. At one point La Guardia shouted at some young people looting a smashed store. They recognized him and, startled, dropped the loot and dispersed. He would spend the rest of the night bustling around and making several radio appeals for calm.

Zoot suited Malcolm Little was strolling down St. Nicholas Avenue when he came upon large numbers of people "hollering and running north from 125th Street…loaded down with armfuls of stuff." He laughed at a handwritten sign in a Chinese restaurant's window: "Me Colored Too." The rioters didn't touch it.

The worst of the rioting had spent itself by dawn, though looting continued for a few more hours. In the early morning light, the dazed, disheveled, bloodied residents of Harlem wandered a neighborhood that looked like a war zone. Fifteen hundred shops had been smashed, gutted, some torched. Smoldering cars lay on their sides on streets littered with glass and rubble. Six people, all black, had been killed. Another seven hundred, including forty cops, were injured. Police made more than five hundred arrests, almost all for looting.

Over the following days there was little agreement on what or who had sparked the event. The *Times* blamed "sinister agitators," others blamed the black press, and J. Edgar Hoover blamed zoot suited hooligans. In fact, the hundreds who were arrested represented a cross section of Harlem residents. Clearly grievances had been building up in the whole community, as White and other black leaders insisted. According to Malcolm Little, very, very few white people ventured into the neighborhood for the rest of the war.

⌢

The riot brought down criticism of another sort on one of the most successful people from Harlem. In 1939, Ted Poston had been the first black journalist in America hired to write full time by a white newspaper. In 1943 he was writing for the domestic propaganda wing of OWI. That was the source of the criticism.

He was born on the Fourth of July in Hopkinsville, Kentucky (also home to Edgar Cayce and Grover Cleveland's vice president Adlai Stevenson, grandfather of the 1950s presidential candidate). In 1919, when he was thirteen, he got his start in journalism as the copyboy for his older brothers' small newspaper, the *Hopkinsville Contender.* After working his way through college as a sleeping car porter, he moved to Harlem in 1928. He waited tables at the Cotton Club and ghostwrote articles on Harlem life for the *Herald Tribune*, which would not give a black writer a byline, before landing a full-time position at the *Amsterdam News*. The paper was struggling to stay afloat in the Depression and his pay was meager. When he headed to Alabama to cover the second trial of the Scottsboro Boys in 1933 he paid his own way. In the courtroom he sat with the other blacks segregated in the balcony, disguised as a local in ragged overalls, because if identified as a black reporter from Jew York he could easily be a target for angry whites.

Back in New York that year, he picked up a *Daily Worker* someone had left on a subway seat and read that the left-leaning, Brooklyn-born journalist Heywood Broun (a role model for Quentin Reynolds) was starting a union for journalists, the Newspaper Guild. Poston signed up as a charter member, and he got the whole editorial staff of the *Amsterdam News* to sign up as well. They joined the picket line at a *Brooklyn Eagle* strike, then went on strike themselves. Broun, Reverend Adam Clayton Powell, and Zora Neale Hurston picketed with them. The *News* fired Poston as a troublemaker. He went to the Federal Writers' Project, where he joined other Harlem writers including Ellen Tarry, Richard Wright, and Ralph Ellison. (Tarry's first book, *Janie Belle*, was published because Poston introduced her to an editor at Doubleday whom he knew through the Guild.)

After Congress ended the FWP in 1939, Poston was hired full time by the liberal, and in this instance pioneering, *New York Post*. Although most of what he wrote was light fare on Harlem life, he was sometimes allowed to dig deeper. One night he got a call from a lawyer he knew, Thurgood Marshall. Marshall had come north from his hometown Baltimore in 1936 to be legal counsel for the NAACP, headquartered on West 135th Street in Harlem. He lived at the fancy 409 Edgecombe where Walter White and other Harlem elites did. Poston met him there and accompanied him out to Queens, where they interviewed black residents who said that local members of the Ku Klux Klan were harassing them. The Klan had been an active presence in Queens since the 1920s. In 1927, a thousand hooded Klansmen held a rally in the Jamaica neighborhood to protest what they claimed was discrimination against white Protestants by Irish Catholic policemen. A handful of men were arrested in scuffles with the cops; one of them was the twenty-one-year-old Fred Trump from the Bronx, Donald's future father.

In 1940 Poston went to Washington to join the so-called Black Cabinet, whose members had two basic jobs. One was to advise federal policy regarding black Americans. The other, possibly of more interest to FDR, was to ensure that black voters appreciated what the president was doing for them and remembered it at election time. Southerners in Congress sniped that Roosevelt was simply pandering to get the black vote. Some black activists argued pretty much the same.

Poston would stay in Washington throughout the war. He started out working under Sidney Hillman at the War Production Board, promoting federal goals for the hiring of black workers in the defense industry. In 1942 Elmer Davis brought him over to the OWI to run the "Negro News Desk." His job was to encourage black participation in the war effort through press releases and pamphlets such as *Negroes and the War*. Southern congressmen complained that the "minority-glorifying" publications were a waste of defense dollars and cut the OWI's publishing budget. (They also cut off funding to prevent another black New Yorker at OWI, the photographer and later filmmaker Gordon Parks, from documenting the achievements of the Tuskegee Airmen.)

Now, in the wake of the riots in Harlem and elsewhere in the summer of 1943, some black activists accused Poston of being an Uncle Tom, promoting the white man's war effort despite the outrageous treatment of blacks in the military. Poston took the blows and decided to keep working for the government.

Well past midnight one night he was walking in a dicey black neighborhood in D.C. when he came upon Eleanor Roosevelt, walking alone after a meeting with a friend, the Black Cabinet member Mary McLeod Bethune. He chastised her for it. "If the wife of the President of the United States were mugged in a Negro section at 3 in the morning," he chided her, "you'd set the cause of race relations back a thousand years." She confessed it hadn't occurred to her. He walked her to where they could flag down a taxi to get her safely back to the White House.

When the OWI was dismantled in the fall of 1945, Poston would return to New York and the *Post*, continuing a long career. He covered the civil rights movement from the 1950s until his retirement in 1972. He died in 1974.

CHAPTER 45

Ghosts

On D-day, June 6, 1944, when more than a hundred and fifty thousand Allied troops invaded Normandy, three notable New Yorkers were with them. One of them, David "Mickey" Marcus, wasn't supposed to be there.

Mickey Marcus was born on Hester Street in 1902, son of a Romanian immigrant pushcart peddler, and grew up in Brownsville. A small kid preyed on by neighborhood bullies, he devoted himself to bodybuilding and boxing. By the time he entered West Point in 1920 he was 135 pounds of iron with a sledgehammer left. After his time in the regular army, he would remain an officer in the National Guard. He earned a degree at Brooklyn Law School and became an assistant to the U.S. district attorney for New York, where he and Tom Dewey became friends.

In 1934, the new mayor Fiorello La Guardia appointed Marcus deputy commissioner of the city's corrections department. Marcus effectively ran the department for the ailing commissioner. One of his first acts was to stage a military-type raid on the old Welfare Island Penitentiary, where the corrupt warden and his staff gave the inmates, including some of the city's top gangsters, free reign to enjoy drugs (brought in by a prisoner's pet homing pigeons), liquor, cigars, and other pleasures. (Welfare Island was renamed Roosevelt Island in 1971.) When La Guardia made Marcus a court magistrate in 1936, he helped Dewey bag Lucky Luciano by the simple expedient of locking up some one hundred Mafia stool pigeons under special guard so Luciano couldn't have them intimidated, or worse.

After Pearl Harbor, Marcus's National Guard unit was posted to Hawaii, where he trained rangers in hand-to-hand jungle fighting. He wanted a field command but was sent instead to the Pentagon to work in the army's Civil Affairs Division (CAD) in 1943, planning for the post-war reconstruction of Europe. In that role he participated in all the major

Allied conferences from Cairo to Yalta and Potsdam, where, at a jovial dinner, the Russian general Zhukov drank all the Americans under the table but Marcus.

In May 1944, the forty-two-year-old Colonel Marcus got himself posted to London to conduct CAD affairs there. On D-day, still itching for combat, he wangled his way onto a C-46 and, without telling his superiors, parachuted into Normandy with the 101st Airborne. It was his first time using a parachute, with no training. He spent a week in combat organizing stray paratroopers into small fighting units, killing and taking enough Germans prisoner that he was already a legend when the Pentagon ordered him home.

As the war in Europe was ending, Marcus would be posted to occupied Germany, where he'd become the U.S. secretary-general for Berlin. He was not previously a Zionist, but a tour of Dachau and his work on resettling displaced Jews convinced him of the need for a homeland in Palestine. He would return to the Pentagon in 1946 to run its War Crimes Division, overseeing legal and security procedures at the Nuremberg trials. What he learned in the process deepened his commitment to the Israeli cause.

In January 1948, using the name Michael Stone, Marcus would go to Palestine to help the outnumbered and outgunned Jewish forces prepare for war with surrounding Arabs. He was appointed the first general of the Israel Defense Forces. Despite knowing very little Hebrew, he trained them in the hit-and-run tactics that were used to fight the Arab forces to a standstill that May and June. Unable to sleep on the night of June 11, 1948, a few hours before a UN-negotiated cease-fire was to begin, Marcus wrapped himself in a sheet and took a walk around the fortified village of Abu Ghosh. A young sentry mistook him for an Arab and called out in Hebrew. Marcus apparently did not understand him and was shot dead. Moshe Dayan brought his body to America and he was buried at West Point.

⌒

Jerome David Salinger was born in 1919 in Harlem to a Jewish father, manager of a successful food importing firm, and an Irish Catholic mother. As the family prospered they moved to a large apartment on Park Avenue near Central Park, and Jerome was sent first to the YMCA's McBurney School on the Upper West Side, later to Valley Forge Military Academy.

Salinger was a twenty-three-year-old struggling writer when the army called him up in the spring of 1942. After two years of training in counterintelligence and a promotion to staff sergeant, he landed with the Twelfth Infantry on Utah Beach the day after D-day. Over the next year he earned five battle stars participating in some of the fiercest fighting as the invasion forces drove the Germans back across Europe. In his intelligence work Salinger interrogated captured military men and Nazi Party members—including a French-German woman named Sylvia Welter, whom he married and brought to New York. His parents, not surprisingly, were unwelcoming. Sylvia returned to Germany in 1946 and filed for divorce.

⌒

Besides participating in planning D-day, Ralph Ingersoll helped to create one of the odder units involved in it.

In June 1942 his draft board had classified him 1-A. He was forty-one, with dependents, but after two years of hawkishness at *PM* he couldn't very well say he wasn't ready to serve. *PM*'s owner Marshall Field intervened and asked for a deferment, arguing that Ingersoll would be of more use to his country at the paper than as a private in a foxhole. When Ingersoll showed up to be inducted he was sent home. Other papers and a few Republicans in Congress howled that Ingersoll was a coward hiding behind his millionaire backer. It made front-page news—at least in *PM*, where Ingersoll took the entire cover to run a giant war-is-over headline, RALPH INGERSOLL VS. DRAFT BOARD NO 44. Inside, his six-thousand-word letter to his draft board took up three full pages. In essence he said he was willing to go, but he charged the conservatives on the board with wanting to put him in uniform chiefly as a way to punish and damage a liberal newspaper they despised.

There was more hooting and snickering in rival papers. In July Ingersoll ended the humiliation by enlisting. At *PM*, as previously at Luce's empire, many staffers greeted Ingersoll's departure with sighs of relief.

Given his engineering background, not to mention his celebrity, the army brass consented to his request to be assigned to a unit called the Engineer Amphibian Command, which was then practicing beach assaults on Cape Cod. Ingersoll later told his biographer that he'd barely arrived when his commanding general received an angry call from Mayor La Guardia, demanding to speak to Private Ingersoll. La Guardia, in one of his excitable fits, shouted down the line that the "goddamned sons of bitches" couldn't keep Ingersoll in uniform. "I'll have you out in twenty-four hours," the mayor yelled. He wanted Ingersoll to run for governor of New York on the ALP ticket. Much as the invitation must have pleased Ingersoll, he declined.

Seeing that a man with Ingersoll's political connections might be useful on his staff, the general quickly bumped him up to first lieutenant and had him working as a kind of in-house publicist. In North Africa to observe amphibious operations there, Ingersoll witnessed a single battle between Allied forces and Rommel's and managed to spin a whole book out of it, the best-selling *The Battle Is the Pay-Off.* It was great publicity for both Ingersoll and army brass, who promoted him to captain.

In 1943 he was sent to Allied Headquarters in London, where, looking the wrong way crossing a street, he was promptly struck by a taxi. On release from hospital he was promoted to major and posted to the American staff planning Operation Overlord, the D-day invasion, with the British. Always confident that he was the smartest guy in any room, he considered British D-day planning disastrously inept. (Then again, so did Stalin when he was shown their ideas.)

Allied Headquarters used an array of deceptions large and small to keep German intelligence confused and distracted in the year leading up to D-day. Major Ingersoll and two other American officers, Colonel William Harris and Captain Wentworth Eldredge, organized one of their own: a "tactical deception" unit that would go in with the invading troops and devote itself solely to hoodwinking the enemy about actual troop sizes and movements. Officially it was the 23rd Headquarters Special Troops, but it was nicknamed the Ghost Army, and got a Casper-ish insignia patch to go along with it.

In unpublished notes he wrote after the war—unpublished because the unit's existence remained top secret until 1996, eleven years after his death—Ingersoll characteristically took sole credit for dreaming up the Ghost Army and proudly called the unit "my con artists." Eldredge conceded that Ingersoll did seem uniquely suited to the deception game, given his penchant for lying.

The concept of tactical deception was at least as old as the story of the Trojan Horse. What distinguished the 23rd Specials unit was that it was formed solely for that purpose, and that it used cutting-edge technologies and a multimedia approach, combining visual and aural trickery with faked radio messages. It was a bit like Special Services, in that many of its eleven hundred men came from the worlds of the arts and entertainment—painters and illustrators, theatrical set designers, recording and radio engineers. Unlike Special Services troops, however, they served on the front lines.

Many in the 350-man camouflage division were artists and art students recruited through the Pratt Institute in Brooklyn. Among them were Ellsworth Kelly, a prominent figure in New York's postwar modern art boom; Bill Blass, a star of its fashion industry; and New Yorker Art Kane, who would go on to be a highly respected photographer of jazz and rock musicians. They deployed inflatable rubber tanks, trucks, jeeps, and artillery pieces to fool German reconnaissance. The decoys were light enough that four men could pick up a fake Sherman tank and carry it into position—which would flabbergast civilians who watched them do it in France. They also used bulldozers to lay down phony tank tracks.

The sonic unit used brand-new recording and broadcast equipment, including giant truck-mounted speakers, to project the sounds of tanks and trucks rumbling by, or ghost engineers hammering together a pontoon bridge. There was even a recording of a ghost sergeant yelling, "Put out that goddamn cigarette, now!" The signal group's false radio transmissions, which they knew German military intelligence would closely monitor, added a crucial layer of verisimilitude.

Eight days after D-day, fifteen men of the 23rd landed at Omaha Beach. They set up dummy artillery pieces a mile ahead of the actual U.S. line, to see if they could draw German fire. It worked. Most of the rest of the Ghost Army arrived the following week. Through the rest of 1944 they crossed France with the advancing army. Their dummy vehicles and guns drew enemy fire away from real ones. They plugged gaps in the advancing line, impersonating actual divisions, concealing weak spots.

Ingersoll, not a man to let the greatest amphibious invasion in human history happen without him, had gotten himself attached to a tank division that rolled onto Utah Beach on June 6. He was with General Omar Bradley's staff in December when the Germans surrounded the 101st Airborne at Bastogne, the beginning of the Battle of the Bulge. As George Patton raced his Third Army to relieve the town, Ingersoll had the Ghost

Army whip up such a blizzard of false radio messages that the Germans were completely confused about Patton's whereabouts. Bradley considered the deception a key element in the rescue of the town; he pinned a medal on Ingersoll for it and promoted him to lieutenant colonel.

Ingersoll had a personal reason to help rescue Bastogne. Theodor Geisel had drawn his last Dr. Seuss cartoons for *PM* at the end of 1942. At thirty-nine, he enlisted in the army. The Information and Education Division assigned him to Frank Capra's signal corps unit, making newsreels and propaganda films in a rented Hollywood studio nicknamed Fort Fox. Late in 1944 he was sent to Europe to show U.S. generals there a training film for occupation troops, *Your Job in Germany*.

At Bradley's headquarters in Luxembourg Geisel met up again with Ingersoll. Geisel would later tell the *New Yorker* that Ingersoll thought he, "like most Stateside tourists, would like to have a peek at some actual fighting while he was in the area—without, of course, getting too dangerously exposed." Ingersoll gave him a driver and jeep and sent him off to see a town he believed was near the front but in no jeopardy—Bastogne. The Germans surrounded it just after Geisel arrived. "Nobody came along and put up a sign saying, 'This is the Battle of the Bulge,'" Geisel told the *New Yorker*. "How was I supposed to know?" He was stuck in the besieged town for three days. Ingersoll was sure he'd gotten Dr. Seuss killed. He was greatly relieved when they met up again at a party in Manhattan five years later.

⌒

Two weeks after the D-day invasion, the first eyewitness report from inside a death camp, from two Slovakian Jews who had escaped Auschwitz, was published worldwide. Although the report merely provided graphic confirmation of what had been known and shrugged off since 1942, the world now reacted with horror.

Six months earlier, Peter Bergson and his supporters had finally prodded Roosevelt into starting an official agency charged with saving the remaining Jews in Hitler's Europe. It came only after much rancorous argument within and without his administration.

In September 1943 the *Times* had run another of Ben Hecht's large ads, his angriest and most outrageously accusatory so far, with a poem called "Ballad of the Doomed Jews of Europe." It began:

Four Million Jews waiting for death
Oh hang and burn but—quiet, Jews!
Don't be bothersome; save your breath—
The world is busy with other news.
**

Four million murders are quite a smear
Even our State Department views
The slaughter with much disfavor here
But then—it's busy with other news.

The last verse was:

Oh World be patient—it will take
Some time before the murder crews
Are done. By Christmas you can make
Your Peace on Earth without the Jews.

The following month Bergson and five hundred Orthodox rabbis from New York and New Jersey marched from Washington, D.C.'s Union Station to the White House, where they asked to see the president. Sam Rosenman, who was on Rabbi Wise's side of the great divide, advised Roosevelt "under no circumstances" to meet with them, reputedly saying that they were "not your kind of Jews." Photos of the gray-bearded marchers huddling outside the White House made the newspapers. Roosevelt was severely miffed, and of course Wise denounced Bergson for putting the chief in such an awkward position.

Meanwhile, representatives of the United States, England, and Russia were meeting at the third Moscow Conference. Among other things, they agreed that after the war the Nazis would be tried for war crimes. They cited the massacres of Czechs, Greeks, Serbs, Russians, French, and Poles but pointedly did not use the word "Jews." Hecht lashed out in a new *Times* ad, in which the ghost of his Uncle Abraham attended the Moscow Conference and had to report to the two million massacred Jews that they were not mentioned there. Uncle Abraham was now, Hecht noted, in the White House, "two feet away from Mr. Roosevelt."

FDR was furious, and he wondered if no one would rid him of these meddlesome Jews. The FBI investigated Bergson, and there were discussions in various federal offices about deporting him back to Palestine, where the British would instantly arrest him; failing that, maybe he could be drafted into the army.

At the same time, friendly congressmen managed to get a bill for the creation of a refugee agency placed before the Foreign Affairs Committee—run by Sol Bloom, still fuming over the Bergson Group's withering critiques of the Bermuda Conference. Bloom called both Bergson and Wise to testify. He needled Bergson about his status as an alien, implying both that he had no business meddling in U.S. policy and that he might be a Communist. To Rabbi Wise he was obsequious.

The bill looked certain to fail. Then, on January 13, 1944, a trio of Henry Morgenthau's staffers at Treasury handed their boss a report on "The Acquiescence of this Government in the Murder of the Jews." John Pehle ran the department's Foreign Funds Control. Josiah DuBois had been a lawyer at Treasury since the 1930s. Randolph Paul was a former Wall Street tax lawyer and director of the Federal Reserve Bank of New York who'd come to Treasury five days after Pearl Harbor. None of the three was Jewish. All were outraged at the foot-dragging they'd experienced from the State Department, and particularly from Breckinridge Long, over the Romanian refugee proposal. They charged Long not just with inaction but with doing everything in his power to "prevent the rescue of the Jews." DuBois warned Morgenthau that if he did not act, he—DuBois—would resign, call a press conference, and "rip the lid off the entire State Department refugee scandal."

Morgenthau had always been disgusted by Long's callousness toward refugees, yet he had never pushed Roosevelt on the issue. He acted now. On January 15 he met with the president in the Oval Office and presented a toned-down version of the report, with the recommendation that under the circumstances it would be a political boon for the president to end-run Congress and State and create his own refugee rescue agency. Five days later FDR signed the executive order creating the War Refugee Board. Pehle was made its director. Long was demoted and quit before the end of the year. Josiah DuBois would go to Nuremberg after the war to help prosecute the directors of I.G. Farben for war crimes.

In April, thousands of the Lower East Side's Orthodox Jews filled up the small Warsaw Synagogue on Rivington Street and spilled out to the sidewalks. They were commemorating the first anniversary of the Warsaw Ghetto uprising. Rabbi Wise was not among them. At the end of the memorial service they marched silently down to City Hall Park and waited forty-five minutes for Mayor La Guardia to come out and address them. He assured them that Allied forces would "go to the rescue of the oppressed peoples in Europe... before long," and "it will not be a case of making an appeal to the Nazi brutes. It will be a matter of the hot bullets of machine guns and then the cold steel of the bayonets... until every Nazi murderer is chased out of Poland."

That May, unbeknownst to La Guardia, SS officers ransacked the apartment of his sister Gemma in Budapest. In 1906, when Fiorello returned to New York, she had stayed in Fiume with their mother, teaching English to adults. She married one of them, Herman Gluck, a Hungarian Jew. They settled in Budapest and raised two daughters. Although Hungary had joined the Axis in 1940, the Glucks, like other Hungarian Jews (under Nazi race law Gemma was Jewish because her mother was), had managed to live relatively unmolested previously. The SS men who rifled the apartment claimed to be searching for a hidden radio transmitter she was using to communicate with her brother. There was no man in America the Nazi leadership despised more than her outspoken brother. Apparently this was meant as a warning and a reprisal for his April speech.

On June 7, the day after D-day, the Nazis returned and arrested the Glucks. Herman was taken to the Mauthausen concentration camp, Gemma to the women's camp at Ravensbrück. She'd never see Herman alive again.

Roosevelt issued a statement on June 12, in which he said, "This nation is appalled by the systematic persecution of helpless minority groups by the Nazis." He promised the "Hitlerite forces" that when the war was over "the fury of their insane desire to wipe out the Jewish race in Europe" would be punished. He was reiterating the threat made at the Moscow Conference in October 1943, but the specific mention of the Jews was new.

It was too little too late. Four out of five Jews in Nazified Europe had already been annihilated. The War Refugee Board's signature achievement was that it provided Raoul Wallenberg the diplomatic cover he used in saving thousands of Jews in Hungary. Overall, the WRB played a hand in rescuing perhaps some fifty thousand Jewish refugees, while the Nazis exterminated hundreds of thousands more in their mad rush to complete the Final Solution in the last months of the war.

CHAPTER 46

The Manhattan Project and Its Moles

On December 18, 1941, ten days after the U.S. committed to war with Japan, atomic research was militarized. A new program code-named S-1 was dedicated to the full-time pursuit of a weapon. Brehon Somervell, by then a general, oversaw it. He was also busy marshaling half a million workers to construct military facilities around the country, including the new Pentagon. His lead man on the Pentagon project was Colonel Leslie Groves, a West Pointer from Albany. Groves was a big, portly, bluff man with a reputation for getting things done and demanding that everyone working for him apply themselves with the same vigor.

In September 1942, Somervell informed Groves that he was putting him in charge of S-1. Groves was disappointed. He had been hoping for a combat command. But he was a lifer who obeyed orders. His one stipulation was a promotion to brigadier general.

S-1 got a new name from its first headquarters, the offices of the Army Corps of Engineers' North Atlantic Division. They were on the eighteenth floor of 270 Broadway, an unadorned twenty-eight-floor federal office tower on Chambers Street near City Hall. Originally the army planned to code-name the project the "Laboratory for the Development of Substitute Materials." Groves didn't think that was secretive enough and decided to call it the Manhattan Engineering District, leading to its commonly being referred to as the Manhattan Project. The building remained the project's headquarters until August 1943, when the administration moved to new offices in Oak Ridge, Tennessee. Also in 270 Broadway were offices of the engineering firm Stone & Webster, which got the contract to design and build a huge plant at Oak Ridge.

Groves launched himself into the Manhattan Project with astonishing speed. His appointment came through on Thursday, September 17, 1942.

His first goal was to secure uranium. He learned that Edgar Sengier, director of a Belgian mining company called Union Minière du Haut Katanga, had offices in the lordly Cunard Building at the foot of Broadway. Union Minière mined uranium in the Belgian Congo. When the Nazis occupied Belgium in 1940, Sengier quickly ordered a huge cache of the ore—some 1,250 tons, in two thousand metal drums—shipped to New York to keep it out of the hands of German atomic scientists. It was secretly stashed in warehouses on Staten Island. On Friday, September 18, Groves bought it all. During the war, another four thousand tons of uranium mined in Canada would be secretly off-loaded on Manhattan's Hudson River waterfront and stored in the large Baker & Williams warehouses on West 20th Street, from where it was distributed to Manhattan Project sites.

On Saturday Groves acquired the sixty-thousand-acre parcel of lonesome land in Tennessee where he would quickly erect Site X, aka Oak Ridge, the Manhattan Project's massive yet top secret facility for the enrichment of uranium. Another site, in Hanford, Washington, known as the Z Plant, produced plutonium. Both types of bombs, uranium and plutonium, would be developed by the Manhattan Project.

Groves flew to Berkeley in early October 1942 to meet Robert Oppenheimer. By the end of the month he'd recruited him to run Site Y, the secret laboratory where the atom bombs would be built. Oppenheimer was not an obvious choice. He and Groves were about as different as two men could be. At thirty-eight, the physicist was still emaciated and fragile-looking, chain-smoking cigarettes as a substitute for food; he had retained the delicate features of a pensive choir boy, lit by brilliant blue eyes, and he could be aloof and arrogant though he could also be charming and personable when he remembered to be. He had never managed any kind of organization larger than a seminar for fifteen students—it was said he "couldn't run a hot dog stand." He was a theoretician, not used to conducting physical experiments. He had no Nobel, which many of the scientists who'd work under him did.

On top of all that, there were his personal associations with Communists: his first girlfriend had belonged to the CPUSA and introduced him to her left-wing circle, with some of whom he was still friends; his wife's former husband was also CPUSA; his brother Frank had joined as well. While he had apparently never joined the party himself, Oppenheimer carried enough of a left-wing taint to give army intelligence serious misgivings.

Groves wanted him despite all that, and General Groves almost always got what he wanted, because he would put it to good use. Army intelligence acquiesced, but they and the FBI would keep a close watch on Oppenheimer throughout the project, including secretly taping his conversations and assigning an agent as his driver and bodyguard.

In November Oppenheimer showed Groves the place he thought Site Y should go: Los Alamos, where a remote boys' boarding school was situated on a mesa not far from Perro Caliente outside of Santa Fe, New Mexico. Groves approved and construction began immediately. By the spring of 1943 Los Alamos was a small government town of wooden barracks and bungalows, with coal stoves and dirt roads, fenced in, gated, and guarded. Some of the world's leading physicists—Fermi, Teller, Bethe, Oppenheimer, and others—would live there in top secrecy over the next two years; others, including Rabi and Bohr, would visit and consult. Los Alamos, Oak Ridge, and Hanford came to be known as the three "atomic cities."

⌣

Even after the Manhattan Project headquarters shifted out of New York, much research and development continued to be done in the city. Up Broadway from Columbia at West 133rd Street is the large, solid Nash Garage Building, which originally housed an auto dealership. Columbia bought it and installed scientific laboratories. At the start of the Manhattan Project scientists tested different methods for separating highly fissionable uranium 235 from the less useful uranium 238. In the Nash building, Columbia physicists and graduate students worked with scientists and employees of the Kellex Corporation to develop a method called gaseous diffusion, in which uranium gas would be passed through filtering material to segregate the isotopes. (Kellex was a subsidiary of the chemical engineering firm M. W. Kellogg, created specifically to work on the top secret research. Kellex's offices were downtown in the venerable Woolworth Building, a couple of blocks from 270 Broadway.)

A young Columbia physicist named Edward Adler was so absorbed in the work that he lived in his Nash lab. Researching a gas filtering material that had a very fine coating printed on it, he spent days across the East River in the industrial area of Long Island City, using the printing presses of the American Chicle Company, which made Chiclets. He enjoyed that the chicle factory smelled of spearmint. James Forde, a seventeen-year-old Kellex lab assistant, was the only African American in the Nash labs. He didn't know the ultimate goal of the research until he read about Hiroshima in the newspapers in August 1945. That was typical of the roughly 130,000 workers ultimately employed on the vast but top secret project.

Kellex's offices in the Woolworth Building were the first stopping point in America for the few dozen scientists of the British Mission, the secret Anglo-American collaboration on the project. Among them was the German theoretical physicist Klaus Fuchs. As a member of the German Communist Party he had feared for his life when Hitler rose to power in 1933 and fled to England. He was living in England—where he'd been interned for a while as a German national at the start of the war—when he volunteered to Soviet intelligence to be a spy. Moscow knew as early as September 1941, a year before the Manhattan Project began, that the Americans and British were having secret discussions about making atomic bombs. Soviet intelligence code-named the project ENORMOZ (Enormous), and made a full-on effort to find out whatever they could, understanding that their American and British allies weren't going to share the knowledge willingly. Fuchs arrived in New York in December 1943 and spent nine months at Kellex, while sending Moscow vital secrets on the gaseous diffusion process.

When future Nobel laureate Richard Feynman first arrived at Los Alamos, Edward Teller knew him only as the kook who kept everyone in the dorm up playing his bongo drums every night. Teller later wrote that he "seemed to be composed in equal parts of physicist and humorist." Feynman himself would later say he made "no big decisions" at Los Alamos and "was always flittering about underneath somewhere." But he possessed a brilliant mind, as well as the fearlessness of a native New Yorker, and famous scientists like Urey, Bethe, and Bohr found they enjoyed arguing and refining their ideas with the feisty young man.

Feynman was born into a nonpracticing Jewish home in 1918 and grew up in Far Rockaway, a small town near the ocean in Queens. He was a brilliant kid who inherited a ceaselessly questioning mind and an irreverent sense of humor from his parents. He set up his own workshop and lab in his home and was an inveterate tinkerer with any electronics or other equipment he could get his hands on. By high school he was displaying a genius for math and puzzle solving. The whole universe seemed to be a puzzle for him to solve, and nothing was above or beneath the reach of his curiosity, from quantum physics to how ants forage, from hypnosis to picking locks.

Despite his obvious brilliance, he was turned down by NYU—the school had filled that year's quota for Jewish admissions. He went to MIT instead, studied physics there, and from there to Princeton for his graduate studies in the fall of 1939. At first he stood out in the school's extremely WASPish social setting as a rough-cut Jewish guy with a New Yawk accent, but his idiosyncratic mind shone through. He was still a graduate student when Wigner arranged for him to give a talk on quantum theory. Wolfgang Pauli and Albert Einstein were in the audience. Pauli was unimpressed; Einstein was kinder.

Feynman was working on his thesis when Robert Wilson, a young professor in the Princeton physics department, recruited him for a top secret project. Wilson was working on how to separate U-235 from U-238. By the end of his first day Feynman found himself an employee of the Office of Scientific Research and Development. He soon met Oppenheimer, Rabi, and others, then took time off to finish his thesis, get his Ph.D., and marry Arline Greenbaum. They had been in love since growing up together in Queens. She was bright, beautiful—and, since the mid-1930s, dying slowly of tuberculosis. When Oppenheimer brought Feynman to Los Alamos in 1943, he also arranged for Arline to go to a clinic in Albuquerque.

Feynman enjoyed testing and tweaking the security arrangements at Site Y. Because censors read all the mail, he and Arline wrote letters in code the censors went mad trying to crack. He also went around to all the safes and locked desks, including Teller's, practicing his lock-picking skills. It wasn't just for fun; he was, in his own way, pointing out security weaknesses.

Through 1944, Feynman hitchhiked from Los Alamos to Albuquerque to visit Arline as often as he could. By 1945 she was clearly fading. In June, he got the message that she was dying. He borrowed an old Buick from a friend at Los Alamos—Klaus Fuchs, who had transferred there from New York in August 1944. As Feynman drove to Albuquerque, the car got one flat tire, then another, then a third. At that point he left it on the road and hitchhiked the rest of the way to the clinic. Arline died a few hours later. He had one more flat tire on the drive back to Los Alamos.

⌒

A week before Fuchs arrived in August 1944, the Soviets had placed another spy inside Los Alamos. He was a young army sergeant and machinist from the Lower East Side named David Greenglass.

As the *New York Times*'s Sam Roberts detailed in his definitive *The*

Brother, David and his older sister, Ethel, were born and raised at 64 Sheriff Street, a poor and crowded street lined with tenements and storefronts that ran from Grand up to Houston Street. After the war it was all but obliterated by new housing complexes and a park. They lived on the ground floor, behind Mr. Greenglass's machine shop, and had the only private toilet in the building; the other tenants used wooden outhouses in the back.

Ethel went to Seward Park High School, then took a secretarial job in the garment district. In 1935, when the Ladies Apparel Shipping Clerks Union went on strike, the strike committee met in her bedroom. She was fired.

The following year she was at a benefit for the International Seamen's Union when Julius Rosenberg introduced himself. Three years younger than Ethel, he'd grown up near her, on Goerck Street. It has now also mostly vanished under housing projects, including the Baruch Houses; the unrecognizable fragment of Goerck Street left was renamed Baruch Place. Julius also went to Seward Park and was now at the City College of New York's school of technology, prepping for a career in engineering. Like Ethel, and many other young people on the Lower East Side, Julius passionately believed that Communism would be the salvation of the world. He joined the CPUSA in 1939, the year they got married at a Sheriff Street Orthodox synagogue. They brought David into the movement with them. He was not as bright as they were, nor as politically committed. He just went along. He also married a girl from the neighborhood, the smart, attractive Ruth Printz, a fellow member of the Young Communist League.

In 1940, Julius got a job as a low-level engineer at the Brooklyn Supply Office of the Army Signal Corps. Around the same time, he began a decade-long career as a spymaster for Soviet intelligence, recruiting and managing a highly productive ring of some dozen agents, mostly engineers working for the military or in defense plants. Four of them he'd known since their time at CCNY: Alfred Sarant, Morton Sobell, William Perl, and Joel Barr. Through the 1940s the Rosenberg ring would pass along to the Soviets significant volumes of classified information on radar, sonar, jet and rocket propulsion, weapons technology—and, the biggest secret of all, the atom bomb. Julius's intelligence on that project was mostly of inferior quality—the Soviets got better information from other sources inside the Manhattan Project, such as Fuchs—but it would prove to be fatal to him and Ethel anyway.

It came from Ethel's brother. David was drafted into the army in 1943. Mentally and physically lethargic, he was no natural warrior, but he had lived his whole young life in machine shops, starting with his dad's, and the modern military had a crying need for mechanics. In June 1944 he was posted to Oak Ridge. He omitted to mention his membership in the Young Communist League when filling out his security clearance papers. In August he was transferred to the Special Engineering Detachment (SED) at Los Alamos. SED was nearly five hundred mechanics, metalworkers, and chemical or electrical engineers. They did the hands-on tooling, fabricating, and wiring that turned the scientists' ideas into actual weapons.

Despite the security and censorship at Los Alamos, David dropped broad hints in his letters home, and Julius was soon reporting to his handlers that his brother-in-law was stationed at a secret facility in New Mexico. Julius didn't know that meant Site Y but the Soviets did. They had doubts about the quality of information a twenty-two-year-old SED mechanic could gather there, but they gave Julius the okay to put David to work, and Ruth as well.

⁀

In January 1945, David returned to New York on a furlough. He reported to Julius everything he'd learned at Los Alamos so far, including the layout of the facility and the identities of scientists working there. He also sketched for him a part of the plutonium bomb he'd worked on, a "lens" to focus the charges that triggered an implosion and nuclear reaction. This was information that wouldn't be declassified until the 1950s. At a meeting in the Rosenbergs' apartment at Knickerbocker Village—a large new complex of affordable units on the Lower East Side, built in the mid-1930s with New Deal funding—Ruth agreed to move to Albuquerque and be the go-between for David and his Soviet courier. She was pregnant and lonely for her husband.

Back at Los Alamos in early 1945, David made stabs at recruiting two other young New Yorkers in the SED, Ben Bederson and William Spindel. His hope of turning them was not entirely unfounded. Bederson was from the Bronx, where he grew up in the United Workers Cooperative Colony housing complex. In a 2015 *New York Times* profile he would remember it as "a Communist neighborhood, or at least a Communist-sympathizing neighborhood—anything from pink to red." At Los Alamos he worked on the ignition switch for the plutonium bomb.

Spindel was a chemist from Brooklyn who tested the purity of Los Alamos's plutonium samples. He and his wife, Sarah, who had taken an apartment in Albuquerque, got friendly with David and Ruth in the spring of 1945. David, Spindel, and another GI bought an old car together. Before then, they'd had to hitchhike, like Feynman, into Albuquerque to see their wives on furlough. David once hooked a ride with General Groves himself. When the car had a flat tire, Groves got out and showed off his marksmanship with a sidearm by shooting tin cans tossed in the air. Only later, Sam Roberts relates, did the oddness of the scene strike Greenglass: a Soviet spy hitching a ride with the pistol-packing head of the Manhattan Project. When Ruth suffered a miscarriage that April, it was on the sofa in the Spindels' apartment.

Both Bederson and Spindel grew weary—and wary—of David. Bederson told the *Times*, "I knew he was pretty radical. He made no bones about it. He was in the next bunk to mine at Los Alamos. We had arguments." In a video interview posted by the Atomic Heritage Foundation in 2013, Spindel recalled that David "actually tried to get me to serve as a spy. The line then was, 'Don't ya think it's not fair of us not to share this with our great Russian allies?'...I said to him, 'David, I'm not necessarily against sharing it with them, but nobody elected us to make these decisions. To do it would be espionage, and you gotta be crazy to do that.'" Eventually, Spindel and Bederson asked to be transferred to a different barracks.

With Ruth laid up, David's courier came to them. He was a pie-faced, easily forgotten schmoe—good camouflage for a spy—Harry Gold, the man to whom Elizabeth Bentley claimed she passed along the troublesome Abe Brothman. Gold had come to New Mexico to be Fuchs's courier. The Greenglasses were an afterthought. He returned to New York City and gave his handler two envelopes. One contained some very useful intelligence from Fuchs on the design of the plutonium bomb. The other held inferior information from Greenglass.

⌣

The Soviets had a third spy at Los Alamos by then. He was also a New Yorker. In fact, he started out in Far Rockaway, like Feynman. His birth name was Theodore Holtzberg but he went by Ted Hall.

Hall was the youngest son of Barnett Holtzberg, a Russian Jewish immigrant who was prospering in New York's fur trade when Theodore was born in 1925. With the crash of '29 few people were buying mink coats anymore, so when Theodore was five Barnett moved his family from their large home on Long Island to a cramped apartment on West 172nd Street in Washington Heights; later they were able to shift out to the leafier Forest Hills in Queens. Ted's brother Ed, eleven years older, was his mentor. Ed was at CCNY at the same time as Julius Rosenberg and his future spies, and he brought home *The Communist Manifesto* and other such literature for his adolescent brother's political education. For his bar mitzvah Ted wanted to give a speech on the dangers of fascism in America, but the rabbi nixed it. The boys started calling themselves Hall as a way to evade the anti-Semitism that was rife at the time.

Precociously brilliant at math—again, like Feynman—Ted skipped some grades and was only fourteen when he entered Queens College, bent on a career in nuclear physics. At sixteen, in 1942, he transferred to Harvard, where James Conant was actively recruiting young scientists for the war effort. While there, Ted joined the campus's pro-Communist John Reed Society—reduced to a handful of true believers after the Stalin-Hitler pact—and continued to absorb Marxist thought. One of his roommates was another New Yorker, Saville Sax. Sax had grown up in a building on the Upper West Side filled with Russian Jewish immigrants, where Yiddish was more common than English and people were as devout about Communism as Judaism. He also leaned toward bohemianism and poetry; one of his best friends in high school was James Baldwin.

Hall was in his senior year at Harvard when he was recruited for the Manhattan Project. When he arrived at Los Alamos in January 1944 he was eighteen, one of the two youngest scientists there. He was working on the uranium bomb when he graduated from Harvard in absentia that June. He was later switched to working on the implosion process that David Greenglass would reveal to Julius.

In October 1944, Ted went to New York for two weeks of leave. Like some others involved in the Manhattan Project, he felt that atomic weaponry was too powerful to be kept in the hands of any one nation, even his own. The knowledge should be shared with the Soviets to preserve the balance of power in the world after the Nazis' defeat. In Manhattan he looked up Saville Sax. The two of them made inquiries at the CPUSA and at the Amtorg Trading Corporation, which was not only the Soviet Union's import-export office but a cover for intelligence operations. Though the Soviets had some misgivings about these two raw youths—their code name for Hall would be Mlad, meaning "youngster" or "kid"—the possible rewards were too great to pass up. They recruited them both, Hall to spy and Sax to be his courier. Sax made his first trip to Albuquerque that December, and Hall passed him important information on the implosion device.

In 1945 the Soviets replaced Sax with a far more experienced agent, Lona Cohen. She was a bona fide working-class hero; the Russians would later put her on a postage stamp. The daughter of Polish immigrant mill workers in Connecticut, she lit out for New York at the age of twelve or thirteen, found work in garment industry sweatshops, and joined the CPUSA in 1935 at the age of twenty-two. She met her future husband, Morris, a CPUSA organizer from East Harlem, at a Madison Square Garden rally for the Spanish loyalists in 1937. A week later he sailed with other volunteers to join the International Brigade and fight for the loyalist cause. He was recruited and trained by Soviet intelligence in Spain. On returning to New York in late 1938, he was employed in the Amtorg cafeteria at Madison Avenue and East 36th Street. Morris told Lona he was a spy after they were married in 1941, and she started working with him. One of their first coups was to turn an engineer at an aircraft factory, who smuggled out part of a newly designed machine gun for them. Apparently, Julius Rosenberg collaborated with the Cohens on that mission. The Cohens also filched information on radar, a technology of great interest to the Soviet military.

When Morris was drafted into the army in 1942, Lona continued spying on her own, while doing various kinds of Rosie the Riveter war work. On one of her jobs, at the Aircraft Screw Products plant in Long Island City, she was elected union shop chairman and made herself an aggravating thorn in management's side. She apparently made two trips to Albuquerque as Hall's courier in 1945. What she brought back to New York, put together with what Harry Gold delivered from Fuchs, effectively gave the Soviets a step-by-step primer on how to build a bomb.

⌒

In 1944 the Allies still had no clear idea of what progress the Germans had made in developing their own atomic weapons. The OSS and military intelligence had in fact made very little effort to find out, partly because, as Richard Rhodes explained in *The Making of the Atomic Bomb*, "to know what to look for, intelligence agents would have to be briefed" at least in the basics of atom bomb technology, "which meant that any agent captured or turned might well give American secrets away."

Directed by George Marshall to proceed anyway, Groves sent an intelligence team—code-named Alsos, Greek for "grove"—to follow Allied troops across Europe after D-day. Progressing through France and Germany, they confiscated tons of uranium ore, secured a cyclotron and an atomic pile, and found Otto Hahn, the man who had first split the atom, waiting with his bags packed to be taken into custody. They concluded that the Nazis had given up on developing atomic weapons as early as 1942. British intelligence concurred.

So did William Donovan's OSS, which had sent its own man in, with orders not just to find Werner Heisenberg, the Nazis' leading atomic scientist, but to assassinate him if necessary.

He was Moe Berg. Donovan had hired Berg as a full-time spy in 1943. None of Donovan's dilettantes was more amateurish than Moe, but none was more enthusiastic either, and he did get some results. Shortly before D-day, a little ahead of the Alsos team, the OSS sent Berg into Europe, also to see what he could find out about the status of Nazi atomic research.

After boning up on physics, Berg made his way to Rome on June 6, 1944—D-day in France and one day after Rome's liberation. There he met a few Italian atomic physicists who were anti-Fascists but had opted to stay in Italy when Enrico Fermi and others left for the United States in the late 1930s. He also tracked down the aeronautics scientist Antonio Ferri, an expert on supersonic flight. When the Germans occupied Rome in 1943, Ferri had sneaked into his lab and destroyed as much equipment and paperwork as he could, then went underground and joined the resistance. Berg found him and arranged for him to go to the United States, where the National Advisory Committee for Aeronautics was very pleased to greet him. He would go on to teach at Brooklyn Polytechnic Institute, work with NASA, and found the General Applied Science Laboratory on Long Island, where he died in 1975.

Early in December 1944 the OSS learned that Heisenberg would be giving a lecture at a technical college in neutral Zurich later that month. Berg and another OSS agent went to Switzerland to attend. Berg's brief was to determine if Heisenberg was anywhere near to completing an atom bomb—and, if so, to assassinate him. Berg was maybe the least likely assassin in the OSS. He carried a pistol but was not familiar or comfortable with firearms, and had previously embarrassed himself by letting his handgun fall out of his pocket or belt in public places. He also carried an "L pill"—a cyanide capsule to take if he was captured.

He got into the lecture pretending to be a Swiss physics student. Heisenberg looked small and frail to him. Although Berg's German was rusty, and his knowledge of physics superficial, by the end of the lecture he concluded that Heisenberg was no threat and there was no need to assassinate him.

Later that week, Berg attended a dinner party at which other physicists harangued a defensive Heisenberg for working inside Hitler's Germany. At the end of the evening Berg walked out with Heisenberg. Still playing the Swiss student, Moe strolled Zurich's dark streets with the scientist and "pestered" him, Heisenberg later recalled, with questions. By the time they parted ways Berg had reconfirmed his opinion that there was no need to assassinate the man.

Despite all the intelligence that there was no Nazi atomic threat, Roosevelt was taking no chances and directed the work at Los Alamos to continue.

Moe did little more spy work during the war. The end of the war would leave him a man without purpose, no longer in baseball, no longer a spy, still a blur. He would hold no serious job and indeed do very little of anything for the rest of his life. In the early 1950s he would conduct a little low-priority snooping for the CIA. But otherwise he would drift through his last quarter century as a kind of celebrity hobo, constantly on the move, mooching off friends and fans, his life as mysterious as in his spy days but nowhere near as dramatic. When he died in 1972 he left no estate, no heirs, and a legacy that's still mostly questions and vagueness.

CHAPTER 47

Clear It with Sidney

The Democrats approached the 1944 presidential election with trepidation. They'd taken a pasting in the 1942 midterm elections. Voters had been unhappy with the way the war was going in its first year, and chafing under wartime restrictions. Turnout was low: only 28 million of 80 million eligible voters. When the 78th Congress got to work in January 1943, Republicans and Southern Democrats were solidly in control and set about dismantling what was left of the New Deal. The most antilabor Congress since the 1920s, they also passed legislation banning strikes and restricting other union activities.

Eleven new Republican governors had also been elected. They included Tom Dewey. He had vacated the DA's office at the end of 1941, set up a private practice, and prepared his gubernatorial campaign. New Yorkers were too preoccupied by the war to pay the governor's race much attention and did not vote in great numbers. Dewey beat Governor Lehman in a landslide. His victory celebration filled the ballroom of the hulking Roosevelt Hotel (named for Teddy) at Madison Avenue and 45th Street. Already looking past the governor's mansion to another run at the White House in two years, he told the crowd, "We are all of us interested in only one victory—total, uncompromising, crushing victory over our country's enemies." Then they all sang a new Spike Jones song, written by a Disney composer for an upcoming Donald Duck cartoon—the wacky "Der Führer's Face," with the lines, "Ven der Führer says, 'Ve iss der Master Race!'/ Ve Heil! [Bronx cheer] heil! [Bronx cheer] right in der Führer's face."

Dewey easily won the Republican presidential nomination in 1944. Willkie mounted a brief and quixotic campaign, but he had alienated too many Republicans by 1944 to be a serious contender. He dropped out in the spring. There was an attempt to get General MacArthur interested in running; he wasn't.

Sidney Hillman had been distressed to see national labor policy veering away from all the goals the CIO had worked toward in the 1930s. In 1943, he invented the country's first Political Action Committee, known as the CIO-PAC. With funds raised from union members' donations, the PAC made a massive effort to ensure that union workers registered and would vote in 1944 for Roosevelt and other Democratic candidates. The PAC printed and distributed some 85 million pamphlets extolling the virtues of democracy and the worker, denouncing corporate greed and war profiteering, and generally mobilizing the two million CIO members to do the right thing when the time came.

For Democrats, the question in 1944 wasn't whether Roosevelt should run for an unprecedented fourth term, but whether he could. He was deteriorating rapidly, both physically and mentally. His heart was weakening, he was prone to infectious diseases like the flu, his hearing was going, and his mind wandered. A *New York Times* reporter visited him in May 1944. He had not seen the president in several months and "was shocked and horrified—so much that my impulse was to turn around and leave... I knew I was looking at a terribly sick man." The consensus among those close to him was that he would never survive four more years in the most difficult job in the country. Eleanor pleaded with him not to run.

Given FDR's fragile condition, the matter of choosing a running mate took on unusual significance. His current vice president Henry Wallace had been a controversial choice, booed by conservative Southern Democrats at the 1940 convention for being too progressive. He was also considered a bit of a loony, being a Freemason (the Masonic Great Seal that has appeared on the back of the dollar bill since 1935 was his idea) with a strong interest in the occult. So Wallace was out.

James Byrnes was a leading candidate to replace him. The South Carolina Democrat was a good friend and adviser to FDR, almost a second Harry Hopkins. FDR had appointed him to the Supreme Court, then tapped him to run the Office of War Mobilization. But for his work there, labor leaders opposed Byrnes as a top figure in the administration's probusiness, antilabor military-industrial cabal. Because of all the support he was getting from Hillman and his CIO-PAC, Roosevelt was very sensitive to labor's opinions in this matter.

As a compromise—the Missouri Compromise, some quipped—Roosevelt considered Senator Harry Truman. He seemed a harmless alternative. As a Missouri senator he'd been an all but invisible backbencher until, on his own initiative, he started a committee looking into the widespread waste and corruption in the defense industry. That made him popular and put him on the cover of *Time* in March 1943.

As Roosevelt and the DNC were deliberating all this, Arthur Krock of the *Times* dropped a bombshell, passing along a rumor that Roosevelt had told the DNC chair to "clear everything with Sidney" before proceeding. Republicans, conservative newspapers, and Hillman's enemies within the labor movement including Dubinsky had a field day. Under the banner "Clear It with Sidney" they denounced Roosevelt for giving so much leverage to a "communistic refugee" and representative of the international Jewish conspiracy. Hearst's *Daily Mirror* railed that Hillman was leading a "Communist conspiracy to take over the U.S.," and the *Herald Tribune* ran a "Sidney Limerick Contest" with entries the likes of:

Clear it with Sidney, You Yanks
Then offer Joe Stalin your thanks
You'll bow to Sid's Rule
No Matter How Cruel
For that's a directive of Frank's

Eventually the Sidney controversy blew over, as progress in the war reclaimed everyone's attention. The first Allied troops entered Germany from the west in September, while Soviet forces advanced from the east. In October, the last of the Japanese navy was effectively wiped out. The question, Dewey now argued, was no longer winning the war but crafting the peace that came after. Republicans jeered at "the Great White Father" and the "fourth termites." They cast the choice as a matter of "youth instead of decadence, vigor instead of cynicism." FDR supporter La Guardia countered that what was needed was "experience, not experimenting."

On October 8, Wendell Willkie died of a heart attack, shocking the nation. He was only fifty-two and had seemed so robust in public, though those close to him knew his heart was weak and he was drinking too much. (In *The Fall of the House of Roosevelt*, Michael Janeway, son of the *Time* magazine business editor and New Deal brains truster Eliot Janeway, relays a story told to him by his father and the actress Miriam Hopkins, who were friends. In 1943 Willkie had gone to see Thornton Wilder's *The Skin of Our Teeth*, one of the most successful plays on Broadway during the war, running from November 1942 to September 1943. He was quite smitten with the southern-born Hopkins, who played the wisecracking maid Sabina. Afterward, Willkie escorted Hopkins to her apartment in Sutton Place. Then, probably drunk, he made such a heavy pass at her that she grabbed a lamp and knocked him out. In a panic, she called the Janeways and said "in her Georgia drawl: 'Elyit, ah think ah've just killed the next Pres'dent of the United States.' " They revived Willkie and put him in a cab.)

In the wake of Willkie's death, the DNC wanted to show that the president still had "vigor"—a question the *New York Times* said was "uppermost in the mind of supporter and detractor alike." On Saturday, October 21, he spent a grueling five hours touring around four of New York City's boroughs (skipping Staten Island). His open car traveled fifty-one miles of New York streets on what the *Times* called a day of "biting cold and whipping rain." He wore his familiar blue cape and a battered hat. Eleanor was with him for most of it, La Guardia for all of it. Ten thousand policemen and a bevy of Secret Service agents provided security.

They started at the Brooklyn Army Terminal a little past 9 a.m., the motorcade rolling slowly past rows of tanks, jeeps, and "rigid lines of soldiers and WACs, both white and Negro." Then it proceeded up to the Navy Yard, where "women riveters, in working hoods and slacks, stood alongside Navy personnel and men workers in their overalls." It was possibly his favorite part of the tour, his open car tooling slowly along the waterfront past "scores of warships and other craft, with crews and workers clinging to turrets, guns, decks and other vantage points."

After that it was Ebbets Field. The car was driven up onto a midfield ramp and parked where he could haul himself up from his seat and grab the heavy lectern, constructed to show him only from the torso up. He was his grinning, joking self as he spoke. "I've got a terrible confession to make to ya," he told the crowd. "I have never been in Ebbets Field before." They cheered him anyway. In the newsreel footage there's a split second when he collapses back into the car looking thoroughly exhausted, then he grins and waves again as it drives off.

After a stop in a Coast Guard garage nearby on Empire Boulevard, where he got a dry suit and a stiff bourbon, the motorcade wound through Brooklyn, with large crowds lining the streets, waving and cheering under black umbrellas. The crowds were thinner in Queens, which was Dewey country, but very large on the streets of the Bronx, where he visited the Hunter College training facility for WAVES. The crowds were "immense," the *Times* reported, from Harlem down Broadway through the garment district and Times Square, where bands played and wet ticker tape fell with the rain. The tour ended at Washington Square in Greenwich Village, where he and Eleanor went into her apartment at 29 Washington Square West to rest up. He addressed the Foreign Policy Association in the Waldorf-Astoria ballroom that night. The NYPD estimated that three million New Yorkers came out in the rain to see the president; Republican sources put the crowd at half that.

On November 7, Roosevelt was reelected by about 26 million votes to Dewey's 22 million. It was his slimmest victory ever in the popular vote. The Democrats held on in the Senate and added twenty seats in the House. Several Republican governors lost as well. Clare Luce held on to her congressional seat in Connecticut.

For Sidney Hillman it was the last triumph. "It was a great campaign," Roosevelt wrote Hillman, "and nobody knows better than I do how much you contributed to its success." Hillman got an hour-long ovation at the next CIO convention, but he had little time to enjoy his revived status as a national player. He suffered three more minor heart attacks in 1945 and died of the fourth one at his vacation cottage in Long Beach in July 1946. He was fifty-nine.

Tom Dewey would run for president again four years later, and lose again, and return again to Albany, where he would continue to serve as a very competent governor through 1954.

⁀

On December 31, 1944, the Nazis' last attempt to place spies in America ended when FBI men arrested Erich Gimpel on a street in midtown Manhattan. Back in 1935, the twenty-five-year-old radio engineer from Berlin had gone to Lima, Peru, to take a job with a German mining company. For his first few years there the young man simply enjoyed the congenial, easygoing life of the port's international milieu. He made good money, learned Spanish and English, danced with the local beauties, and drank with British and American sailors. When Germany pushed Europe into war, the German legation in Lima recruited him to observe traffic in the harbor. He sent his reports by shortwave to Chile, where they were transmitted to U-boats prowling the Pacific.

When the United States entered the war, Gimpel was arrested and deported at the request of the American embassy. He spent two months in an internment camp in Texas, then went home to Germany in a prisoner exchange. He was immediately recruited by German intelligence and went through long, intensive training in all facets of spycraft. By the time his first big assignment, an ambitious plan to blow up the Panama Canal, was aborted by his superiors, the Allies had landed at Normandy. Gimpel's next and last assignment came from Der Führer himself. Hitler was frantic to know how far the Americans had gotten with their atomic bomb project, and whether they planned to drop the bomb on Germany. Gimpel's job was to find out and transmit his reports by shortwave.

He was assigned a partner, William Colepaugh, a weedy twenty-six-year-old American defector. Born on the Connecticut shore of the Long Island Sound, Colepaugh was raised by his German mother after his American father left them. He went to the Admiral Farragut Academy, the naval prep school in New Jersey, then MIT. The German consul in Boston became a surrogate father figure; Colepaugh celebrated Hitler's birthday with him at the consulate in April 1941. He dropped out of MIT and was drafted into the navy in 1942, then discharged the following year because of his German sympathies. He took a job on a Swedish vessel, jumped ship in Lisbon, and defected at the German consulate there, saying he wanted to join the German army. Instead, he was recruited and trained by German intelligence.

Gimpel didn't much like or trust the twitchy "Billy," but there was no time to find a substitute. They crossed the Atlantic on the *U-1230*, which slipped into Frenchman Bay on the Maine coast on November 29. That night the captain inched the U-boat to within a few hundred yards of the shoreline. At one point a car parked near the water within shouting distance and the Germans stared incredulously at the couple inside making out, oblivious to the U-boat standing just offshore. By the time the car drove away a snow squall had blown up. Sailors rowed Gimpel and Colepaugh ashore in a dinghy. The two spies wore trench coats and carried suitcases, revolvers, several thousand dollars in cash, and a supply of diamonds in case the cash ran out.

They were standing on the side of the shore road when seventeen-year-old Harvard Hodgkins passed them on his bike, riding home through the snow from a Boy Scout sing-along. By late 1944 no one on the East Coast was keeping a vigilant eye out for Nazi spies and saboteurs anymore—except Boy Scouts. Suspicious of the hatless pair standing out in the night on the lonely road, Hodgkins followed their footsteps in the snow down to the waterline, then raced his bike to the local police station. The cops laughed him off. Next morning he reported his sighting to the FBI, which shrugged it off as well.

The spies hitched a ride to Bangor and trained from there to Boston and on to Grand Central, arriving in New York on day three. They got a room in a hotel near Gramercy Park, and Gimpel went around to various radio shops to buy the parts for a transmitter. Once a cab he was riding in struck a woman pedestrian and knocked her to the pavement. A crowd formed and two cops arrived. Gimpel panicked and ran. A woman shouted, thinking he was the driver. He heard police whistles behind him but got away.

Colepaugh meanwhile went on a weeklong bender in various Manhattan bars, then vanished. A few days later, he drunkenly told a friend why he'd returned to the country, and the friend contacted the FBI. The Bureau was very eager to nab Colepaugh. During the week, the *U-1230* had sunk a Canadian freighter off the New England coast. The FBI remembered the Boy Scout who'd reported seeing spies put ashore and agents rushed to reinterview Hodgkins. They were on the lookout for the two mysterious men when Colepaugh fell into their laps.

Gimpel was going about his task, collecting what information he could gather on the Manhattan Project in the city. He built his transmitter and got off one coded transmission. Then on December 31, working leads Colepaugh had freely given them, FBI agents picked up Gimpel on a midtown street. He joined Colepaugh behind bars at Fort Jay on Governors Island.

In January the *New York Journal-American* trumpeted Harvard Hodgkins's contribution to the case. He was flown to Manhattan, where La Guardia gave him the key to the city. He took in some Broadway shows and got to meet Joe Louis and Babe Ruth.

Colepaugh and Gimpel were tried by military court on Governors Island in February, and both were sentenced to be hanged. Then Roosevelt died in April and all state executions were suspended for a month of mourning. Gimpel was moved to Leavenworth. He was there when Truman commuted his and Colepaugh's sentences to life. He was moved again, to Alcatraz, where he played chess with Machine Gun Kelly. Released in 1955, Gimpel was brought back to New York and put on a ship bound for West Germany. In 1957 his memoir *Spy for Germany* was published in England. It would not be published in the United States until 2003, under the new title *Agent 146*. By then he had moved to Brazil, where, at the age of one hundred, he would die in 2010. Colepaugh was paroled in 1960. He moved to suburban Philadelphia, opened a small retail business—and became a volunteer with the Boy Scouts. He died in 2005.

CHAPTER 48

Endings

By the Yalta Conference, in February 1945, at which the Allies discussed how to reorganize Europe after the war was won, Roosevelt was dying and Harry Hopkins was not in much better condition. Hopkins spent most of the conference in bed; the rest of the U.S. team gathered around it for meetings with him. When the conference ended, Hopkins felt too ill to sail straight for America with FDR and the team. Roosevelt, who had depended on Hopkins so much for so long, was peeved. He wanted Harry to sail back with him and help him with some speeches. Hopkins refused. It was a rare spat, and they would have no time to patch it over.

With Hopkins bedridden, Robert Sherwood stepped in as the president's unofficial emissary. General MacArthur barely communicated his plans or ideas with FDR, so Sherwood flew to the Philippines to ask the general his thoughts on how to deal the coup de grâce to Japan, and how to govern it afterward. He reported this to the president in the White House late in March. He found Roosevelt "in much worse shape than I had ever seen him before... unnaturally quiet and even querulous."

The president proceeded to Warm Springs. He died there of a cerebral hemorrhage on April 12. Eleanor was not with him. Lucy Mercer, now the widowed Lucy Mercer Rutherfurd, was. She had quietly resumed her friendship with him during the war.

Harry Hopkins was not with him either. He was back at the Mayo Clinic.

New Yorkers heard the first radio announcements at 5:49 p.m.—rush hour. For twenty or thirty minutes, the *Tribune* reported, people weren't sure they believed it; the White House and a cooperative press had done a good job of concealing the president's crumbling health from the public. People huddled around newsstands, waiting for late editions to confirm the news. They poured up out of subway stations and hopped off buses, asking strangers if it was true. "Shock and disbelief were in faces everywhere." One young woman on the street, when told the news, snapped, "How dare you say that? What a rotten thing to say!" When the manager of the Embassy newsreel theater on Broadway near 47th Street interrupted the programming to make the announcement, men and women cried aloud, and some rushed out to the sidewalk to tell passersby. The same happened to the three hundred soldiers waiting for the evening's entertainment at the Stage Door Canteen.

The *Amsterdam News* reported:

> A woman rushed into a drug store at Eighth and 138th, extremely nervous and crying.
>
> "Doctor," she screamed to the druggist behind the counter, "did you know that President Roosevelt is dead?"
>
> "No, no," he replied. "It isn't true, it can't be true. Calm yourself. Excitement like that won't help that heart of yours."

Mayor La Guardia was at the Plaza on Fifth Avenue, about to address a meeting of the Sons of the American Revolution, when he was told. He looked like "a man who had suffered a stunning blow," a *Tribune* reporter observed.

That Saturday, the president's funeral in Washington, D.C., began at 4 p.m. At 3:55, all of New York City went still and silent. "Trolley cars stopped and subway cars were halted between stations," Lorraine B. Diehl writes. "Planes scheduled to take off at LaGuardia Field remained on the ground and in the Times Tower the presses that rolled out the news were silenced." At four o'clock, people all over the city bowed their heads or knelt. Before dawn that Sunday morning, Roosevelt's funeral train passed quietly through Penn Station on its way to Hyde Park.

On April 28, the aircraft carrier USS *Franklin*, severely damaged by a dive-bomber attack just fifty miles off mainland Japan, crawled up the East River, slid under the Brooklyn Bridge, and eased in at the Brooklyn Navy Yard. Although yard workers would repair it, it never saw active duty again and was decommissioned in 1947.

On Sunday, April 29, the day after Mussolini's defiled and battered corpse hung upside down from a rusty beam outside a gas station in Milan, La Guardia was at the Navy Yard for the christening and launch of a new supercarrier, the USS *Franklin D. Roosevelt*, soon nicknamed the *Swanky Franky* by her crew. Workers at the yard had spent two years on it.

Two days later, the headline of the *World-Telegram* shouted HITLER IS DEAD. People milling through Times Square at rush hour looked up in a chill afternoon rain to see the same news crawl across the Zipper and "to shrug in disbelief, before they dived like moles into the subway," the *Times* noted. "There was no cheering, only subdued gloating."

"It would have been good news twenty years ago," a cop said. "Late now."

⁓

On May 5, La Guardia announced that he would not run for a fourth term. Three had already been unprecedented, and the third had been marked with much frustration and disappointment. He was sixty-two and had held the second-toughest job in America since he was fifty.

Two days later, a little past 9:30 on the morning of Monday, May 7, news began to spread through the city that Germany had surrendered. It was premature—the surrender wouldn't be officially announced until the next day—but New Yorkers didn't care. New York "let itself go," the *Herald Tribune* reported, and "staged a five-borough, five-hour show of delirious elation." With "shouting and paper throwing, with horn-tooting and dancing, with banners and bottle," an estimated one million packed into Times Square. As a thousand tons of confetti fell in "blinding storms," the crowd passed liquor bottles around, snake danced, sang "Roll Out the Barrel" and "When Johnny Comes Marching Home." "The carmine blaze of lipstick showed on many a service man's face." Inevitably, "hawkers of flags, horns and V-E day buttons sprang out of nowhere and began to sell busily." A vast crowd celebrated in the Wall Street district as well. Thousands more went to their churches and synagogues. At 3:15 that afternoon, La Guardia went on WNYC, his voice sounding strained as it came out of the station's public address speakers in Times Square, and appealed to the crowds to disperse and wait for the official word. A hush fell. Some booed. The party was over.

On Tuesday Truman made it official, and some New Yorkers partied again, mobbing Times Square bars at lunchtime and again after work and drinking some of them dry. The War Production Board made the announcement New Yorkers had long been waiting for: the dimout was over. That night, in the harbor, the floodlights at the base of the Statue of Liberty blazed on fully. (The torch had already been brought back to full illumination.) In Times Square, which had been so gloomy for four years, thousands cheered as all the neon ads and theater marquees flashed on. Washington also announced that the national midnight curfew imposed during the war was over. New York City had never observed it anyway. La Guardia declared that all the bars and clubs could go back to staying open until 4 a.m.

Large crowds turned out again on Tuesday, June 19, to greet General Eisenhower. A quarter of a million jammed into City Hall Park and surrounding streets and buildings to watch La Guardia award Eisenhower a gold medal as an honorary citizen of the metropolis, and they let out a roaring cheer that was measured by General Electric's new noise meter as equaling "the noise of 3,000 loud peals of thunder sounding at the same time." Millions thronged Broadway and leaned out of windows as the general and the mayor motored slowly up to Gracie Mansion in an open car.

Early the next afternoon, the deep bellow of a foghorn rolled around the harbor, from Red Hook to Sandy Hook and the canyons of lower Manhattan. Out of a bank of fog that lay across the Narrows at the entrance to the harbor, into a bright and sunny afternoon, glided the majestic *Queen Mary*, still painted wartime gray. Over the past four years she had carried half a million Americans to the war zone. Tens of thousands of people who stood lining the waterfront on all sides burst into cheers at her appearance now, and a traffic jam of cars on Brooklyn's waterfront streets tootled their horns. Tugboats scuttled around her; fireboats shot jets of water into the air, where a navy dirigible hung like a silver cloud; the Staten Island ferry shuttled out of her path. A WAC band on a small boat trundling alongside serenaded her with pop songs, such as "Don't Fence Me In."

From the *Queen Mary*'s many decks and portholes, 14,526 men and women in uniform waved and cheered back. They were the first returnees from the war in Europe. Many of them held up handwritten signs with messages: "I Made It, Mom." One pretty blonde, a second lieutenant with a nursing unit, waved "a strictly unsoldierly pair of black lace panties." The party continued after the *Queen Mary* nestled up to Pier 90 at the foot of West 50th Street and the vets came down the gangplanks into the waiting crowd. Most were only on furlough and would be reposted to the Pacific, but that didn't dampen the festivities. Many more tens of thousands would be sailing into the harbor in a steady stream now, aboard the *Queen Mary* and the *Queen Elizabeth* and less famous troopships.

⌒

In July, La Guardia made a couple of his last gestures as mayor. The first was a small one, yet it's the one he would be most often and affectionately remembered for. On June 30 the truckers who delivered the city's daily newspapers went on strike. It lasted until July 17. La Guardia decided that it was one thing for adults to be cut off from their daily diet of ink, but worse for New York's kids to be "deprived" of their comic strips "due to a squabble among the adults." And so—making sure that there were plenty of newsreel cameras there to capture it—the mayor read *Dick Tracy* to the kids on his regular Sunday afternoon WNYC broadcast. In the newsreels, which were shown before feature films in theaters around the country, he's pictured having a ball. He narrates, does all the voices and sound effects, bangs his fist on his desk for the crash of an iron pot on a character's head, and adds his own moral at the end: "Dirty money never brings any luck." The broadcasts won him such goodwill and good press that the following Christmastime, when he was just a few days short of vacating the mayor's office, he reprised them by reading "A Visit from St. Nicholas" ("'Twas the night before Christmas..."), written in New York in 1823.

At the end of July, he led a giddy parade of Broadway performers a couple of blocks from the 44th Street Theatre to the Stage Door Canteen's new home in the Hotel Diplomat on 43rd Street. The Times Company had closed the 44th Street Theatre and the building was torn down to make way for a new printing plant. Duke Ellington's orchestra and the cast of *Carousel* would perform on the Canteen's final night, October 29.

⌒

In May, Harry Hopkins had made one last, and for him grueling, trip to Moscow, to get Stalin's agreement on U.S. and British plans for the Potsdam Conference in Germany. When Truman, Churchill, and Stalin met at the conference that July, Hopkins was too ill to go. He retired from federal service that month and moved back to Manhattan, renting a house on Fifth Avenue near the Metropolitan Museum. Sam Rosenman had gotten him a one-day-a-week job as a mediator between the unions and management in the garment industry, and Harper & Brothers offered him a healthy advance to begin writing two or more books about his experiences. But his candle was burning out. He would die on January 29, 1946. The next day's *Times* ran Churchill's comment on his "profound grief" at the death of "a man not only of wide ranging vision but piercing eye. He always went to the root of the matter...He was a true leader of men, and alike in ardor and in wisdom in time of crisis, he has rarely been excelled...We shall not see his like again." Robert Sherwood would incorporate notes and papers Hopkins left behind into his voluminous *Roosevelt and Hopkins: An Intimate History*, published in 1948.

⌣

Ralph Ingersoll returned to New York as soon as the fighting in Europe ended. He immediately hired three stenographers and kept them busy while he dictated his next book. Part of it was pithy descriptions of his personal wartime experiences. The rest was classic Ingersoll opinionating, advancing Omar Bradley as the genius of the European war and criticizing Eisenhower, Montgomery, and Patton. Called *Top Secret*—even though he couldn't mention his most secret project, the Ghost Army—it would come out in the spring of 1946 to much controversy and mixed reviews. Some praised him for having the courage to tell the truth about the levels of incompetence in Allied command, while others panned the book as grandstanding twaddle.

In January 1946 he returned to *PM*, in its new offices at 21 Hudson Street in what's now called Tribeca. In the four years he'd been away, the editorial staff had fallen into squabbling pro- and anticommunist camps, while owner Marshall Field had wrangled with the Newspaper Guild. Wartime price controls had meant that the paper actually made a small profit, but in 1946 it was back to losing as much as $25,000 a day. In November of that year, Field announced that the paper would start accepting advertising. Ingersoll, who had never felt comfortable back at the paper, resigned that day. Field struggled on for a while, then folded *PM* in the spring of 1948. Ingersoll faded from the limelight after that. From the 1950s into the 1970s he ran a successful chain of small, conventional newspapers. He died in 1985 at the age of eighty-four.

⌣

The morning of July 28 New York City was blanketed in swirling fog. Although it was a Saturday, people were at work in the Empire State

Building. A few seconds before 9:49, some of them heard the roaring engines of an aircraft and went to the north-facing windows, above 34th Street. To their horror they saw a twin-engine B-25 army bomber appear from the fog, heading straight for them. The plane smashed into the north side of the building between the seventy-eighth and seventy-ninth floors.

The pilot, Captain William Smith, was a combat veteran. He was on a routine run from New Bedford to LaGuardia Field, with a copilot and one passenger, a navy machinist who had hitched a ride. The fog was so thick at LaGuardia that Smith decided to go on to Newark. He was in a banking turn over midtown Manhattan when the fog cleared enough for him to see that he was flying much too low, heading straight into a forest of skyscrapers. He was trying to turn and climb when he crashed into the building.

The wings were sheared off as the fuselage and engines punched an 18- by 20-foot hole in the wall. Burning fuel poured out of the hole, swept through the seventy-ninth-floor offices of the National Catholic Welfare Council, and raced down stairwells. An elevator plunged from that floor all the way to the bottom of its shaft. Miraculously, rescuers found the twenty-year-old operator, Betty Lou Oliver, alive. For a moment, the force of the explosion cleared the fog, and people down on 34th Street could see flames belching out the gaping wound three-fourths of the way up the tower. One engine skidded clear across the floor, punched out the south wall, and landed on the roof of a twelve-story office building on 33rd Street, destroying a sculptor's penthouse studio. The other plunged down an elevator shaft to the subbasement. Fourteen people—including the three men in the plane and clerical workers, mostly females, of the NCWC on the seventy-ninth floor—died, their bodies horrifically mangled and burned. More than twenty-five others were injured.

Mayor La Guardia arrived and, as he always had, plunged straight in. He took an elevator to the sixtieth floor, then climbed the stairs to the seventy-ninth. A *Brooklyn Eagle* reporter found that floor a scene of carnage, with charred bodies and body parts piled on desks. One body from that office was found down on a seventy-second-floor deck; he had either jumped or been blown out a window.

⌒

Fritz Kuhn was brought to Ellis Island in September, put on a ship, and deported. When he arrived in West Germany he was jailed again, and he would remain behind bars very nearly until his death in 1951.

Preparations for the Nuremberg war crime trials of Nazi leaders were well under way by September. Several New Yorkers in addition to Mickey Marcus played key roles. The legal approach adopted by the prosecutors came from Lieutenant Colonel Murray C. Bernays, a New York lawyer who was serving in the army's office of the chief of staff in Washington. He was born Murray Cohen in Lithuania, came with his parents to New York in 1900, and studied law at Harvard, Columbia, and Fordham. In 1917 he married Hella Bernays, a New York–born niece of Sigmund Freud. Because she wanted to preserve her family name, Murray agreed to change his surname to Bernays. It made for a small article in the *Times*, "Bridegroom Takes Name of His Bride." He went off to serve in the first world war and returned to cofound a prosperous law firm.

In July 1943 he was back in uniform, sitting behind a desk in Washington and collecting evidence of SS crimes against American POWs, when his friend Sam Rosenman asked him to consider how to prosecute Nazi leaders after the war. Churchill argued they should simply be shot on sight, but Roosevelt and Stalin wanted show trials. Bernays developed the theory that the Nazis should be handled like a criminal organization and tried on conspiracy charges. Convicting the organization of conspiracy to commit war crimes would "serve as prima facie proof of the guilt" of individual members. Bernays presented this argument to Henry Stimson, who liked it well enough that it came to be known as the Stimson Plan.

Early in April 1945, FDR had sent Rosenman to London to get the British on board; he was still in London when Roosevelt died. Truman agreed there should be a trial and appointed the Supreme Court justice Robert Jackson to head the prosecution.

Jackson brought in William Donovan. As a small-town lawyer in Buffalo and a faithful Roosevelt Democrat, Jackson had long known and not always gotten along with the high-flying Wall Street Republican. Yet Donovan commanded mountains of evidence the OSS had been collecting since as early as 1942, and he had considerable experience as a trial lawyer as well. So Jackson took a chance on Wild Bill. Donovan would bring 172 OSS staffers onto the team with him.

The Soviets wanted to hold the trials in Berlin, which they controlled. The Americans and British wanted a site outside the Soviet sector. Donovan and his OSS team suggested the Bavarian city of Nuremberg (Nürnberg), the symbolic heart of the Nazi regime, where Hitler had staged his most impressive rallies, captured by Leni Riefenstahl in her film *Triumph of the Will.* Donovan and Jackson flew there in June 1945 to inspect it. Much of the city had been bombed to a lunar landscape of craters and rubble, and hundreds or even thousands of corpses still lay under the ruins, filling the air with a hideous stench. But the large Palace of Justice, a complex of courtrooms and jail cells, still stood. The British and Soviets approved.

If there was going to be a show trial, with the whole world watching, it needed an appropriately grim but grand stage setting. The OSS Visual Presentation Branch was brought in. The courtroom that was created elevated the judges in a row, gazing down at the defendants across the room, with the legal teams between them. A large screen covered one wall for projection of OSS-prepared charts and films of Nazi crimes. Stark and dramatic as a set for a Wagner opera, it was the Presentation Branch's final project, though the courtroom for the 1946 war crime trials of Japanese leaders would be an almost exact replica.

One of Jackson's assistants at Nuremberg was Murray Gurfein, who had helped the navy with Operation Underworld. To direct the pretrial interrogations of the twenty-four Nazi leaders and supporters, Jackson called on John Harlan Amen. In August, Amen began the interrogation of the leading figure among the defendants, Hermann Göring. In nearly three dozen sessions they faced off across a plain table in a bare cell. Amen sat in shadow, with a bright light in Göring's eyes. Amen repeatedly gave Göring the traditional gangbuster third degree, but the shrewd, portly Nazi remained evasive and supercilious.

William Donovan thought he could do better. In October, without Amen's consent, he began his own series of meetings with Göring, more negotiation than interrogation, trying to coax a confession out of him. As he often did, Donovan had an ulterior motive. In September, he had flown to Washington to be told face-to-face by President Truman that the OSS was finished and he had ten days to clear out his desk. For Donovan, who had been dreaming up grandiose plans for his agency in the postwar world, it was a steep fall from grace. He saw Nuremberg as a chance to redeem himself. Besides intruding on Amen's interrogations, he lobbied Jackson for a role in the courtroom as the chief prosecutor, even as he sharply criticized Jackson's preparations for the trial. By November he had managed to turn Jackson totally against him. Jackson forced his resignation from the team.

Donovan never fully recovered from those two falls of the autumn of 1945. Bitter and shut out of world politics, he would return to his Wall Street law firm. In 1953 President Eisenhower gave him a minor posting as ambassador to Thailand, but he resigned in just under a year. His physical and mental health deteriorated in the following years, and he died, aged seventy-six, suffering dementia, at Walter Reed Army Medical Center in 1959.

CHAPTER 49

To Trinity and Beyond

Despite Germany's surrender in May, Truman's government never gave serious consideration to ending the atomic bomb project. The first bomb was almost ready to test, and Japan was still at war.

Oppenheimer, General Groves, and company conducted that first A-bomb test in predawn darkness on July 16, 1945, at the Alamogordo Army Air Field (renamed Holloman Air Force Base after the war). It was a flat, secluded spot in a desolate stretch of desert presciently named by the conquistadors Jornada del Muerto, Journey of the Dead (or Dead Man's Journey). Oppenheimer code-named the test Trinity, from a religious sonnet by John Donne that begins, "Batter my heart, three-person'd God." The site was called Zero or Ground Zero.

More than five hundred scientists, technicians, officers, and GIs were at the site. Only one journalist was allowed to observe: William Laurence, science writer for the *New York Times*.

Back in April, General Groves had privately communicated with Arthur Sulzberger, asking him to release Laurence for a top secret war assignment. Shortly, Laurence arrived at Los Alamos to observe and document the final stages of developing the bombs—not for the *Times* but for the War Department. Sulzberger agreed that nothing Laurence wrote would appear in public until the government had cleared it for viewing. He further agreed that whatever the *Times* did eventually print would be distributed free to other newspapers. This made the *New York Times* the world's first source for insider information on the atomic bomb—and, as it turned out, the government's principal conduit for disseminating propaganda and even outright lies about it. (One other journalist, Drew Pearson, the syndicated columnist in Washington, learned what was going on with the bomb. He voluntarily kept the government's secret but couldn't resist dropping a broad hint in his radio show a week before Hiroshima.)

In Laurence, Groves had once again picked exactly the right man for the job. Laurence was born Leib Wolf Siew in Lithuania in 1888, in a shtetl where he studied the Talmud and learned to read English, German, and Russian. At seventeen, he avoided conscription into the czar's hated army by hiding in a pickle barrel that was shipped to Germany. When he sailed into the New York harbor in 1905 the only English he knew was the Shakespeare he'd read. He went on to Harvard Law, renaming himself William for Shakespeare, Leonard for Leonardo da Vinci, and Laurence for a street he lived on. In the mid-1920s he came to New York City to write for the *World*, and in 1930 the *Times* hired him as the first science writer in an American newspaper. That June he wrote a full-page article, "The Quest of Science for an Atomic Energy," a full eight years before the first atom was split. From then on he was an enthusiastic and awestruck booster for the potential of atomic energy. In the winter of 1939 he was as excited as any physicist to hear that nuclear fission had been achieved. He wrote numerous articles that year and into the spring of 1940 about the atom-smashing that Fermi and others were doing. Then the government clamped the lid on press about atomic research. Laurence wouldn't write about it again in the *Times* until after Nagasaki.

Laurence's exclusive, top secret assignment inside the Manhattan Project—his "119 days behind the atomic curtain," he called it—was a dream job for a man who'd been fascinated with atomic power since it was only theory. He happily wrote reports for Washington and even press releases for Groves, "in effect functioning as the Manhattan Project's public-relations man," as the historian Paul Boyer put it. It was a role he'd continue even when he was back at the *Times* after the war ended.

The bomb they tested at Trinity was the plutonium one. Observers used sheets of welders' darkened glass to protect their eyes from the expected brightness of the blast. Reasoning that it wasn't the brightness of the flash that could damage the eye but the ultraviolet light, Richard Feynman "got behind a truck windshield, because the ultraviolet can't go through glass, so that would be safe, and so I could *see* the damn thing...I'm probably the only guy who saw it with the human eye." In fact, one or two others took the same risk.

Ted Hall and Klaus Fuchs were there. David Greenglass was not. He slept in. Years later, he'd tell Sam Roberts he figured it would either go off or it wouldn't, and that he'd find out either way.

William Laurence's article about Trinity, not published in the *Times* until September 26, 1945, was reverential. "The Atomic Age began at exactly 5:30 Mountain War Time on the morning of July 16, 1945," Laurence commenced. He went on to rhapsodize about it as a "great moment in history, ranking with the moment in the long ago when man first put fire to work for him and started on his march to civilization." He described the explosion as "a burst of flame such as had never before been seen on this planet, illuminating earth and sky for a brief span that seemed eternal," and the roar "like the grand finale of a mighty symphony," "as if the earth had spoken and the suddenly iridescent clouds and sky had joined in one mighty affirmative answer. Atomic energy—yes." Afterward, he wrote, "One felt as though he had been privileged to witness the Birth of the World—to be present at the moment of Creation when the Lord said: Let there be light." In this very long article, he scarcely mentioned that it was also a moment of destruction, and he made only a fleeting, offhand reference to radioactivity.

Because no one knew how big the Trinity explosion was going to be, Groves had Laurence write four alternate press releases in advance, depending on what the sparse population around Alamogordo might experience, from a loud bang with no damage to a catastrophic explosion with damage and lives lost. All versions lied, saying that the explosion was caused by an accident in a large cache of traditional ammunition on the base. Therefore there was no need to mention the possibility of radioactive fallout.

President Truman was in Germany for the Potsdam Conference when he was told that Trinity had gone off successfully. He waited a week before telling Stalin that the United States now had a weapon "of unusual destructive force." He was bemused when Stalin merely nodded and thanked him. Of course Stalin already knew all about the bomb.

⌒

The bombing of Nagasaki on August 9 was followed by what the *Times* would characterize as "five days of waiting, of rumor, intimation, fact, distortion—five agonizing days" when it was not yet clear that Japan would surrender. All morning and afternoon of Tuesday, August 14, a crowd built in Times Square. Some milled around, alert to every rumor. Others stood under the Zipper, waiting and watching. Still others got the drinking and partying started early.

Then, at 7:03 p.m., the Zipper flashed: "Official—Truman Announces Japanese Surrender."

The crowd, which was estimated at over a million, exploded into deafening cheers. More people raced into the area, boosting the crowd to an estimated two million. The biggest, loudest, most raucous street party New York had ever seen went on all night. The partying on VE Day back in May, jubilant as it was, had been tempered by Roosevelt's recent death and the awareness that the war in the Pacific was still on. Now people totally let loose. Elsewhere around the city, "Greenwich Village was a madhouse," Hirohito was hung in effigy from Bronx streetlamps, they did a dragon procession in Chinatown, there were impromptu parades in the other boroughs, and on the Lower East Side "juke boxes were hauled onto the sidewalks to furnish music for jitterbug dancing in the streets." After partying until dawn, the crowds rested, then restarted the festivities, a bit more subdued and many no doubt hungover, on Wednesday afternoon. Some restaurants and bars decided to close until the revelry died down, while others were mobbed. Subway and bus service were reduced on Wednesday because there were so many absentees. Four people around the city died in the merrymaking, including a soldier who fell out a window in Brooklyn. Almost nine hundred others did themselves some injury, the *Times* reported, "130 of them requiring hospitalization." More than a hundred false fire alarms were turned in and seventy-eight cars were stolen.

During the afternoon, as the crowds and excitement mounted, every newspaper and magazine in the city sent photographers to Times Square. *Life*'s Alfred Eisenstaedt was one of them. He'd spent the war documenting the home front. Now he sought one image to symbolize war's end. On Broadway he saw a sailor grab a slim brunette nurse. The sailor wrapped her in an aggressive hug, bent her crooked, and planted a big kiss on her lips. People around them grinned. There were a lot of strangers kissing that day. Eisenstaedt snapped four quick shots. Nearby, a navy lieutenant named Victor Jorgensen also shot the couple. Then they all moved on, scattered in the swirl.

Jorgensen's photo ran in the *New York Times* the next day. Eisenstaedt's took up all of page 27 of the August 27 *Life*. Neither attracted much comment at first. But over the years, as *Life* kept reprinting Eisenstaedt's shot, it became one of the most widely recognized images of the war era, and trying to determine the identity of the sailor and the nurse would become a national pastime. Neither Eisenstaedt nor Jorgensen had tried to meet the couple or get their names. It was street photography, quick and impromptu. As the decades passed, various men and women would come forward to claim that they were the sailor and the nurse. Some seemed more credible than others.

In 2012 the Naval Institute Press in Annapolis published *The Kissing Sailor*, in which coauthors Lawrence Verria and George Galdorisi claimed to solve the mystery. The sailor, they wrote, was George Mendonsa, son of a Portuguese fisherman from Rhode Island. He was on his last day of leave in New York on August 14, 1945, got a little drunk, and grabbed a pretty young woman for a celebratory kiss. The young woman, they said, was Greta Zimmer, a Jewish refugee from Austria, and not a nurse. Sent to America by her parents to escape the Nazis in 1939, she lived with relatives in New York, went to the Central Needle Trades High School, volunteered as an air raid warden, and found a job as a dental assistant in an office a few blocks from Times Square. At lunchtime on August 14, wearing her dental assistant's whites, she walked over to Times Square to see what was going on and found herself in the iconic embrace. *The Kissing Sailor* made a compelling but not quite conclusive case, and doubts and counterclaims remain.

⌒

Rosie the Riveter's cheers and tears were as heartfelt as anyone's on VJ Day. But for the majority of women war workers the taste of victory was bittersweet. Four out of five were hoping to keep their new jobs, but every woman knew she was legally required by the Veterans' Preference Act to step aside if a man returning from the war wanted it. In addition, as the economy shifted back to peacetime production, many wartime jobs might disappear altogether.

At the Brooklyn Navy Yard, there were sixty-nine thousand workers on VJ Day. A year later there were just under fifteen thousand. The firings had started immediately. Women and black workers were the first to be let go. Even the flag loft, the one traditional spot for women in the yard, was all male by 1946.

It was the same all over the city and country. "Despite some ineffectual protests from laid-off workers," Maureen Honey reported in *Creating Rosie the Riveter*, "women found themselves at the end of the war in nearly the same discriminatory situation they had faced prior to Pearl Harbor." Half the women who had been employed in higher-paying durable goods industries during the war lost those jobs in the year after VJ Day. Half a million women in "craftsmen and foremen" positions were quickly let go.

More women continued to find work out of the home in the postwar years than had before the war, but they also found themselves channeled back into traditional "woman's work." "By April 1947," Honey writes, "the prewar employment pattern had been reestablished and most employed women were clerical workers, operatives, domestics, and service workers."

When the signing of the Japanese surrender documents took place on September 2, 1945, it was on the deck of the USS *Missouri*, launched at the Brooklyn Navy Yard in 1944, produced by Rosies working alongside males.

⌒

Polls conducted in the fall of 1945 indicated that more than 80 percent of Americans supported the decision to use the atom bombs on Japan. They believed Truman when he said that one hundred thousand deaths from the bombings prevented the million who would have died if the United States had been forced to invade. Of the major opinion-shaping newspaper columnists, Dorothy Thompson was virtually alone in even hinting at a slight moral doubt.

One reason for the widely positive responses was that even after Laurence's "atomic curtain" was parted the government continued carefully censoring and stage-managing what Americans read and heard about atomic weapons. There was a special effort to deny the effects or even the existence of radioactive fallout from the explosions. The government encouraged Americans to think of the atomic bomb as just a bigger version of conventional explosives, not a new terror weapon that spread lingering death and disease. This made it easier for Americans both to accept that the bombings in Japan were justified and to acquiesce to the future testing, on American soil, that the government planned to conduct. Laurence and the *New York Times*, the "paper of record," were major collaborators in this deception. The *Times* ran 132 bomb-related items in the first five days after Hiroshima. Only one of them mentioned the danger of radioactivity—and only to refute it.

In 1946 a few magazines would begin running stories of people who had survived the bombings, giving Americans for the first time a personal idea of what the devastation had been like—and the lingering effects of radiation. The fullest account would appear more than a year after the bombings, taking up the entire August 31, 1946, issue of the *New Yorker*: John Hersey's "Hiroshima."

Hersey, like Henry Luce, was born in China to Christian missionaries. He was ten when the family moved to New York in 1924. He started writing for Luce at *Time* and *Life* in 1936. During the war he covered both the Pacific and European theaters, and he also wrote the 1944 novel *A Bell for Adano* about GIs occupying a Sicilian town, which won him a Pulitzer. He went to Hiroshima a couple of months after the bombing and began interviewing survivors, six of whom he featured in his thirty-thousand-word article. After the years of propaganda, Hersey's portraits of his subjects—two doctors, a tailor's widow, a female factory clerk, a Methodist minister (all Japanese), and a German Jesuit priest—were startlingly understated, almost deadpan. He simply recorded in reportorial detail their memories of that day and how they had been living since. The impact was in the details: naked people wandering the streets in a daze, with the patterns of the suspenders or flowery kimonos they'd been wearing blazed into their skin; people trapped in rubble, calling out with unfailing Japanese politeness, "Help, if you please!"; a group of soldiers in a "nightmarish state: their faces were wholly burned, their eye sockets were hollow, the fluid from their melted eyes had run down their cheeks."

Within two weeks of the blast, four of Hersey's six interviewees began showing symptoms of the radiation sickness that the American government, Oppenheimer, and the *New York Times* had all denied. So did many other people—hair falling out, wounds not healing, sterility, miscarriages.

The "Hiroshima" issue of the *New Yorker* quickly sold out, and the magazine took requests for reprints from around the globe. ABC had the piece read on air, word for word, in four half-hour installments. Alfred A. Knopf published it as a book, which went on to sell millions of copies.

PART FOUR

The Big Bonanza

New York is the biggest, richest city the world has ever seen.

—Time *(1948)*

It is a miracle that New York works at all. The whole thing is implausible.

—E. B. White, "Here Is New York" (1949)

CHAPTER 50

The Wonder City

The period from 1945 into the 1960s was New York City's twentieth-century apex. In 1948, to mark the fiftieth anniversary of the consolidation of the five boroughs into one metropolis, *Time* ran a paean titled "New York: The Big Bonanza." (The "Big Bonanza" was what people called the immense Virginia City silver lode in the 1860s and '70s. It was also the title of a 1944 Hollywood western.)

> In the boom year, 1948, New York is the biggest, richest city the world has ever seen. Almost eight million people live in its boroughs, almost 13 million in its metropolitan area—at least three million more than in Greater London. Its wealth is incalculable. Its physical assets are worth as much as all the real estate in the eleven western states. Its 157 banks and 94 insurance companies handle treasures which would ransom an army of maharajas. It is the world's greatest port, the world's greatest tourist attraction, the world's greatest manufacturing city and the world's greatest marketplace.

Time was not exaggerating. Postwar New York was "the de facto world capital of art, architecture, literature, medical research, finance, advertising, philanthropy, and that befuddling new medium, television," the historiographer Kevin Baker writes. "It was still the country's—and the world's—greatest manufacturing center, with over one million workers toiling in 40,000 factories. It was the capital of both retail and wholesale, where one-fifth of all of the nation's wholesale transactions took place. Forty percent of everything imported to America came through its waterfront, and it housed the headquarters of 135 Fortune 500 companies."

Unlike so many of the world's great cities, New York emerged from the war entirely unscathed. Large sections of London, Berlin, Tokyo, Moscow, Leningrad, Rome, Paris, and many other cities lay in ruins. (Paris had avoided destruction by the Germans when France capitulated so early in the war, and again when German officers ignored Hitler's directive to burn it to the ground as they evacuated in 1944. But the Allies bombed large areas of its industrial outskirts that year.) New York was pristine, all lights blazing, all shops and offices and bars and restaurants open for business.

Although investing on Wall Street lagged a bit behind the boom, the rest of New York's business sector surged. The big corporations, like ITT, grew bigger still, consolidating other companies into mammoth conglomerates. They started building new monuments to themselves, soaring glass and steel towers that burst up like stalagmites in midtown Manhattan.

The garment industry hummed, the waterfront bustled. It was a golden age on Madison Avenue as well. Industry easily shifted back from wartime production to consumer goods—cars and refrigerators, televisions and bicycles, plus new products that came out of technologies developed for war, such as deodorant in aerosol spray cans, synthetic detergents, and anything that could be made out of or packed in plastic. Consumers, who had stored up tremendous reserves of spending money during the war years, went on a wild and sustained shopping spree. Because of the advertising agencies' ingenious shift to propaganda, ad spending had increased somewhat during the war; it now shot up 100 percent in just the five years from 1945 to 1950.

Already the most diverse city in the world, New York grew more so. Its black community expanded in the postwar years to three-quarters of a million people. And a new group of immigrants arrived: Puerto Ricans, whose numbers approached two hundred thousand by 1950. They began to transform neighborhoods as upwardly mobile and suburb-bound groups, such as the Italians, moved out.

New York had long been the nation's nerve center of all media, entertainment, news. Now it was the world's intellectual and art capital as well. The cream of European academic and creative life had fled to New York in the 1930s and war years: Kurt Weill, Lotte Lenya, Hannah Arendt, Vladimir Nabokov, W. H. Auden, Christopher Isherwood, Max Ernst, Marcel Duchamp, Piet Mondrian, André Breton, Salvador Dalí, Yves Tanguy, André Masson, Fernand Léger, Claude Lévi-Strauss, Erich Fromm, Wilhelm Reich, Lisette Model... the list goes on and on. Their collective impact on New York's culture was incalculable. Some of them taught at the New School, where returning veterans—a good number of whom would never have gone to college previously—could take classes for free, thanks to the GI Bill.

When Peggy Guggenheim opened her Art of This Century gallery on West 57th Street in 1942, it was in effect the gallery-in-exile for European modern art. In the postwar years, a generation of New York artists who had been influenced and inspired by the exiles created the first avant-garde art movement in America, including what Robert Coates offhandedly named the Abstract Expressionist movement in a 1946 *New Yorker* review of Hans Hofmann's paintings. (He wrote that Hofmann, who had come to New York in 1932, was "one of the most uncompromising representatives of what some people call the spatter-and-daub school of painting and I, more politely, have christened abstract [*sic*] Expressionism.") By the 1950s New York had succeeded Paris as the modern art capital of the Western world. Across the board, the city became an intense laboratory for artistic experimentation in theater, music, literature, dance, photography, and film, and for the next quarter of a century the world looked to New York to lead the way. It was also the powerhouse of more mainstream and pop culture pursuits. The Brill Building and Broadway, the national TV and radio networks, the nightclubs and the fashion industry all added to the city's now unrivaled reputation as the fountain of all that was fun, new, stylish.

Politically, the city no longer exerted quite the influence in the White House it had for FDR's twelve years there. But then again it sent more representatives to Congress in 1945 than the state of California did. And if it was no longer the shadow capital of the United States, when it lured the United Nations headquarters to Manhattan it became, by unanimous consent, something more: the capital of the world.

A 1945 newsreel called it "The Wonder City." In 1947, the British writer J. B. Priestley offered the opinion that the "glittering cosmopolis belongs to the world, if the world does not belong to it." (No unalloyed fan, he also called New York "Nineveh and Babylon piled on Imperial Rome.") In his ubiquitously cited 1949 essay "Here Is New York" for the magazine *Holiday*, E. B. White wrote that "the city makes up for its hazards and its deficiencies by supplying its citizens with massive doses of a supplementary vitamin—the sense of belonging to something unique, cosmopolitan, mighty and unparalleled." One European visitor called New York simply the "capital of everything."

It would not last forever. Starting in the 1960s and accelerating in the 1970s, factors external and internal would send the city into a long, deep decline. But from the end of the war until then, New York City reigned supreme, the unchallenged queen of the world.

⌒

Even at its postwar height it was not a problem-free city by any means. The mob roared back with everyone else, ensuring decades more of violence, corruption, and heroin addiction. Juvenile delinquency was still a great worry. Black veterans came home to find racial inequalities as entrenched as ever, while black defense workers learned how ephemeral their wartime advances had been. Union and municipal workers went on crippling strikes. There were lingering shortages of some basics, including telephones and winter coal. The subway system was dangerously rickety. Adding a million new residents just as the city's veterans came home created a severe housing crisis. The municipal budget was a mess.

The Wonder City elected a new mayor in the fall of 1945 to deal with it all. In January of that year, John Pehle had stepped down as director of the War Refugee Board, and Roosevelt appointed William O'Dwyer to replace him. O'Dwyer filled that role until Germany surrendered in May, then returned to a hero's welcome in Brooklyn, where his job as DA was waiting for him. When La Guardia announced that same month that he wouldn't seek reelection, O'Dwyer announced his candidacy for the Democratic nomination.

Although his great popularity seemed to make him a shoo-in, he committed one tactical error. In August, he resigned as Brooklyn DA, and Governor Dewey leapt at the chance to appoint a Republican as interim DA, a talented Brooklyn lawyer named George Beldock. Beldock went for O'Dwyer's head. He immediately impaneled a grand jury to dredge up O'Dwyer's suspicious handling of Reles and Anastasia and other questionable actions. Although Beldock's grand jury handed up a preelection presentment charging O'Dwyer and his office with "gross laxity, inefficiency and maladministration," the larger implications of corruption and outright collusion with the mob did not stick. The war was over, O'Dwyer was one of its heroes, and Beldock's fulminating looked calculated and partisan. O'Dwyer won in a sweeping Democratic landslide.

Beldock meanwhile lost the election for Brooklyn DA to his Democratic opponent Miles McDonald. He did not go out without a fight. After the elections, his grand jury handed down a far more blistering presentment, calling O'Dwyer's failure to prosecute Anastasia "revolting" and a "shocking" abuse of the public trust. Mayor-elect O'Dwyer waved it off as political grandstanding, and a Democratic Brooklyn judge conveniently had the presentment stricken and expunged from the record. O'Dwyer had successfully navigated those shoals but he seemed to intuit that his past was not entirely done haunting him.

Mayor O'Dwyer turned his attention first to fixing the city's crumbling infrastructure and finding homes for returning vets and their families. More than three million New Yorkers rode the subway every morning, and again every night, every day but Sunday, and its maintenance and repair had been neglected out of fiscal necessity through the Depression and war years. Some of the city's hospitals and other public buildings hadn't seen a lick of paint or roofing tar in the same period and had grown shamefully dilapidated. Veterans meanwhile were living more like war refugees than war heroes. Housing was so short that families doubled or tripled up in apartments, or wandered from hotel to hotel, or packed the Ys. Some people slept in the subways or Turkish baths.

The city's master planner and builder had little interest in such mundane problems. The day after O'Dwyer was elected, Robert Moses presented him with a $1.5 billion proposal for building more of what he really liked building—highways, bridges, and tunnels. Pressed to come up with some solution to the housing crisis, Moses's response was to set up hundreds of military surplus Quonset huts on empty lots strung around Brooklyn and Queens and put veterans and their families in them. They were cold in winter, leaked when it rained, and far more amenable to barracks life than family life. Up the Hudson in Rockland County, Camp Shanks, which had been the largest staging area for the New York Port of Embarkation, was renamed Shanks Village and also housed vets' families in Quonsets.

In a few years, some New York City vets would be able to use the GI Bill to buy homes in sprawling new suburbs, notably Levittown, out on Long Island, begun in 1947. Some vets, but not black ones: Levittown was by design and deed whites-only. In 1953, Levittown's seventy thousand residents represented the largest community in the country without a single black person living among them. After many court battles the first black couple would move there in 1957.

Black vets didn't have to trek out to Long Island to face housing discrimination. There was a classic example right in Manhattan. In 1943 La Guardia had announced Robert Moses's plan to create Stuyvesant Town, a massive apartment complex on the east side above 14th Street. Moses used eminent domain to clear away the gas tanks that gave the area its name, the Gas House District, along with blocks of old town houses and storefronts. Metropolitan Life Insurance partnered with the city to build the complex. There was one stipulation: Met Life intended to exclude blacks. "Negroes and whites don't mix," Met Life's chairman Frederick Ecker flatly declared. The argument was that integrating the housing would mean trouble and depress property values all around it.

Moses, never inclined to let social or moral quibbles get in the way of his plans, agreed. So did the *New York Times* and *Herald Tribune*. La Guardia, who was no racist but foresaw clearly the city's looming housing crisis, acquiesced.

Every liberal organization in the city expressed dismay and outrage, frequently using the terms "fascist" and "Hitlerian." Adam Clayton Powell Jr. addressed a mass rally at Madison Square Garden, calling for the mayor's impeachment, to wild applause. The plan went through, and the first buildings opened in 1947. Lawsuits, including ones brought by black veterans, would pressure Met Life into allowing a few black families to rent in the complex in 1950, but it would remain almost entirely white through the 1960s.

To address the subway problem, O'Dwyer was forced to propose something that struck New Yorkers as downright sacrilegious: raising the fare from five cents to ten. New Yorkers had cherished the nickel subway ride as an inalienable birthright since 1904. In 1948, facing a massive budget deficit plus wage demands from the transit workers' CIO union, O'Dwyer bit the bullet and doubled the fare.

Despite that insult, New Yorkers liked O'Dwyer. After twelve years of the frenetic, splenetic La Guardia, his cheery, smiling-Irish-eyes manner was calming. They called him Bill-O. *Time* put him on the cover of the "Big Bonanza" issue. He was handily reelected in November 1949, when one of his opponents was Vito Marcantonio.

It was Bill-O's last easy victory. The following month, Brooklyn DA McDonald started a grand jury probe into the widespread practice of the borough's police shaking down big gambling operations for protection payoffs. In July 1950, one precinct captain under suspicion shot himself in the head with his service revolver. Six thousand officers attended his funeral, as did Mayor O'Dwyer, who denounced McDonald as a homegrown Hitler conducting a witch hunt.

If O'Dwyer was hoping to quash McDonald's investigation he failed. A month later, O'Dwyer resigned the office of mayor. He claimed poor health, which had some legitimacy, but the more obvious motive was fear that any probe of corruption in Brooklyn would inevitably lead once more to him. Truman appointed him ambassador to Mexico. He got a ticker-tape sendoff on lower Broadway and left the country, hoping to leave his troubles behind him.

⁀

In 1946, former mayor Fiorello La Guardia got a new job. At President Truman's request, he took over directing the United Nations Relief and Rehabilitation Administration (UNRRA) from former governor Herbert Lehman, who had run it since its start. Despite its name, the UNRRA predated the founding of the United Nations. FDR had created it in the fall of 1943, got forty-three other nations to sign on, and asked his old comrade Lehman, who left the governor's mansion at the end of 1942, to run it. Roosevelt saw it as a training program in international cooperation for the full UN to come later.

At the beginning its goal was to provide war victims with food, shelter, medicine, and other necessities. By the time La Guardia took charge, resettling the world's millions of war refugees was its major focus. For La Guardia, there was a personal aspect to this: Gemma was one of them.

Because she was his sister, when the Nazis arrested Gemma in 1944 they had at first considered executing her, then decided it was better to keep her alive as a possible bargaining chip should the war continue to go badly for them. On April 15, 1945, three days after FDR's death, they transferred her to the Gestapo prison in Berlin. In May, Russian troops opened the prison. Shortly after, she spoke with her brother by telephone for the first time in twenty years, asking him to help her get to America. He was clipped and officious with her, telling her she had to wait her turn, "for I won't make any exceptions." She was still waiting when he took over at the UNRRA in 1946, which only made him even more of a stickler. That year she learned that her husband had been beaten to death at Mauthausen.

It wasn't until May 1947 that she finally arrived in New York City. She didn't have much time with her brother. He had been diagnosed with cancer, and he died on September 20, 1947. Close to ten thousand mourners packed the Cathedral of Saint John the Divine for his funeral. They ranged from foreign diplomats to John D. Rockefeller Jr.; some of La Guardia's old Tammany enemies; and Mrs. Laura Stockton, who had been his first elementary school teacher in Prescott, Arizona. He was buried at Woodlawn Cemetery in the Bronx.

Gemma lived on in the apartment her brother had arranged for her in Queensbridge Houses, a large public housing complex in Long Island City where he had laid the cornerstone in 1939. In 1961 her memoirs, *My Story*, came out. She died the next year.

⁓

When the war ended, the Bergson Group refocused efforts on the creation of a Jewish homeland. This brought them into direct conflict with the British authorities in Palestine, who set up a naval blockade to keep boatloads of Jewish "displaced persons" from entering. In 1946, while Bergson went to Paris to set up a Hebrew government-in-exile, Ben Hecht wrote another stage pageant, *A Flag Is Born*, with music again by Kurt Weill. Playing war refugees trying to enter Palestine were Paul Muni and a twenty-two-year-old whom Stella Adler admired, Marlon Brando. It packed houses on Broadway and then toured. The press in England denounced it as "the most virulent anti-British play ever staged in the United States." "Britain may be able to patrol the Mediterranean," Hecht replied, "but she cannot patrol Broadway."

Bergson, Hecht and the others used proceeds from the play to buy a war surplus ship. They had it refitted in Brooklyn's Gowanus Canal and rechristened it the SS *Ben Hecht*. FDR's son Elliott Roosevelt volunteered to captain it, but Eleanor nixed that. Most of the nineteen crewmen were volunteers from Brooklyn, both Jews and Gentiles. In 1947 the *Ben Hecht* sailed to southern France, picked up six hundred displaced Jews, and was carrying them to Palestine when it was seized by the British. The refugees and the crew were imprisoned. Deeply embarrassed by the ensuing international headlines, the British released the crew after a few weeks. They returned to a heroes' welcome in New York, with a ceremony at City Hall followed by a grand banquet thrown by Hecht. As Irgun attacks on the British increased, Hecht wrote his most incendiary ad yet, "Letter to the Terrorists of Palestine," cheering them on. The *Times* refused to run it but the *Tribune* and liberal *Post* did. Hecht and his works were banned in England.

Hillel Kook dropped his Peter Bergson pseudonym and entered the new state of Israel in 1948. He joined the first Knesset but, still a gadfly and provocateur, was soon ousted. He went to his grave in 2001 still blaming Rabbi Wise (who had died in 1949, aged seventy-five) and mainstream American Jews for the deaths of millions.

CHAPTER 51

Treason on Trial

In August 1948, in Room 1400 of the Commodore Hotel near Grand Central, a bizarre confrontation took place between Alger Hiss and Whittaker Chambers. The suave, self-controlled persona that Hiss had been showing the world for decades cracked, and a desperate, fearful man showed through. An ambitious young congressman named Richard Nixon was in the room to take note of it. Nixon had arranged the meeting, but its roots went back to the last days of the war, and to Elizabeth Bentley.

Jacob Golos's death in 1943 had deeply shocked and depressed Bentley. She fell to drinking and became a problem for her Soviet handlers. In 1945, summoned to Moscow, she had been fearful, as Chambers had once been, that the trip to Moscow could be her last. She gave herself up to the FBI in August, just as the war was ending. It took several interviews over several months for them to take her seriously as she reeled off some three dozen names of wartime contacts in the federal government.

One of them was Alger Hiss, though she initially remembered him as "Eugene" Hiss. All through the war, Hiss had continued to feed intelligence to the Soviets as he rose up the ranks at State. In 1944 he was the executive secretary of the Dumbarton Oaks international conference that laid out the plans for the United Nations. High-level documents from him and a few other agents gave Stalin a clear idea in advance of the postwar plans FDR and Churchill would present at the Yalta Conference in February 1945, which Hiss attended. In April 1945 Hiss presided over the UN charter conference in San Francisco as temporary secretary-general, then sailed with the U.S. delegates to London for General Assembly meetings.

By the spring of 1946, aware that the FBI was keeping tabs on him, Hiss resigned his State Department position and moved back to New

York City in 1947 to be president of the Carnegie Endowment for International Peace, a prestigious think tank where John Foster Dulles chaired the board. It was excellent cover, but the FBI continued fattening its file on him.

It took until the autumn of 1947 for the government to feel it had gathered enough information to convene a federal grand jury in Manhattan to hear Bentley's testimony. The closed-door hearings went on into 1948, but Bentley made such a poor impression on the jurors that no indictments resulted. Bentley, her life falling apart, took a new tack. She went public, speaking to reporters at the *World-Telegram*, which ran a sensational front-page story in July 1948, "Red Ring Bared by Blond [*sic*] Queen."

That piqued the interest of the House Un-American Activities Committee. Now dominated by Republicans, HUAC was actively seeking proof that the Democrats FDR and Truman had allowed Communists to infiltrate the federal government. They called Bentley in and she repeated in public what she'd been saying in private until then.

The committee summoned William Remington to testify. While others invoked the Fifth Amendment, Remington admitted knowing Bentley but categorically denied all her charges against him.

Next, HUAC subpoenaed Whittaker Chambers. He was now a highly respected senior editor at Time-Life, a stout cold warrior with extremely anticommunist opinions. All the while, he continued to worry that the Soviets wanted him dead. He bought a small farm in Westminster, Maryland, as a safe house for himself and his family. He carried a pistol at all times and moved every night from one hotel to another when he was in Manhattan. He got around the city by a laborious process of taking taxis and the subway in various directions to shake tails, real or imagined. His Time-Life colleagues believed him psychotically paranoid, but he was such a fine writer and editor they shrugged it off.

Chambers was loath, with good reason, to air his past not just as a Communist but as a Communist *spy*. But he could not ignore the HUAC subpoena. He reluctantly appeared and named Alger Hiss as one of the Soviet agents he'd run in the 1930s.

Hiss and his family were living in Greenwich Village at the time. He fired off an outraged telegram, categorically denying knowing Chambers and asking the opportunity to appear before the committee, who were only too happy to grant his request. "I am not and never have been a member of the Communist Party," he said in his opening statement. "The statements made about me by Mr. Chambers are complete fabrications." Yet by the end of his testimony he had appeared cagey and evasive in ways that roused the suspicion of the most junior member of the committee—freshman congressman Richard Nixon of California.

With Hiss denying ever having met Chambers, Nixon arranged for them to meet face-to-face in Room 1400 at the Commodore. Hiss started out acting extremely evasive, demanding to hear Chambers speak and even examining his teeth. Then he exploded into a rage that verged on physical violence. Nixon was convinced he had his man.

A week later, Hiss and Chambers faced off again in a televised HUAC hearing. Hiss had regained his composure and appeared trim, proper, and righteously aggrieved. The slovenly, lugubrious Chambers, clearly very uncomfortable, looked so squirmy by contrast that many people watching on TV were convinced he was mentally unstable and a liar. When Chambers then went on *Meet the Press* and named Hiss as a spy, Hiss sued for libel.

It was a fatal error. As Chambers was being deposed by Hiss's libel lawyer, he produced the manila envelope he'd left with his Brooklyn in-law back before the war. Among other documents it contained notes in Hiss's hand. Then he led a team of Nixon's investigators to a pumpkin patch on his Maryland farm, and, as their mouths dropped open, pulled five rolls of film out of a hollowed-out pumpkin. The film contained images of State Department documents from 1938. The press dubbed them the Pumpkin Papers.

All this was terribly embarrassing to Henry Luce. His star anticommunist writer had turned out to have been a Communist spy. Walter Winchell could not contain his glee. "Gee Whittaker! Time Marxes on," he crowed in one column. Under pressure from Luce, Chambers agreed to resign. Then he went out to the family home on Long Island, where his aged mother still lived, and tried to commit suicide by inhaling rat poison fumes. All he got was a terrible headache.

Brought before a grand jury in Foley Square, Hiss denied ever passing any documents to Chambers. The jury indicted him for perjury. His first perjury trial in the spring of 1949 ended in a hung jury. Retried the winter of 1950, Hiss was convicted on two counts and sentenced to five years in prison. He managed to stave off the start of that sentence until 1951.

In 1952, Whittaker Chambers's *Witness*, combining memoirs with dire warnings about the Communist threat, was a smash bestseller. In

1955, William F. Buckley Jr. started the conservative *National Review* and hired Chambers as a senior editor. He died of a heart attack on his farm in 1961.

⁀

While the Hiss trials went on, a grand jury indicted William Remington for perjury for having denied his Communist past. On the day after Christmas 1950, New York's federal district attorney Irving Saypol and his young assistant Roy Cohn brought Remington to trial at the federal courthouse. Elizabeth Bentley testified in detail about sensitive documents Remington had passed her. Nine other witnesses said he'd been a Communist. He was convicted and given the maximum five years in prison. He won on appeal, would be retried in1953, reconvicted, and sentenced to three years. To the hardcase felons in the Lewisburg federal penitentiary in Pennsylvania he was a commie and a traitor. A couple of them beat him to death in his cell in 1954.

⁀

The biggest spy trial of the century got under way at Foley Square on March 6, 1951. Two years earlier, an army intelligence program called Venona had cracked codes used by Moscow intelligence and new information on Soviet espionage in the United States came pouring out. Working with the FBI, the army identified the sender of one message from Los Alamos as Klaus Fuchs, who was back in England. He was confessing to Scotland Yard by January 1950. Among other things, he described his American courier, whom he knew as Raymond. The FBI went back to its Bentley files and identified Raymond as Harry Gold. They arrested Gold in May and he quickly confessed. It made the front page of the May 24 *Herald Tribune*, complete with photo.

Julius Rosenberg, who had continued running spies after the war, was duly alarmed. He tried to convince David and Ruth Greenglass to flee the country. David, lazy as ever, dawdled. Following up on leads provided by Gold, the FBI picked him up in his Rivington Street apartment in June. Cooperative to the point of ingratiating under questioning, David and Ruth portrayed themselves as Julius's dupes. Julius was arrested in July; when he refused to cooperate, the authorities arrested Ethel a month later. She wouldn't talk either. A grand jury was convened.

The rest of Julius's spy ring scattered. Alfred Sarant and Joel Barr defected to the Soviet Union, where they would help create the Soviet computer industry. Morton Sobell made it to Mexico before he was captured and brought back. William Perl, who was designing jet fighters in Cleveland for the NACA (later NASA), was also arrested. Testifying before the Rosenberg grand jury he denied knowing them.

The grand jury indicted Julius, Ethel, and Sobell on charges of conspiracy to commit espionage. If convicted, they could be sentenced to anything from thirty years' imprisonment to death. The evidence against Ethel was very thin, but the prosecutors—once again, U.S. attorney Irving Saypol and his assistant Roy Cohn—hoped that by threatening Ethel with death they could frighten her or Julius into a confession. It did not work. David, who had confessed and waived a trial, would be sentenced separately, and in return for his cooperation Ruth was never charged.

The trial was held in Room 107 of the federal courthouse, Judge Irving Kaufman presiding. One day while Julius was being uncooperative on the witness stand, a crowd of newsmen outside buzzed around the tall, trim figure of Alger Hiss. He had appealed his perjury convictions all the way to the Supreme Court and lost. He had now come to Foley Square to surrender himself to the authorities and be remanded to the Lewisburg prison, which he would share with Harry Gold and William Remington.

The jury found Julius and Ethel Rosenberg and Morton Sobell guilty. Judge Kaufman spent a week deliberating and soul-searching about their sentences, especially Ethel's. Though various states, including New York, had executed more than thirty women in the twentieth century, no federal judge had sentenced a woman to death in that time. Worse, she was the mother of two young boys who would be orphaned. No husband and wife team had ever been executed together. But the jury had found her just as guilty as Julius, and the winds of the Red Scare were blowing at gale force. Kaufman gave Sobell thirty years behind bars and condemned the Rosenbergs to die in the electric chair. In a separate hearing, Kaufman gave David Greenglass fifteen years.

The Rosenbergs were sent to Sing Sing. For two years they languished there, steadfastly proclaiming their innocence while their lawyer used appeals and other stratagems to stave off their executions. The Supreme Court turned down the lawyer's appeals over and over. President Eisenhower declined to grant pardons. As the final date of Friday, June 19, 1953, drew close, someone called the NYPD claiming to have hidden a bomb in Judge Kaufman's apartment building. Five thousand protesters gathered in Union Square and heard speakers denounce the "bloodthirsty" Eisenhower and praise the couple as "little people who have become giants because they refused to crawl."

It was all for naught. That Friday evening, the Rosenbergs, described in the *Times* as "stoic and tight-lipped to the end," were electrocuted.

The funeral was held that Sunday at the Jewish I. J. Morris Funeral Home on Church Avenue at Rockaway Parkway in the Brownsville neighborhood of Brooklyn. Twelve thousand mourners filed past the coffins, where four uniformed color guards stood at attention bearing American flags. During the Orthodox service, the crowd booed and hissed the aged rabbi who asked them to "bear no rancor or hatred" toward the government. They "murmured approval" when the Rosenbergs' lawyer declared that "America today is living under the heel of a military dictatorship" that had murdered the two "sweet, intelligent, gentle, cultured people." No one from the Greenglass family attended. A cortege of two hearses, three buses, and an estimated three hundred cars wended its way through Brooklyn and out to Wellwood, a Jewish cemetery farther out Long Island. Sobell's wife and W. E. B. Du Bois spoke at the gravesite as the summer sun beat down and the temperature rose toward the mid-90s.

In 1996 *Times* reporter Sam Roberts—who had seen the Rosenberg cortege as a six-year-old in Brownsville—tracked down and conducted extensive interviews with David Greenglass, who had been living under a new identity since his release from prison in 1960. In the 2000s, Roberts and others interviewed Sobell, who was in his nineties and living in the Bronx. He confessed for the first time that he had spied for Julius.

⁓

Along with Alger Hiss's appearance during Julius's testimony, there was one other spectacular distraction during the Rosenbergs' trial. On March 12 through 21, 1951, the period when David Greenglass was testifying, the Senate Committee to Investigate Crime and Interstate Commerce, chaired by Estes Kefauver of Tennessee, held televised hearings into organized crime in a room upstairs at the federal courthouse. Formed in 1950, the committee had gone on the road in January 1951, holding hearings in several major cities, fascinating and scaring the nation with its allegations that organized crime might be even more of a menace to the American way of life than Communism was, and could, "if not curbed, become the basis for a subversive movement which could wreck the very foundations of this country."

The public found the fact that the hearings were televised at least as interesting as the hearings themselves. They'd never seen anything like it. "Broadcast live during the day by five of New York's seven stations," the historian Thomas Doherty writes, "and in its entirety by DuMont affiliate WABD, the hearings became an obsession in New York... During the two-week run of the Kefauver Committee in New York, most of the city stopped to watch the riveting real-time, real-life television drama. Human interest sidebars in the tabloid press vied with each other for wild tales of metropolitan obsession: taxi drivers cruised deserted streets, housewives neglected housework, and apartment dwellers held 'Kefauver block parties.'"

On Broadway—where *Guys and Dolls* had been sweeping them in—box offices tanked. ("Kefauver Blitzes Eastern B.O.," was how the *Hollywood Reporter* put it.) Movie theaters gave in and showed the hearings on big televisions. At Fabian's Fox Theater on Flatbush Avenue, management asked an audience whether they wanted to stick with the hearings or switch them off for the scheduled movie. Four out of five voted to keep watching the hearings.

The two high points of the broadcasts were the testimonies of Frank Costello and William O'Dwyer. When Costello refused to appear on camera, Kefauver agreed that his face would not be televised, only his hands. Millions of viewers fixated on those hands. As one TV critic commented at the time, "Somehow the camera view of the headless Mr. Costello's exquisitely tailored chest, his spotless pocket handkerchief, his manicured hands nervously picking at his faultlessly-turned lapels or toying with his eyeglasses only accentuated the impression that he is indeed a sinister figure." A very unhappy and uncooperative witness, Costello ducked and dodged most questions about both his political connections and his Mafia activities, sticking to his role as just an honest businessman. Needled by the committee to name one thing he had done for his country, he drew snickers from the gallery when he grumbled, "Paid my tax."

O'Dwyer, who thought he had left his troubles behind him when he went to Mexico City in 1950, came back with great reluctance and truculence. He sparred grumpily with committee members as they grilled him about his own connections to Costello. One evening in December

1942, when O'Dwyer was still a major in the army, he had paid a visit to Costello at the Majestic. He claimed that he merely went to question Costello about a military contractor with possible ties to the mob. They spoke for fifteen minutes, he said, and when Costello denied any knowledge of the business O'Dwyer left.

Few people believed him. It seemed more likely that his actual purpose was to secure Costello's backing, and that of the Tammany leaders O'Dwyer admitted were at the apartment that evening, for his next shot at the mayor's office in 1945.

The Kefauver committee also dredged up all the Anastasia and Murder Inc. business again. O'Dwyer was unforthcoming, but a few of his former associates and underlings sank him. The committee would report its damning conclusion that his "defense of public officials who were derelict in their duties, and his actions in investigations of corruption, and his failure to follow up concrete evidence of organized crime, particularly in the case of Murder, Inc., and the waterfront, have contributed to the growth of organized crime, racketeering, and gangsterism in New York."

O'Dwyer's past had finally caught up with him. He would resign as ambassador in 1952 but continue to live in self-exile in Mexico City until 1960. He died in New York's Beth Israel Hospital of heart failure in 1964, and, for his war service, he was buried at Arlington.

CHAPTER 52

World Capital

On April 25, 1945—two weeks after Roosevelt died and two weeks before final victory in Europe—delegates from fifty Allied nations convened in San Francisco to begin drafting a charter for the new United Nations. Alger Hiss presided as temporary secretary-general. The OSS's Visual Presentation Branch produced all the charts, films, exhibits, and publications used during the two-month conference. Oliver Lundquist and Joseph Mielziner dressed the stage for the final signing ceremony, and Donal McLaughlin designed what's still the official seal of the United Nations.

The one woman in the U.S. delegation was Virginia Gildersleeve. Only a handful of women had been sent by other nations; the Soviet Union, for example, sent none. Gildersleeve and Elizabeth Reynard drafted the American-tinged opening lines of the charter's preamble: "We the peoples of the United Nations, determined to save succeeding generations from the scourge of war, which in our time has brought untold sorrow to mankind..." Gildersleeve also took the lead in the creation of the UN's Commission on Human Rights.

In *Capital of the World*, the historian Charlene Mires relates that although the diplomats did not yet even consider where the new organization's permanent home should be, three places in America were already vying for the honor: San Francisco itself, Philadelphia, and, less plausibly, the Black Hills region of South Dakota, home to Mount Rushmore and some irrepressibly optimistic boosters.

The delegates reconvened in London in the fall. Among the Americans sailing from New York to London on the *Queen Elizabeth*—which, like its sister the *Queen Mary*, was still wearing wartime gray—were Alger

Hiss, serving as an adviser, and Eleanor Roosevelt. Truman had asked her to replace Gildersleeve on the U.S. delegation. Eleanor would chair Gildersleeve's Human Rights Commission and serve with the delegation until President-elect Eisenhower asked her to resign in December 1952. (For her part, Gildersleeve went on to be a leading figure in the American anti-Zionist movement that opposed the creation of Israel, arguing that it dangerously destabilized the Middle East.)

An international committee in London was charged with recommending a permanent location for the organization. They rejected war-ravaged Europe and suggested the United States. Instantly, some eighty cities, towns, and states across the country were jockeying for consideration. Besides the original three, they included Boston, Chicago, Denver, Miami, St. Louis, and Atlantic City. The town of Claremore, Oklahoma (home of Will Rogers), and the plantation of Possum Poke, Georgia (winter home of Michigan governor Chase Osborn), joined in. A number of them sent representatives to London to make formal presentations, armed with promotional films, elaborate brochures, architectural renderings, and, if their locales could afford it, spending money for wining and dining delegates. Being Americans, they were motivated at least as much by dreams of profit as by dreams of world peace. Bringing the world organization to your community, they imagined, would also bring huge windfalls in real estate, construction, and tourism.

Barraged with sales pitches, the committee focused on the East Coast, from Maine to Delaware, where there were some thirty or forty contenders. At first, civic leaders in New York were so confident that the city was the obvious and logical choice that they didn't bother to join the lobbying fray. The giant metropolis was already the "capital of everything," hub of international business, finance, shipping, and communications. International politics was just one more component to plug in. Robert Moses already knew where it would go. The world's fair site at Flushing Meadows was cleared, prepped, and ready to build on.

There was only one problem: New York City was the last place some members of the international site committee thought the UN should go. New York was too big, too crowded, too distracting—too New York. Their preference was for creating an entirely new "world capital," on its own land somewhere out in the suburbs or countryside, convenient to but at a distance from any city.

A site inspection team landed, ironically but conveniently, at LaGuardia and were whisked straight to the Waldorf-Astoria, where they spent the next few weeks. The team's leader, Stoyan Gavrilovic of Yugoslavia, knew the city very well. Fleeing the Nazis in 1941, he and his family had found refuge in New York. But even he didn't think it was a suitable home for the UN.

Mayor O'Dwyer very much wanted the UN in the city. He appointed Robert Moses to chair a blue ribbon booster committee that included Grover Whalen; Bronx borough president James "Jimmy" Lyons; Nelson Rockefeller; Rockefeller's uncle Winthrop Aldrich, president of Chase National Bank and former member of Vincent Astor's spy club; Arthur Hays Sulzberger of the *Times*; Frederick Ecker of Metropolitan Life, who had outraged black New Yorkers with the segregated Stuyvesant Town project; and IBM's chairman and CEO Thomas J. Watson. At City Hall they made a pitch that featured a brochure "two feet square, bound in blue leather, with a map folding out ten feet in length and five feet wide."

Still, the diplomats would not be deflected from exploring the countryside. That's when things started to turn in New York's favor. Outside of Boston, the site committee was charmed by the postcard village of Concord, home to Walden Pond, but the residents there decided that a mass influx of foreigners disrupting their bucolic peace was the last thing they wanted. The very wealthy people of Greenwich, Connecticut, felt the same way. The committee turned to the counties of Westchester in New York and Fairfield in Connecticut. Both were home to large country estates, many of them the weekend and summer retreats of rich New Yorkers. Some of these landed gentry, including Clare Luce, said they might be willing to sell their land in the interests of world peace, while others, such as Gene Tunney, flatly refused. When the committee showed serious interest, those landowners willing to sell made it clear they weren't going to sell cheap. They were holding prime real estate and they knew it.

Boosters in Poughkeepsie made a proposal for the Roosevelt estate at Hyde Park, ten miles north of their city. They had sent a team to London with a handsome brochure and had continued to lobby since. The Roosevelt estate and burial place had an obvious sentimental attachment to the very idea of the UN. Eleanor's friend and biographer Joseph Lash wrote that she privately enlisted the aid of President Truman and Harry Hopkins to get the diplomats to give it serious consideration but felt she should offer no public opinion. The site committee did visit but, once again, not everyone in the area wanted the UN to come, and there were logistical problems.

⌒

Deadlines loomed. The UN Security Council was scheduled to begin its work in March, the General Assembly in the fall. Until a permanent home was built, a temporary meeting place, offices, and housing were needed. Robert Moses offered a plan. The large New York City Building, the only world's fair structure left standing at Flushing Meadows, had been converted to an indoor ice rink. It could easily and relatively cheaply be reconverted into a UN meeting hall. For offices, there was a large plant Sperry Gyroscope had expanded into during the heady war years and was now vacating. It was at Lake Success, on Long Island just east of the Queens border in Nassau County, not a terrible drive from Flushing Meadows. Housing for the diplomats and their hundreds of staffers would be more of a headache, given the shortage in the city, but the suburban building boom in the outer boroughs and Long Island was about to start. Implicit in all this was the notion that once the UN settled in the city "temporarily" it would never leave.

While the delegates discussed Moses's plan, the Security Council's March meeting date rushed up. Jimmy Lyons offered to let the Security Council meet in the Bronx. In fact, he opined that the Bronx would make a fine permanent home for the full UN. It was a quixotic proposal from a man who was on one level a typical Tammany pol but also showed an independent and eccentric streak. He was born in 1890 into a working-class home in the Irish section of Greenwich Village but raised in the Bronx from the age of three. He drove a pony cart with his dad delivering produce, and after graduating elementary school he got a job selling shoe leather. He was first elected borough president in 1933 and would never lose after that, holding the job into the 1960s. Lyons loved the Bronx and saw himself as the chief salesman for a borough the city's power elite tended to dismiss as a hilly mess of poor neighborhoods distinguished only by Yankee Stadium and the Bronx Zoo. In 1939 he and his chauffeur planted a Bronx flag on a rocky outcrop in Marble Hill, one of the area's nicer neighborhoods. Politically and historically, Marble Hill was (and is) incorporated into Manhattan though located at the southern end of the

Bronx. Lyons claimed it for his borough. The *Times* derided him as the "Bronx Führer" invading his own Sudetenland, and nothing but publicity came of the stunt.

Going after the UN was a similar stunt on a grander scale. With nowhere else to go, the Security Council acceded to Lyons's idea of leasing the Bronx campus of Hunter College, which the navy had vacated after training all those WAVES there during the war. In a little over two weeks the gym was converted to a meeting hall, complete with radio and television booths, and classrooms were outfitted as offices. Lyons had the streets and subway stations in the area cleaned up and festooned with welcome banners. At the same time, he kept promoting his larger vision that Riverdale, the Bronx's upscale suburban neighborhood on the Hudson, would make an excellent permanent home for the Capital of the World.

His dream quickly faded. Diplomats and their staffs, who preferred living wherever they could in Manhattan, found the daily commute on the Bronx's infamously tangled streets a nightmare. Within weeks they were close to revolt. Moses pressed again for his plan, and now the UN accepted. Marshaling some of the top architectural and design talent in the country and an army of construction workers, Moses transformed the ice rink at Flushing Meadows into a handsome meeting hall. When the General Assembly met there for the first time in October 1946, some three thousand delegates sat at walnut desks, facing a raised dais behind which spread a magnificent blue and gold map of the world, 60 feet wide and 35 high. A cafeteria, offices, and other support spaces were added onto the building. Where the Trylon and Perisphere once stood was now a broad circular plaza ringed with the flags of all the participating nations.

Living quarters remained a dire problem. The fall start of the Broadway, shopping, and convention season meant that hotels in Manhattan, where many UN personnel wanted to live, were packed to bursting. Then there was the commute. The city organized a fleet of limousines to ferry the delegates and staffers across the East River and seven miles out to Flushing Meadows, farther still to the offices at Lake Success.

While Moses drew up handsome plans to build the UN a permanent home at Flushing Meadows, many delegates were unhappy and unconvinced. Moses's plan was dead by November. The search for a permanent home outside of the city resumed, much to the New Yorkers' dismay. Philadelphia leapt back into the fray with a very persuasive offer of land and support services. It was soon clear that if the UN stayed in New York it had to be in Manhattan—where real estate was scarcest and most expensive. Philadelphia's prospects looked brighter every day.

At the eleventh hour, two new figures stepped up to keep the UN in New York. One was the forty-year-old real estate developer William Zeckendorf. In some ways a Trump for his time, Zeckendorf was described in *Life* as "a big, brash man...with a baronial paunch and a temperamental disinclination to do business in amounts of less than seven digits...Not since Napoleon III redesigned the city of Paris in the 1850s has anybody indulged a more grandiose appetite for real estate." He was born in Paris, Illinois, where his Jewish father ran a hardware store. The family moved to New York when he was three, and he went into real estate after leaving NYU. He made his first huge score during the war, when he reorganized Vincent Astor's vast but ailing real estate empire in the city.

That was nothing compared to Zeckendorf's postwar dreams. Early in 1946 he proposed transforming Manhattan's West Side from 24th to 71st Streets into a mammoth, $3 billion, three-runway airport, elevated ten stories above street level, with hangars and associated airport buildings underneath. At the same time he was buying some of the Turtle Bay area on the East River waterfront between 42nd and 49th Streets. While parts of Turtle Bay featured blocks of lovely town houses (homes to Dorothy Thompson, Katharine Hepburn, and Tyrone Power, among others), Zeckendorf's strip along the waterfront was a depressed industrial zone of reeking slaughterhouses, rotting piers, and a gigantic Con Edison steam power plant. He proposed to knock all that down and build "X City," a city-within-a-city to rival Rockefeller Center. Renderings showed soaring residential towers, a heliport, an opera house, restaurants, and shops, with subway and roadway connections belowground.

On Friday, December 6, 1946, while reading about Philadelphia's UN hopes in the *Times*, Zeckendorf suddenly had a new idea for Turtle Bay. He called Mayor O'Dwyer and offered to sell the land for $8.5 million, which was little more than he'd paid for it. O'Dwyer contacted Nelson Rockefeller, who spoke to his father, John D. Rockefeller Jr.; John D. Jr. agreed to buy the land and gift it to the world. Within a week, all the relevant deals were struck, and the question of where the Capital of the World would be was answered.

Getting all parties to agree on the architectural plans took the following year. Removals and demolitions began in 1948. The slim, elegantly modernist box of the Secretariat building rose first. On October 24, 1949, the fourth anniversary of the General Assembly's first meeting at Flushing Meadows—and ten years after the world's fair's first season ended—President Truman, Governor Dewey (who had made his last run for the White House against Truman in 1948), various diplomats, and ten thousand onlookers in rows of folding chairs gathered at the foot of the tower to lay the granite cornerstone. The building was still just a tall latticework of beams and girders. Construction of the complex would go on for another three years.

A brass band played "The Sidewalks of New York." Truman called the complex "the most important buildings in the world," and a *Times* editorial called it "the dream made visible." The flags of fifty-nine nations flanked the blue UN symbol Donal McLaughlin had designed in San Francisco.

The *Times* conceded that not all nations interpreted "the dream" the same way; that "our international differences have wide and sinister frontiers." Two months earlier, the Soviets had made their first successful test of an atomic bomb. Seated next to Eleanor Roosevelt at a gala reception, India's prime minister Jawaharlal Nehru offered the sobering prediction that capitalism and communism "could not exist together indefinitely in the same world," and eventually one would have to defeat the other.

It was the start of a new era. In 1947, W. H. Auden, who had stayed in New York and taken U.S. citizenship, published an epic narrative poem about four loners who meet up in a shabby Third Avenue bar one night and reflect on the times, an age "tamed by terror," a grim world "Of convulsion and vast evil,/ When the Cold Societies clash." The poem's title, "The Age of Anxiety," was adopted by some as a name for the troubled postwar times. But it was Bernard Baruch that same year who gave the period its more commonly used label, the Cold War.

⌒

For nearly a decade after being asked to step out of the UN in 1953, Eleanor continued to be a leading speaker and writer on world issues. In 1958 she bought her last place in Manhattan, the imposing town house at 55 East 74th Street. Two years later, as she was crossing Eighth Avenue in Greenwich Village on her way to a speaking engagement, a driver backing up knocked her down. When she saw that the driver was a young black man, she told him to drive off to avoid an ugly scene with the white people who were gathering. Then she limped to her talk. Despite failing health in her last two years she kept up a packed public schedule as long as she could, still Public Energy No. 1, until her heart gave out in 1962.

She was seventy-eight. When she was buried in the rose garden at Hyde Park she lay down beside her husband for the first time in decades.

Notes on Sources

BOOKS

Albright, Joseph, and Marcia Kunstel. *Bombshell: The Secret Story of America's Unknown Atomic Spy Conspiracy*. New York: Times Books, 1997.

Alexander, Charles C. *Breaking the Slump: Baseball in the Depression Era*. New York: Columbia University Press, 2002.

Alonso, Harriet Hyman. *Robert E. Sherwood: The Playwright in Peace and War*. Amherst: University of Massachusetts Press, 2007.

Alvarez, Luis. *The Power of the Zoot: Youth Culture and Resistance during World War II*. Berkeley: University of California Press, 2008.

Baker, James C. *The Bank for International Settlements: Evolution and Evaluation*. Westport, CT: Quorum Books, 2002.

Baruch, Bernard. *Baruch: My Own Story*. New York: Holt, Rinehart and Winston, 1957.

Bates, Beth Tompkins. *Pullman Porters and the Rise of Protest Politics in Black America, 1925–1945*. Chapel Hill: University of North Carolina Press, 2001.

Bennett, David H. *The Party of Fear: From Nativist Movements to the New Right in American History*. Chapel Hill: University of North Carolina Press, 1988.

Bennett, Scott H. *Radical Pacifism: The War Resisters League and Gandhian Nonviolence in America, 1915–1963*. Syracuse, NY: Syracuse University Press, 2003.

Bergreen, Laurence. *As Thousands Cheer: The Life of Irving Berlin*. Boston: Da Capo Press, 1996.

Berkman, Ted. *Cast a Giant Shadow*. New York: Doubleday, 1962.

Berner, Thomas F. *The Brooklyn Navy Yard*. Charleston, SC: Arcadia Publishing, 1999.

Bernstein, Arnie. *Swastika Nation: Fritz Kuhn and the Rise and Fall of the German-American Bund*. New York: St. Martin's Press, 2013.

Bernstein, Bernard. *Report on the Investigation of IG Farben Industry AG*. Office of Military Government, U.S. (Germany), 1945.

Beyer, Rick, and Elizabeth Sayles. *The Ghost Army of World War II*. New York: Princeton Architectural Press, 2014.

Block, Alan. *East Side, West Side: Organizing Crime in New York, 1930–50*. New York: Routledge, 1983.

Bourke-White, Margaret. *Portrait of Myself.* New York: Simon & Schuster, 1963.

Boyer, Paul. *By the Bomb's Early Light: American Thought and Culture at the Dawn of the Atomic Age.* Chapel Hill: University of North Carolina Press, 1994.

Brandt, Nat. *Harlem at War: The Black Experience in WWII.* Syracuse, NY: Syracuse University Press, 1997.

Breuer, William. *Nazi Spies in America.* New York: St. Martin's Press, 1989.

Brinkley, Alan. *The Publisher: Henry Luce and His American Century.* New York: Alfred A. Knopf, 2010.

Bullock, Steven R. *Playing for Their Nation: Baseball and the American Military during World War II.* Lincoln: University of Nebraska Press, 2004.

Burt, Kendal, and James Leasor. *The One That Got Away.* New York: Ballantine Books, 1958.

Butler, Smedley. *War Is a Racket.* New York: Round Table Press, 1935.

Cannistraro, Philip V., and Gerald Meyer, eds. *The Lost World of Italian American Radicalism: Politics, Labor, and Culture.* Westport, CT: Praeger Publishers, 2003.

Carlson, John Roy. *Under Cover.* New York: E. P. Dutton, 1943.

Carson, Julia M. H. *Home Away from Home: The Story of the USO.* New York: Harper & Brothers, 1946.

Casey, Steven. *Cautious Crusade: Franklin D. Roosevelt, American Public Opinion, and the War against Nazi Germany.* New York: Oxford University Press, 2004.

Churchill, Sarah. *Keep On Dancing.* New York: Coward, McCann & Geoghegan, 1981.

Churchill, Winston S. *The Grand Alliance, vol. 3.* New York: Houghton Mifflin, 1950.

Clavin, Tom. *The DiMaggios.* New York: HarperCollins, 2013.

Clinard, Marshall B. *The Black Market: A Study of White Collar Crime.* Montclair, NJ: Patterson Smith, 1969.

Coates, Robert M. *The Bitter Season.* New York: Harcourt, Brace and Company, 1946.

Colman, Penny. *Rosie the Riveter: Women Working on the Home Front in World War II.* New York: Crown, 1995.

Conot, Robert E. *Justice at Nuremberg.* New York: Harper & Row, 1983.

Conradi, Peter. *Hitler's Piano Player: The Rise and Fall of Ernst Hanfstaengl, Confidant of Hitler, Ally of FDR.* New York: Carroll & Graf, 2004.

Cooke, James J. *American Girls, Beer, and Glenn Miller: GI Morale in World War II.* Columbia: University of Missouri Press, 2012.

Cotter, Bill. *The 1939–1940 New York World's Fair.* Charleston, SC: Arcadia Publishing, 2009.

Curtis, Tony, with Peter Golenbock. *American Prince: A Memoir.* New York: Harmony Books, 2008.

Dawidoff, Nicholas. *The Catcher Was a Spy: The Mysterious Life of Moe Berg.* New York: Pantheon, 1994.

DeLisa, Michael. *Cinderella Man: The James J. Braddock Story.* Wrea Green, UK: Milo Books, 2005.

Dellinger, David. *From Yale to Jail: The Life Story of a Moral Dissenter.* New York: Pantheon, 1993.

Diehl, Lorraine B. *Over Here! New York City During World War II.* New York: HarperCollins, 2010.

Diggins, John P. *Mussolini and Fascism: The View from America.* Princeton, NJ: Princeton University Press, 1972.

Dobbs, Michael. *Saboteurs: The Nazi Raid on America.* New York: Alfred A. Knopf, 2004.

Doherty, Thomas. *Cold War, Cool Medium: Television, McCarthyism, and American Culture.* New York: Columbia University Press, 2003.

Doyle, William. *Inside the Oval Office: The White House Tapes from FDR to Clinton.* New York: Kodansha America, 1999.

Dubois, Josiah. *The Devil's Chemists.* Boston: Beacon Press, 1952.

Duffy, Peter. *Double Agent.* New York: Scribner, 2014.

Dunn, Susan. *1940: FDR, Willkie, Lindbergh, Hitler—the Election Amid the Storm.* New Haven, CT: Yale University Press, 2013.

Enyeart, Stacy. *America's Home Front Heroes: An Oral History of World War II.* Santa Barbara, CA: Praeger, 2009.

Fermi, Laura. *Illustrious Immigrants: The Intellectual Migration from Europe, 1930–41.* Chicago: University of Chicago Press, 1968.

Feynman, Richard P. *"Surely You're Joking, Mr. Feynman!"* New York: W. W. Norton, 1985.

Fraser, Steven. *Labor Will Rule: Sidney Hillman and the Rise of American Labor.* New York: The Free Press, 1991.

Fry, Varian. *Surrender on Demand.* Boulder, CO: Johnson Books, 1997.

Gabler, Neal. *Winchell: Gossip, Power and the Culture of Celebrity.* New York: Alfred A. Knopf, 1994.

Gallagher, Dorothy. *All the Right Enemies: The Life and Murder of Carlo Tresca.* New Brunswick, NJ: Rutgers University Press, 1988.

Gara, Larry, and Lenna Mae Gara, eds. *A Few Small Candles: War Resisters of World War II Tell Their Stories.* Kent, OH: Kent State University Press, 1999.

Gilman, Sander L., and Steven T. Katz, eds. *Anti-Semitism in Times of Crisis.* New York: New York University Press, 1991.

Gimpel, Erich. *Agent 146.* New York: St. Martin's Press, 2003.

Gluck, Gemma La Guardia. *Fiorello's Sister.* Syracuse, NY: Syracuse University Press, 2007.

Goldberg, Vicki. *Margaret Bourke-White: A Biography.* New York: Harper & Row, 1986.

Goldstein, Richard. *Helluva Town: The Story of New York City During World War II.* New York: Free Press, 2010.

Goodwin, Doris Kearns. *No Ordinary Time: Franklin & Eleanor Roosevelt: The Home Front in World War II.* New York: Simon & Schuster, 1994.

Grant, James. *Bernard Baruch: The Adventures of a Wall Street Legend.* New York: Simon & Schuster, 1983.

Greenberg, Cheryl Lynn. *Or Does It Explode? Black Harlem in the Great Depression.* New York: Oxford University Press, 1997.

Gregory, Raymond F. *Norman Thomas: The Great Dissenter.* New York: Algora, 2008.

Hamilton, Charles V. *Adam Clayton Powell, Jr.* New York: Collier Books, 1991.

Hegarty, Marilyn E. *Victory Girls, Khaki-Wackies, and Patriotutes: The Regulation of Female Sexuality during World War II.* New York: New York University Press, 2008.

Higham, Charles. *Trading with the Enemy.* New York: Barnes and Noble, 1983.

Hodgson, Godfrey. *The Colonel: The Life and Wars of Henry Stimson, 1867–1950.* New York: Alfred A. Knopf, 1990.

Holsinger, M. Paul. *War and American Popular Culture: A Historical Encyclopedia.* Westport, CT: Greenwood Press, 1999.

Honey, Maureen. *Creating Rosie the Riveter: Class, Gender, and Propaganda during World War II.* Amherst: University of Massachusetts Press, 1984.

Hoopes, Roy. *Ralph Ingersoll: A Biography.* New York: Atheneum, 1985.

Hortis, C. Alexander. *The Mob and the City.* Amherst, NY: Prometheus, 2014.

Ingersoll, Ralph. *Report on England, November, 1940.* New York: Simon & Schuster, 1940.

Isaacson, Walter, and Evan Thomas. *The Wise Men: Six Friends and the World They Made.* New York: Simon & Schuster, 1996.

Janeway, Michael. *The Fall of the House of Roosevelt.* New York: Columbia University Press, 2004.

Jeansonne, Glen. *Women of the Far Right: The Mothers' Movement and World War II.* Chicago: University of Chicago Press, 1996.

Jeffers, H. Paul. *The Napoleon of New York: Mayor Fiorello la Guardia.* New York: Wiley, 2002.

Johnson, Niel M. *George Sylvester Viereck: German-American Propagandist.* Urbana: University of Illinois Press, 1972.

Jones, John Bush. *The Songs That Fought the War: Popular Music and the Home Front, 1939–1945.* Waltham, MA: Brandeis University Press, 2006.

Jordan, David M. *FDR, Dewey, and the Election of 1944.* Bloomington: Indiana University Press, 2011.

Kaskowitz, Sheryl. *God Bless America: The Surprising History of an Iconic Song.* New York: Oxford University Press, 2013.

Keever, Beverly Ann Deepe. *News Zero: The New York Times and the Bomb.* Monroe, ME: Common Courage Press, 2004.

Kelly, Cynthia C., and Robert S. Norris. *A Guide to the Manhattan Project in Manhattan.* Washington, D.C.: Atomic Heritage Foundation, 2012.

Kersten, Andrew E. *Labor's Home Front: The American Federation of Labor during World War II.* New York: New York University Press, 2006.

Kessner, Thomas. *Fiorello H. La Guardia and the Making of Modern New York.* New York: McGraw-Hill, 1989.

Koszarski, Richard. *Hollywood on the Hudson: Film and Television in New York from Griffith to Sarnoff.* New Brunswick, NJ: Rutgers University Press, 2008.

Kurth, Peter. *American Cassandra: The Life of Dorothy Thompson.* New York: Little, Brown and Company, 1990.

Lash, Joseph P. *Eleanor and Franklin: The Story of Their Relationship, Based on Eleanor Roosevelt's Private Papers.* New York: W. W. Norton, 1971.

———. *Eleanor: The Years Alone*. New York: W. W. Norton, 1972.

Laurie, Clayton D. *The Propaganda Warriors: America's Crusade Against Nazi Germany*. Lawrence: University Press of Kansas, 1996.

Lease, Donald E. *Theodor Seuss Geisel*. New York: Oxford University Press, 2010.

Leff, Laurel. *Buried by the Times: The Holocaust and America's Most Important Newspaper*. New York: Cambridge University Press, 2005.

Lepore, Jill. *The Secret History of Wonder Woman*. New York: Alfred A. Knopf, 2014.

Lewis, Sinclair. *It Can't Happen Here*. New York: Doubleday, 1935.

Loesser, Susan. *A Most Remarkable Fella: Frank Loesser and the Guys and Dolls in His Life*. New York: Donald I. Fine, 1993.

Lowenstein, Steven M. *Frankfurt on the Hudson: The German-Jewish Community of Washington Heights, 1933–1983, Its Structure and Culture*. Detroit: Wayne State University Press, 1989.

MacDonnell, Francis. *Insidious Foes: The Axis Fifth Column and the American Home Front*. New York: Oxford University Press, 1995.

Mahl, Thomas E. *Desperate Deception: British Covert Operations in the United States, 1939–44*. Dulles, VA: Brassey's, 1998.

Manning, Frankie, and Cynthia R. Millman. *Frankie Manning: Ambassador of Lindy Hop*. Philadelphia: Temple University Press, 2007.

Mappen, Marc. *Prohibition Gangsters: The Rise and Fall of a Bad Generation*. New Brunswick, NJ: Rutgers University Press, 2013.

Margolick, David. *Beyond Glory: Joe Louis vs. Max Schmeling, and a World on the Brink*. New York: Alfred A. Knopf, 2004.

Marino, Andy. *A Quiet American: The Secret War of Varian Fry*. New York: St. Martin's Press, 1999.

Mauro, James. *Twilight at the World of Tomorrow*. New York: Ballantine Books, 2010.

May, Allan R. *Gangland Gotham: New York's Notorious Mob Bosses*. Santa Barbara, CA: Greenwood Press, 2009.

May, Gary. *Un-American Activities: The Trials of William Remington*. New York: Oxford University Press, 1994.

McEuen, Melissa A. *Making War, Making Women: Femininity and Duty on the American Home Front, 1941–1945*. Athens: University of Georgia Press, 2011.

McGovern, Charles F. *Sold American: Consumption and Citizenship, 1890–1945*. Chapel Hill: University of North Carolina Press, 2006.

McGurn, Barrett. *Yank: Reporting the Greatest Generation*. Golden, CO: Fulcrum Publishing, 2004.

McPherson, Nelson. *American Intelligence in War-Time London: The Story of the OSS*. London: Frank Cass, 2003.

Medoff, Rafael. *Militant Zionism in America: The Rise and Impact of the Jabotinsky Movement in the United States, 1926–1948*. Tuscaloosa: University of Alabama Press, 2002.

Mehra, Jagdish. *The Beat of a Different Drum: The Life and Science of Richard Feynman*. Oxford, UK: Clarendon Press, 1994.

Milkman, Paul. *PM: A New Deal in Journalism, 1940–1948*. New Brunswick, NJ: Rutgers University Press, 1997.

Miller, Dorothy Laager. *New York City in the Great Depression: Sheltering the Homeless*. Charleston, SC: Arcadia Publishing, 2009.

Miller, Marvin D. *Wunderlich's Salute*. New York: Malamud-Rose, 1983.

Minear, Richard H. *Dr. Seuss Goes to War: The World War II Editorial Cartoons of Theodor Seuss Geisel*. New York: The New Press, 1999.

Mires, Charlene. *Capital of the World: The Race to Host the United Nations*. New York: New York University Press, 2013.

Morris, Jan. *Manhattan '45*. Baltimore: Johns Hopkins University Press, 1986.

Morris, Sylvia Jukes. *Price of Fame: The Honorable Clare Boothe Luce*. New York: Random House, 2014.

———. *Rage for Fame: The Ascent of Clare Boothe Luce*. New York: Random House, 1997.

Newark, Tim. *The Mafia at War: The Shocking True Story of America's Wartime Pact with Organized Crime*. New York: Skyhorse Publishing, 2012.

O'Brien, Kenneth Paul, and Lynn Hudson Parsons, eds. *The Home-Front War: World War II and American Society*. Westport, CT: Greenwood Press, 1995.

O'Dwyer, William. *Beyond the Golden Door*. New York: St John's University Press, 1987.

Offley, Ed. *The Burning Shore: How Hitler's U-Boats Brought World War II to America*. New York: Basic Books, 2014.

Olmstead, Kathryn S. *Red Spy Queen: A Biography of Elizabeth Bentley*. Chapel Hill: University of North Carolina Press, 2002.

Olson, Lynne. *Citizens of London: The Americans Who Stood with Britain in Its Darkest, Finest Hour*. New York: Random House, 2010.

Ossian, Lisa L. *Forgotten Generation: American Children and World War II*. Columbia: University of Missouri Press, 2011.

Papas, Phillip, and Lori R. Weintraub. *Port Richmond*. Charleston, SC: Arcadia Publishing, 2009.

Pasachoff, Naomi. *Frances Perkins: Champion of the New Deal*. New York: Oxford University Press, 1999.

Patchen, Kenneth. *The Collected Poems of Kenneth Patchen*. New York: New Directions, 1968.

———. *The Journal of Albion Moonlight*. New York: New Directions, 1961.

Peiss, Kathy. *Zoot Suit: The Enigmatic Career of an Extreme Style*. Philadelphia: University of Pennsylvania Press, 2011.

Peretti, Burton W. *Nightclub City: Politics and Amusement in Manhattan*. Philadelphia: University of Pennsylvania Press, 2007.

Pernicone, Nunzio. *Carlo Tresca: Portrait of a Rebel*. Oakland, CA: AK Press, 2010.

Persico, Joseph E. *Casey: From the OSS to the CIA*. New York: Viking, 1990.

———. *Roosevelt's Secret War: FDR and World War II Espionage*. New York: Random House, 2001.

Pfau, Ann Elizabeth. *Miss Yourlovin: GIs, Gender, and Domesticity in World War II*. New York: Columbia University Press, 2008.

Phillips, Kimberley L. *War! What Is It Good For?: Black Freedom Struggles and the U.S. Military from World War II to Iraq*. Chapel Hill: University of North Carolina Press, 2012.

Piller, Emmanuel A. *Time Bomb.* New York: Arco Publishing, 1945.
Pizzitola, Louis. *Hearst over Hollywood: Power, Passion, and Propaganda in the Movies.* New York: Columbia University Press, 2002.
Polaski, Leo, and Glen Williford. *New York City's Harbor Defenses.* Charleston, SC: Arcadia Publishing, 2003.
Powell, Adam Clayton, Jr. *Adam by Adam.* New York: The Dial Press, 1971.
Powers, Thomas. *Heisenberg's War: The Secret History of the German Bomb.* New York: Alfred A. Knopf, 1993.
Puzo, Mario. *The Godfather Papers and Other Confessions.* New York: G. P. Putnam's Sons, 1972.
Quigley, Carroll. *Tragedy and Hope: A History of the World in Our Time.* New York: Macmillan, 1966.
Quinn, Susan. *The Furious Improvisation: How the WPA and a Cast of Thousands Made High Art out of Desperate Times.* New York: Walker Books, 2008.
Rapoport, Louis. *Shake Heaven & Earth: Peter Bergson and the Struggle to Rescue the Jews of Europe.* Jerusalem: Gefen Publishing House, 1999.
Rattray, Jeannette Edwards. *Perils of the Port of New York.* New York: Dodd, Mead & Company, 1973.
Reynolds, Quentin. *A London Diary.* New York: Random House, 1941.
———. *The Wounded Don't Cry.* New York: E. P. Dutton, 1941.
Rhodes, Richard. *The Making of the Atomic Bomb.* New York: Simon & Schuster, 1986.
Ro, Ronin. *Tales to Astonish: Jack Kirby, Stan Lee, and the American Comic Book Revolution.* New York: Bloomsbury, 2004.
Roberts, Nancy L. *Dorothy Day and the Catholic Worker.* Albany: SUNY Press, 1984.
Roberts, Randy. *Joe Louis: Hard Times Man.* New Haven, CT: Yale University Press, 2010.
Roberts, Sam. *The Brother: The Untold Story of the Rosenberg Case.* New York: Simon & Schuster, 2001.
Roll, David L. *The Hopkins Touch.* New York: Oxford University Press, 2013.
Rollins, Richard. *I Find Treason: The Story of an American Anti-Nazi Agent.* New York: William Morrow, 1941.
Ronnie, Art. *Counterfeit Hero: Fritz Duquesne, Adventurer and Spy.* Annapolis, MD: Naval Institute Press, 1995.
Rose, Kenneth. *Myth and the Greatest Generation: A Social History of Americans in World War II.* New York: Routledge, 2007.
Rosenbaum, Robert A. *Waking to Danger: Americans and Nazi Germany, 1933–1941.* Santa Barbara, CA: Praeger, 2010.
Rosenman, Samuel I. *Working with Roosevelt.* New York: Harper & Brothers, 1952.
Roza, Mathilde. *The Life and Literary Works of Robert M. Coates.* Columbia: University of South Carolina Press, 2011.
Ryan, James G. *Earl Browder: The Failure of American Communism.* Tuscaloosa: University of Alabama Press, 1997.
Sanders, Roland. *The Days Grown Short: The Life and Music of Kurt Weill.* New York: Holt, Rinehart and Winston, 1980.
Schacht, Hjalmar. *My First Seventy-Six Years: Autobiography.* London: Wingate, 1955.

Shaw, Irwin. *Bury the Dead*. New York: Random House, 1936.

Sherwood, Robert E. *Roosevelt and Hopkins, an Intimate History*. New York: Harper & Brothers, 1948.

———. *Idiot's Delight*. New York: Charles Scribner's Sons, 1936.

———. *There Shall Be No Night*. New York: Charles Scribner's Sons, 1940.

Shulman, Irving. *The Amboy Dukes*. New York: Doubleday, 1947.

Smith, Richard Norton. *Thomas E. Dewey and His Times*. New York: Simon & Schuster, 1982.

Snyder-Grenier, Ellen M. *Brooklyn! An Illustrated History*. Philadelphia: Temple University Press, 1996.

Sperber, A. M. *Murrow, His Life and Times*. New York: Fordham University Press, 1998.

Still, Bayard. *Mirror for Gotham: New York as Seen by Contemporaries from Dutch Days to the Present*. New York: New York University Press, 1956.

Stossel, Scott. *Sarge: The Life and Times of Sargent Shriver*. Washington, D.C.: Smithsonian Books, 2004.

Strong, Donald S. *Organized Anti-Semitism in America: The Rise of Group Prejudice during the Decade 1930–40*. Washington, D.C.: American Council on Public Affairs, 1941.

Sullivan, Dean A., ed. *Middle Innings: A Documentary History of Baseball, 1900–1948*. Lincoln: University of Nebraska Press, 2001.

Sweeny, Charles. *Sweeny: The Autobiography of Charles Sweeny*. Canterbury, UK: Harrop Press, 1990.

Tanenhaus, Sam. *Whittaker Chambers*. New York: Random House, 1997.

Taylor, Nick. *American Made: The Enduring Legacy of the WPA*. New York: Bantam, 2008.

Teller, Edward. *Memoirs: A Twentieth-Century Journey in Science and Politics*. Cambridge, MA: Perseus Publishing, 2001.

Thorn, William J., Phillip M. Runkel, and Susan Mountin, eds. *Dorothy Day and the Catholic Worker Movement: Centenary Essays*. Milwaukee: Marquette University Press, 2001.

Thorpe, Charles. *Oppenheimer: The Tragic Intellect*. Chicago: University of Chicago Press, 2006.

Treadwell, Mattie E. *The Women's Army Corps*. Washington, D.C.: Center of Military History, 1991.

Turkus, Burton B., and Sid Feder. *Murder, Inc: The Story of the Syndicate*. New York: Farrar, Straus and Young, 1951.

Tuttle, William M., Jr. *Daddy's Gone to War: The Second World War in the Lives of America's Children*. New York: Oxford University Press, 1995.

Twing, Stephen W. *Myths, Models & U.S. Foreign Policy: The Cultural Shaping of Three Cold Warriors*. Boulder, CO: Lynne Rienner, 1998.

Underhill, Robert. *The Rise and Fall of Franklin Delano Roosevelt*. New York: Algora, 2012.

Urofsky, Melvin I. *A Voice That Spoke for Justice: The Life and Times of Stephen S. Wise*. Albany: State University of New York Press, 1982.

Verria, Lawrence, and George Galdorisi. *The Kissing Sailor*. Annapolis, MD: Naval Institute Press, 2012.

Volo, James M. *A History of War Resistance in America.* Santa Barbara, CA: Greenwood Press, 2010.

Waller, Douglas. *Disciples: The World War II Missions of the CIA Directors Who Fought for Wild Bill Donovan.* New York: Simon & Schuster, 2015.

———. *Wild Bill Donovan.* New York: Simon & Schuster, 2011.

Walsh, George. *Public Enemies: The Mayor, the Mob, and the Crime That Was.* New York: W. W. Norton, 1980.

Ward, Nathan. *Dark Harbor: The War for the New York Waterfront.* New York: Farrar, Straus and Giroux, 2010.

Weinstein, Allen, and Alexander Vassiliev. *The Haunted Wood: Soviet Espionage in America—The Stalin Era.* New York: Random House, 1998.

Wertheim, Albert. *Staging the War: American Drama and World War II.* Bloomington: Indiana University Press, 2004.

Whalen, Grover. *Mr. New York: The Autobiography of Grover A. Whalen.* New York: G. P. Putnam's Sons, 1955.

Whalen, Robert Weldon. *Murder, Inc., and the Moral Life: Gangsters and Gangbusters in La Guardia's New York.* New York: Empire State Editions, 2016.

White, E. B. *Here Is New York.* New York: Harper & Brothers, 1949.

White, G. Edward. *Alger Hiss's Looking-Glass Wars: The Covert Life of a Soviet Spy.* New York: Oxford University Press, 2004.

White, Walter. *A Man Called White.* New York: Viking, 1948.

Wigley, Mark. *Buckminster Fuller Inc.: Architecture in the Age of Radio.* Zurich: Lars Müller Publishers, 2015.

Williams, Mason B. *City of Ambition: FDR, La Guardia, and the Making of Modern New York.* New York: W. W. Norton, 2013.

Winchell, Walter. *Winchell Exclusive.* Englewood Cliffs, NJ: Prentice-Hall, 1975.

Winfield, Betty Houchin. *FDR and the News Media.* Urbana: University of Illinois Press, 1990.

Wouk, Herman. *Sailor and Fiddler: Reflections of a 100-Year-Old Author.* New York: Simon & Schuster, 2016.

X, Malcolm, with Alex Haley. *The Autobiography of Malcolm X.* New York: Grove Press, 1964.

Zieger, Robert H. *The CIO, 1935–1955.* Chapel Hill: University of North Carolina Press, 1995.

ARTICLES AND ESSAYS

Bylined, by Author

Aruga, Natsuki. "An' Finish High School: Child Labor During World War II." *Labor History*, vol. 29, 4 (1988).

Baker, Kevin. "Glamour Girls, Murder, and the Mayor." *NYPR Archives and Preservation,* November 24, 2014.

Barron, James. "A Manhattan Project Veteran Had a Unique View of Atomic Bomb Work." *New York Times*, July 26, 2015.

Belair, Felix, Jr. "King Tries Hot Dog and Asks for More." *New York Times*, June 12, 1939.

Berger, Meyer. "City Takes Report of Death in Stride." *New York Times*, May 2, 1945.

Birchall, Frederick T. "Dorothy Thompson Expelled by Reich for 'Slur' on Hitler." *New York Times*, August 26, 1934.

Bowles, Chester. "The Deadly Menace of Black Gasoline." *New York Times*, July 30, 1944.

Busch, Noel F. "Joe Di Maggio." *Life*, May 1, 1939.

Coates, Robert M. "Big Night." *New Yorker*, May 27, 1944.

Conklin, William R. "Pair Silent to End." *New York Times*, June 20, 1953.

Connors, Anthony. "Then & Now the Yorkville Casino." *New York Daily News*, March 29, 1938.

Darnton, Byron. "Vast Throng Jams the Mall to Cheer American Day Fete." *New York Times*, May 19, 1941.

Dixon, Carolyn. "Harlem Weeps with World Remembering a Great Man." *Amsterdam News*, April 21, 1945.

Dorwart, Jeffery M. "The Roosevelt-Astor Espionage Ring." *New York History Quarterly Journal*, vol. 62, no. 3 (July 1981).

Dunlap, Orrin E., Jr. "Ceremony Is Carried by Television as Industry Makes Its Formal Bow." *New York Times*, May 1, 1939.

Feinberg, Alexander. "All City 'Lets Go.'" *New York Times*, August 15, 1945.

———. "9,500 at St. John's at La Guardia Rites." *New York Times*, September 23, 1947.

Fimrite, Ron. "The Play That Beat the Bums." *Sports Illustrated*, October 20, 1997.

Franklin, Ronald E. "The Stage Door Canteen and African Americans in WW2." Owlcation.com. https://owlcation.com/humanities/The-Stage-Door-Canteen-and-African-Americans-in-WW2.

Gray, Christopher. "A Notable Block with a Hole in Its Heart." *New York Times*, July 16, 2006.

Groth, Gary. "Jack Kirby Interview." *The Comics Journal*, February 1990.

Gunnison, Walter B., and Walter Crosby. "13 Dead, 24 Injured in Skyscraper Crash." *Brooklyn Daily Eagle*, July 29, 1945.

Herrick, Elinore M. "With Women at Work, the Factory Changes." *New York Times*, January 24, 1943.

Hinckley, David. "Deadly Aim: Sinatra at the Paramount, 1944." *New York Daily News*, October 31, 2004.

Hitler, William. "Why I Hate My Uncle." *Look*, July 4, 1939.

Horne, George. "Queen Mary in with 14,526, Who Get Raucous Welcome." *New York Times*, June 21, 1945.

Katz, Barry. "The Arts of War: 'Visual Presentation' and National Intelligence." *Design Issues* 12, no. 2 (Summer 1996).

Kay, Hubert. "Wendell Willkie." *Life*, May 13, 1940.

Kennedy, Paul P. "Rosenberg Ruling Likely Tomorrow." *New York Times*, June 14, 1953.

Krock, Arthur. "The War in Pictures." *New York Times*, October 8, 1941.

Laurence, William. "Drama of the Atomic Bomb Found Climax in July 16 Test." *New York Times*, September 26, 1945.

———. "The Quest of Science for an Atomic Energy." *New York Times*, June 29, 1930.

Maney, Richard. "*Life* Goes to Bleeck's." *Life*, November 26, 1945.

McAllister, Gertrude. "City Patrol Corps Calms Girls' Fears of Muggers." *Brooklyn Daily Eagle*, March 8, 1943.

Moses, Robert. "The Saga of Flushing Meadow." April 11, 1966. Nywf64.com. http://www.nywf64.com/saga02.shtml.

Mushnick, Phil. "Giants Player Gave Career, Life for Country." *New York Post*, May 28, 2010.

Norwood, Stephen H. "Marauding Youth and the Christian Front: Antisemitic Violence in Boston and New York During World War II." *American Jewish History*, vol. 9, no. 2 (June 2003).

Parmet, Herbert. "What Should We Make of the Charge Linking the Bush Family Fortune to Nazism?" *History News Network*, November 17, 2003.

Philologos, "The Truth About Einstein's Boat." *Forward,* August 8, 2007.

Potter, Robert W. "General Becomes Honorary Citizen." *New York Times*, June 20, 1945.

Powell, Adam Clayton, Jr. "Soap Box." *Amsterdam News*, May 27, 1939.

Roberts, Sam. "New York 1945; The War Was Ending. Times Square Exploded. Change Was Coming." *New York Times*, July 30, 1995.

Robertson, Ben. "Hail of Nazi Bombs Turned London into Hell on Earth." *PM*, September 9, 1940.

Rosenberg, Elliot. "Fiorello's Army." *Seaport*, Summer 1995.

———. "Undead." *New York Daily News*, April 5, 2005.

———. "Woodwork." *New York Daily News*, June 2, 2005.

Rosenberg, Rosalind. "Virginia Gildersleeve: Opening the Gates." *Columbia Magazine*, Summer 2001.

Rumsey, Spencer. "Einstein's Long Island Summer of '39." *Long Island Press*, February 1, 2013.

Sassaman, Richard. "Nazi Spies Come Ashore." *America in WWII*, October 2005.

Schmalacker, Joseph H. "Crowds Estimated at 3,000,000 Cheer President in 65-Mi. Tour." *Brooklyn Daily Eagle*, October 22, 1944.

Selmer, Robert. "The Man Who Wants to Build New York Over." *Life*, October 28, 1946.

Shalett, Sydney M. "Use of Fair's Steel in Defense Likely." *New York Times*, August 19, 1940.

Simon, John J. "Rebel in the House: The Life and Times of Vito Marcantonio." *Monthly Review*, vol. 57, no. 11 (April 2006).

Simonsen, Clarence. "The Clayton Knight Committee." Lest We Forget. https://athabaskang07.wordpress.com/2014/11/22/the-clayton-knight-committee/.

Slayton, Robert A. "Children in Europe Are Europe's Problem!" *Commentary*, October 1, 2014.

Smith, Harold. "Rosenbergs 'Murdered,' Their Lawyer Says at Funeral." *Brooklyn Daily Eagle*, June 22, 1953.

Sparr, Arnold. "Looking for Rosie: Women Defense Workers in the Brooklyn Navy Yard, 1942–1946." *New York History*, vol. 81, no. 3 (July 2000).

Taylor, Robert Lewis. "The Kampf of Joe McWilliams." *New Yorker*, August 24, 1940.

Urwin, Cathy K. "No Liquor, But Damned Good Anyway." *America in WWII*, August 2006.

Unattributed, by Date

"Captain Duquesne Is Slain in Bolivia." *New York Times*, April 27, 1916.

"Capt. Duquesne Found Wounded; Will Recover." *New York Times*, May 8, 1916.

"Bridegroom Takes Name of His Bride." *New York Times*, October 16, 1917.

"Hitler Seized Near Munich." *New York Times*, November 13, 1923.

"Mussolini to Furnish Italian House Here." *New York Times*, January 20, 1926.

"Disturbers Foiled at Nobile Welcome." *New York Times*, July 19, 1926.

"10,000 at Funeral of Slain Fascisti." *New York Times*, June 5, 1927.

"Militant Jewish Rally Here Opens National Drive Against Hitlerism." *New York Herald Tribune*, March 20, 1933.

"55,000 Stage Protest on Hitler Attacks on Jews; Nazis Order a New Boycott." *New York Times*, March 28, 1933.

"May Day Is Quiet Throughout World; 50,000 Parade Here." *New York Times*, May 2, 1933.

"Fusion Supporters Overtax Garden." *New York Times*, November 3, 1933.

"Welfare Island Raid Bares Gangster Rule Over Prison." *New York Times*, January 25, 1934.

"Riot Squads Guard 20,000 in Nazi Rally at the Garden." *New York Herald Tribune*, May 18, 1934.

"20,000 Nazi Friends at a Rally Here Denounce Boycott." *New York Times*, May 18, 1934.

"Storm Cools City As 91° Heat Kills 3." *New York Times*, July 4, 1934.

"Ivy Lee German Advisor at $25,000 Yearly Pay, House Hearing Reveals." *New York Herald Tribune*, July 12, 1934.

"Ivy Lee, as Adviser to Nazis, Paid $25,000 by Dye Trust." *New York Times*, July 12, 1934.

"Jeering Nazis Pack Congress Hearing." *New York Times*, October 18, 1934.

"Jews Are Beaten by Berlin Rioters; Cafes Are Raided." *New York Times*, July 16, 1935.

"Town Goes Mad Over Joe Louis." *Amsterdam News*, September 28, 1935.

"Police Muss Up Marcantonio, Balk Parade of 10,000 Idle." *New York Herald Tribune*, February 16, 1936.

"WPA Aims to Stage 'Can't Happen Here.'" *New York Times*, August 22, 1936.

"New York: La Guardia v. Hitler." *Time*, March 15, 1937.

"900 N.Y. Nazis Parade; 1,500 Police on Guard." *New York Herald Tribune*, October 31, 1937.

"Seven Are Injured at Nazi Rally Here When Legionnaires Heckle Speaker." *New York Times*, April 21, 1938.

"Nazi Riot Suspect Freed by Jew's Aid." *New York Times*, April 22, 1938.

"Hunt Four Nazi Thugs Who Beat Boro Editor." *Brooklyn Daily Eagle*, April 23, 1938.

"Reich Withdraws from World's Fair." *New York Times*, April 27, 1938.

"Mike Jacobs Is the Big Boss of the Boxing Business Today." *Life*, June 20, 1938.

"Camp Siegfried Loses." *New York Times*, July 17, 1938.

"40,000 at Nazi Camp Fete." *New York Times*, August 15, 1938.

"Spies." *New York Times*, December 1, 1938.

"Marble Hill Area Annexed to Bronx." *New York Times*, March 12, 1939.

"Kin of Hitler, Here, Are Cool to Fuehrer; Nephew Calls Chancellor 'a Menace.'" *New York Times*, March 31, 1939.

"Jail 4 World's Fair Pickets." *Amsterdam News*, April 8, 1939.

"Act to Halt Opening of Fair." *Amsterdam News*, April 29, 1939.

"Vision Earth Rocked by Isotope Blast." *New York Times*, April 30, 1939.

"Trade: In Mr. Whalen's Image." *Time*, May 1, 1939.

"The President of the United States Opens the World's Greatest World's Fair." *New York Times*, May 1, 1939.

"Willy Hitler." *New Yorker*, July 29, 1939.

"F.B.I. Arrests 18 Here for Plot to 'Seize U.S., Set Up a Dictator.'" *New York Herald Tribune*, January 15, 1940.

"Hitler's Trouble Shooter Here to Patch Up Broken Trade Ties." *New York Herald Tribune*, April 13, 1940.

"President-Maker." *New Yorker*, June 8, 1940.

"Ten Hurt by Bombs Here Near Red, Nazi Agencies." *New York Times*, June 21, 1940.

"Guard Consulates After Explosions." *PM*, June 21, 1940.

"'Bomb' on Train Is Only a Sample Shell Left by Absent-Minded Arms Salesman." *New York Times*, June 26, 1940.

"What Nazi Bombs Could Do to a Brooklyn Street." *PM*, July 9, 1940.

"Colonel Donovan Leaves on the Atlantic Clipper." *New York Times*, July 15, 1940.

"U.S. Opens Its Homes and Heart to Refugee Children of England." *Life*, July 22, 1940.

"Thomas Denounces Both Rivals on Draft." *New York Times*, October 5, 1940.

"Brooklyn Airman with R.A.F. Lost." *New York Times*, February 18, 1941.

"Navy Closing Deal for a Great Base at Bennett Field." *New York Times*, April 27, 1941.

"*Life* Calls on Mrs. Natalie Wales Latham." *Life*, May 19, 1941.

"29 Are Held as Nazi Spies in Roundup by F.B.I." *New York Herald Tribune*, June 30, 1941.

"Women Spy Suspects Are Jeered in Prison." *New York Times*, July 4, 1941.

"Lindbergh Sees a 'Plot' for War." *New York Times*, September 12, 1941.

"Murrow Sees End of War in Our Hands." *New York Times*, December 3, 1941.

"First Leaflets on Civil Defense Given Out Here." *Brooklyn Daily Eagle*, December 8, 1941.

"*Normandie* Keels Over After Surviving Fire; One Dead, 168 Injured; Sabotage Is Denied." *New York Herald Tribune*, February 10, 1942.

"U-Boat Sinks U.S. Destroyer Off Cape May; All But 11 Lost." *New York Times*, March 4, 1942.

"Business: Bootlegging Is Back." *Time*, May 4, 1942.

"More War Orders Sought for City." *New York Times*, June 3, 1942.

"Threat to 3-A Men Backfires on Mayor." *Brooklyn Daily Eagle*, June 27, 1942.

"First Women Hired in Navy Yard Shops." *New York Times*, September 14, 1942.

"3,500 Women Apply for Shipyard Jobs." *New York Times*, October 4, 1942.

"59 Women Hired by Todd Shipyard." *New York Times*, October 11, 1942.

"'Zoot Suit' Youths Guilty of Murder." *New York Times*, November 20, 1942.

"Zoot Suit Killers Start for Sing Sing." *Brooklyn Daily Eagle*, December 4, 1942.
"Life Presents R. Buckminster Fuller's Dymaxion World." *Life*, March 1, 1943.
"Save Doomed Jews, Huge Rally Pleads." *New York Times*, March 2, 1943.
"Now Is the Time." *Amsterdam News*, May 15, 1943.
"Zoot Lore." *New Yorker*, June 19, 1943.
"Spy Here Admits He Sent Nazis Data on Arms and Ships." *New York Times*, June 29, 1943.
"FBI Traps Engineer Who Gave Nazi Spy Data on U.S. Arms." *New York Times*, June 30, 1943.
"Women in Steel." *Life*, August 9, 1943.
"Thousands Mourn Victims of Ghetto." *New York Times*, April 20, 1944.
"Home-Bound Crowds Hushed by Death News." *New York Herald Tribune*, April 13, 1945.
"City Lets Go for 5-Hour Victory Fete." *New York Herald Tribune*, May 8, 1945.
"Statue of Liberty's Lights Go on Tonight, Brighter Than Ever." *New York Herald Tribune*, May 8, 1945.
"Bomber Hits Empire State Building, Setting It Afire at the 79th Floor; 13 Dead, 26 Hurt; Wide Area Rocked." *New York Times*, July 29, 1945.
"V-J Revelry Erupts Again with Times Sq. Its Focus." *New York Times*, August 16, 1945.
"Brooklyn: 'An Atlantic Coast Port.'" *Brooklyn Daily Eagle*, December 9, 1945.
"Churchill Lauds Hopkins' Wisdom." *New York Times*, January 30, 1946.
"New York City's Dream Airport." *Life*, March 18, 1946.
"A Bronx Campus Makes a Dignified World Capital." *Life*, April 8, 1946.
"La Guardia Is Dead; City Pays Homage to 3-Time Mayor." *New York Times*, September 21, 1947.
"New York. The Nickel's Last Ride." *Time*, May 3, 1948.
"New York: The Big Bonanza." *Time*, June 7, 1948.
"Eisenhower Denounced to 5,000 in Union Sq. Rally." *New York Times*, June 20, 1953.
"Children's Friend." *New Yorker*, December 17, 1960.
"Lady Malcolm Douglas-Hamilton." *The Telegraph*, March 10, 2013.
"The Brooklyn Housing Shortage." *The Brownstone Detectives*, April 21, 2017.
"New York Enclave Finally Ends Nazi-Era Policies." *New York Post*, May 20, 2017.

Acknowledgments

Tremendous thanks to my editor, Sean Desmond, and to Rachel Kambury, Bob Castillo, and everyone else at Twelve for making this, my second book with them, such a great pleasure. And to Donald Kennison for his superb copy editing and fact checking.

Big thanks to my agent, Chris Calhoun, for making the arrangements.

As always, friends and colleagues helped in many ways as I researched and wrote this book. William Monahan came through as a true friend at a critical point in the process. Rasha Refaie reviewed and fact-checked various draft iterations. William Bryk, Brian Berger, and Elliot Rosenberg each graciously gave me the benefit of his deep knowledge of New York history. Chris George at the International Center of Photography let me spend a few days leafing through his extensive archive of *PM*. Ken Swezey pointed me in the direction of some excellent research materials. Daniel Riccuito let me try out some passages at his marvelous history site *The Chiseler* (chiseler .org). Thanks also to Lauri Bortz, Richard Byrne, Lisa Kearns, Laura Lindgren, Don MacLeod, Diane Ramo, Jane Strausbaugh, James Taylor, and Christine Walker. Couldn't have done it without all of you.

Photo Credits **1:** Manuscripts and Archives Division, The New York Public Library, Astor, Lenox and Tilden Foundations. **2, 5, 10, 11, 13, 14, 16, 20:** Library of Congress. **3:** *New York Daily News* Archive, *New York Daily News* (Getty). **4, 8, 17, 22:** Bettmann (Getty). **6:** The Imperial War Museum. **7:** Andreas Feininger, The LIFE Picture Collection (Getty). **9:** Photography Collection, Miriam and Ira D. Wallach Division of Art, Prints and Photographs, The New York Public Library, Astor, Lenox and Tilden Foundations. **12:** Billy Rose Theatre Division, The New York Public Library for the Performing Arts, Astor, Lenox and Tilden Foundations. **15:** Margaret Bourke-White, The LIFE Picture Collection (Getty). **18:** CORBIS/Corbis via Getty Images. **19:** Hulton Archive / Stringer (Getty). **21:** Courtesy of *The New York Times*.

Index

About the Author

John Strausbaugh has been writing about the culture and history of New York City for a quarter of a century. *City of Sedition*, his singular history of New York City's role in and during the Civil War, won the Fletcher Pratt Award for Best Non-Fiction Book of 2016; *The Village*, his epic history of Greenwich Village, has been widely praised and was selected as one of *Kirkus Review*'s best books of the year (2013). His previous books include *Black Like You*, a history of blackface minstrelsy; and *E: Reflections on the Birth of the Elvis Faith*.